HUMAN DIGNITY AND POLITICAL CRITICISM

Many, including Marx, Rawls, and the contemporary "Black Lives Matter" movement, embrace the ambition to secure terms of coexistence in which the worth of people's lives becomes a lived reality rather than an empty boast. This book asks whether, as some believe, the philosophical idea of human dignity can help achieve that ambition. Offering a new fourfold typology of dignity concepts, Colin Bird argues that human dignity can perform this role only if certain traditional ways of conceiving it are abandoned. Accordingly, Bird rejects the idea that human dignity refers to the inherent worth or status of individuals, and instead reinterprets it as a social relation, constituted by affects of respect and the modes of mutual attention which they generate. What emerges is a new vision of human dignity as a vital political value, and an arresting vindication of its role as an agent of critical reflection on politics.

COLIN BIRD is Professor of Politics at the University of Virginia. He is author of *The Myth of Liberal Individualism* (Cambridge University Press, 1999), *An Introduction to Political Philosophy* (Cambridge University Press, 2006, 2020), and numerous journal articles.

HUMAN DIGNITY AND POLITICAL CRITICISM

COLIN BIRD

University of Virginia

CAMBRIDGE
UNIVERSITY PRESS

University Printing House, Cambridge CB2 8BS, United Kingdom

One Liberty Plaza, 20th Floor, New York, NY 10006, USA

477 Williamstown Road, Port Melbourne, VIC 3207, Australia

314–321, 3rd Floor, Plot 3, Splendor Forum, Jasola District Centre, New Delhi – 110025, India

103 Penang Road, #05–06/07, Visioncrest Commercial, Singapore 238467

Cambridge University Press is part of the University of Cambridge.

It furthers the University's mission by disseminating knowledge in the pursuit of education, learning, and research at the highest international levels of excellence.

www.cambridge.org
Information on this title: www.cambridge.org/9781108832021
DOI: 10.1017/9781108937597

First published 2021

A catalogue record for this publication is available from the British Library.

ISBN 978-1-108-83202-1 Hardback

It is said, quite correctly, that in antiquity there existed no such notion as respect for a person. The ancients thought far too clearly to entertain such a confused idea.

SIMONE WEIL

The only intelligible language in which we converse with one another consists of our objects in their relation to each other. We would not understand a human language and it would remain without effect. By one side it would be recognized and felt as being a request, an entreaty, and therefore a humiliation, and consequently uttered with a feeling of shame, of degradation. By the other side it would be regarded as impudence or lunacy and rejected as such. We are to such an extent estranged from man's essential nature that the direct language of this essential nature seems to us a violation of human dignity, whereas the estranged language of material values seems to be the well-justified assertion of human dignity that is self-confident and conscious of itself.

KARL MARX

CONTENTS

vii

PREFACE AND ACKNOWLEDGMENTS

When we follow the threads of political argument dominant in the new millennium back to their root assumptions, we sooner or later encounter claims about "human dignity" and the "respect" it is supposed to command. These categories are now the dominant vehicle for expressing a commitment to humanitarian improvement, pretending to a significance at once universal and foundational for late modern politics and its avowed project of civilization. Social criticism and protest, democratic deliberation, as well as our efforts to manage our deepest ethical disagreements now all seem unthinkable apart from these categories. Our very consciousness of ourselves as enjoying legal, moral, and civic standing today speaks the language of respect and human dignity. Few would find it easy to explain the significance of other key political concepts – justice, freedom, autonomy, impartiality, reciprocity, equality, rights, property, cruelty, tolerance, civility – without at some point speaking of the "equal respect due to all," the "dignity of the human person," the importance of "mutual respect," and so forth. Today, it seems, no social and political practice can vindicate itself except before the tribunal of human dignity.

Confronted with the charge that political "theorizing" had little application to political "practice," the Abbé Sieyès is said to have offered a memorable response: "Theories," he reportedly replied, "are the practice of centuries; and their practice is the theory of the passing moment."[1] The special political relevance enjoyed in modern times by concepts of dignity and respect perfectly illustrates Sieyès's point. The belief that human dignity consists in a certain kind of self-disciplining autonomy that commands "mutual respect" is by now a fundamental presupposition of our social forms and ethical consciousness. Our legal systems reflect it, and our moral codes lay claim to it: no adequate account of these and other well-established social practices could ignore it. That belief informs our resentments and feelings of indignation; our attitudes to envy and social comparison; our understandings of certain public complaints as urgent and others as comparatively trivial; our investments in norms

---

[1] Murray Forsyth, *Reason and Revolution: The Political Thought of the Abbé Sieyès* (New York: Holmes & Meier, 1987).

ix

of personal responsibility, independence, and equality; our recognition and experience of abuse, degradation, insult, dehumanization, and humiliation; our feelings of acceptance and rejection; and how we encounter ourselves and others as centers of "worth." In these ways, our consciousness of the respect we are owed and the dignity we possess reflects a Sieyèsian "practice of centuries," while simultaneously rendering "passing moments" intelligible as episodes of fulfillment or aberration.

Sieyès's brilliant insight not only captures the profound interconnection of theory and practice but also explains why it is often difficult to understand socially dominant ideas from a position of critical detachment. The overwhelming cultural credibility of what I will call "Dignitarian Humanism" is beyond dispute. But how far, and when, is it deserved? If so, in what form and to what effect? We cannot hope to answer these questions without achieving a measure of critical distance on its distinctive commitments.

This book attempts to step back and open a fresh angle on this dignitarian humanist orthodoxy, and on the social practices it purports to legitimate and cast into doubt. More specifically, it is concerned with its place, character, strengths, and limitations as a guiding framework for critical reflection about politics. The prestige and currency of dignitarian humanism are as obvious in the writings of recent moral and political theorists as they are in the wider public culture. What follows is an assessment of these efforts to put dignitarian humanist ideas to a distinctively philosophical use in political criticism. What theoretical work can they really perform in political reflection? Are they ever anything more than rhetorical ornaments on arguments whose real substance lies elsewhere? Do the intellectuals who today earnestly mobilize these elevated categories indulge a naïve idealism that has no place in sophisticated political understanding? Are they victims of an ideology?

"Dignitarian humanism" is a term of my own devising, and does not – so far as I am aware – appear in the writings of any political theorist. I find it a helpful term for capturing a set of loosely affiliated normative postures that recur in much contemporary political thought, thereby lending large sectors of it a distinctive character. Later, I attempt to detail commitments that typify dignitarian humanist varieties of political theory. However, pulling a range of political arguments together under an artificial covering label of this kind may encourage a misconception that it is important to preempt at the outset. Specifically, the project does not assume that ideas about dignity and respect crop up in political reflection always in a single, simple way. Nor need it presuppose that "dignitarian humanism" is an internally coherent view to be accepted or rejected as an integrated package, so that a critique of the sort offered in this book must seek to overturn it, *en bloc*, from some adversarial external position.

To the contrary, this book offers a critique in the proper sense of that term, aiming to clarify and vindicate as much as reject. Among other things, it hopes to discriminate between those elements of dignitarian humanist political thinking worth keeping and those that may be more strained or even politically damaging. Such a critique is quite compatible with a sympathetic appreciation for leading dignitarian commitments. And, in accepting that they admit of a variety of uses and interpretations, it presupposes that those commitments are both diverse and complex. Exhibiting that complexity and understanding its implications for various political arguments are accordingly among the book's main preoccupations.

Still, and keeping these provisos very firmly in mind, it will be useful to provide a provisional summary of this book's critical target. For the purposes of this book, then, dignitarian humanist varieties of political theory are characteristically committed to the following:

1. Human agents have inherent dignity, not price; their "worth" is therefore of a special kind, distinct from and irreducible to exchange value, preference, utility, and considerations of instrumental rationality; at the same time, human "worth" is in principle an entirely secular, nonreligious, category.
2. This inherent "dignity" or worth is not a value to be promoted but rather an object of respect and disrespect; the relevant respect/disrespect is disclosed in visible forms of treatment that express certain inner attitudes toward other human beings.
3. This respectful treatment is owed to persons as such; the respect at issue is therefore not like that commanded by specific individuals for particular attributes (achievements, moral virtue, prowess, etc.) but is an entitlement owed equally and unconditionally to all.
4. The dignity and worth of human individuals is bound up with their autonomy and independence as persons and so the respect it commands requires an acknowledgment of their equal status as free agents.
5. The dignity and worth of individuals condition not only the treatment they must receive from others but also reflect vital human needs, including the preservation of self-respect and avoidance of self-contempt, the ability to affirm one's worth, importance and status, and to obtain appropriate recognition in the eyes of potentially oppressive, limiting, others.
6. All of these (points 1–5) are central to our concept of persons' public worth and standing. As such:
   a. these stipulations jointly define a very basic, uncontroversial set of standards that public institutions must at all costs satisfy; they therefore comprise a privileged, authoritative critical standpoint
      i. from which existing political arrangements should be impartially judged legitimate or wanting; and
      ii. that excludes at least some other purported critical standards (e.g., utilitarian ones) that might be applied to assess the legitimacy of social and political arrangements with different results;

b. they are distinct from the forms of standing and worth relevant in private settings, connected to forms of love, friendship, loyalty, beneficence, concern, social and professional recognition, appreciation, and so on.

I stress again that this is a preliminary outline that will have to be elaborated, qualified, and refined in due course and whose internal coherence is not being presumed. Obvious ambiguities in, and questions about, the formulations mentioned above (often giving rise to disagreements between different philosophers) will require careful consideration and in some cases radical revision. However, even if it is a ladder we will eventually have to kick away, it gives us enough height to spy the road ahead.

Our question, stated very broadly, is the adequacy of point 6(a), mentioned earlier. Should we agree that a principle of respect for human dignity can serve as an impartial critical standard by which political philosophers can reach authoritative judgments about the merits and legitimacy of political arrangements? If so, how, and to what effect?

* * *

This book has suffered a long and often tortured gestation, and over the years I have incurred very many debts. I thank all of those who have supported this research, financially, intellectually, and psychologically, for their faith and patience. The book began life during a sabbatical year at the University Center for Human Values at Princeton University, where I held a Laurance Rockefeller visiting fellowship in 2001–02. A second sabbatical year was spent as an NEH Fellow at the National Humanities Center in North Carolina in 2008–09. These two years of freedom provided crucial respite from my regular academic duties, and I am enormously grateful to these institutions for hosting me and my family, and to the University of Virginia for granting me these leaves. Special thanks are due to Joe Davis and Tal Brewer for organizing a mini-conference on Dignity hosted by the Institute for Advanced Studies in Culture at the University of Virginia in the fall of 2018, at which I received invaluable feedback as the project entered its final stages. However, as always with such endeavors, I have benefited the most from conversations with the many teachers, colleagues, and students who have generously offered their intellectual advice, criticism, comradeship, and kindness during the period in which the book was conceived and written. The following list is surely incomplete (and I apologize to anyone I have omitted by mistake), but I wish to particularly thank Bob Amdur, the late John Arras, Charles Beitz, Geoff Brennan, Mark Bevir, Susan Bickford, Matthias Brinkmann, Richard Boyd, Tal Brewer, Susan Brison, Natalie Broome, Brookes Brown, Dan Brudney, Trevor Burnard, Susan Brison, Ian Carter, Emanuela Ceva, David Ciepley, Tom Christiano, Rich Dagger, Joe Davis, Remy Debes, Florence Dore, John Doris, Suzi Dovi, Julia Driver, Anthony Duff, Chris Eberle, Adam Etinson,

Harrison Frye, Mary Floyd-Wilson, Anna Elisabetta Galeotti, Pablo Gilabert, Susan Gubar, the late Thomas Haskell, Kate Jackson, Alex Jech, Colin Kielty, Krishan Kumar, Cécile Laborde, David Lefkowitz, Lily Li, Ian Maclean, Chuck Mathewes, the late Joe Miller, Ross Mittiga, Paul Morrow, Nancy Hirschmann, Des Jagmohan, Peter Jones, Michael Kates, George Klosko, David Kovacs, Mina Lee, David Levy, Jacob Levy, Loren Lomasky, Michelle Mason, Ashley Mehra, Margaret Moore, Illan Nam, Serena Olsaretti, S. Douglas Olson, Alan Patten, Carmen Pavel, Ryan Pevnick, Tom Porter, Jon Quong, Kelly Rohe, Michael Rosen, Arya Royal, Jen Rubenstein, Andrea Sangiovanni, Micah Schwartzmann, Dave Schmidtz, Parker Shipton, David Shoemaker, Daniel Silvermint, John Simmons, Peter Singer, Quentin Skinner, Houston Smit, Jeff Spinner, Becky Stangl, Annie Stilz, Shruta Swarup, Jade Tan, Jackie Taylor, Richard Tuck, Jeremy Waldron, Steve Wall, Stephen White, Jo Wolff, Nick Wolterstorff, Liya Yu, and Frederico Zuolo. Audiences at the Universities of Oxford, Edinburgh, Pavia, Bologna, Georgetown, and Virginia provided helpful sounding boards for some of the arguments presented in this book.

I am indebted also to several anonymous referees for Cambridge University Press for providing vital feedback; this is certainly a better book for their guidance. Hilary Gaskin has, as always, mixed forbearance with trenchant editorial advice, and I greatly appreciate her assistance in seeing this project through to completion, as well as the help of Hal Churchman in the final stages. Finally, I above all thank my wife Adrienne; my children Nicholas, Teddy, and Tatiana; my parents Graham and Louise; and my brother Michael for their unstinting love, tolerance, and kindness. I dedicate this book to my family, with unbounded gratitude.

This book includes material previously published in the following four articles, and I am grateful for permission to use it here.

Bird, Colin. 2013. "Dignity as a Moral Concept." *Social Philosophy and Policy* 30 (1–2): 150–76.
    2013. "Does Religion Deserve Our Respect?" *Journal of Applied Philosophy* 30 (3): 268–82.
    2004. "Status, Identity, and Respect." *Political Theory* 32 (2): 207–32.
    2018. "The Theory and Politics of Recognition." In *The Oxford Handbook of Distributive Justice*, edited by Serena Olsaretti, 235–55. Oxford: Oxford University Press.

PART I

The Contours of Dignitarian Humanism

1

The Tribunal of Human Dignity

In 1971, two starkly contrasting books appeared. One was B. F. Skinner's *Beyond Freedom and Dignity*, a popular yet intellectually sophisticated manifesto for behaviorist social reform. As its title indicates, Skinner's book urged that inherited ideas about the dignity and freedom of the person be discarded as obsolete relics from the prescientific past. Addressing himself to the concerns of C. S. Lewis and other humanists that the progress of science and technology is "abolishing Man," Skinner replied:

> There is clearly some difficulty in identifying the man to whom these expressions refer. Lewis cannot have meant the human species, for not only is it not being abolished, it is filling the earth. (As a result it may eventually abolish itself through disease, famine, pollution, or a nuclear holocaust, but that is not what Lewis meant.) Nor are individual men growing less effective or productive. We are told that what is threatened is "man qua man," or "man in his humanity," or "man as Thou not It," or "man as a person not a thing." These are not very helpful expressions, but they supply a clue. What is being abolished is autonomous man – the inner man, the homunculus, the possessing demon, the man defended by the literatures of freedom and dignity. His abolition has long been overdue. Autonomous man is a device used to explain what we cannot explain in any other way. He has been constructed from our ignorance, and as our understanding increases, the very stuff of which he is composed vanishes. Science does not dehumanize man, it de-homunculizes him. . . . To man qua man we readily say good riddance. Only by dispossessing him can we turn to the real causes of human behavior. Only then can we turn from the inferred to the observed, from the miraculous to the natural, from the inaccessible to the manipulable.[1]

If Skinner was hoping to persuade the intellectuals of his generation to abandon the category of "human dignity" and invest in a program of utilitarian social reform based exclusively on the efficient "manipulation" of behavior, he failed completely. The last quarter of the twentieth century witnessed a sudden resurgence of interest in dignitarian ideas within the human sciences, and especially within political theory. The pivotal moment in this revival was the

---

[1] B. F. Skinner, *Beyond Freedom and Dignity*, (Indianapolis: Hackett, 2007), pp. 199–200.

3

virtually simultaneous publication of a second book: John Rawls's *A Theory of Justice.*

Rawls's book both revitalized political theory as an academic enterprise and catapulted dignitarian categories to a prominence in moral and political philosophy that they have not relinquished to this day.[2] It did so in virtue of its strong and intuitively compelling rejection of utilitarianism. For Rawls and many of those he influenced, the utilitarian tradition represented, in its most philosophically systematic and plausible form, the technocratic vision of public policy-making that dominated the period of postwar reconstruction in the West, and of which Skinner's radically behaviorist program was an extreme example. Rawls's early work had operated within a utilitarian framework, but the failure of his efforts to devise a fully satisfactory version of the doctrine led him to a damning conclusion: utilitarianism is not only philosophically problematic but also politically dangerous. Here, it is important to recall the political context of the Cold War. During this period, the West was not only

---

[2] John Rawls, *A Theory of Justice*, 2nd edition (Cambridge, MA: Belknap Press: An Imprint of Harvard University Press, 1999). The explosion of subsequent work on ideas of human dignity attests to the high currency enjoyed by that idea today. To cite the tip of the iceberg: Aharon Barak, *Human Dignity: The Constitutional Value and the Constitutional Right* (Cambridge: Cambridge University Press, 2015); Charles R. Beitz, "Human Dignity in the Theory of Human Rights: Nothing But a Phrase?," *Philosophy & Public Affairs* 41, no. 3 (June 1, 2013): 259–90; Marcus Düwell et al., eds., *The Cambridge Handbook of Human Dignity: Interdisciplinary Perspectives* (Cambridge: Cambridge University Press, 2014); Jeremy Waldron, *Dignity, Rank, and Rights*, ed. Meir Dan-Cohen, Reprint edition (Oxford: Oxford University Press, 2015); Jeremy Waldron, *The Harm in Hate Speech*, (Cambridge, MA: Harvard University Press, 2014); Jeremy Waldron, "How Law Protects Human Dignity," *The Cambridge Law Journal* 71, no. 1 (March 2012): 200–22; George Kateb, *Human Dignity* (Cambridge, MA: Harvard University Press, 2011); Remy Debes, *Dignity: A History* (Oxford University Press, 2017); Remy Debes, "Dignity's Gauntlet," *Philosophical Perspectives* 23, no. 1 (December 1, 2009): 45–78; Pablo Gilabert, "Human Rights, Human Dignity, and Power," in *Philosophical Foundations of Human Rights*, ed. Rowan Cruft, Matthew Liao, and Massimo Renzo (Oxford: Oxford University Press, 2015), pp. 196–213; Pablo Gilabert, "Labor Human Rights and Human Dignity," *Philosophy & Social Criticism* 42, no. 2 (February 1, 2016): 171–99; Pablo Gilabert, "Facts, Norms, and Dignity," *Critical Review of International Social and Political Philosophy* 22, no. 1(November 23, 2017): 1–21; Michael Rosen, *Dignity* (Cambridge, MA: Harvard University Press, 2012); Michael Rosen, *Dignity: The Case Against* (Oxford: British Academy, 2013); Stephen Darwall, *The Second-Person Standpoint: Morality, Respect, and Accountability* (Harvard University Press, 2009); Nicholas Wolterstorff, *Justice: Rights and Wrongs* (Princeton, NJ: Princeton University Press, 2008); Michael Goodhart, "Constructing Dignity: Human Rights as a Praxis of Egalitarian Freedom," *Journal of Human Rights* 17, no. 4 (August 8, 2018): 403–17; Neomi Rao, "On the Use and Abuse of Dignity in Constitutional Law," *Columbia Journal of European Law* 14 (2008): 201–56; Neomi Rao, "Three Concepts of Dignity in Constitutional Law," *Notre Dame Law Review* 86 (2011): 183–272; Christopher McCrudden, *Understanding Human Dignity*, Reprint edition (Oxford: British Academy, 2014).

defining itself in opposition to the totalitarian regimes of the communist Eastern bloc but was also struggling to come to terms with the atrocities of the two world wars, which, in the idiom of the day, were often gathered under the heading of assaults on "human dignity." How had the cradle of Enlightenment civilization descended so rapidly into the barbarism of trench warfare, *blitzkrieg*, and genocide? As commentators wrestled with this question, they canvassed a variety of hypotheses about the complicity of various philosophical ideas in promoting political oppression, authoritarianism, and tribalism – political phenomena that had systematically ground the dignity of the human individual under their wheels in the early twentieth century. These writers of the postwar generation accordingly hoped to foster a political culture that would "never again" overlook the fundamental importance of respect for individuals' basic dignity as human beings.

Rawls's critique of utilitarianism resonated powerfully with this aspiration because it raised the specter of a society that could permit violations of human dignity (e.g., sacrificing, coercing, manipulating, or exploiting individuals) in order to satisfy the maximizing demands of the utility principle. He argued that the utilitarian effort to reduce all political values to welfarist calculation cannot fully guarantee the dignity of the individual person, because a society committed to it would be willing to sacrifice them to the idol of "aggregate utility," as if the welfare of society *as such* matters more than the lives of the individuals comprising it. In effect, Rawls suggested that, as long as we remain utilitarians, we will still not have fully turned our back on the intellectual seductions responsible for the crises that marked the first half of the twentieth century.[3] With the Vietnam War and its Orwellian euphemisms for "acceptable loss" providing rich grist for his mill, Rawls insisted that a genuinely just society would refuse, on principle, to violate the entitlements and claims grounded on the basic dignity of the individual even if overall welfare was reduced as a result.

He was aware of course that no sophisticated utilitarian would deny that indignity, humiliation, disrespect, and personal violation carry a prohibitive cost in terms of human happiness, and therefore that utilitarian policy-makers should be extremely reluctant to entertain them. Yet, he claimed, far from imposing a principled prohibition on such violations, utilitarianism merely describes conditions under which they might be legitimate. Rawls thought that, even if rarely activated, such a permission runs against a considered conviction that "each person possesses an inviolability founded upon justice

---

[3] In this sense, we should think of Rawls's work as growing out of the Cold War liberal critique of totalitarianism represented by such authors as Isaiah Berlin, Jacob Talmon, and Karl Popper. For more on that historical background, see David Ciepley, *Liberalism in the Shadow of Totalitarianism* (Cambridge, MA: Harvard University Press, 2006); Colin Bird, *The Myth of Liberal Individualism* (Cambridge: Cambridge University Press, 1999).

that not even the welfare of society as a whole can override." Accordingly, he took the special urgency of principles of justice to be grounded upon "the value of persons that Kant says is beyond all price." In appealing to this powerful Kantian distinction between the "dignity of persons" and the "price of things," Rawls thus reinstated the very idea of "man" that Skinner had hoped to exorcise.

Thanks to Rawls's massive influence within at least mainstream Anglophone and European political philosophy, that dignitarian humanist distinction has become so axiomatic that it is hard, looking back from our vantage point, for us to imagine that it was not a fixture of Enlightenment modernity from the beginning. To be sure, Rawls was certainly not the first to appeal to the inviolable worth and dignity of the human person: rather, he tapped into a familiar dignitarian idiom that enjoys the broad cultural credibility I described at the outset. Yet, as a number of scholars have begun to remind us, the entrenchment of a secular ideal of human dignity within political *philosophy* is a rather recent development. Before the twentieth century, dignitarian ideas had little philosophical currency outside Western theism, and they were often implicated in very hierarchical practices and modes of thought ill-suited to the egalitarian temper of contemporary political thinking. Even when used after the war as descriptors for atrocities (genocide, the mass slaughter of modern warfare, slavery and racial oppression, religious persecution, etc.), their role was less diagnostic or philosophical than declamatory. The assaults on human dignity to which the postwar generation reacted were anyway so flagrant that it occurred to virtually no one that a dignitarian *theory* was needed to amplify their significance. While that generation sought to understand the causes and conditions of the indignities inflicted during the early twentieth century, it rarely attached much independent philosophical or explanatory significance to the category of human dignity itself.

Rawls changed all this. Before him, the dignitarian humanist idiom performed a largely negative function, identifying the gravest atrocities falling outside the stockade of civilization. After him, it was increasingly recruited in intellectual argument to address more controversial questions about how life within the stockade should best be arranged. Rawls deployed complex philosophical argumentation to explain what, in his view, a society that refused to compromise human dignity would have to look like, how it would instantiate justice, and why we should affirm it for that reason. Under his influence, securing the conditions of human dignity accordingly became not only a goal to be achieved but also one whose realization can be furthered by philosophical reflection about its content. In a way that echoed not only classical utilitarianism but also (as we shall see) Marx, intellectual speculation here stepped forward as a mode of politically engaged philosophical criticism, albeit now representing the cause of human dignity and its purported centrality to the realization of a just and decent social order.[4] In turning away from the welfarist approach of the utilitarian tradition, then, Rawls launched a quite distinctive and in many ways novel mode of political criticism, one centered on principles of "equal respect," the "social bases of self-respect," and a conception of persons and their lives as centers of "inviolable" worth and dignity.

We Are All Dignitarians Now

Although developed in opposition to utilitarianism, Rawls's dignitarian turn nonetheless shares an important formal affinity with it. Both he and the utilitarians proceeded from assumptions that they take to be virtually self-evident: that transgressing human dignity is indefensible; and that it is always rational to spare sentient beings unnecessary suffering. By speculating on the intuitive force of these primitive axioms, each approach canvasses a putatively authoritative and impartial standpoint from which to critically assess moral, social, and political practices. Both think of themselves as, in a broad sense, progressive paradigms, offering a framework to guide critical reflection about which political arrangements should be retained, abandoned, or reformed. In neither case is this hope obviously unreasonable, for it is hard to see what could possibly be said for practices that cause unnecessary suffering or that undermine human dignity. The challenge, of course, is to move beyond uncontroversial platitudes about suffering and indignity ("agony is bad," "torture is humiliating," etc.) and to defend more interesting, controversial conclusions about what overall welfare or a concern for "human dignity" concretely require or forbid.

Rawls charted a path for dignitarians to answer that challenge – one that he thought could rival utilitarianism in sophistication while repairing its alleged dignitarian deficit. His signal conceptual innovation was to devise a way to model the intuition that persons bear an inviolable worth philosophically that permitted (as he saw it) a definitive account of the norms and principles that ought to guide the practice of a truly just society. Rawls's heavy investment in a form of contractualism reflected this dignitarian intuition, for he believed it can correct the utilitarian tendency to equate the requirement of ethical impartiality between persons with a merely formal expectation that each count equally in the consequentialist calculus. For Rawls, impartiality between persons is a more demanding value, entailing a substantive ideal of "equal

---

[4] For other elaborations of a similar dignitarian approach, see Avishai Margalit, *The Decent Society* (Cambridge, MA: Harvard University Press, 1998); Ronald Dworkin, *Justice for Hedgehogs* (Cambridge, MA: Belknap Press of Harvard University Press, 2011); Ronald Dworkin, *Is Democracy Possible Here? Principles for a New Political Debate* (Princeton, NJ: Princeton University Press, 2008).

respect," linked to the values of fairness and dignity, that precludes treating agents merely as "means" toward collective ends like "aggregate welfare." Contractualism in his view honors that ideal by conferring on each party to his social contract the standing to veto principles, proposals, and practices that conflict with their reasonable desire to ensure that their lives are not subjugated to the needs of some impersonal abstraction with which they cannot identify.[5] Rawls understood this procedural requirement of reasonable agreement as precluding "even the tendency to regard men *(sic)* as means to one another's welfare."[6] In this way, as Paul Weithman has put it, Rawls's contractualist project assumes that "the grounds of human dignity include capacities which are properly respected only by consulting those who have those capacities about their own basic entitlements."[7] Not only did Rawls develop his contractualist model with unparalleled rigor, he also brought it to bear on highly salient public debates about the role of state power in regulating markets, about the proper constitution of a "free society," about how far inequalities of income and wealth are just, and about the terms on which redistribution of wealth from the affluent to those suffering social and economic disadvantage can be legitimate.

The systematic elaboration of this model, which carried controversial implications at both a methodological and political level, stimulated a storm of debate. Some sought to defend his contractualism; some to amend it; some to explore its implications for issues Rawls himself didn't recognize; some to reject it in favor of alternatives; some to urge that his whole approach is misguided and to try something quite different.[8] The resulting philosophical

---

[5] Rawls, *Theory of Justice*, p. 27; Nozick, *Anarchy, State and Utopia* (New York: Basic Books, 1974) pp. 32–33.

[6] Rawls, *Theory of Justice*, p. 183.

[7] Paul Weithman, "Two Arguments from Human Dignity," in President's Council on Bioethics, *Human Dignity and Bioethics: Essays Commissioned by the President's Council on Bioethics*, 1st edition (Washington, DC: U.S. Independent Agencies and Commissions, 2008), pp. 439–40.

[8] Thanks especially to the influence of Jürgen Habermas, the same period witnessed a parallel development within the "Frankfurt School" of critical theory. Like Rawls, Habermas found untapped critical potential in the Kantian tradition that earlier critical theorists had viewed with deep suspicion. As a result, ideals of human dignity played an increasingly prominent role in the amended version of critical theory he pioneered. Axel Honneth, "A Society without Humiliation?," *European Journal of Philosophy* 5, no. 3 (December 1, 1997): 306–24; Axel Honneth, *The Struggle for Recognition: The Moral Grammar of Social Conflicts* (MIT Press, 1996); Axel Honneth, *Disrespect: The Normative Foundations of Critical Theory* (John Wiley & Sons, 2014); Nancy Fraser and Axel Honneth, *Redistribution or Recognition? A Political-Philosophical Exchange* (London: Verso, 2003); Jürgen Habermas, "The Concept of Human Dignity and the Realistic Utopia of Human Rights," *Metaphilosohy* 41, no. 4 (July, 2010), pp. 464–480; Ernst Bloch, *Natural Law and Human Dignity*, trans. Dennis J. Schmidt, Revised edition (MIT Press, 1987); Rainer Forst, *The Right to Justification: Elements of a Constructivist*

ferment brought political theory back to life after a lengthy period of decadence.

However, in all this the underlying assumption that a principle of respect for the dignity of the person is central to critical reflection on political institutions has gone largely unquestioned. Even those who repudiate, not only Rawls's methods but also his whole philosophical orientation, frequently endorse the importance of respect for human dignity.[9] Few of the forms of political theory being actively pursued today can be called "Rawlsian"; yet inasmuch as many incorporate Rawls's dignitarian humanist starting point in some way, they share an important family resemblance. The intellectual historians of the future will be struck that the rebirth of political philosophy at the end of the twentieth century spawned thoughtforms that, for all their diversity, appear to share a similar dignitarian DNA. The implicit assumption that intellectually serious political criticism succeeds to the extent that it properly codes a dignitarian humanist genome is one we owe to Rawls.[10]

The Crisis of Dignitarian Humanism

A critical assessment of these ideas has become urgent because, as the novelty of Rawls's fresh start has worn off, appeals to human dignity in political argument have become victims of their own success. Following the Rawlsian model, proponents of contending political views have come to expect dignitarian humanist ideas to do definite philosophical work in political criticism: to tell us, for example, whether the untrammeled operation of commercial capitalism secures or undermines human dignity; to determine whether a welfare state is needed to ensure that citizens receive the respect appropriate to their share in human dignity; to explain what forms of organized violence (if

---

Theory of Justice, trans. Jeffrey Flynn, Reprint edition (New York: Columbia University Press, 2014); Rainer Forst, "The Ground of Critique: On the Concept of Human Dignity in Social Orders of Justification," *Philosophy & Social Criticism* 37, no. 9 (November 1, 2011): 965–76; it is worth mentioning also the "personalist" turn in Catholic social thought associated especially with Karol Wojtyła, who later became Pope John Paul II.

[9] William E. Connolly, *Identity, Difference: Democratic Negotiations of Political Paradox*, Expanded edition (Minneapolis, MN: University of Minnesota Press, 2002), pp. x, xxvi. On this, see also Stephen K. White, *The Ethos of a Late-Modern Citizen* (Cambridge, MA: Harvard University Press, 2009).

[10] Some have missed the centrality of dignitarian ideals in Rawls's project. Moyn, for example, claims that Rawls and Rawlsians "have not focused" on it. See S. Moyn, "The Secret History of Constitutional Dignity," *Yale Human Rights and Development Law Journal* 17 (2014): 39, 64. Moyn's book is primarily interested in the intellectual history of the idea of "human rights," which played little role in Rawls's original argument, concerned as it was mainly with the *domestic* ordering of a just society. But, as we have already seen, the Kantian idea that persons bear an inviolable dignity that must at all costs be respected was absolutely central to his project.

any) are required or prohibited by a concern for the dignity of offenders and their victims; to pinpoint the nature of abuse, exploitation, and oppression that we might otherwise overlook; to establish the sense in which agents' dignity is at stake in different models of toleration and respect for citizens' diverse convictions and identities; or to identify those forms of treatment to which agents can claim a "human right."

Yet, as the categories of "dignity" and "respect" have been stretched and reinterpreted to support a wide range of political conclusions about many different questions, the original idea that dignitarian principles are somehow impartial, above the fray, has inevitably come into question. The wide agreement on the fundamental political significance of an imperative of respect for human dignity now coexists with wildly divergent views about how to do political philosophy, and about what that imperative recommends in concrete political contexts. In this sense, dignitarian humanism has become an intellectual, political, and ideological battleground, a site at which commentators struggle to redescribe the terms of "respect for human dignity" so that they align with their favored political conclusions. It is not unusual to find completely incompatible political recommendations defended alike in the name of respect for human dignity.

Examples are legions. For every Rawls who regards a welfare state as justified for the sake of human dignity, we find a Nozick who sees redistributive taxation as no less disrespectful of persons than "forced labor." While the Vatican calls capital punishment an "affront to human dignity," some Kantians still follow their mentor in regarding the failure to inflict the death penalty (when deserved) as a denial of the offender's dignity. And what goes for capital punishment specifically goes, too, for controversy not only about retributive punishment more generally but also about what forms of conduct are crimes and abuses grave enough to warrant a penal response.

Similarly, some think that respect for human dignity requires that public policy be as far as possible "blind to difference";[11] they are opposed by others who see dignity "in" difference and so call for a respect that honors agents' particularities and collective identities.[12] For some, respect for persons requires a moratorium on appeals to controversial ethical and religious beliefs in public deliberation;[13] others resent such a moratorium as disrespecting religious

---

[11] Brian M. Barry, *Culture and Equality: An Egalitarian Critique of Multiculturalism* (Cambridge, MA: Harvard University Press, 2002); Brian Leiter, *Why Tolerate Religion?* (Princeton, NJ: Princeton University Press, 2013).

[12] Carol Gould, "Diversity and Democracy: Representing Differences," in *Democracy and Difference*, ed. Seyla Benhabib (Princeton, NJ: Princeton University Press, 1996), p. 182; Charles Taylor, *Multiculturalism*, ed. A. Gutmann (Princeton, NJ: Princeton University Press, 1994), p. 8; Iris Marion Young, *Justice and the Politics of Difference* (Princeton, NJ: Princeton University Press, 1990), p. 163.

[13] John Rawls, *Political Liberalism*, Expanded edition, Columbia Classics in Philosophy (New York: Columbia University Press, 2005); John Rawls, *The Law of Peoples: With*

believers by requiring that they practice an intolerable self-censorship in political discourse.[14] Many see the case for an extremely permissive right to free speech, including even very offensive speech, as turning on an appeal to human dignity. Others, like the judge who was prepared to prohibit a South African newspaper from publishing notorious Danish cartoons satirizing Islam, think that prohibitions on "hate-speech" or public intolerance are justified for the sake of dignity.[15]

This list of claims and counterclaims, which could be indefinitely extended, attests to the cultural credibility that dignitarian discourse enjoys in contemporary consciousness of progress and reaction, of function and dysfunction, of institutional reform and abuse, of emancipation and subjugation, and of justice and injustice. However, as that discourse has swept the field and acquired ever more intense political charge, critics have understandably found it ever harder to see the constituent ideas of dignitarian humanism as capable of performing any deep critical role. Even Rawls came to think, in his later work, that in any strongly Kantian form, dignitarian humanism is a "comprehensive" ethical outlook too controversial to serve as a suitably impartial premise for political evaluation.[16] Many would now generalize Rawls's view about the Kantian position and suggest that all deployments of these concepts must be similarly partisan.[17] Like other important political concepts, they often say, ideals of "human dignity" and "respect for persons" must be "essentially contested": they give rise to indefinitely many legitimate, but mutually exclusive, interpretations of the same basic conceptual material that cannot be decisively vindicated against each other. Yet, if there are as many partisan construals of ideals of human dignity and respect as there are defensible political positions, the suggestion that they can themselves assume

"The Idea of Public Reason Revisited," (Cambridge, MA: Harvard University Press, 2003); Jonathan Quong, "On the Idea of Public Reason," in eds. Mandle, J., and Reidy, D., *A Companion to Rawls* (Wiley-Blackwell, 2014), pp. 265–80; Jonathan Quong, *Liberalism without Perfection* (Oxford University Press, 2010); Charles Larmore, "The Moral Basis of Political Liberalism," *The Journal of Philosophy* 96, no. 12 (1999): 599–625; Charles Larmore, "Respect for Persons," *Hedgehog Review* 7, no. 2 (Summer 2005): 66–76; Charles E. Larmore, *Patterns of Moral Complexity* (Cambridge: Cambridge University Press, 1987); Robert Audi and Nicholas Wolterstorff, *Religion in the Public Square: The Place of Religious Convictions in Political Debate, Point/Counterpoint* (Lanham, MD: Rowman & Littlefield Publishers, 1997).

[14] Audi and Wolterstorff, *Religion in the Public Square*; Michael J. Perry, *The Political Morality of Liberal Democracy* (Cambridge University Press, 2010); Steven Douglas Smith, *The Rise and Decline of American Religious Freedom* (Cambridge, MA: Harvard University Press, 2014).

[15] See Nazeem M. I. Goolam, "The Cartoon Controversy: A Note on Freedom of Expression, Hate Speech and Blasphemy," *The Comparative and International Law Journal of Southern Africa* 39, no. 2 (2006): 346; Waldron, *The Harm in Hate Speech*.

[16] Rawls, *Political Liberalism*.

[17] Connolly, *Identity, Difference*, p. x.

the role of an impartial adjudicator, refereeing their respective merits from a critical point of view, becomes harder to sustain and the decision to embrace or reject particular conceptions of dignity will come to seem largely strategic, but not of any philosophical import.[18]

In the face of all this, many today follow Steven Pinker in thinking that it is simply "stupid" to assign "human dignity" the critical weight that many claim for it; the category is simply too "squishy" to bear it, and we should abandon the idea that it can afford any genuinely impartial standard of political judgment. Dignity-skeptics like Pinker can of course concede that dignitarian idioms are powerful tools of political mobilization, affording useful rhetorical intensifiers to rally waverers around any number of political causes. Clearly, though, that concession cannot show that they play any significant role in *justifying* the political positions to which they are recruited.[19]

Other skeptics will go further still, asserting that the constituent ingredients of dignitarian humanism can only ever be "ideological" categories in Marx's pejorative sense. Here, they will say, limp philosophical abstractions (persons as ends-in-themselves, "project pursuers," "self-originating sources of valid claims," as self-owners, etc.) are cashed out with metaphors imported uncritically from contingent social practices ("dignity," "respect," "standing," etc.). A more propitious breeding ground for ideological obfuscation is hard to imagine, and even a cursory review of historically influential uses of the language of dignity indicates that it has carried strongly divergent implications at different times. Won't the "dignity" of the human person wear the three-piece suit of the bourgeois under capitalist conditions, and the bishop's miter when the theistic hierarchies of feudalism reign? Perhaps, then, Skinner was right all along: the turn to dignitarian ideas is always a symptom of a failure, and perhaps a refusal, to engage politically on suitably unsentimental, scientific, or realist terms. So construed, dignitarian humanism merely flatters our limited self-understanding with mystifying illusions, wishful thinking, and vain fantasies of personal value and standing, impeding rather than promoting any genuinely critical perspective on the concrete circumstances of human politics.

Still, dismissing dignitarian humanism as so much ideological froth is a difficult bullet to bite. Imagine a person who returns from a visit to

---

[18] William E. Connolly, *The Terms of Political Discourse* (Princeton, NJ: Princeton University Press, 1993); Mirko Bagaric and James Allan, "The Vacuous Concept of Dignity," *Journal of Human Rights* 5, no. 2 (July 1, 2006): 257–70; Philippe-André Rodriguez, "Human Dignity as an Essentially Contested Concept," *Cambridge Review of International Affairs* 28, no. 4 (October 2, 2015): 743–56.

[19] This is the view discussed extensively (and critically) in Beitz, "Human Dignity in the Theory of Human Rights." A sophisticated recent version of that view is developed in A. Sangiovanni, *Humanity without Dignity: Moral Equality, Respect, and Human Rights* (Cambridge, MA: Harvard University Press, 2017).

Auschwitz with a vivid impression of the massive assault on human dignity the Nazis' "final solution" represented. To suggest that this reaction is merely sentimental and communicates no important critical information about the character of organized genocide does not immediately ring true. The indignity, dehumanization, humiliation, and social defeat implicated in genocide may be neither strictly "material" phenomena nor susceptible of a behaviorist analysis. Yet they need not be, for that reason, empty abstractions, rhetorical gloss, or just convenient shorthand like using the phrase "Uncle Sam" to refer to the US Federal Government. Many will insist, to the contrary, that these dignitarian concepts capture something fundamental about the real character of injustice, oppression and personal abuse, and more generally about what it is for peoples' lives (whether black or white, like or unlike ours) to fail to *matter*. For them, the expectation of respect for the dignity and worth of all people is not merely an illusion of the epoch but a sine qua non for civilized coexistence. It lies, they suppose, at the core of our moral and political consciousness, the closest thing secular modernity has to a universally valid humanist depth-grammar for political criticism.[20]

So our commitment to the cause of human dignity today carries with it a profound ambivalence. When we wish to critically interrogate the social practices that surround us, we instinctively reach for claims about human dignity for trustworthy and informative guidance. We presume them to constitute an authoritative tribunal to which social and political institutions must answer. Yet we are haunted by an insistent and intensifying fear that it is a kangaroo court, its judgments tainted by the partialities and illusions of the judges appointed to its bench.

This book aims to resolve this ambivalence about philosophical ideals of human dignity, to move us beyond the *impasse* framed in 1971 by Skinner and Rawls. It tries to establish when, how, and in what form, dignitarian humanist arguments might carry philosophical conviction and when, in contrast, they function as little more than empty pieties mystifying political consciousness, or merely as self-serving ideologies protecting suspect social practices from critical scrutiny.

The Road Ahead

The argument of the book unfolds in three parts. Part I, which comprises this Chapter 1, and the next three (Chapters 2, 3, and 4), constitutes an overview of the dignitarian humanist paradigm and my own approach to it. Chapter 2 outlines the methodological orientation of the book, which is distinctive in rejecting several approaches widely accepted today. Chapter 3 asks why one

---

[20] It is, in Moyn's sense, a "last utopia." Samuel Moyn, *The Last Utopia: Human Rights in History* (Cambridge, MA: Harvard University Press, 2012).

might invest in dignitarian humanism at all as an approach to political criticism. By detailing both its attractiveness as a basis for critical argument in politics, and the most serious challenges it faces as such, it sets the agenda for the subsequent discussion. Among the most important strengths of dignitarian humanism, I argue there, is that it gestures in the direction of what I will call a "timanthropic" approach to political criticism, one centered on claims about the *worth* of persons and their lives as against other possible loci of value (commodities, gods, animals, states of affairs, forms of desirable experience, etc.). As I propose to construe it, then, dignitarian humanism in political theory aims to specify the appealing yet vague idea that legitimate political institutions and practices must value people and their lives for their own sakes.

Drawing on the analysis of Chapter 3, Chapter 4 develops a typology of four concepts of dignity, locating within it the leading features of what I will call a "traditional" account of human dignity that I go on to reject in the following chapters, and creating space for a "revisionist" alternative that I will try to reconstruct and partly defend later on. These alternative construals differ along two dimensions: whether we should think of "human dignity" as transient and vulnerable or as an immutable property of persons and their mutual relations; and whether we should conceive it as something "possessed" by, or inherent in, the person as opposed to being an ambient, social quality, somehow diffused across "humanity" and its common life.

The three chapters comprising Part II (Chapters 5, 6, and 7) reject "traditional" accounts of human dignity. These accounts construe the relation between dignity and respect as "reactive": they postulate that respect is a proper response to the antecedent presence of human dignity, which they presume to be immune to change. Chapter 4's typology allows us to distinguish two variants of the traditional approach: the first treats "human dignity" as an "inalienable," inherent, property of the individual person; the other identifies it with a fixed relation of equal status pertaining between agents. Part II shows that these traditional accounts of human dignity are deeply problematic, fail to capture what is important, bog political argument down in metaphysical abstraction, and denude the category of human dignity of any significant critical force in political argument. It therefore lends credence to the dignity-skepticism that is increasingly voiced in many quarters.

My fourfold typology suggests, however, that nontraditional ways of understanding human dignity might be available. Until we have shown that this possibility is also a cul-de-sac, the failure of traditional understandings cannot be dispositive of dignitarian humanism *as such*. Finally, Part III is devoted to exploring such an alternative, "revisionist," approach. My proposed dignity-revisionism turns the traditional view on its head. It regards the relation between respect and dignity as "performative" rather than "reactive," because it theorizes human dignity as an emergent property resulting from enacted forms of respect, and not (as in traditional views) a property that itself commands respect as a response. Performative views therefore conceptualize human dignity as a transient, rather than immutable, phenomenon. They assert that it can be weakened, strengthened, enhanced, and diminished according as respect and disrespect are socialized, and that the point of dignitarian social criticism is to analyze these dynamics and their consequences for human life.

Chapter 8 outlines that approach, and identifies not only the central challenges it faces but also some important reasons to take it seriously. Chapters 9 and 10 introduce and develop two ideas: First, that human dignity is constituted by the affective repercussions of interpersonal encounters, specifically those involving the emotion of respect; and second, that those repercussions can be seen as the site of what David Graeber has called a "human" as opposed to a "commercial" economy. Drawing on Marx's value-theory, I argue that the human dignity is a function of the way human lives are "valorized" or "devalorized" within affective economies of respect and disrespect. Chapters 11 and 12 accordingly explain the sense in which we can think of "tokens" of respect and disrespect as a kind of currency by which the relative social value of human beings is partly determined. This proposal challenges a cherished dignitarian assumption: that the value of persons and their lives is noncomparable (Kant: "beyond all price"). Since this claim is likely to invite strong resistance from precisely those most sympathetic to a dignitarian approach, a central concern of Chapter 12 is to explain how, in attending affectively to persons as objects of their respect and love, agents *do* implicitly compare their value along a particular dimension.

On my account, these comparisons partly determine how human beings are valorized in their form of life; properly understanding how this happens, and why this matters, I believe, holds the key to ultimately vindicating human dignity as a fundamental category in political criticism. I argue that we should face up to the reality of these comparisons, and need not bury it behind the traditional insistence that the worth of persons refers to some "absolute" or "incommensurable" form of value that forbids any and all evaluative comparisons between persons. That traditional insistence is motivated by an understandable refusal to "commodify" persons, to reduce their value to something like price or exchange-value. But I suggest that one can reject such commodification without asserting that personal worth stands beyond all comparison. Ultimately, I will argue that dignitarian humanism cannot succeed as an agent of political criticism unless it abandons that traditional assertion.

Chapter 13 lays out the revisionist conception of human dignity, describes some of the social forms in which it resides (and can therefore come under threat), and shows how it offers a forceful diagnosis of the Nazi genocide – a central archetype of radical indignity. Chapter 14 argues that the revisionist view makes better sense of the standard dignitarian requirement that decent social forms value human lives "for their own sakes" than do their more traditionalist interlocutors. The concluding Chapter 15 describes what a practice of dignitarian political criticism informed by dignity-revisionism would look like, and how it differs from, and in important respects improves on, several paradigms of critical reflection that dominate mainstream political theory today. It tries to show how the revisionist approach developed in the book might orient political argument toward the value of human dignity in a powerful and attractive way.

An important goal of the concluding chapter, and the book as a whole, is to argue that while the motives animating the dignitarian turn in recent political thinking are sound, executing it successfully requires that we think about human dignity in terms quite different from those to which contemporary political philosophers have accustomed us. Rawls and his successors were, I believe, correct to reject the instrumentalizing impetus of utilitarianism, and to seek a mode of political reflection better attuned to the ways that modern social forms can and do fail to value people and their lives humanely, and for their own sakes. However, as this book tries to document, they have invested in assumptions and theoretical frameworks that conspire to mystify that very commitment. As a result, political theorists in the present generation have not only lost sight of that commitment but also surrendered to concrete social and political tendencies that directly threaten human dignity in the contemporary world.

Human dignity, I therefore claim, needs protection not only from concrete social and political forces but also from intellectual paradigms that misperceive and distort it. In setting itself the immodest goal of rescuing "human dignity" from some of its most ardent philosophical defenders, then, the book is both dignity-skeptical and dignity-enthusiastic. To the extent that traditional ways of understanding humans likely thwart the effort to step back from regnant social forms and evaluate them honestly, we should be dignity-skeptics. Yet a reconstructed conception of human dignity, loyal to our ordinary convictions about why it matters, can still deserve its place in critical reflection on politics. Once the weeds obscuring its path have been removed, it may still help specify an otherwise elusive aspiration that, for all their other differences, many modern critics, from Marx to Rawls, have shared: the search for organized forms of coexistence in which the worth of all human lives becomes, as far as possible, a lived reality rather than an empty boast.

2

Some Remarks on Method

By now, dignitarian humanism in political philosophy has become closely associated with several well-entrenched theoretical assumptions which, in my view, conspire to obscure both what is compelling and what is problematic about its place in political evaluation. To begin to open a fresh angle on it, therefore, this chapter flags three assumptions, common in several currently influential genres, that this book refuses. The second half of the chapter describes and defends my own approach.

Contractualism and Liberalism

First, while Rawls's work was crucial in propelling dignitarian ideas to prominence within recent political theory, I won't assume that dignitarian humanism stands or falls with the distinctive form of contractualism that he developed. Indeed, I will ultimately argue that his contractualist approach threatens rather than secures its own dignitarian rationale. Making room for that claim will require isolating the dignitarian grounds on which Rawls rejected utilitarianism from his case for contractualism. Once we have unpicked the knot by which Rawls and others have hitched contractualism and human dignity together, we will be in a position to appreciate why, although motivated by powerful dignitarian intuitions, contractualism cannot in the end do them justice.

Second, and relatedly, this book refuses to conflate the assessment of dignitarian humanism with judgments about the adequacy of a "liberal" tradition of political thought. Today, commentators routinely identify Rawls's dignitarian turn with a distinctive kind of "philosophical liberalism" around which much recent debate within Anglophone political theory continues to swirl vainly. The resulting fixation on a "liberal tradition" has however obscured what was most important and exciting about Rawls's initial intervention: its demonstration that philosophical investigation into the justification-conditions of social and political arrangements need not prostitute "objective" academic inquiry to "subjective" political preference or sentiment, as an earlier generation of emotivists and logical positivists might have said. That demonstration depended crucially on the assumption that the raw materials on which his theory is built command attention independent of one's partial preferences, or one's allegiance to this or that political or ethical perspective. At least as originally presented, Rawls's theory seemed to satisfy that condition by appealing fundamentally to a "considered conviction," integral to any reasonable political view, that individuals possess an inviolable dignity and worth that commands unconditional respect.

Relativizing that conviction to a "liberal tradition," however, immediately denudes it of real philosophical interest, threatening the ambition to transcend the confines of any particular ideological outlook and assess political life from some more impartial, encompassing, standpoint. Rawls himself encouraged this tendency, recasting his theory in its later versions as a form of "Political Liberalism," despite his original book's admirable disinterest in establishing the "liberal" credentials of its view. This, I believe, was a regrettable and muddled disavowal of the original aspiration described in *A Theory of Justice*.[1] In beating that retreat, Rawls himself surrendered to a wider intellectual current determined to cast "liberalism" in a leading role – whether as hero or villain – in political discussion.

If human dignity matters for political theory, it is because people and their lives matter in a way that dignitarian categories are uniquely equipped to capture. The important question is: how, and with what implications for political organization? Translating that question into one about the adequacy of a supposed "liberal" tradition (as if, contrary to all evidence, we share any clear and settled understanding of what "liberalism" even is) only alienates us from the substance of the issue and artificially limits efforts to investigate it. The question deserves consideration on its own terms, and we should not assume that dignitarian ideals, whatever their content, are ones on which any particular theoretical tradition, "liberal" or otherwise, has an exclusive claim.

Political Criticism and "Applied Ethics"

Third, I will not assume that any critical force the concept of human dignity has in political judgment must reflect its standing as a source of unconditionally binding duties, obligations or rights for whose violation assignable agents are morally accountable. That this assumption has become virtually axiomatic in large areas of contemporary political philosophy is due to the confluence of several mutually reinforcing factors which have, I submit, conspired to distort perceptions of the likely relevance of dignitarian humanism in political argument.

---

[1] See also, for a similar line of thinking, Charles Larmore's characterization of "political liberalism" as drawing "on an underlying view of human dignity and of the respect that we thereby owe each and every human being." Larmore, "Respect for Persons," 71. See also Larmore, "The Moral Basis of Political Liberalism," 599–625.

Perhaps the most basic of these factors is the tendency to subsume critical reflection on politics under the field of "moral philosophy," (or sometimes simply "ethics") as it has been understood by academic philosophers from the mid-twentieth century down to the present. Peter Singer has recently defined that field as "a study of what we ought to do, not of what is the case." Following Sidgwick, and much of the "moral philosophy" of the intervening period, Singer construes such inquiry as aiming to justify "a rational procedure by which we determine what individuals 'ought' – or what it is "right" for them – to do, or to seek to realize by voluntary action."[2] Twentieth century "moral philosophy" encouraged the belief that such a "criterion of right action" must enjoy a natural priority in all practical judgment. On that view, when we move beyond purely theoretical and empirical investigation and enter the domain of "practical reasoning," the question "how should I (we) conduct myself (ourselves) if I (we) am (are) to act rightly?" enjoys immediate primacy, so that all other practical judgments – including those sought in critical reflection on politics – ultimately derive from, or be constrained by, prior criteria guiding moral deliberation about voluntary action. In other words, before we can make headway on any other normative questions, including political ones, we must first establish such criteria and then specify decision rules that individuals or institutions can use to approximate their recommendations. Under this dispensation, a certified algorithm for individual moral deliberation becomes the unique gateway through which all critical reflection on social and political life must first pass. This implies that "moral philosophy" in the Sidgwick-Singer sense must be foundational for critical reflection on politics, and therefore that political philosophy is simply one of its branches.[3]

This view powerfully shaped the intellectual milieu within which Rawls (during the 1950s and 60s) developed the arguments that would eventually coalesce into his theory of "justice as fairness." Not surprisingly, therefore, questions about the moral propriety of voluntary action are central to his philosophical concerns, despite Rawls's interest in the rule-governed

---

[2] Katarzyna de Lazari-Radek and Peter Singer, *The Point of View of the Universe: Sidgwick and Contemporary Ethics*, 1st edition (Oxford: Oxford University Press, 2014).

[3] This view need not imply that whatever criteria are entitled to determine the eligibility of voluntary actions are *sufficient* to decide all questions addressed in political criticism. Nor need it deny that the concrete decision-rules agents should follow in ordinary life might, for practical purposes, diverge from the underlying "criterion of right action" recommended by the best moral theory. Proponents of such a view could accept, following Mill, that it might be more effective in practice to encourage agents to follow certain "secondary" rules or precepts, rather than attempt to apply the relevant "criterion of right action" directly as they deliberate about what to do. But the underlying suggestion that such a criterion must be settled first does require that valid critical judgments about politics and society be shaped by some antecedently established account of the conditions of justified voluntary action and cannot be adequately pursued without it.

institutional practices comprising (what he called) the "basic structure of society." This focus is particularly evident at two points in his theory.

On the one hand, Rawls presumes the addressees of his theory to be moved by a "sense of justice." Such agents have a "reasonable principle-dependent" desire to do justice for its own sake: they are motivated to act rightly, disposed to respect each other as "free and equal moral persons," and will feel guilty about "acknowledged" wrongdoing. The purpose of Rawls's theory is then not to answer agents who doubt the rationality of acting on such motives, but rather to specify the content of the public principles they should follow when "the constraints of morality are imposed on them in circumstances which give rise to questions of justice."[4] The clear implication is that the theory of justice is a special case to which more general criteria for determining whether voluntary action is morally required, permitted, or forbidden apply. Such a theory is needed, on his account, because no pre-reflective consensus exists on exactly how those criteria condition conduct in public settings, even among agents who agree on basic principles of *individual* probity.

On the other hand, especially in his later writings on "public reason," Rawls stressed the question of how democratic societies may permissibly resolve on public decisions in a way that conforms with a "duty of civility" requiring that citizens respect each other as "free and equal" citizens. Although Rawls did not regard that duty as legally enforceable, he presupposed that the legitimacy of public institutions depends on the moral character of the deliberation preceding voluntary democratic action. Indeed, his point was precisely that democratic decisions are truly "voluntary" and hence politically legitimate only to the extent that citizens fulfill that duty of mutual respect. In concentrating on the ethical propriety of political decision procedures, then, his account of public reasoning assumes that the circumstances of morally permissible voluntary choice deserve pride of place in political evaluation, even though the latter focuses on *collective,* rather than individual, decisions.[5]

This focus is also discernible in other recently influential theories, including ones that reject many of Rawls's particular conclusions. Consider, for example, Robert Nozick's insistence that, as long as no one is guilty of wronging anyone, the routines of social interaction must be basically legitimate by dignitarian lights. This Nozickean position again treats the "moral permissibility" of

---

[4] J. Rawls, *Collected Papers*, ed. S. Freeman (Cambridge, MA: Harvard University Press, 1999), p. 97

[5] This line has been extensively developed by several later figures. See Kevin Vallier, *Liberal Politics and Public Faith: Beyond Separation* (New York: Routledge, 2014); Christopher J. Eberle, *Religious Conviction in Liberal Politics* (Cambridge, UK: Cambridge University Press, 2002); Gerald Gaus, *The Order of Public Reason: A Theory of Freedom and Morality in a Diverse and Bounded World*, Reprint edition (Cambridge, NY: Cambridge University Press, 2010); Quong, "On the Idea of Public Reason"; Quong, *Liberalism without Perfection*; Larmore, "The Moral Basis of Political Liberalism."

voluntary choices as the most fundamental desideratum that legitimate political arrangements must satisfy.

Theorists like Rawls and Nozick were also pushed in this direction by their strong commitment to a Kantian outlook on politics. Kant's ethical theory clearly conforms to the moral philosopher's paradigm just described, in which a "criterion of right action" enjoys a kind of lexical priority within all normative reflection. On a Kantian account, after all, practical reasoning *as such* ultimately reposes on the categorical imperative – a principle that conditions, and is unthinkable apart from, first-personal deliberation about how to act.

This doesn't mean that the imperatives of the Kantian "moral law" are exclusively concerned with prescribing private conduct, because they also turn out to imply various necessary conditions for the legitimacy of public institutions. Most importantly, since the Kantian view regards coercing and manipulating people as violating the autonomy on which their dignity as moral agents purportedly depends, it will permit state coercion only under very special conditions (i.e., when it is used like a virus in a vaccine, hindering its own operation so as to immunize society against it). Indeed, it carries the very strong implication, beloved of libertarians today, that political coercion is legitimate only when used to prevent wrongful coercion by private parties. On the resulting view, the purposes of the state must be limited to holding open a protected domain of free and voluntary exchange. That domain is implicitly conceived by Kantians as a condition not only for individual moral probity and an allied conception of personal dignity but also for a regime of political liberty that guarantees such dignity. As Nozick put it: if we "are inviolate individuals, who may not be used in certain ways by others as means or tools or instruments or resources . . ., " then we are morally required to treat each other "as persons having individual rights with the dignity this constitutes."[6]

These background factors have profoundly shaped contemporary perceptions of dignitarian ideas in political philosophy. Yet, as I now suggest, they have also limited them by encouraging precisely the assumption that I wish to question – that claims about respect and human dignity must figure in critical reflection about politics primarily as sources of certain unconditional moral requirements to which the voluntary choices of agents or institutions are answerable.

One important reason to resist that assumption has been canvassed in the recently influential "realist" critique of Rawls and Nozick's approach. Echoing Marx, such self-described "realists" as Bernard Williams and Raymond Geuss have objected that these Kantian positions indulge a problematically "moralizing" approach to political criticism.[7] In their view, Kantian views exemplify

---

[6] Nozick, *Anarchy, State and Utopia*, pp. 333–34.
[7] B. A. O Williams, *In the Beginning Was the Deed: Realism and Moralism in Political Argument*, ed. Geoffrey Hawthorn (Princeton, NJ: Princeton University Press, 2005).

a superficial "applied ethics" or "ethics-first" stance capable of recognizing only those shortcomings in social and political practice that materialize as someone's failure to attend to their moral duties or to the rights of equal persons. The problem with this moralizing orientation, the critics complain, is that the social pathologies most urgently inviting critical attention are precisely not of a kind that can be analyzed as species of culpable wrongdoing. As writers within the various branches of critical theory that grew out of classical Marxism have repeatedly emphasized, oppression, exploitation, dehumanization, objectification, commodification, structural racism, and many other abuses can be endemic even when all participants in the social system fulfill their conventionally recognized moral duties or do nothing that could be described as wicked. Marx was surely correct that systems of social control can be deeply problematic even though (and perhaps precisely in that) none involved is guilty of "acknowledged" wrongdoing. Focusing on the moral propriety of voluntary action, and on its deliberative conditions, is therefore from a realist standpoint superficial, limiting, and likely ideological.

Although this realist line makes an important general point about the scope of critical reflection in politics, it only gets us so far, for it cannot itself tell us whether dignitarian humanist approaches in political philosophy necessarily exemplify the sort of "ethics-first" approach they reject. Indeed, to the extent that its exponents identify dignitarian humanism with the Kantian views they revile, as they invariably do, the realist critique actually reinforces, rather than queries, the standard assumption that appeals to human dignity in political argument must indulge a narrow, moralizing mode of political criticism.

Consider in this regard Marx's characterization of the "bourgeois" ethic of freedom, equality, and voluntary exchange that he believed prevails under capitalist conditions. In that ethic, he claimed,

> [s]ubjects are posited as exchangers, equals ... [such that] they themselves are of equal worth, and assert themselves in the act of exchange as equally worthy ... whatever other individual distinction there may be between them ... [T]hey are, as equals, at the same time also indifferent to one another; whatever other individual distinction there may be does not concern them; they are indifferent to all their other individual peculiarities. Although individual A feels the need for the commodity of individual B, he does not appropriate it by force, nor vice versa, but rather they recognize one another reciprocally as proprietors ... With that, then, the complete freedom of the individual is posited: voluntary transaction; no force on either side ... the exchange of exchange values is the productive, real basis of all *equality* and *freedom*. As pure ideas they are merely the idealized expressions of this basis [commercial society]; as developed in

Raymond Geuss, *Philosophy and Real Politics* (Princeton, NJ: Princeton University Press, 2008).

juridical, political, social relations, they are merely this basis to a higher power.[8]

There is little in the picture Marx paints here from which Nozickean libertarians and other apologists for commercial society need dissent. Hayek expressed essentially the same view when he claimed that a "society that does not recognize that each individual has values of his own which he is entitled to follow can have no respect for the dignity of the individual and cannot really know freedom."[9] The equal worth and dignity of the free, choosing agent is understood on all sides as a common attribute, one that transcends the myriad differences between individuals, their tastes, values, talents, powers, and outlooks on life.

The remarkable overlap in these views is striking: Kant, Nozick, Hayek, and Marx all seem to agree that "human dignity" enters political argument as a distinctively *moral* value in that it is concerned fundamentally with the permissibility of voluntary individual action; they just differ over whether its status as such is grounds for enthusiasm or suspicion. So, where Kant, Hayek, and Nozick suppose that a dignitarian principle of equal "respect for persons" provides a decisive reason to approve of market relationships, Marxians deny that such principle is in any interesting sense distinct from the capitalist social and economic formation in which they have historically emerged. They are simply of a piece with it, faithfully recording the contours of a "bourgeois" scheme of voluntary exchange while ideologically concealing its real limitations from view. In a sense, then, Marx agrees with Nozick that the right to engage in "capitalist acts among consenting adults" is grounded on a moral obligation of respect for the personal dignity of autonomous choosers. Indeed, viewed from this angle, Kantian ethics may have been the bourgeoisie's greatest gift to historical materialism: for it provides convenient circumstantial support for Marx's hypothesis that modes of economic production give rise to moral ideologies purporting to legitimate their standard operation.

I will later partly substantiate Marx's complaint that strongly Kantian accounts of "human dignity" stand in a problematically ideological relation to market society. The point relevant now, however, is that the fierce debate over realism, ideology, and "applied ethics" in political philosophy deflects attention away from an outstanding question that remains to be considered: Must all interesting forms of dignitarian humanism display an "ethics-first" structure? If not, the realist critique may reach only strong Kantian versions of dignitarian humanism; other nonmoralizing ways to bring claims about the conditions of human dignity to bear in political criticism might be available. To keep that possibility open, this book refuses to assume that principles of

[8] K. Marx, *Grundrisse* (London: Penguin, 1973), pp. 241–45.
[9] F. A. Hayek, *The Constitution of Liberty: The Definitive Edition*, ed. Ronald Hamowy (Chicago: University of Chicago Press, 2011), p. 141.

respect for the dignity of the person must figure in political argument as "side-constraints" on morally appropriate voluntary choice.

Metaphor and Social Criticism

So much for assumptions that I reject. How then does this book proceed instead? For one thing, I take it that in most of its multifarious uses, the concept of "human dignity" functions in political argument as a *metaphor*. I will therefore approach the question of whether dignitarian humanism is fit to inform critical reflection on politics as one about when, and on what terms, the concept of human dignity, and some closely related concepts like "respect," can serve as politically useful metaphors. What does it mean to assess the "political use" of dignitarian metaphors, and how should we go about making the assessment?

Metaphors look in two directions. On the one hand, they have *targets* – something that the speaker wishes to communicate (e.g., my distress about a lost love). On the other hand, metaphors draw on linguistic *source material* – a fund of images, analogies, connotations, idioms, figures, symbols, and so on – that the speaker recruits from ordinary language to characterize their target (e.g., a "broken heart"). In general, the purpose of uniting targets and source material in a metaphor is to orient listeners' conscious attention in a particular direction for some communicative (usually practical) purpose. In using a metaphor, one selects hopefully apt linguistic content from its source material in order to pick out some relevant fact or feature of the world of putative concern to both speaker and listener – its target.

Metaphors are indispensable in ordinary life: the information available to us at any given moment is massively superabundant; to navigate an extremely complex world, we need frameworks that enable us to hone in efficiently on information that bears immediately on our situation. Metaphors afford one way of doing this,[10] and our concern here will be to understand how different dignitarian metaphors attempt to draw political attention in some directions rather than others, and to move some considerations into the foreground while ignoring others. Whether a metaphor succeeds or fails, is apt or inapt, is helpful or an obfuscating hindrance, depends on whether or not it efficiently and propitiously directs our attention toward something that we have good reason to be concerned about.

Although the ways in which any given concept or idea might serve as a metaphor are virtually infinite, their metaphorical uses are constrained to a greater or lesser extent by the content available in their source material. That source material is ultimately constituted by ordinary language, and so whether

---

[10] George Lakoff and Mark Johnson, *Metaphors We Live By* (Chicago: University of Chicago Press, 2003).

a particular metaphor "works" or not will often depend on what ordinary use allows us to say. The choice of particular source material in a metaphor is also often *committing*: once one has begun to use a particular set of metaphors to characterize something, this may rule out using other metaphors to describe the same thing. Especially when, as in the case of human dignity, a metaphor or complex of metaphors acquires prominence within a specific discourse, it is also usually possible to determine, at least within broad parameters, what communicative work their users hope it will perform.

Together, these factors can shed light on the success and utility of particular metaphorical uses, and they will all play a role in the following assessment of the ways political philosophers commonly use the metaphor of human dignity. I will argue that some dignitarian metaphors can indeed propitiously guide political judgment. However, I will also suggest that many familiar ones fail. Some, for example, are simply too vague, as many dignity-skeptics charge; some commit one to assumptions (particularly that human dignity is an unchanging quality) that frustrate, rather than further, the critical aims of dignitarian humanism; still others miss the intended target of dignitarian argument by focusing attention on formal status as opposed to human worth.

I stress that this book assesses the adequacy of dignitarian metaphors from a *practical* rather than descriptive, metaphysical, or epistemic point of view. The fundamental question is not whether metaphors of human dignity accurately describe the world, but whether interpreting our political condition in their light can help us evaluate it more intelligently, diagnose its failings more precisely, or discharge common responsibilities more wisely than we could if we did without them.[11] This normative aim is anyway what motivates

---

[11] I presume, therefore, that social criticism and political argument normally proceed by looting natural language for apt metaphors for justice and injustice, legitimate and illegitimate institutions, forms of life that oppress or emancipate, etc. Some of the metaphors the critic deploys for these purposes may work, others not; but whether they help agents better appreciate the virtues and vices of their political situation or obfuscate them, some may catch on and gradually become integrated into conventional political consciousness. In that latter case, the relevant metaphors often attain (for good or ill) axiomatic status within settled discourses, thereby becoming "literalized" platitudes anchoring standard linguistic uses and shared cultural understandings. This is how, for example, terms originally denoting aspects of feudal social organization ("estate," "sovereign," reciprocal "bonds" of "service and protection") became metaphors characterizing the authority that the modern state claims over its subjects. By now, they have ossified into "dead" metaphors that are nonetheless sedimented deeply within conventional self-understanding. Once they have evolved into familiar archetypes in this way, their original vitality as metaphors eventually wears off, and we no longer even recognize them as such; they become "common knowledge," acquiring – as Rorty has put it – a familiar "place in a pattern of justification" such that they can be "used in argument, cited to justify beliefs, treated as counters within a social practice, employed correctly or incorrectly." Richard Rorty, *Objectivity, Relativism, and Truth: Philosophical Papers Vol. 1* (Cambridge: Cambridge University Press, 1991), p. 171.

dignitarian humanists themselves. As we shall see, they have deployed human dignity as a metaphor for many different things, but all of them bring practical judgments about the good society into view: justice and injustice; rights and entitlements; the special urgency of certain abuses and grievances; liberty and personal independence; the value of human beings and their lives; the status of "free and equal" persons; and the sense of a common humanity. Our question is whether dignitarian metaphors help or hinder social criticism directed toward these values.[12]

Minding, Mattering, and Ordinary Language

I propose to think of dignitarian consciousness as constituted by a master metaphor: we *mind* how people and their lives *matter*. Stated so generally, however, this metaphor is not very informative; what we want to know is when lives fail to matter in ways that we should mind because somehow human dignity is at stake. A central assumption of this book is that the analysis of ordinary language is an essential resource in unpacking this powerful but vague idea. As Jonathan Lear says in a discussion of the later Wittgenstein, analyzing ordinary use allows us to "how we are 'minded' ... by moving around self-consciously and determining what makes more and less sense."[13] Accordingly, the account that follows frequently refers to the way concepts of dignity and respect figure in everyday natural language.

Even today, some doubt that ordinary language is a source of valuable philosophical insight. This reflects the long-standing prejudice, particularly common among "social scientists," that everyday discourse lacks precision and

---

[12] Thinking of concepts like "respect" and "dignity" as nothing more than metaphors may seem deflationary, implying that they are merely figurative, or fictive, interpretations that are distinct from some independent reality that must in the end be understood on some nonmetaphorical, "literal," basis. However, like Davidson, Rorty, and others, I deny that metaphors have a meaning that is somehow distinguishable from the "literal" meaning of the words used in the metaphor. Davidson is right that "since in most cases what [a] metaphor prompts or inspires is not entirely, or even at all, recognition of some truth or fact, the attempt to give literal expression to the content of the metaphor is simply misguided." D. Davidson, "What Metaphors Mean," in Davidson, *Inquiries into Truth and Interpretation* (Oxford: Oxford University Press, 1984), p. 247. Once one accepts, as he puts it, that "metaphors mean what the words, in their most literal interpretation, mean, and nothing more," one can focus more clearly on their practical uses and the distinctive communicative functions they perform. When Lepore and Stone say that metaphors highlight "real relationships among things that only metaphorical thinking can bring us to notice," (E. Lepore and M. Stone, "Against Metaphorical Meaning," *Topoi* 29, no. 2 (October 2010): 165–80) they are not necessarily referring to "reality" any descriptive, empirical, or problematic metaphysical sense. In practical contexts, it is simply elliptical for "what really matters."

[13] Jonathan Lear, *Open Minded: Working Out the Logic of the Soul* (Cambridge, MA: Harvard University Press, 1998), pp. 247–81.

sophistication. As B. F. Skinner put it: "the vernacular is clumsy and obese; its terms overlap with each other, draw unnecessary or unreal distinctions, and are far from being the most convenient in dealing with the data."[14] In the present context, one sees something like Skinner's attitude at work whenever theorists trying to articulate the meaning and significance of ideas of dignity and respect instinctively seek guidance in the work of fellow intellectuals from the past and present without pausing to consider pertinent ordinary language first. They may turn immediately (for example) to the theological tradition of thinking about human dignity, to such Renaissance humanists as Petrarch, Manetti, Ficino, and Pico, or to the modern German philosophical tradition of Pufendorf, Wolff, Kant, Schiller, Fichte, and Hegel.

This impulse is easy enough to understand, and these philosophical traditions are certainly often illuminating. Yet, as Austin pointed out, relying exclusively on them is often a symptom and cause of an undesirable scholasticism.[15] We must remember that the concepts of respect, disrespect, dignity, indignity, honor, dishonor, as well as closely adjacent categories like love, contempt, admiration, intimidation, and awe are not fundamentally the property of any philosophical framework or scholastic tradition. Ultimately, they belong to the everyday language of face-to-face interaction, expectation, and complaint, an arena moreover that is historically rich and anthropologic-ally quite varied. They are unlikely to have been coined, established, and developed *arbitrarily*; their survival and sedimentation in ordinary use pre-sumably reflects longstanding struggles to enforce and explain social expect-ations, and to negotiate recurring challenges of everyday human existence. In the end, these are *our* words, a poetry of concepts woven in a homeland of day-to-day social exchange. We are, I believe, more likely to recognize a human dignity worth fighting for in that homeland than in the often unworldly constructions of scholars, social scientists, and theologians. Accordingly, rather than sneering condescendingly at vernacular usage, this book takes very seriously how ordinary concepts of "respect," "love," "dignity," and "indignity," actually function in everyday discourse.

To illustrate just how far ordinary language can take us in delineating the contours of our target concepts, consider the rather complex metaphorical "physics" implicit in our everyday dignitarian consciousness. Dignity has weight and mass – the dignified have "gravitas" and are difficult to describe simultaneously as "lightweights."[16] Dignitarian idioms also characteristically connote elevation and altitude. Yet, although dignity cannot survive burial or

---

[14] B. F. Skinner, *The Behavior of Organisms* (New York: Appleton Century, 1938), p. 7.
[15] J. L. Austin and Geoffrey Warnock, *Sense and Sensibilia* (Oxford: Oxford University Press, 2010), p. 3.
[16] The connection between dignity and "gravity" is no mere pun. See also Aurel Kolnai, "Dignity," *Philosophy* 51, no. 197 (1976): 255, and Margalit, *The Decent Society*, p. 43.

submergence in dank, subterranean, or cramped spaces, it does not flutter airily or delicately on the wind like a butterfly. Rather, it hoists itself skyward like a snow-capped mountain, impressive precisely because what is held up is heavy like rock and ice, not insubstantial like an insect's wing. In this and other ways, it draws attention to itself, sometimes inspiring awe, although not through dissembling or illusion. Thus it cannot fade deceptively into the background like camouflage; it has a luster that radiates, but is not flashy; it can rust and tarnish; it is unyielding, not limp. Dignity also has a speed, or at least a tempo: it is stately, not hasty; there is no dignity in convulsing, rapid twitching, or pangs of agony. As I will try to show, although apparently remote from politics, these and similar observations can shed new light on our central question: How, if at all, might dignitarian idioms propitiously inform political criticism?

This is not to say, of course, that considering ordinary use is sufficient to resolve any particular philosophical issue, nor to deny that technical terms are ever helpful. Indeed, this book will advance quite a few technical categories of its own, some of which are entirely new, and many of which (I'm afraid) are aesthetically displeasing. But ordinary language analysts have never been opposed in principle to the introduction of technical terms. Austin was responsible, after all, for such terms as "performative," "behavitive," "exercitive," and "perlocutionary" while openly acknowledging their rebarbative character. The turn to ordinary language is then not a matter of style. The point is rather to insist that any technical terms one deploys be reined in by attention to pertinent ordinary uses, and not become a vehicle for suppressing common sense or confining our theoretical imagination. The enemy is not technical jargon *as such*, but rather technical jargon that has become so scholastic and detached from ordinary concerns as to become a source of philosophical distortion and prejudice.

Healthy Skepticism

So far, I have spoken of "dignitarian humanism" as if it were a relatively well-defined doctrine, and in the Preface, I gave a rough and ready sketch of our target. Still, that outline is a simplifying heuristic adopted for convenience: in truth, there is no clear position that is recognized as *the* "dignitarian humanist" view, only a cluster of commitments whose elective affinity can at best be inferred from political arguments that invoke it. It is precisely the evanescence of that cluster that breeds the corrosive dignity-skepticism I associated earlier with figures like B. F. Skinner and Steven Pinker. If they are right, dignitarian humanism is a conceptual morass that comprises only vapid generalities subject to virtually unlimited strategic or ideological manipulation.

A skeptical attitude is certainly appropriate given our effort to interrogate the place of appeals to "human dignity" in political argument. Yet, so sweeping a skepticism is ultimately of limited value: discounting the possibility that dignitarian humanism affords propitious metaphors for humane, just, emancipated, and decent forms of life from the outset leaves too much unexplained. To presume that its widespread popularity reflects only blundering confusion is both uncharitable and question-begging. As ordinary language analysts will rightly insist, speakers don't arbitrarily express their concerns in this idiom; they presume it to highlight certain problems and not others. They might have trouble articulating why and be prepared to admit that the relevant intuitions are vague. But they are unlikely to concede that their disapproval could be expressed just as well in other terms. They would insist that, before reaching so downright a conclusion, we should at least make some effort to unpack and charitably reconstruct the intuitions involved. To make progress in that direction, Chapter 3 teases out, in a schematic form, several immediately compelling elements in dignitarian humanism that together recommend its adoption by political philosophers and therefore partly explain its contemporary popularity.

3

Pressure Points

This chapter paints a composite portrait of the leading features of what I call dignitarian humanism. I again stress that there is in fact no single doctrine to which this label refers, still less any canonical understanding of how central dignitarian commitments fit together. For the time being, however, I make the artificial assumption that we can recover the view of a representative "dignitarian humanist" whose position we are seeking to sympathetically reconstruct but critically assess. As the argument proceeds, and we tease out those aspects of dignitarian consciousness that are worth keeping while dropping others, my hope is that we will wind up with a compelling dignitarian view that does have a genuine doctrinal integrity.

My reconstruction focuses on three consistently recurring features of dignitarian thought:

(1) The suggestion that the demands of human dignity have *unconditional* importance for the organization of social and political life;
(2) The claim that dignitarian expectations carry *universal* human significance in practical judgment; and
(3) A commitment to taking the *worth* of people, their lives, and perhaps "humanity" as such, seriously.

In each case, I will identify key points at which dignitarian humanist commitments come under pressure. My hope is that, by viewing these pressure points against the backdrop of virtues dignitarian humanists can legitimately claim for their view, we can come to appreciate more clearly its promises and perils.

To highlight the strengths of a dignitarian humanist approach, I will suggest that several common or tempting objections to it are not decisive. But clearing away these unsuccessful objections only exposes more serious difficulties that remain to be answered. My aim, then, is to replace the wholly destructive, and hence uninformative, dignity-skepticism of figures like Skinner and Pinker with a more productive skeptical attitude: one that faces up to the serious objections that confront dignitarian humanists without prematurely dismissing the possibility that they are worth answering.

The Adamant Claims of Human Dignity

I assume, first of all, that to object that some social or political institution attacks human dignity is not to draw attention to some minor flaw with which societies could conceivably live in order to achieve some countervailing benefit. It is, rather, to allege a vitiating defect that cannot be tolerated under any circumstances, something in the orbit of an outrage, even an atrocity. In other words, the dignitarian humanist regards securing human dignity not just as a discretionary end, but as a sine qua non, grounding categorical constraints and expectations. This doesn't require her to believe that human dignity is the only value claiming such unyielding stringency, nor to believe that its claims can always be fully met. Her point, rather, is that the claims of human dignity do not enjoy their importance at the sufferance of any more fundamental value or principle. They form for her a self-sufficient, basic, and adamant set of desiderata defining the outer limit of humane and civilized association.

In line with the resolution adopted in Chapter 2, I won't commit the dignitarian humanist to thinking that the violation of these categorical expectations must always correspond to the failure, on the part of some culpable agent, to fulfill an assignable moral or legal duty. No doubt this correspondence often holds. However, we have no immediate reason to presume that the adamant disapproval that affronts to human dignity invite is only activated by culpable wrongdoing. While the Kantian view that respect for human dignity is a categorical moral obligation derives such plausibility as it has from the deeper underlying assumption that human dignity makes adamant demands of us, that assumption itself doesn't entail that those demands must immediately crystallize as obligations.

A common way of expressing the adamant quality of dignitarian claims is to assert that "human dignity," and those entitled to its protections, are "inviolable."[1] However, that familiar formulation is potentially misleading because "inviolability" has distinct *normative* and *descriptive* uses that must be disambiguated. Sometimes it implies (normatively) "*shall* not be violated"; sometimes it means (descriptively) "is always *inviolate*, whatever anyone does." The potential for slippage between these alternatives has sown confusion, encouraging the illicit inference that human dignity is an unconditional value *because* it is an inalienable, immutable property of persons.

That inference rests on a suppressed, but unsound, premise: that a prohibition becomes stronger to the extent that what it protects, or grounds it, is something permanent and unchanging. It is unsound because that relation can and more usually does flow in exactly the opposite direction. For example, most think that our reasons to look after children are particularly

---

[1] As the German "Basic Law" states. For another clear statement of this view, see Perry, *The Political Morality of Liberal Democracy*, p. 11.

weighty and uncompromising. But surely it is not children's invulnerability, but precisely their great vulnerability, that gives those reasons their overriding weight. The same might apply to "human dignity": the adamant force of dignitarian claims in political criticism could reflect, not the invulnerability of "human dignity," but precisely its vulnerability.

The view that human dignity is vulnerable, and can therefore be damaged or enhanced, win victories or suffer setbacks, and so on, conflicts with the familiar claim, clearest in traditional theism and its secular Kantian offshoot, that "human dignity" refers to an immutable attribute inherent in the individual person that always commands unconditional respect. Not surprisingly, dignity-skeptics like Pinker frequently exploit the tension between these two very different patterns of thought. Hence he despairs of the "outright contradictions" one finds when "we read that slavery and degradation are morally wrong because they take someone's dignity away. But we also read that nothing you can do to a person, including enslaving and degrading him, can take his dignity away."[2] Pinker is correct to notice this tension, which shows up both in philosophical writing about dignity and in ordinary use. However, rather than seeing in it an automatic reason to dismiss dignitarian arguments out of hand, one might instead think of it as an invitation to dignitarian humanists to confront this choice. In later chapters, I push on this key pressure point and force them off the fence. I will argue that they should drop the traditional view of human dignity as immutable in favor of one in which it is a transient, vulnerable, quality. As we shall see, this does not require that they cease to regard its demands as adamant.

Why Adamance?

Some may object that in attributing to dignitarian humanism the view that the demands of respect and "human dignity" are adamant, I depict it in needlessly robust terms. Why saddle it with claiming that affronts to human dignity are never defensible when it might instead adopt the more relaxed position that there is merely a potent but rebuttable presumption against them? After all, the supposedly adamant quality of dignity-claims is by no means consistently reflected in ordinary use. Many routine medical examinations involve a certain indignity, but patients willingly submit to them in order to detect disease early. Humiliation and disrespect are moreover fairly familiar experiences; all of us have at some point suffered them, and sometimes the experience has a salutary effect. It may jolt agents into making more effort next time, or incline them toward greater compassion for other victims. One might conclude that dignitarian values are governed ultimately by a logic of cost

---

[2] Stephen Pinker, "The Stupidity of Dignity," http://pinker.wjh.harvard.edu/articles/media/The%20Stupidity%20of%20Dignity.htm.

and benefits and hence there can only be only a rebuttable presumption, not an adamant prohibition, against contravening them.

Yet such a dilution of the dignitarian humanist position cannot be reconciled with the principled anti-utilitarianism of at least recent dignitarian humanist thought. Downgraded to the level of a mere presumption, disapproval of conduct and practices that imperil human dignity would lose any overriding urgency and instead be treated as just another cost, albeit doubtless significant, to be balanced in the calculus of welfare interests. Utilitarians have never denied that indignity, humiliation, disrespect, and so on are bad, but they do deny that they have the adamant priority in political judgment that dignitarian humanists claim for them, grounding an insistence that "every human being is of infinite importance, and therefore that no consideration of expediency can justify the oppression of one by the other."[3]

It is also worth observing that actual political debate over the political implications of an adamant commitment to "human dignity" rarely turns interestingly on the question of whether that insistence is too strong. The real controversy is not over whether someone could reasonably think that its claims can be ignored or outweighed, but rather over what, precisely, *counts* as a violation of, or affront to, human dignity. The issue is difficult to settle once one moves beyond various uncontroversial archetypes of human indignity – vindictive cruelty, torture, enslavement, genocide, rape, violent assault, abject humiliation, forced labor, and so on. Chapter 1 noted several examples. In none of these familiar disputes (over retributive punishment, abortion, human rights, etc.) is the unconditional, adamant, character of dignitarian expectations seriously in dispute. To the contrary, these disagreements take their zest from the shared assumption that once we agree that something *is* a violation of human dignity, we can no longer find it defensible. The value of human dignity is not calculable in a utilitarian way, such that we may ever accept a certain amount of its sacrifice even in order to maximize its overall availability.

Far from being too strong, then, the dignitarian humanist's claim that attacks on human dignity are indefensible is, as it stands, platitudinously weak. The most urgent challenge facing those who think "human dignity" can play an important role in critical reflection about politics comes not from contrarians and provocateurs who call such platitudes into question ("*ok, genocide/torture/rape etc. undermine human dignity: so what?*"), but rather from those who doubt that philosophical elaborations of "human dignity" can justify interesting, nontrivial conclusions about what public institutions should and shouldn't do in its name in more controversial cases. Unlike contrarians, such skeptics aren't suggesting that, just because they are truistic,

[3] R. Tawney, *Richard Tawney's Commonplace Book*, ed. J. M. Winter and D. M. Joslin (Cambridge: Cambridge University Press, 2006), p. 67. Although Tawney does not mention the word dignity here, he was a dignitarian humanist, albeit of a theist kind.

claims about the indignity suffered by (say) rape or torture victims are some-how false, misleading, or to be dismissed. These are, after all, very important platitudes: societies are decent and civilized insofar as they simply take them for granted. The most troubling forms of dignity-skepticism concede this much, but then deny that, rhetorical value aside, the idiom of human dignity has any further critical import.

Universalism and Its Critics

Like the utilitarian position it seeks to replace, dignitarian humanism claims to speak from a universal point of view. Complaints on behalf of *human* dignity are presumed to be globally, rather than merely locally, intelligible, their force appreciable by all agents regardless of their membership in some historically, geographically, or culturally specific community. Thus a Scottish college professor teaching in Virginia can find himself debating with a Taiwanese graduate student whether mullahs in Iran are entitled to complain of disrespect and indignity when a cartoonist in Copenhagen represents the Prophet in a satirical fashion. Clearly, when dignitarians affix the word "human" to the word "dignity," the adjective functions in this context as an *intensifier*, picking out a particularly significant category of abuses from a larger set of "disres-pectful," "undignified," "degrading," and "humiliating" phenomena recog-nized in ordinary language. These abuses, whatever they are, form a special class of indignities so severe and overwhelming that they invite universal condemnation. The problem is to explain when and why their aversive features can become so pronounced that they constitute an assault on our very human-ity without implicitly appealing to the putatively universal psychology of experience, pain, and pleasure postulated by utilitarians.

Both the content and history of dignitarian idioms as well as currently fashionable skepticism about universalist claims put this familiar stance under immediate pressure. One problem is the sheer historical contingency and cultural particularity of modern dignitarian idioms. The suggestion that respect for human dignity is a universal requirement, owed equally to all humans regardless of their culture, beliefs, historical milieu, personal charac-teristics, virtues or vices, fairly obviously secularizes an older, though no less historically specific, theist tradition in which persons are considered to be creatures who partake equally in the image of God. It may seem sacrilegious to entertain the possibility that these ideas are merely local prejudices but the historical record forces one to take it seriously: the conventional practices of many societies, past and present, have often implicitly denied and indeed sometimes explicitly rejected modern intuitions about a universal human dignity. Many socialized into these cultures would regard the very notion that dignity could be a universal human attribute shared equally by all human agents as absurd or even abhorrent. So, one might reasonably worry that, rather than affording a genuinely independent standpoint from which to step back and assess existing social practices, dignitarian humanism merely begs the question of their value, ideologically repackaging contemporary prejudice. Chapter 15 notes that Marxian social critics, for whom dignitarian humanism does little more than summarize the "bourgeois" ethic of voluntary exchange, often take just this line.

The problem, moreover, is not just that the egalitarian universalist outlook associated with contemporary ideals of human dignity is alien to many cultures and epochs; it is also that their constituent concepts lack any inherently egalitarian or inclusive accent and seem equally at home in hierarchical contexts. Indeed, one might be tempted to suggest, in a Nietzschean vein, that these traditions have effected a transvaluation of categories that originally carried, and can still carry, a very different resonance.

Consider first the concept of respect, which started life as a rather colorless Latin verb ("respicere," "respectare") with a number of vaguely related basic meanings: to "look back or behind," to "look again (at something)," to "gaze" at a thing "repeatedly" or "intently," to "consider," to "wait," or to "expect." Circumstance, culture, and the evolution of ordinary use have however built a variety of rather more specific meanings onto this rather nondescript linguistic base. Although diverse, most of these usages display at least a loose affinity with its original Latin roots. For example, when we say "in this respect, his efforts were a huge success" or "in several respects this view resembles Marx's," the term refers to some particular to which we want to draw attention, often one that we won't notice unless we consider something closely or intently. Similarly, to urge respect for the power of hurricanes, unpredictable adversaries, and dangerous mountains is to advise caution and vigilance in their presence. Although such usages are quite distant from the original Latin we can still usually trace a family resemblance – respect as fearful caution after all involves the need to "watch one's back" and pay special heed. At the core of the concept, then, is the deployment of metaphors of visual perception ("looking") to express notions of careful consideration and directed attention.

Nothing in this conceptual format points uniquely toward an egalitarian or inclusive outlook. To the contrary, it has just as often served to express the demand that certain people, institutions, or objects should take precedence over others and therefore be treated differently. A sign saying "quiet, respect please" at the doorway of a cathedral or mausoleum indicates that one is entering a sacred space that is not to be treated as casually as a railway station or public convenience. Bowing, genuflecting, and other honorific gestures are archetypes of respect. The language of respect saturates the discourse of authority, where it invariably signifies deference, submission, reverence, homage, and obedience. Respect usually looks upward; contempt, its clearest antonym, looks down.

The familiar contemporary idea that respect for persons is a matter of treating people as one ought to treat anyone would therefore have puzzled many in former times. Indeed, in the King James Bible, "respect of persons" refers to partiality and favoritism – the sin of "prosopolepsia."[4] Those who "respect persons" in this sense accord them undue priority in virtue of their outwardly impressive attributes – that that their "persona" or "prosopon" ("mask" or "face") refracts to others, for example, their recognizable authority, apparent power, merits, visible success, social rank, and wealth.[5] God is no "respecter of persons" in that His attention is unswayed by comparisons between persons made on these bases and judges impartially, "without respect" to them. According to this usage at least, "respecting persons" appears to be exactly the converse of treating individuals impartially in the egalitarian Kantian sense of "respect for persons."[6] Blackstone in the Commentaries uses the term in the same antiKantian way, praising the Common Law for its refusal to "respect persons" by ignoring privilege and social status in the context of legal adjudication.[7]

Hierarchical and anti-egalitarian implications are even more evident when we turn to the concept of dignity, originally a Latin word used in ancient Rome to describe social elites.[8] Persons of dignity enjoy special status, belong to a privileged class, are a cut above. Even today, we distinguish between state dignitaries, who sometimes enjoy such privileges as diplomatic immunity, and ordinary citizens who (unlike diplomats) cannot normally break speed limits and traffic laws with impunity. In these basic uses, dignity is inherently bound up with hierarchy, distinction, privilege, social intimidation, and invidious exclusion.

A related and similarly troublesome aspect of the concept's historical pedigree is its affinity with practices involving violence, combat, and struggle. It is

[4] For example, Rom 2:11, Ephes. 6:9, Col 3.25, James 2:1; *The Bible: Authorized King James Version* (Oxford: Oxford University Press, 2008).

[5] In his commentaries on Deuteronomy, in which the biblical prohibition on *prosopolepsia* first appears (1:17), Luther defends social privilege as a "just principle of public order … lest everything be uniform and equal … the world has need of these forms, even if they appear to have a show of inequality, like the status of servants and maids or workmen and laborers. For not all can be kings, princes, senators, rich men, and freemen … While before God there is no respect of persons [*ansehen der person*], but all are equal, yet in the world respect of persons and inequality are necessary." Martin Luther, *Lectures on Deuteronomy*, ed. J. Pelikan (St. Louis: Concordia Publishing, 1960), p. 145.

[6] For Weber, the imperative to not "respect persons" was integral to the bureaucratic ethos of the modern civil service. See M. Weber, ed. H. H. Gerth and C. Wright Mills, *From Max Weber* (Oxford: Oxford University Press, 1958), pp. 215–16.

[7] Blackstone, *Commentaries*, Book 4, Chapter 29.

[8] See M. Griffith, "Dignity in Roman and Stoic Thought" and P. Rankine, "Dignity in Homer and Classical Greece," in Debes, *Dignity: A History*, pp. 19–67; J. Ober, "Meritocratic and Civic Dignity in Greco-Roman Antiquity," in Düwell et al., *The Cambridge Handbook of Human Dignity*, pp. 53–63.

not for nothing that criminal organizations like the Mafia are heavily invested in honor, dignity, and respect. Psychiatrist James Gilligan has documented how the idiom of dignity recurs in the outlook of the violent offenders he treated in Massachusetts prisons, implicated at a deep level in their dispositions toward violence and aggression.[9] In the past, dignity was central to the irrational and self-destructive practice of dueling, and even today fuels petty, yet often dangerous, diplomatic squabbles between nations over perceived slights.[10] One might worry, then, that dignitarian humanism is mired in prideful and power-craving prejudices of "honor-culture" and must therefore view social organization under an obsolete, violent,[11] combative, and often sexist optic.[12]

Doubts along these lines chime with a more general skepticism about universalism itself that has become increasingly influential as a result of the so-called post-modern turn taken by the human sciences over the past half-century. The post-modern critique has been directed above all at what its exponents regard as the "Enlightenment" quest for universal, rational foundations for knowledge, ethics, and political legitimacy. This they regard as a modern delusion. Among its central symptoms, according to the critics, has been the repeated attempt to approximate, by means of dispassionate reason alone, an impartial, "God's-eye" perspective on the world that can somehow transcend the particularities of specific human traditions, cultures, and identities. In repudiating all such attempts as foredoomed, the post-modern turn has fostered an intellectual culture mistrustful of universal claims, ever-ready to take "difference" seriously, hostile to "metaphysical" extravagance, determined to be maximally sensitive to the particularities of context, and confident that agents always see the world from some partial, non-mandatory perspective, shaped as much by the peculiarities of identity and emotion as by generally accessible rational insight. Given the close association between dignitarian humanism and the Enlightenment tradition, this intellectual culture is bound to approach the claim that "human dignity" is a universal value with deep suspicion. All of the characteristics of dignitarian idioms just enumerated would appear to be grist for the post-modern mill.

---

[9] J. Gilligan, *Violence: Reflections on a National Epidemic* (New York: Vintage Books, 1997).

[10] See Barry O'Neill, *Honor, Symbols, and War* (Ann Arbor: University of Michigan Press, 2001).

[11] See R. Cantanzaro, *Men of Respect: A Social History of the Italian Mafia* (New York: Free Press, 1992). See also the Unabomber manifesto: "To many of us, freedom and dignity are more important than a long life or avoidance of physical pain. Besides, we all have to die some time, and it may be better to die fighting for survival, or for a cause." T. Kaczyniski, *Industrial Society and its Future* (Berkeley, CA: Jolly Roger Press, 1995), para. 168.

[12] Mika LaVaque-Manty, "Dueling for Equality: Masculine Honor and the Modern Politics of Dignity," *Political Theory* 34, no. 6 (December 2006): 715–40.

Answering the Critics

Fashionable though they are, these doubts need not trouble the particular sort of universalism that I take dignitarian humanists to intend. As I emphasized in Chapter 2, the purposes guiding the effective deployment of dignitarian metaphors are fundamentally *practical*: as such, they differ crucially from the more narrowly epistemic concerns that have motivated the main line of post-modern criticism. In asking how dignitarian metaphors shepherd critical attention in political argument, we are not assessing their adequacy as scientific or metaphysical descriptions. Rather, we are investigating whether viewing agents' political situation under a dignitarian optic can help them – and us – achieve wiser, more discerning, more critically aware, attitudes to it.

There is no reason to think that dignitarian humanism cannot perform this function just because it is a historical construction rather than a "natural kind," given a priori by supposedly transcendent standards of rationality. The activity of critical reflection requires only the capacity to open distance between the standpoint from which existing practices are being evaluated and the practices themselves, including any prevailing positive moralities implicated within them. Admitting the contingent emergence of some historical constellation of ideas does not automatically disqualify it from serving in this capacity. All that is needed is that it be suitably independent of the particular social and political practices under scrutiny, at least in that (a) it doesn't beg the question of their adequacy; and (b) it cannot be debunked as a complicit ideological illusion attached either to the social practices under scrutiny or to any other historically existing formation of a comparable kind.

As at least some post-modern writers have implicitly recognized, satisfying these conditions of independence does not require the critic to trespass into suspect "metaphysical" territory. Consider, for example, Richard Rorty's effort to generalize and extend a "liberal" prohibition on cruelty as widely as possible. He canvasses this view while claiming to "abandon [...] universalism," in that he is prepared to admit that "liberalism" is a contingent historical construction. Yet in one important sense Rorty's disavowal of universalism is misleading. Presumably, he does not intend the view that immunity from cruelty is a privilege only to be enjoyed by the select few living in the "rich, lucky, bourgeois democracies." While not universal in its foundations, his proposal still aspires to something like universal application. I take the dignitarian humanist to embrace universality of exactly this sort.

We should therefore not confuse "contingency of emergence" with "parochiality of application." From the fact that a network of concepts has a historically local origin, it does not follow that its force in practical reflection is similarly bounded. Contingency also is compatible with the possibility that certain values are common to many, perhaps all, actual human cultures.[13]

Dignitarian Affects

Her resolutely practical focus also allows the dignitarian humanist to dispel another source of post-modern disquiet about "Enlightenment" thought – its (alleged) tendency to fetishize reason to the exclusion of affective engagement. It is not only its historical association with the Enlightenment that might lead one to connect dignitarian humanism with the quest for a dispassionate, unemotional stance, for something of the impassive Stoic sage remains in our immediate stereotypes of personal dignity. And certainly, being overwhelmed by powerful, uncontrolled, emotions is one way to lose a dignified bearing.

On reflection, however, dignitarian consciousness itself carries rich affective resonance and is largely unintelligible without it. Dignity and indignity are as much felt as reasoned upon. Relevant here is Hume's point that, although passions can be relatively calm or inflamed, their motivational effectiveness need not correlate with that dimension of intensity. As he saw, calm passions can successfully master more ardent impulses, and this, rather than a total absence of emotional engagement, often seems to characterize the quality of personal dignity. Moreover, the dignitarian's central category of "respect" is plainly an affective one, bringing emotions of fear, intimidation, and awe into view. This is clear even in Kant's ethical theory, which, despite its partly deserved reputation as obsessively rationalistic, shows a keen awareness of the emotional resonances of the idea of "respect." We have also already noticed that our intuitive sense of indignity and humiliation implicates strong emotions of dread, fear, and anxiety – especially about maintaining bodily integrity.

Given all this, it is difficult to pin the antiseptic, disembodied, dispassionate conception of deliberative rationality stereotypically associated with the modern Enlightenment on the dignitarian humanist, even if one agrees with the critics in rejecting it. Indeed, although we have noted the worry that honor, respect, and dignity bring with them a troubling approval of violence, intimidation, and hierarchical exclusion, the emotional atmosphere surrounding

---

[13] I have in mind here something like Hart's "minimum content of natural law," which replaces the classical claim that the necessary validity of the "natural law" can be established by the light of reason alone with the more modest empirical generalization that, given the limitations of earthly existence (roughly captured in Hume's "circumstances of justice"), it is predictable that virtually all societies will establish basic legal prohibitions on force, fraud and theft. H. L. A. Hart, *The Concept of Law*, 2nd edition (Oxford: Oxford University Press, 1994), pp. 193–200.

dignitarian consciousness has at least some welcome features given the aims of social criticism.

Here the dignitarian humanist can cite to her advantage the striking conceptual connections between personal dignity and a commitment to freedom. Even strong dignity-skeptics like B. F. Skinner appreciate this linkage, as the title of his book *Beyond Freedom and Dignity* itself attests. One might similarly note the centrality of autonomy in Kant's strongly dignitarian ethical theory, and the recurring emphasis on personal responsibility, conscience, promise-keeping, courage, truth-telling, and steadfastness of will within honor culture. More generally, in ordinary language, being manipulated, dominated, controlled, bullied, subjugated, oppressed, and intimidated normally exclude dignity; being in charge, staying true to oneself, maintaining confident self-possession, and refusing to compromise one's integrity are standard incidents of dignity.

In many ways, the best statement of this ideal of personal dignity as self-authorship remains that of Pico della Mirandola in his fifteenth century *Oration on the Dignity of Man*. There, Pico describes the human person as "a creature of indeterminate image"; "a free and proud shaper of [their] own being"; and "born into [a] condition of being what [they] choose to be." He asks: "Who then will not look with awe upon this our chameleon . . . this nature capable of transforming itself?"[14] Pico's remarks, which are entirely representative of dignitarian ideas down to the present, imply that our reasons to *mind* assaults on human dignity reflect a deep commitment, buttressed by emotions of pride, awe, and self-respect, to protect the human chameleon from forces that limit or contort the myriad forms in which it might freely express itself. Clearly, embracing the cause of human dignity in the name of freedom in this way need not be to view politics from a coldly detached perspective. It suggests, rather, that emancipating individuals and communities from the indignity of subjugation, oppression, manipulation, and intimidation is a basic species-responsibility reflecting sympathy and fellow feeling as much as reasoned reflection.

Viewed in the light of this emancipatory impetus, the affective connotations of intransigence and truculence carried by dignitarian categories seem, not troubling, but actually highly congenial. There is dignity in standing up for oneself and one's freedom with courage and self-respect. In contrast, meekly accepting the yoke and refusing to resist subservience or domination compound the indignity of unfreedom with that of cowardice. In this context, then, the association between dignity, self-vindication, and stubborn resistance seems worth embracing. The value of dignitarian metaphors may consist as much in their entanglement in the affective psychology of militancy as in their

---

[14] Pico della Mirandola, *Oration on the Dignity of Man*, ed. Russell Kirk (Chicago: Henry Regnery, 1956), pp. 4–8.

conventional image as means of communicating abstract normative principles (e.g., in a programmatic legal declaration).

The Common Standpoint of Humanity

Pico's human chameleon is infinitely variegated and diverse, but I take the dignitarian campaign to obstinately defy forces that limit its free expression to have an importantly different structure from a dominant contemporary paradigm that purports to protect identity, difference, and pluralism.[15] That paradigm is an avowedly "agonist" one; it postulates agents struggling to define their "identities" against Schmittian adversaries, and tends to define the "political" in terms of such struggles. Yet, however it is construed, "human dignity" is not plausibly an "identity" so much as a more general condition for the healthy and emancipated expression of particular identities. Nor is it a form of "difference," because securing that condition is difficult to conceive except as a common responsibility, shared by all. Pico's dignitarian paean to "this *our* chameleon" (emphasis added) thus captures something that currently fashionable idioms of "identity-politics" often miss – the importance of speaking from a common, human, point of view that is accessible to individuals whose experiences and situation are admittedly sharply different.

Recognizing the different ways that specific groups can suffer oppression (as in racism, homophobia, chauvinism, and economic domination) is obviously important. Yet it is, in my view, a mistake to follow that recognition up by relativizing our reasons to oppose such abuse to the standpoints occupied by the relevant identity groups. This can erode a sense of common cause and threatens to undermine inclusive coalitions committed to the struggle for dignified terms of human existence. A strength of dignitarian humanism is its emphasis on quite general reasons to *mind* the presence of such indignities and to appreciate the urgency of eliminating them.

Under the influence of an "agonist" outlook, however, the spokespersons of marginalized and subordinated constituencies today often insist that their mistreatment can only ever be partially acknowledged by others with opposing identities, especially those presumed to enjoy positions of relative advantage: thus those tarnished by "whiteness" or "white privilege" are told that their insight into the character of racism must be limited, males or "cisnormative"

---

[15] Chantal Mouffe, *The Return of the Political*, Radical Thinkers (London: Verso, 2005); Chantal Mouffe, ed., *The Challenge of Carl Schmitt*, Phronesis (London: Verso, 1999); Chantal Mouffe, Elke Wagner, and Chantal Mouffe, *Agonistics: Thinking the World Politically* (London: Verso, 2013); Connolly, *The Terms of Political Discourse*; Connolly, *Identity, Difference*; William E. Connolly, *Pluralism* (Durham: Duke University Press, 2005); William E. Connolly, Samuel Allen Chambers, and Terrell Carver, *Democracy, Pluralism and Political Theory* (London: Routledge, 2007); Bonnie Honig, *Political Theory and the Displacement of Politics*, Contestations (Ithaca: Cornell University Press, 1993).

individuals that they cannot understand the challenges faced by members of marginalized genders, atheists that they cannot fully comprehend what it is to suffer religious persecution, and so on. The resulting esoterism of "you can never understand" (Are we sure? How do we know?) risks fragmentation, tending to isolate the subjugated both from each other and from those whose support is apt to be dismissed as in "bad faith" because they can be identified as enemies implicated in their subjugation. The point is not to map, and remap, deathless struggles between adversaries ranged across a field of "difference," but to repair to a common standpoint from which seeming adversaries can be brought to see that the grievances of marginalized constituencies are legitimate. Rousseau was right to worry that the "frenzy to distinguish oneself" and to make everyone "competitors, rivals, or ... enemies" can allow "politics to restrict the honor of defending the common cause."[16]

This is *not* to deny the opacity of others' experiences – this is after all an absolutely basic feature of the human condition, although not one that affiliation or disaffiliation based on "identity" has any general tendency to diminish or aggravate. Nor is it to repudiate the insight of "standpoint epistemology" that vital information about the character of a society can be gleaned only by taking up the perspective of those subordinated within it. The unfortunate splintering encouraged by the discourse of "identity" is less a matter of how one might acquire pertinent knowledge than it is a problem about the unwarranted diffusion of emotional attention. Highlighting what differentiates racist, homophobic, and chauvinist abuse can lead one to lose sight of what those who suffer abuse, for whatever reason, *share* in virtue of their subjection, and to obscure the powerful reasons to form nonpartisan coalitions that stand adamantly against them. Such common features are genuine, not sham: female rape-victims and males who were sexually abused by priests at Catholic school have not undergone wholly incommensurable experiences; those who go through life shunned and ridiculed for some physical deformity acquired at birth know something of what it is to be mocked and abused for one's visible racial characteristics; heretics persecuted by representatives of a majority religion share something of the predicament of LGBTQ individuals confronting systemic homophobic zealotry; and surely *anyone*, any *human being*, should unconditionally oppose all of this.[17]

---

[16] Rousseau, *Basic Political Writings*, ed. D. Cress and D. Wootton (Indianapolis, IN: Hackett, 2011), pp. 88–89.

[17] These remarks are *not* to be assimilated to so-called conservative attacks on "identity-politics" advanced by figures like Douglas Murray or Jordan Peterson (I am grateful to an anonymous reader for pressing me for clarification). The point I am making is that the progressive impetus of social movements mobilized in defense of oppressed identity groups is weakened insofar as the *urgency* of their grievances is treated as fully appreciable only from inside the perspective of group members. Recent global protests against racially

The classical utilitarians hoped that a psychologically informed account of the conditions of human happiness, buttressed by sympathy for the suffering of others, might provide a general grammar of social reform subsuming all of this on generally accessible terms. However, as worries about the vacuity and commensurability of the utilitarians' notion of "welfare," as well as substantive doubts about their willingness to accept the suffering of the few for the sake of the happiness of the many, gained ground, social critics have often lost sight of, and confidence in, the underlying ambition to criticize the social system from a position both detached enough to be impartial and yet critically incisive. Partly for that reason, and for some time now, the intellectual fashion has been to scoff at the ambition itself.

Yet it is difficult in the end to understand what the point of political criticism could be without it. The famous remark about "purity of heart" that concludes Rawls's *A Theory of Justice* expresses the hope that his "Original Position" argument might assist agents to "see clearly" a set of concerns and interests that are not uniquely their own, but ones they share with all human beings, even those who are in all other respects strangers. In this sense, Rawls's thought experiment is an effort to contrive a mutually intelligible perspective, drilling through layers of social contingency to excite a nerve of fellow feeling from which critical reflection on public life might proceed on a commonly accessible basis. Even as I write these words, I can hear the knowing sneers of my academic colleagues. But the effort to find commonality in mutual estrangement should not be despised; it is central to the very enterprise of political criticism. The recent emergence of the concept of human dignity reflects that effort. The interesting question is not whether the aspiration is worth

---

abusive police tactics exposed in George Floyd's killing have been heartening precisely because they haven't only been motivated by solidarity based on identity, but also by a quite general outrage at the manifest indignity he, and those he represents, suffer. When we reflect on the magnificent slogan "Black Lives Matter!" we should not be distracted by the conservative red herring: "but don't all lives matter?" – as, *of course,* they should. The question is not, *which* lives matter, picking and choosing according to more or less exclusive categories ("all," "Black," "Blue," etc.) with which the speaker identifies. We should instead ask: "matter *to whom*?" It isn't *only* those who are already members of the targeted group or who otherwise have first-hand experience of racism, who should mind that, under racist conditions, Black lives don't matter. The power of the "Black Lives Matter!" slogan derives from its implicit addressees: those who, whether or not they are themselves victims, are in a broad sense responsible for the institutional framework of the US and who, as such, have unconditional reasons to eradicate the systematic indignities to which members of the African-American community have been for a very long time subjected. It is a mistake, in this context, to say: "you can never understand." Instead, one should emphasize that *anyone* can understand why the indignities they have faced, and still face, are adamantly unacceptable. For all his indulgence of agonist tropes, even Marx thought it important to construe the proletariat as a "universal class," bearing historical responsibility not only for emancipating itself, but humanity *as such.* See also note 20 in this chapter.

pursuing, but whether that concept is of any real philosophical help in further-
ing it and, if so, how.

Reactive and Performative Accounts

Worthwhile as it is, the dignitarian effort to somehow represent a "common
humanity"[18] *as such* nonetheless contains a key internal ambiguity. One
possibility, which I take to be the dominant, traditional view, regards
"human dignity" as inherent *in* the individual person, so that it is in some
sense possessed equally by each. The common standpoint of humanity is here
construed as that of an assembly of persons each of whom shares an attribute in
virtue of which they enjoy an equal standing commanding mutual respect.

This more traditional view moreover typically presupposes what I call
a *reactive* account of dignity and respect, in that the latter is understood as
the proper response to the former. Reactive views presuppose, as Charles
Taylor puts it, some

> account of what it is that commands our respect. ... [It] ... tells us, for
> instance, that human beings are creatures of God and made in his image,
> or that they are immortal souls, or that they are all emanations of divine
> fire, or that they are all rational agents and thus have a dignity which
> transcends any other being, or some other such characterization; and that
> *therefore* we owe them respect.[19]

Different theories displaying that structure might identify human dignity
with different personal qualities. But they agree in conceiving of dignity as
inherent in the person, a property, or possession that itself commands respect.

On the other hand, however, one might think of "human dignity" as an
ambient quality that is diffused across humanity itself such that individuals
may then be said to share in, or exemplify, it, perhaps to greater or lesser degrees.
Here one construes dignity not as an inherent property of the person to which
respect reacts, but as "abroad among," persons, emerging (or failing to emerge)
according as interaction between them is characterized by respectful conduct
and attitudes. I will call this second approach a "performative" one because it
conceives of the presence and protection of "human dignity" as resulting from
enacted practices of respect. Together with the earlier introduced distinction
between conceiving of dignity as a vulnerable or immutable quality, this contrast
between reactive and performative accounts plays a central role in the typology
of dignity concepts I present in the coming chapters.

In no interesting sense are these *ontological* options. In line with the
approach adopted here, we should instead think of each as a distinctive

---

[18] Raimand Gaita, *A Common Humanity: Thinking about Love and Truth and Justice*
(London: Routledge, 2000).
[19] Charles Taylor, *Sources of the Self* (Cambridge: Cambridge University Press, 1989), p. 5.

metaphorical structure purporting to specify an otherwise very abstract human self-image: as creatures seeking to live together in ways worthy of their humanity. One might therefore describe them as efforts to elaborate a kind of communal amour-propre, each entailing distinctive political expectations. So construed, they afford alternative explanations of how the human species *as such*, as opposed to some narrower community of agents, should have and show self-respect.

One emphasizes formal membership: we properly respect ourselves as human beings by respecting each other as beings who all *possess* a qualifying trait – dignity – that makes us worthy of respect and inclusion as comembers. The other thinks of human dignity as consisting, not in a common attribute possessed separately by individual members of the human community, but rather in realized patterns of interaction, such that an adamant commitment to approximating or preserving those patterns becomes a condition for species self-respect. This second, performative, way of thinking about dignity is obviously the more complex and challenging. However, I will argue that dignitarian humanism can serve a useful critical role in political argument only to the extent that it adopts that more challenging account.

Timanthropic Criticism

The third and final aspect of dignitarian humanism that I want to highlight is its special concern with the *worth* of people and their lives. To suffer indignity is to be *devalued* or *debased* in some important way; to respect persons and their dignity is to value them for their own sake. I will use the term "timanthropic" to capture this focus on the valuation of lives and people. I coin that term by combining the Greek words for "honor," "esteem," "worth" (even "price"), (τιμή, timé) and for humankind (ἄνθρωπος, anthrópos). Since there are many ways in which persons might be said to have "worth," value, honor, valor, or to be "worthy," I take the category of the "timanthropic" to be related to the notion of "human dignity" as a type to a token, or (perhaps better) as genus to species. Exactly how one might understand the particular kind of "worth" to which "human dignity" refers is obscure, and still remarkably undertheorized (though I will try to remedy that lacuna in later chapters). Still, as noted in the Preface, most would recognize the Kantian contrast between dignity and price as the keystone of the dignitarian humanist's timanthropic arch, holding many of the other elements of her position already mentioned in place: thus the dignitarian "worth" of persons is somehow unconditional and adamant, "beyond all price," to be prized *for its own sake*; it attaches to human beings *as such*, not in virtue of any particular traits or attributes that distinguish some individuals from others; and it is connected to our concept of personal freedom, because to be commodified, traded, objectified, or treated simply as a resource to be exploited to gratify others, are at once indignities and affronts to one's autonomy.

Standing behind all this is an extremely powerful intuition: that any adequate form of organized life must be one in which its power-structures, modes of self-reproduction, and animating ambitions are subordinated to, and made to secure rather than threaten, the independent worth of people and their lives.[20] Human beings must be valued *for their own sakes*; their worth stands in its own right and must never be made subservient to some inhuman, impersonal, or collective entity. For agents to have any warranted consciousness that they and their lives matter for their own sakes, they must be assured that they are *not* merely being exploited as fodder for the hive. As we shall see in a moment, it is precisely such an assurance that, according to Rawls, any institutionalized form of utilitarianism cannot ever give. That timanthropic charge also echoes a central theme in Marx: his identification of political criticism with the aspiration "to overturn all circumstances in which the human is a degraded, a subjugated, a forsaken, a contemptible being."[21] Perhaps it's not purely coincidental that two of Marx's favorite passages from Shakespeare, both reflecting critically on the corrupting effects of money, come from *Timon of Athens*.[22] The name "Timon," ironically, is itself

---

[20] Thus Judith Butler urges us to "stand for the value and dignity of human life, to react with outrage when lives are degraded or eviscerated without regard for their value as lives (Butler, *Frames of War* (London: Verso, 2016), p. 77)." The dignitarian import of the struggle on behalf of marginalized groups is invariably, and most plausibly, couched in terms of "social value" (Lebron, C., *The Color of Our Shame* (Oxford: Oxford University Press, 2015), pp. 44–51). Thus, according to Derrick Darby, the "dignitary injustice" of racist educational practices "impugns [the] inner worth of" black students (Derrick Darby and John L. Rury, *The Color of Mind: Why the Origins of the Achievement Gap Matter for Justice* (Chicago, IL: University of Chicago Press, 2018), p. 148), Anderson defends her "imperative of integration" as a way to counteract the stigmatizing and demeaning quality of racist or sexist prejudice (Elizabeth Anderson, *The Imperative of Integration* (Princeton, NJ: Princeton University Press), p. 20), and Tommie Shelby approvingly cites King's view that the dignitarian "insult" of poverty undermines the "intrinsic worth" of the poor (Tommie Shelby and Brandon M. Terry, eds., *To Shape a New World: Essays on the Political Philosophy of Martin Luther King, Jr.* (Cambridge, MA: Harvard University Press, 2018), p. 195).

[21] Here, I use (for largely aesthetic reasons) the translation used by Plaice, Plaice, and Knight, in their English edition of Ernst Bloch, *The Principle of Hope, Vol. 3*, trans. Neville Plaice, Stephen Plaice, and Paul Knight, Reprint edition (Cambridge, MA: MIT Press, 1995). The original passage is from Marx's "Contribution to the Critique of Hegel's *Philosophy of Right*: introduction." See Karl Marx and Friedrich Engels, *The Marx-Engels Reader*, ed. Robert C. Tucker, 2nd Revised and enlarged edition (New York: W. W. Norton & Company, 1978), p. 60, which has instead, "abased, enslaved, abandoned, and contemptible."

[22] Marx and Engels, *The Marx-Engels Reader*, pp. 102–03; Karl Marx and Ernest Mandel, *Capital: Volume 1: A Critique of Political Economy*, trans. Ben Fowkes, Reprint edition (London: Penguin Classics, 1992), pp. 229–30.

derived from our orienting Greek word τιμή, yet here applied to a character who winds up hating mankind.

Rawls's objection to utilitarianism was that, like Timon, it is misanthropic: utilitarians cannot give an appropriate account of the dignity or worth of the individual and his or her life because in their view all that ultimately matters is the net balance of pleasure over pain. Individuals and their claims become subject to the "calculus of social interests," at risk whenever the greater good requires their sacrifice. Sometimes Rawls is interpreted just as saying that utilitarianism puts certain basic rights at risk, but he was actually making a much deeper point. Whether or not it resulted in the violation of individuals' rights, the public recognition of utilitarian principles is anyway likely to undermine individuals' (sense of their own) value. As he put it, "in a public utilitarian society men (*sic*), particularly the least advantaged, will find it more difficult to be confident of their own worth."[23]

Rawls presented this thesis as grounded upon "general facts of moral psychology" whose implications become clear when we consider the "basic structures" of society from the point of view of individuals able to decide on its design before having to live within them. One way to proceed in political philosophy, he thought, is to make explicit the view of one's own value that one would have to endorse in order to accept different principles for ordering political interaction. According to Rawls, the effects of performing this con-tractualist operation on utilitarian principles are devastating. To endorse utilitarian principles as the primary regulators of the basic structure of society is necessarily to endorse a conception of oneself and one's life simply as a resource for others. It is to see oneself as a relatively trivial cog in a larger social mechanism whose ultimate purpose – the maximization of overall welfare – transcends the confines of any one life. Rawls feared that this would express a kind of contempt for individuals and their personal aspir-ations; the public application of utilitarian principles is therefore likely to erode the "social bases of self-respect." The point of his famous "Original Position" is to specify a standpoint for political judgment from which individ-uals and their lives matter only for their own sakes, and never for the sake of something else.

Set against his loathing of Bentham, Marx's complaint in *The Communist Manifesto* that "the bourgeoisie has resolved all personal honor and dignity into exchange value" in some ways foreshadows Rawls's later stance against utilitar-ianism. Notwithstanding their many differences, both Marx and Rawls charge their major critical interlocutors with idolatry in relation to timanthropic expectations. Just as Rawls's utilitarian is willing to sacrifice persons to an abstract idol – aggregate welfare – so Marx's capitalism "mutilates" people into "mere fragments" of human beings in forcing them to submit to the impersonal

---

[23] Rawls, *Theory of Justice*, p. 158.

domination of the market, as if it deserves worship for its own sake. That is why he characterized the operation of market power as a fetishizing form of idolatry, in which the circulation of commodities becomes a source of dominant, but mystifying, metaphors for relations of humane mutual concern and service.

Timanthropic Ambiguities

Appealing as it is, the timanthropic dimension of dignitarian humanism poses several immediate problems. Perhaps the most basic of these concerns the suggestion that human dignity consists in the incomparable, infinite, worth of persons. The dignity of persons, as Kant famously said, "is exalted above all price, and so admits of no equivalent." But what does it mean to say that personal worth is beyond all such comparison – "invaluable?" Given the ubiquity of comparative judgment in everyday practical reflection, this idea is very difficult to pin down. What is this value that cannot be valued, this worth beyond worth?

The problem is connected to the contrast drawn earlier between conceptions of human dignity as vulnerable (and hence subject to change) or invulnerable (and hence unchangeable). Talk of persons' noncomparable, "unconditional worth" implies a kind of infinite value that cannot be diminished or altered. Apart from its metaphysical extravagance and religious overtones, such talk raises an immediate philosophical difficulty: how can human dignity be both immune to change *and* of urgent practical importance? We tend to care most about what is fragile, mortal, and insecure. But if human dignity is an infinite, limitless, value, we don't need to worry that it will drain away; it can have no career, no past in which it had to be fought for, no uncertain future. Why should we then think of it as making unconditional, adamant, demands on practical judgment?

This is another major pressure point in dignitarian humanism. Many today cope with it, albeit in two diametrically opposed ways, by simply accepting that the claims of human dignity have a religious, mystical, quality. On one side are those who embrace their ineffability and thereby give up on secularism. These (typically theist) commentators argue in effect that the contemporary popularity of dignitarian ideals attests to a yearning to "re-enchant" modernity by restoring the "mystery of being" to center stage. On the other side are those who agree that faith in human dignity requires faith in God, but go on to draw the opposite conclusion: we should give up the sacred and focus entirely on material welfare. This, broadly speaking, is the position taken by utilitarians, consequentialists and behaviorists like B. F. Skinner. Yet many atheists, who have no wish to indulge mysticism, would say that Rawls was right to reject utilitarianism in the name of human dignity. But how exactly is the dignitarian notion of "incalculable worth" specifiable on a strictly secular basis? One might worry that dignitarian humanists are engaged on a hopeless quest to secularize the sacred.

As I have already hinted, the psychology of affective response provides the obvious alternative source for elaborating a coherent dignitarian humanist position within this middling terrain. In developing this line, the dignitarian humanist can turn to an old idea already present in Plato: that our psychological dispositions are tripartite, reducible neither to inclinations to secure our material interests nor our need to comprehend the world and sate our rational curiosity, but often reflecting a third, discrete, locus of concern and ambition – Plato's "*thymos.*" This is the seat of emotions reflecting our hopes for love, respect, honor, and recognition, generating powerful feelings of resentment, anger, indignation, and desires for acceptance. Since they often, if not always, reflect the need to be and feel valued in the eyes of significant others, these are to a large extent timanthropic affects.

The notion that our timanthropic affects constitute a psychologically independent aspect of ordinary practical consciousness has recurred throughout the history of moral and political thought after Plato. Aristotelian (and later Christian) understandings of the virtues presuppose it; Hobbes's suggestion that even in a state of nature, devoid of any settled conventional morality, agents would be jealous of their "glory" and therefore disposed to resent perceived insults exemplifies it; Mandeville's analysis of "honor" as a symptom of "self-liking" that is distinct from material self-interest appeals to it; Rousseau's suggestion that "amour-propre" (unlike "amour-de-soi") leads us to live "in the opinions of others" reflects it; Smith's account of the "impartial spectator," chiding agents into respectability mobilizes it; the overawing role of "respect" as the defining affective orientation of Kant's "kingdom of ends" appeals to it; and Nietzsche's genealogical attempt to read implicit judgments about the "order of rank" among *persons* into everyday understandings of morally good *actions* also represents it.[24]

Rooting dignitarian political criticism in the domain of affect, however, brings its own problems. If there is one theme that emerges most prominently from all the sources just cited, it is that the relevant emotional dispositions form a roiling, unruly, broth of vanity, pride, and partiality. This instability has at least two sources: on the one hand, the invidious and often incorrigible character of affects of mutual evaluation, which makes biases in this area at once endemic yet difficult to adjudicate; on the other, the frequently positional

---

[24] More recent authors who have explored these themes include: (Oxford: Oxford University Press, 2009). P. Blau, *Exchange and Power in Social Life* (London: Routledge, 1964);Arthur Lovejoy, *Reflections on Human Nature* (Baltimore: Johns Hopkins University Press, 1961); G. Brennan and P. Pettit, *The Economy of Esteem: An Essay on Civil and Political Society* (Oxford: Oxford University Press, 2005); F. Fukuyama, *Identity: The Demand for Dignity and the Politics of Resentment* (New York: Farrar, Straus and Giroux, 2018). R. Frank, *Choosing the Right Pond: Human Behavior and the Quest for Status* (New York, NY: Oxford University Press, 1986); R. Frank, *Luxury Fever: Why Money Fails to Satisfy in an Era of Excess* (New York, NY: Free Press, 1999).

quality of social status and esteem. In Gore Vidal's succinct summary: "It is not enough to succeed; others must fail." The most extreme version of this view is Nietzsche's claim that the point of view of the few and that of the many are inherently opposed.[25] One might infer from such unsentimental realism about the affective conditions of timanthropic judgment that familiar, consoling, talk about the "equal worth" of all human beings is little more than an insipid fantasy. Even Gaita, an eloquent contemporary exponent of dignitarian humanism, admits that there is something "sickly" and embarrassing about talk of the "preciousness" of individual lives.[26]

The underlying issue about the stability of timanthropic judgment is a final major pressure point that dignitarian humanists must somehow address. Although it represents a formidable problem, I conclude by noting an import-ant asset available to dignitarian humanists in addressing it: our ordinary notions of personal dignity exclude being in the grip of illusion, vanity, fantasy, and pretense. One cannot be a dupe, hypocrite, or naïf, without some indig-nity. Dignity is often a kind of grandeur, but *delusions* of grandeur are disqualified: a deluded grandeur is sham dignity. This allows us to hypothesize that (1) whatever kind of "worth" or personal value the concept of dignity denotes, it can be genuine or counterfeit; and (2) the relevant standards of authentication have something to do with the presence/absence of honesty, sincerity, vainglory, and illusion.

Earlier, I noted that timanthropic political arguments often amount to a charge of idolatry, as in Rawls's objection that utilitarianism submits agents to the needs of an impersonal abstraction (overall welfare) and in Marx's complaints that the fetish of commerce causes the "process of production" to acquire "mastery over man, rather than the opposite." For all the obvious differences in their positions, both implicitly connect the struggle to liberate agents from idolatry with the effort to specify the conditions under which they can achieve an honest, undeluded, and demystified appreciation of how people matter. Idolatry involves overvaluation or misevaluation: it occurs when agents worship (derived from "*worth*ship") the wrong things and/or do so excessively. And it is just such a concern that Marx and Rawls both express. They each wish to expose the irrational spoilage of human energies on causes and practices whose claims to importance turn out to be vain, delusive, or sham because they fail to properly value the persons and lives enmeshed within them. One reason to think that dignity must be integral to that ambition is that it names a form of personal value to which fantasy, pretense, and idolatry are always detrimental. Viewed in that light, dignitarian humanism in political philosophy aims to specify the social conditions in which the common currency of personal worth is authentic not forged.

---

[25] F. Nietzsche, *On the Genealogy of Morality: A Polemic* (Indianapolis, IN: Hackett, 1998), pp. 33–34.

[26] Gaita, *A Common Humanity*, pp. xxiii–xxiv.

Four Concepts of Dignity

Chapter 3 described, in schematic form, the basic contours of the dignitarian humanist ideas latent in much contemporary political philosophy. It tried to highlight where those ideas hold promise as well as the outstanding challenges they face as vehicles of political criticism. This chapter develops a fourfold typology of dignity concepts that will allow us to consider how dignitarians might best meet those challenges. The typology teases out, from our ordinary notions of dignity, several contrasting ways in which dignitarian metaphors can work. Doing this will enable us to bring into sharper focus traditional accounts of human dignity that construe it as an inherent trait of persons to which respect is the appropriate response while creating space for the revisionist alternative that I will later elaborate and partly defend.

Dignity: A Typology

Two important dimensions of ambiguity in our concepts of human dignity emerged from Chapter 3. One concerns whether dignity should be construed as immutable or vulnerable, and hence transient; the other, whether we should think of it as "inherent in" the person or "abroad among" them. Putting them together yields the following four possible combinations, each corresponding to a particular way of conceiving of human dignity.

Human Dignity change→ ↓locus	Transient Vulnerable to Damage/ diminishment	Fixed Invulnerable to Damage/ diminishment
Inherent within the person	A	B
Ambient among persons	D	C

Before I explicate these alternatives, two points about this typology deserve emphasis. First, the four alternatives it picks out are not offered here as rival hypotheses or generalizations vying with each other to capture the "essence" of human dignity. The point is rather that they help to clarify the modalities of actual dignitarian consciousness, allowing us to distinguish different ways in which dignity can figure in our repertoire of practical concerns. The hope is that exposing the conceptual mechanics by which different metaphors for dignity are held in place helps to determine when and how they might serve the goals of critical moral reflection and when not. "Utility for critical reflection," not "fidelity to a dignitarian essence," is the standard relevant to the argument of this book.

Second, the typology should not be taken too rigidly. It is merely a provisional map on which more detailed cartography (of various kinds) can later be performed, for various purposes. The borders defining the cells in the table moreover form permeable membranes, and so when recruited within specific political arguments, conceptions of human dignity may defy confinement within any one quadrant. Nor, as long as we are clear about the different senses in which we use them, must we *choose between* these options. Still, as long as we keep these caveats in mind, the typology affords a serviceable guide.

This chapter works through the possibilities in a roughly clockwise direction, starting in the Northwest corner.

A-Dignity

Sometimes we find indignity in agents who lose their "cool," or "temper." For example, "at this remark, all dignity deserted him, and he exploded into a raging tantrum." We also often speak of those who find themselves in some humiliating predicament as seeking to extricate themselves from it with their "dignity intact" or a "shred of dignity." In a more serious vein, we similarly intimate that physical torture or cruelty takes victims' dignity away.

These formulations presuppose a notion of dignity that is inherent but vulnerable. One's "cool" refers to a disposition of serene and confident self-possession; "temper" implies something similar. Both are lost when we are overwhelmed by some impulse that undermines them (uncontrollable sobbing, flying off the handle, screaming in agony, etc.). Talk of dignity as something that can be "shredded" uses bodily laceration as a metaphor for damage to such aspects of one's "dignity" as, for example, one's self-confidence, credibility, or moral character. Such dignitarian metaphors also often concern the ability to maintain control over physiological functions such as defecation, urination, or perspiration. Suggesting that torture or physical cruelty takes someone's dignity away similarly implies that it was somehow with them in the first place.

Two initial clarifications are in order here. First, it is vital not to confuse the *vulnerability* of some property (like dignity) with mere *variation* in its instantiation across persons. The essential contrast between the Western and Eastern columns in our diagram is a matter of the former, not the latter. For, it is concerned with *changes* that a given quality of dignity may or may not undergo. In B and C, on the Eastern side of our typology, dignity is understood as *fixed*, and hence not subject to change. But the claim that dignity is a fixed property doesn't entail that everyone possesses it to the same degree or in the same way. For example, lords and peasants can vary in their dignity but their respective dignitary standing may nonetheless be fixed and immutable. If your earldom is an inalienable birthright, it becomes immune from all change, and so cannot exemplify A-dignity. Of course, I can always kill you, but this no more alters your dignity (in the sense of undermining your nobility) than Jack Nicklaus's murder would deprive him of his eighteen major tournament titles. Although they were at some point no one's, as yet unwon, they don't somehow revert to the commons upon his demise; they remain his forever. In this case, claims about whether someone is alive or physically present and ones about their title to certain honors move on completely independent planes.

On the other hand, insofar as we are speaking of A-dignity, drawing any such clear distinction becomes *much* harder (perhaps not impossible). For, construed in mode A, dignity must share the physical location of the agents possessing it, almost as if it were integral to, or an accoutrement of, their bodies, like arms, glands, stature, natural beauty or ugliness, a knapsack and its contents, visible symptoms of health, disease, stress or mood, dress, demeanor, bearing, gait, and so on. We carry A-dignity around with us as we go, in various modifiable characteristics.

For example, suppose you are part of a stately procession, presenting a dignified manner. Something trips you up, causing you to stagger out of line, graze your knee on the gravel and bleed profusely through your now torn uniform. The gravitas you hoped to display is now undermined by a pained and embarrassing limp. Here, various physical properties in which your A-dignity consists are interrupted at a particular place and for some period of time. Similarly, if A-dignity consists in maintaining bodily integrity, self-command, and physical comportment, then dismemberment, crucifixion, and post-mortem putrefaction diminish it.

To say that A-dignity is something that we carry around with us need not require that it consists in simple physical or material properties. It can consist, for example, in a person's "temperament," "personality," "powers," "autonomy," and "character." Even though not purely physical, we can usually only consciously conceive of these qualities as sharing your location. I resisted the temptation to lose my rag *here*, despite *her* outrageous provocations on *that* occasion; you displayed your charming personality during last night's speech; *these* decisions were taken autonomously in that they reflected the exercise of your own judgment in this situation; your generosity was shown in *these* contributions, made under *those* circumstances. Insofar as we recognize a loss or gain in dignity in any of these transactions, we are in the orbit of A-dignity, for they involve changes to something physically copresent with the person.

A vital implication of this point, to which I return in the concluding chapters, is that A-Dignity requires that agents actually enjoy the physical space necessary for them to express the relevant attributes. One way to threaten someone's A-Dignity, in other words, is to deny them that space. That is one reason why the picture of a person bound, blindfolded, and gagged, so that they cannot orient themselves or control their actions, is an image of indignity. In other words, our consciousness of A-dignity is one of the points at which concerns about freedom and dignity intersect.

Contrast all this with a person's reputation, which doesn't have to be expressed in the space occupied by them and can be encountered even in their absence. Although certainly *yours*, a reputation can spread far beyond, and quite independently of, your physical presence. That is how, for example, your reputation can "precede" you, arriving at your host's door even before you have physically left home. This is possible because reputational attributes are in my sense "abroad" rather than inherent; others can be its carriers without it becoming *their* reputation. Like Nicklaus's major titles, their locus is essentially public, consisting in social relations that preserve public information about him. Not only can those relations, and the information about Nicklaus they record, persist even in his absence, they can also survive his death. However, your character, temperament, autonomy, powers, and so on are not diffused in this way, and can survive only as memories. Any A-dignity they comprise dies with you.

The modifications to which qualities, physical or otherwise, falling under A-dignity are liable should also not be equated with variation in the degree to which a person's A-dignity or indignity is manifest or concealed. Goffman's classic work *Stigma* discusses many cases of the latter kind, in which persons bearing a stigma (e.g., illiteracy or illegitimacy) successfully conceal it, allowing them to "pass" among their fellows even though it would, if recognized, impugn their respectability and social standing.[1] In such cases, as Goffman puts it, a gap opens between a person's "virtual social identity," constituted by an automatically extended presumption of social adequacy, and their "actual social identity," marred by a stigma whose public exposure would override that presumption. The social fortunes of a stigmatized person can thus rise and fall according as they more or less successfully conceal their "actual" identity. These changes in the management of appearances, however, are not of the kind involved in the vulnerability of A-dignity, though they may, as we shall see, be relevant to other types of dignity.

---

[1] E. Goffman, *Stigma: Notes on the Management of Spoiled Identity* (New York: Simon & Schuster, 1986).

Suppose, for example, that Arthur's A-dignity was undermined yesterday afternoon, when he flew into an unobserved rage after receiving an irritating email. Now, the presence of witnesses might well have compounded Arthur's indignity with embarrassment. But the presence or absence of observers does not determine, given A-dignity, whether or not Arthur's conduct *is* such an indignity in the first place. Even if successfully concealed from observers, it remains a loss of A-dignity, and Arthur can be ashamed of it as such just on his own account.

This leads me to the second important clarification mentioned earlier. Although, as a member of the northerly row of my diagram, A-dignity "inheres" in persons, it isn't usually an "inner" or "inward" quality, at least if these metaphors of inwardness imply something deep, hidden, or unobservable. We note in Chapter 6 that modern Western thinking about human dignity has increasingly treated it as an innate, often nonempirical, feature of the person (the *imago Dei*, "noumenal" self, the "human essence," particular latent capacities like rationality, agency, etc.). But it would be misleading, I think, to see this tendency to locate dignity in such inward profundities necessarily as a turn toward A-dignity. As the cases we have considered under this heading indicate, the qualities in virtue of which our A-dignity is vulnerable to change are rarely "inward" ones in this sense. Consider again Arthur, cringing at his own undignified, yet unobserved, tantrum. He is not, I submit, noticing any alteration in a hidden "intrinsic" or "innate" feature. Rather, he simply becomes conscious of the temporary interruption of his normally dignified demeanor.

To be sure, his conscious access to this change is itself introspective. We can assume that, while in the throes of his rage, Arthur was not simultaneously engaged in self-conscious monitoring and hence that, in the moment, he felt no embarrassment. His embarrassment comes only in later conscious recollection. But while Arthur's memory is in this sense introspective, this does not mean that what he is remembering was an alteration of an innate or inward quality. The cause of his embarrassment is, rather, an observable change in outward behavior, which required Arthur's physical presence at a particular time and location. He can hardly fume with rage *anywhere else*. Contrast this with criminal conviction, demotion, or removal from office, all of which can befall Arthur even *in absentia*.

It makes no difference that the behavior was not actually observed by anyone else. The point is that it was *observable*, and not a change in some occult, intrinsic, inner feature to which Arthur himself enjoys privileged introspective access. To the contrary, his memories of this earlier eruption won't be interestingly different, in terms of content, from what others, had they witnessed it, might themselves recollect of it. Psychologists have noted that our conscious memory of events in our own lives is very often autoscopic. That is, when I recall a childhood holiday at the beach the specific contents of my experiences from within my point of view at the time – the direct sensations of being in the water, of the salt stinging my eyes, of the hot sun on my exposed skin, and so on – are not what primarily come to mind. Rather, as often in dreams, I observe myself playing on Newquay beach, building sandcastles, gingerly paddling in the cold water, running from the waves, enjoying an ice-cream on the promenade, and so on, as if from a space station above. Insofar as such autoscopic "excerption" is endemic in conscious memory, no sharp contrast between recalling something in one's own past and remembering others' behavior can be drawn.[2]

Goffman proposed the useful category of "body gloss" to describe manifest outward behavior that allows observers to "glean" information about a person's attitudes or dispositions at a given time without verbal explanation.[3] A shrug, for example, may indicate that my consent is reluctant or grudging. Ostentatiously checking my watch while standing on a street-corner (Goffman's own example) lets others know that I am waiting for someone rather than behaving suspiciously. Though it is often about much more than a person's dignity, body gloss is, I suggest, a more felicitous metaphor for phenomena in the neighborhood of A-dignity than are trad-itional ideas about such hidden, intrinsic, "inner" qualities as "rational agency" or the *imago Dei*. A-dignity is typically far more superficial; while it is "glossed" in distinctive behaviors, *what* they gloss (grace, poise, self-possession, demeanor, disposition, etc.) remains, as it were, at or near a person's surface. For, although the gloss is outwardly manifest, it represents neither something abroad (like reputation) nor any deep feature of a person or the self. Whatever it exactly consists in, A-dignity is typically a skin-deep, and often fragile, quality that accompanies persons as they move physically through a world that continually threatens it.

B-Dignity

It is only when we look east, and consider the category of B-dignity, that human dignity takes on the quality of inwardness familiar in, for example, Kantian and Christian ethics. Here belongs the idea of human dignity as an invulnerable "inner worth," lodged within the person, categorically constrain-ing proper treatment while remaining unchanged regardless of whether those constraints are respected. This standard view has the challenging implication that no wrongdoing can be so extreme nor any humiliation, agony, or cruelty so severe as to alter or tarnish the dignity inherent in the personality of those

---

[2] J. Jaynes, *Origins of Consciousness in the Breakdown of the Bicameral Mind* (New York: Houghton Mifflin, 1976), pp. 29–30.
[3] E. Goffman, *Relations in Public: Microstudies of the Public Order* (New Brunswick, NJ: Transaction Publishers, 2010), pp. 122–37.

who perpetrate or suffer them. Dignity is here an inner *possession* that one cannot lose, buried so deeply in the self that nothing that befalls a person can touch it.

Dignitarian moral philosophers, theologians, and political theorists have historically spurned A-Dignity for this more inward perspective. Their standard concern is that A-dignity names qualities too ephemeral to ground a bedrock presumption of "equal moral worth" and associated protections enjoyed unconditionally by all human beings *as such*. Alan Gewirth's complaints against (what he calls) "empirical dignity" are representative:

> In this sense, dignity is a characteristic that is often also signified by its corresponding adjective, "dignified"; it is, variously, a kind of gravity or decorum or composure or self-respect or self-confidence .... Thus, we may say of some person, "he behaved with great dignity on that occasion," or "she generally comports herself with dignity." Such dignity is a contingent feature of some human beings as against others; it may be occurrently had, gained and lost.[4]

Gewirth accepts, of course, that these are perfectly valid ways of talking, and that A-dignity can be a source of genuine practical concern. He need not deny that undermining someone's composure just for the fun of it ("winding them up") is unkind and cruel. But like others committed to interpreting human dignity in terms of B-dignity, he regards such concerns as too superficial to perform any significant philosophical role in political argument.

One reason why Gewirth and others deny A-dignity any significant critical moral standing is that they fear that it cannot yield a suitably egalitarian, universal, or unconditional notion of personal worth. As Gewirth says, the qualities involved "are not always had by all human beings, let alone equally." These considerations not only push dignitarian humanism toward B-dignity but also explain why that move is almost always simultaneously an "inward" turn. This inward pressure is generated as follows. B-dignity is, by hypothesis, inherent, and so has to be thought of as somehow "possessed" by persons. To be genuinely universal and unconditional in the needed sense, however, it cannot be identified with any traits that vary from person to person, or within a person at different times. It is notoriously difficult, and likely impossible, to specify any empirically detectable trait that can meet this condition.

Nicholas Wolterstorff's criticism of secular concepts of human dignity presses this point to great effect and helps explain why proponents of B-dignity have been driven inward, to some nonempirical conception of it.[5] As he and others have pointed out, once one equates "dignity" with an empirical referent, one immediately faces the problem that different people

---

[4] Alan Gewirth, *Self-Fulfillment* (Princeton, NJ: Princeton University Press, 1998), p. 167.
[5] Wolterstorff, *Justice.*

display the relevant trait to greater and lesser degrees. Consider the "capacity for rational agency," which, Wolterstorff notes, secular dignitarians often canvass as the locus of "human dignity." Construed empirically, however, that capacity is a "graded trait," unequally distributed among persons. Babies and Alzheimer's patients for example largely lack it. Very bright people possess it to a high degree.

One might object that such traits can be construed in very broad terms, so that even a patient with incurable, late-stage, Alzheimer's counts residually as a center of "rational agency" just in virtue of her membership in a species of rational beings. Anticipating that objection, Wolterstorff notes that thinning out the relevant trait in this way threatens to empty it of all practical significance. To ground unconditional, urgent, and overriding ethical pro-hibitions (human rights, etc.), in the way that Gewirth and others propose, human dignity must be a suitably impressive consideration. But this requires a highly concentrated, rather than diluted, dignitarian solvent. The more one waters it down into a mere homeopathic residue, the less such a trait should impress our practical judgment in the adamant way to which "human dignity" pretends.

Indeed, Wolterstorff in some ways understates the problem, for embracing some empirically more demanding conception of the traits comprising B-dignity raises the even more troubling specter of what Margalit has called "trait-racism." Views incorporating trait-racism postulate a "trait such that only creatures possessing that trait are worthy of basic respect as human beings, while those who lack it are considered subhuman and unworthy of such respect."[6] The bare idea of B-dignity – of a fixed, unchangeable, personal trait that determines how its bearers should be treated – is unfortunately not sufficient to preclude trait-racism. This is so because, as noted earlier, it is one thing to maintain that a person's dignity is fixed and unalterable and another to admit variation in the degree to which different individuals instantiate it. So, alas, the concept of B-dignity allows one to think that, although no one can take away or damage the inherent human dignity of those who fully possess it, not everyone actually does in fact fully possess it.

White supremacism, I take it, exemplifies trait-racism of this sort, although so far as I am aware, it has rarely presented itself in explicitly dignitarian terms. Still, it is disconcerting to find that a recurring trope in white supremacist rhetoric can easily be reconciled with a commitment to B-dignity: the metaphor of "races" as hierarchically ranked castes, such that "whites," "Aryans," and so on constitute a kind of racial aristocracy, with an inborn right to dominate "lower" races. This is often connected to the Hitlerian precept that "races" stand in an inherently antagonistic relation (Schmittian "friends" and "enemies") and so are inevitably engaged in

---

[6] Margalit, *The Decent Society*, pp. 80–83.

a continual struggle for domination, glory, and lebensraum. Whether or not they are rendered in explicitly dignitarian terms, such nauseating claims effectively assimilate racial categories to ancien régime hierarchies in which groups are ranked by their relative "dignities." True, the idea that social groups, whether defined racially or not, must fight to attain de facto supremacy or superiority over subordinates is hard to reconcile with that of B-dignity, for it implies that the dignity of different people and groups can change with the outcomes of their mutual struggles. Still, the assumption that, in virtue of sharing some empirically discernible racial trait (e.g., skin color or facial appearance), some groups or "types" of people have a de jure title to superiority or supremacy over others is quite consistent with a commitment to B-dignity. It makes no difference that that assumption is spurious; the point is that, when hitched to some set of empirical traits, B-dignity permits such nonsense.

In the face of these difficulties, those who turn to B-dignity to render the ideal of an equal and unconditional worth inhering in persons *as such* have little choice but to abandon any suggestion that B-dignity is an empirically discernible property. According to Wolterstorff, this establishes that that ideal cannot be a purely secular one and hence, the only adequate accounts of it must be theist ones. I will suggest later that Wolterstorff is likely correct that a fully inclusive concept of B-dignity is an inherently religious idea, but he moves too quickly in assuming that non-empirical properties must be ipso facto religious ones. As it stands, the conclusion to draw, then, is not that a fully inclusive, universal, concept of B-dignity must be a religious idea, but that preserving the unconditional egalitarianism that its protagonists normally intend requires that it be construed as a non-empirical possession of the person. I submit that the pressure driving B-dignity "inward" reflects the struggle on the part of theorists committed to it to make this rather perplexing notion of a "non-empirical possession" intelligible.

We see this very clearly in Kantian ethical theories, which have recognized but side-stepped the issues raised by Wolterstorff and "trait-racism" by simply denying that moral dignity is any sort of empirical property. Kantians insist that the moral point of view is not one from which we *observe* persons as if from outside, from a third person's view, but one constituted by a special kind of reflexive attention. It involves the cultivation of a set of attitudes, dispositions, and forms of deliberation that appear appropriate, and sometimes compulsory, when rational agency consciously *attends* to itself in the right way, and thereby comes to appreciate, with a sense of wonder and awe, the dignity of a self-legislated "moral law." But on the Kantian view, the conscious process by which this dignity comes to our attention, triggering reverential awe, is not an encounter with an object of empirical experience, presenting various properties to our senses. As Richard Sorabji rightly points out, to attend to something one perceives "is not an extra bit of perception," any more than to "realize that I saw my friend after my friend is no longer there to be seen" is to somehow *see* her.[7]

Strictly Kantian views radicalize this contrast between perceiving and attending, insisting that consciousness of anything (including a person) as an empirical object precludes attending to it (or them) as a locus of moral worth. Metaphors of inwardness seem irresistible in this context for three reasons: first, the relevant quality of B-dignity is accessed introspectively, through conscious attention to our concept of ourselves and others as rational agents. B-dignity thus takes on some of the inwardness that accompanies all conscious interiority. Second, such introspection (if it goes as Kantians claim it must) exposes B-dignity as a *presupposition* of ordinary ethical self-consciousness, buried somewhere in its foundations. Third, in order to play any critical role in authenticating (or invalidating) the norms and expectations of positive morality, B-dignity must be recognizable apart from any conventional moral expectations about how persons should be treated. Otherwise it will merely express, rather than serve as an independent basis on which to critically evaluate, such positive moral conventions. So the requisite introspection must turn away from the outward expression of a "form of life" and into the precincts of the individual selves that allegedly "possess" an intrinsic, unchanging, dignity. If that presupposition is not to be found in a person's empirical characteristics, nor in the external normative conventions that surround and socially bind them, how else can we be conscious of it except as somehow "within?" There is no other direction left in which the relevant consciousness can move; the ubiquity of metaphors of inwardness in this context reflects this.

C-Dignity

I have suggested that those who invest in some notion of B-dignity as a metaphor for the unconditional, equal, worth of persons are naturally driven to conceive of dignity as an inward quality. However, it does not follow that this is the only way dignitarian humanists might deal with the challenges posed by Wolterstorff and Gewirth. They might instead pursue, and as we shall see have in fact often adopted, some version of C-Dignity. An account of human dignity in this south-eastern quadrant retains the idea that a person's dignity cannot be changed. But in turning from the northerly row to the southerly one, it abandons the idea that it simply *inheres in* them, claiming instead that it is ambient among persons, a function of their outward relations. Before considering the character of theories that have actually embraced such a view, then, we need first to clarify the operative notion of "ambience" to which we have alluded but not yet fully explained.

[7] Richard Sorabji, *Self: Ancient and Modern Insights about Individuality, Life, and Death* (Chicago: University of Chicago Press, 2006), p. 260.

We have already encountered some cases of qualities that are ambient or "abroad" in my intended sense: a person's reputation, their title to honors (like Nicklaus's major championships), and their status as "dignitaries." As these examples hopefully make clear, to say that these qualities are "ambient" or "abroad" does not preclude their belonging to, or being identified with, particular individuals. Your reputation is still *yours* even though it is also in some sense an external quality. But on reflection the precise meaning of such claims is not obvious. How can something outside you nonetheless be yours or be identified with you?

A fruitful initial clue is provided by the strained relation in ordinary use between the categories of reputation and *possession* (which naturally affiliates with the notion of inherence). The statement, "He possesses a high reputation" sounds odd; while it is not, strictly speaking, an abuse of language, it is aberrant, or at least elliptical for more precise and natural formulations: for example, that he "has gained or won . . . , " "enjoys . . . , " "achieved . . . , " or has "built . . . " such a reputation. We have already noticed one reason why these descriptions are better: "reputation" does not have to be physically co-present with its bearer. One might then hypothesize that the difference between attributes that are inherent rather than abroad is that the former share the physical location of those who display them while the latter don't.

This hypothesis is on the right lines, but it cannot be the whole story. For one thing, we can often be said to "possess" things that are physically remote from our present location: my washing machine remains mine even when I am on holiday in the mountains, for example. Conversely, even items with no determinate physical position can have inherent properties. Consider the *Aria* that opens and closes J. S. Bach's *Goldberg Variations*. It is the center of gravity of the whole piece, presenting the ground on which the subsequent variations are based with unsurpassed elegance, grace, and clarity. Its return at the end of the set is one of the most moving moments in Western music, as the listener is reminded of the basic thematic material from which the whole germinated, leaving her with a sense of a journey of discovery that has reached fruition and fulfillment and therefore need go no further. When heard at the start, it gently arrests the listener, like an intriguing path beckoning her to explore. When heard again at the end, its budding welcome has become an autumnal gesture of grateful farewell.

Imagine two concert-goers coming away from a performance of the piece, marveling at the dignity of the *Aria*, and of the variations it frames. Clearly, the *Goldberg Variations* has no clear spatial location, yet there remains a clear sense in which they are talking about the dignity *of* the music. If it isn't *there*, inherent in the composition, where else can it be?

My answer turns on the idea that a central function of metaphors is that of *excerption*. When our concertgoers discuss the dignity of the piece, they are, I submit, excerpting the piece in their minds using dignitarian metaphors to make it consciously available for conversation. They are conscious of the dignity of the music as inherent because in this case it is possible to excerpt the piece as a freestanding object, independent of any relations to anything outside it, and locate its dignity "there" (even though, strictly speaking, there is no physical "there" there).

Suppose their conversation now shifts into a discussion of the place of the *Goldberg Variations* in the pantheon of Western music. One reports that it is a "masterpiece of the highest order." Now, while it may sound a little strained to describe its elevated status in the keyboard repertoire as a kind of dignity, certainly musicians speak of it with great reverence. In discussing its standing as a recognized masterwork, our concert-goers are again excerpting the *Goldberg Variations*. However, whereas their previous comments excerpt the piece itself, what has now come into view is the *relation* between the piece and an appreciative audience. We might say that the effort to consciously excerpt the piece itself as a stand-alone object of scrutiny is here partial or incomplete, for what is now in view is not the music and its inherent character but the relation between the music and a community of informed musicians. This is not to say that the excerption is partial or incomplete in the second case; rather it is to say that to successfully excerpt a feature like reputation or status, one must be excerpting a *relation* between at least two differentiated things. Here, too, what is excerpted is not a strictly physical quality: clearly, the esteem in which the *Goldberg Variations* is held is not an event or feature with a clearly defined spatiotemporal location. Even so, it would be misleading to regard it as inherent in the music itself. It is, rather, "abroad" within the community of musicians, a musical res publica.

This, then, is how I propose to construe the contrast between features of an object that inhere in it and those that are "ambient." Consciousness of A-dignity and B-dignity presumes that we can excerpt their bearers as free-standing sites in which dignity consists. That of C-dignity and D-dignity rather imputes it to some excerpted *relation* between at least two items.

Stephen Darwall's attempt to conceive of moral dignity in terms of "second-personal authority" is perhaps the clearest contemporary example of a theory that construes it in terms of C-dignity.[8] Although it is theirs to wield, "second-personal authority" in his sense is not simply an inherent feature of agents, but rather an aspect of their relation to the "moral community" they jointly constitute with all other agents. In his account, moral practices (complaints, forms of resentment and indignation, ascriptions of wrongdoing, the recognition of moral duties, etc.) presuppose, and thereby in a sense constitute, the second-personal authority of all agents. The character of both wrongdoing and the appropriate reaction to wrongdoers is properly understood only from

---

[8] S. Darwall, *The Second-Person Standpoint: Morality, Respect and Accountability* (Cambridge, MA: Harvard University Press, 2006).

within this "second-person standpoint." Yet neither those who wrong nor those who are wronged are thereby ejected from the moral community: in his account, nothing anyone can do can ever revoke or change anyone's standing within that community.

While Darwall's second-personal dignity is in this way invulnerable, it is nonetheless ambient, diffused across the norms and moral psychology of common life. We cannot excerpt agents as executors of "second-personal authority" independently of their relation to others who are accountable to that authority, and who also have the same moral authority to demand respect for their status as "self-authenticating sources of valid claims," to use a Rawlsian formulation. To be sure, your "second-personal authority" is indeed *yours* on his account, but it does not straightforwardly inhere in an excerpted "you," as the dignity of Bach's *Goldberg Variations* inheres in the music. For such authority is yours only because it is also ours. So, like Kantian notions of B-dignity, then, Darwall's account sees the relevant form of dignity as an unalterable presupposition that can be recovered by introspectively attending to certain ethical commitments. But unlike B-dignity, it is presupposed, not within an excerpted conception of persons considered *as such,* apart from any social relations, but rather in our consciousness of them as mutually accountable members of a speech-community.

Rawls's contractualism is tacitly committed to something like this view, for it is built around the idea of a "reasonable person" moved by the "principle-dependent desire" to seek reciprocity and mutual respect for their own sake. Such people acknowledge, as Darwall puts it, "the common dignity that all persons share."[9] They are prepared to submit themselves to expectations ratified by contractualist agreements because the fact that they survive such scrutiny establishes that they can be reconciled with the reasonable claims of all who share in a primordial equal status. The salient aspect of Rawlsian "reasonableness," then, does not only look inward, to an attribute inherent in the person, but also outward, to an irreducibly relational ideal of cooperation structured by fairness and reciprocity. Human dignity is here implicitly construed, not simply as an individualized possession, but rather as a diffused relation of equal status which then constrains how human communities may legitimately organize themselves.

Jean Hampton's intriguing defense of retributivist punishment also appeals to C-Dignity (not coincidentally, as she was one of Rawls's students). We see this in her distinction between treatment that is merely "demeaning" and treatment that actually "diminishes." Hampton asserts that

> there is a difference between being demeaned and being literally lowered in value [diminishment]. A prince who is mistaken for a pauper and who

---

[9] Ibid., p. 136 (also pp. 22–23, 25, 138, 147, 203, 274, 299).

therefore fails to receive royal treatment will regard this treatment as demeaning, not because he will believe or even worry that the treatment literally ... causes him to lose his princely status, but because he will believe the treatment is too low for him *given* that princely status. It is because he believes he is *not* lower in status that he regards the treatment as insulting.[10]

Insofar as the dignity of Hampton's prince is a matter of his royal status, we have here a conception that exemplifies C-dignity. For it seems impossible to specify "royal status" simply as an inherent feature of the prince. It is rather a relational property, one that depends on his social recognition as royalty.

Darwall's notion of second-personal authority, and the closely allied Rawlsian notion of "reasonable" persons who share a "sense of justice," appropriate the same idea for the non-hierarchical ideal of a community of equal persons. Of course, reasonable people can disagree about what, exactly, is required to attend appropriately to persons construed as moral equals, just as there is room for debate in a monarchy about exactly what forms of deference are called for in the presence of members of the royal family. But these disagreements are *not* about what is necessary to *preserve* the C-dignity either of princes and princesses or agents who wield "second-personal authority." For, by hypothesis, their dignitarian status is fixed and not subject to change. The only remaining question is what social rules agents must follow, and on a contractualist view ratify, in order to show due respect for the relevant status.

D-Dignity

To specify D-dignity we need only retain the idea that dignity consists in diffused relations between agents but relax Darwall's assumption that they are invariant. Reputation and fame are qualities of the relevant sort, for they are at once alterable, socially diffused, yet attached to particular individuals. Honor culture, a historically very diverse yet remarkably consistent, phenomenon, provides a convenient point of reference for D-dignity. Schopenhauer's famous definition is helpful here: "Honor is, objectively, the opinion others hold of our worth, and, subjectively, the fear which this opinion inspires in us." To understand the implications of this definition for D-dignity, consider *scandals* and the way in which they disgrace public figures or institutions and thereby effect dishonor.

Simply committing an offence does not automatically disgrace the perpetrator. Nor is it enough that an infraction is known or suspected, even by many people. Indeed, it is rarely the case that individuals are completely unaware (consider gossip, rumor-mills, and grapevines) of conduct that later causes

---

[10] J. Hampton and J. G. Murphy, *Forgiveness and Mercy* (Cambridge: Cambridge University Press, 1988), p. 45.

a scandal. The examples of child abuse in the Catholic church, phone hacking in the British press, and the cases of sexual harassment recently brought to light by the "me-too" movement illustrate this point very clearly. When a scandal "breaks," the critical factor is not the bare dissemination of compromising information but rather the way in which it becomes publicly present and hence an object of common knowledge. Members of the public not only come to know that an offence has been committed but also become conscious of themselves as a collective audience to the offence. On the assumption that the objectionable nature of the offence is not in dispute within that audience (as it rarely is in most scandals), they thereby come to know that others' disapproval and outrage is actively focused on the offending party. This converts mere wrongdoing into "disgrace," and thereby effects dishonor because, as analysts of honor cultures attest, honor is crucially about one's standing in the "eyes of society."

While wrongdoing is dishonorable, then, it only effects actual dishonor when, as in a scandal, it becomes common knowledge within some observing "honor group." To clarify how this bears on the construal of D-dignity, recall Goffman's account of agents' struggles to manage gaps that sometimes open up between their "virtual identity" (some idealization of respectable person-hood) and their "actual identity," which includes some shameful or conventionally discrediting stigma. Agents in this position will seek to conceal such stigmas from public view, but, as already noted, their success or failure in this endeavor need not measure any change to their dignity. Indeed, this predicament often arises, and will be particularly acute, when a person's dignity is understood as fixed, as in either mode B or C.

Consider trait-racist or caste societies in which agents' dignity is unalterably fixed according to their possession of relevant traits (B-dignity) or class position (C-dignity). Suppose that you live in one or other of these societies, and that your traits or pedigree disqualify you from the full privileges of dignity. Assume further, however, that you are in a position to conceal the relevant traits or pedigree; as long as you can hide them, you are able to evade the consequences of your (B- and C-) indignities coming to light. Here, the stigma that you are trying to conceal is precisely the "fact" of your indignity (identified by some account of B- or C-dignity). To be sure, the exposure of your stigma under these conditions would lead to your dishonor. For all we have said so far, however, what is at stake here is the extent to which patterns of respect and tokens of honor exchanged among agents genuinely track their *actual* dignity. We have not yet reached D-dignity because none of this requires the relevant forms of dignity to be alterable.

For honor culture to serve as a model approximating D-dignity, then, we must take the more radical step of seeing the respect and contempt that agents actually receive as somehow *determining* their honor. In other words, we must entertain exactly the possibility that Gewirth repudiates when he says that the "existence and nature of dignity cannot be constituted by respect; on the contrary, it is because humans have inherent dignity that respect is demanded or required of other persons as the recognition of an antecedently existing worth."[11] Goffman's terminology is again useful here. Insofar as an agent's D-dignity is identified with their social honor, it consists in, and varies with, their "virtual identity," the image they refract in the eyes of society. As they are respected, and as the fact of others' respect becomes "common knowledge," their honor is enhanced; as any humiliation and contempt to which they are subject similarly crystallizes as "common knowledge," they are dishonored.

As Gewirth's comment illustrates, moral and political theorists have often been highly allergic to any suggestion that human dignity is well-construed on this model. The association with honor culture is itself a major historical reason for this hostility. But there is also a more philosophical reason: if D-dignity is truly an *ambient* property, diffused across social relations like fame, honor, and reputation, then there is an immediate ambiguity about its location. An advantage of theorizing human dignity as D-dignity is that it would seem to capture the idea that it is somehow a species-property, spread across the human community. But then human dignity must be importantly *unlike* qualities like honor, fame, and reputation: we have no concept of "human honor," "human fame," or "human reputation." It is *my* reputation that alters as I attract plaudits or derision; no judgment about the reputation of humanity is implied. So in this sense, the logic of human dignity seems importantly different from other categories that fit in the southwestern quadrant of our typology.

At the same time, we do often want to say precisely that it is *my* human dignity that is taken away, violated, or abused when I am tortured, raped, enslaved, targeted for extermination in a genocide, and so on. So it seems plain that honor, reputation, and fame must at best be imperfect models for an account of human dignity as D-dignity. Such an account would have to explain how it is both like and unlike honor, reputation, and fame. I think that uncertainty about how to iron out these equivocations is another reason why philosophers have neglected – indeed scorned – the possibility that something like D-dignity could be a propitious metaphor for human dignity. Since I will ultimately be arguing that it is, this is a problem I will have to solve in future chapters.

---

[11] Gewirth, *Self-Fulfillment*, p. 167.

PART II

Against Traditional Accounts of Human Dignity

5

The Inherent Dignity of the Person

According to the *Universal Declaration of Human Rights,* recognizing "the inherent dignity and . . . the equal and inalienable rights of all members of the human family is the foundation of freedom, justice and peace in the world." This statement expresses what we can call the traditional view of human dignity, according to which "dignity" inheres in personality and grounds inalienable entitlements to be treated with respect. Recast in timanthropic terms, this view implies that human dignity is a kind of intrinsic worth

- that all persons *as such* possess equally and at all times, regardless of (1) any differentiating personal characteristics, (2) their socially recognized legal status, or (3) the actual treatment they receive at the hands of public or private agents; and
- that always commands the unconditional respect of all other persons and any institutions they represent.

This traditional account has an important affinity with the "just price" theory of the medieval scholastics. For a just price theorist, "overcharging" and "underpayment" are specified, in part, in relation to the intrinsic worth of the goods or services being exchanged; fair exchanges are answerable to some value *in* the objects being exchanged. While neoclassical economics has dropped this metaphysical postulate about intrinsic value in favor of a "subjectivist" one in which (at least economic) "value" is the result, rather than the ground, of human valuation, something like it lives on in traditional accounts of human dignity. For, on these accounts, human dignity refers to an inner worth possessed by individual persons, and to which the conduct of persons and institutions is accountable.

Much as the "just price" theorists took economic valuation to be answerable to the inherent value of goods and services, then, traditional dignitarian accounts impute to persons *as such* an attribute of dignity to which "respect" is the appropriate reaction. This reactive view of dignity and respect clearly doesn't imply that agents *will* automatically receive the respect they are due, any more than that the just price theory guarantees that goods exchange at their true value. Whatever actually occurs, however, such accounts analyze legitimate (permitted or required) treatment of persons in terms of the respect properly commanded by their dignity; conversely, they diagnose abuse as the symptom of a failure to pay it appropriate heed. Traditional views of dignity are thus built around two terms, one constant and one variable: the constant is dignity; the variable is the degree to which agents recognize and properly respect it. Dignity here is judge and jury, representing the standpoint from which dignitarian political judgments are to be made; in the dock are social practices, institutions, and individual conduct that stand accused of failing to respect persons and their lives appropriately. So construed, dignitarian political criticism aims to determine whether or not they are guilty as charged.

Chapters 5, 6, and 7 argue that the account of political criticism implicit in this approach cannot succeed. To establish this, they interrogate the two concepts of dignity comprising the easterly column of the typology laid out in Chapter 4 – B-dignity and C-dignity. Only if these concepts can be shown to have critical utility can dignity-traditionalism be vindicated. This chapter and Chapter 6 consider B-dignity and various views in its orbit; their sequel turns to C-dignity.

B-Dignity and Nonempirical Introspection

Chapter 4 identified one reason to be suspicious of the idea that agents possess the sort of inherent, fixed, dignity falling within the "B" quadrant of our typology. We noted there the disturbing truth that a commitment to B-dignity cannot rule out "trait-racism," the view that there is some empirically discernible feature of persons that constitutes basic dignity, but that not all actual human beings possess or possess to the same degree. A residual "trait-racism" seems to me implicit even in traditional "chain-of-being" views that locate the class of "humanity" in an intermediate position between divine superiors (angels, Gods, etc.) and "animal" inferiors. One proponent of this traditional line, John Finnis, says that human dignity "denotes a rank of being, and all beings of this rank have . . . [equivalent] worth. . . . Differences of innate intelligence and aptitude . . . are . . . quite irrelevant to this dignity of the human over all that is subhuman, and to the human rights to equal concern and respect, life, and so forth."[1] Finnis is probably right that such a view need not in principle draw any invidious distinctions between human beings, but as his striking use of the term "subhuman" indicates, to use this idiom is to play with fire. As soon as *any* blurring of the boundaries defining the rank of "humanity" is introduced, the possibility that some human beings have "marginal" status will become troublesome. One recalls Orwell's *Animal Farm*: "Four legs good, two legs better!"

---

[1] John Finnis, "The Priority of Persons Revisited," *The American Journal of Jurisprudence* 58 (2013): 45.

The problem is to explain how, if dignity reposes on some reasonably encompassing but empirically variable trait like "rationality" or "autonomy," we are not committed to treating human dignity as something that more and less rational or autonomous individuals display to greater or lesser degrees. While acknowledging that some senses of "dignity" are indeed hierarchical in this way, most dignitarian humanists today insist that the sort of dignity that matters for political judgment does not vary between persons in that way. A variety of ways of dealing with the problem on these terms[2] have been canvassed, but none is entirely without difficulty.

As we noted earlier, however, a Kantian approach has struck many as affording traditional dignitarian accounts a way to circumvent this problem. Central to Kant's ethical theory is the intuition that moral dignity is not, and cannot be, an empirical category at all. Persons can be said to bear or possess it, but not because of anything about them that is empirically perceptible. For Kant, rather, the dignity of persons is disclosed to us when we take up the practical standpoint – the point of view from which we consider how to conduct ourselves – and reflect consciously on what that standpoint presupposes. Kant claimed that attending in this way to our concept of ourselves as agents, capable of recognizing and responding (in)appropriately to practical reasons, exposes an absolutely fundamental postulate to which we are implicitly committed: that dignity and worth inhere in persons in virtue of their possessing the basic capacities of responsible agency (autonomy, deliberative rationality, moral sensibility, and such emotional dispositions as respect, indignation, resentment, etc.). Once made explicit, the resulting conception of the inherent worth of persons reveals itself as the cornerstone of the whole system of practical reasoning: it motivates a categorical distinction between the worth of persons and the price of things, and grounds agents' most basic moral entitlements in the former; it directly commands a humbling awe and respect that check self-love and activate principled concern for others; it unconditionally prohibits the subordination of persons to the status of "mere means" or instruments for the realization of others' ends; it marks coercion, manipulation, and other autonomy-infringing conduct as the most urgent threats to human dignity; and it points toward a condition of social freedom as a necessary desideratum of any just and legitimate political order. But, according to Kant, none of these conclusions depend on any empirical generalizations or causal predictions about human psychology, institutional life, or the typical course of events. They commend themselves (as Kant would have said)

---

[2] For example, Rawls's "range-property" argument (For discussion, see J. Waldron, *God, Locke, and Equality: Christian Foundations in Locke's Political Thought* (Cambridge: Cambridge University Press, 2002), pp. 76–81, 108, 111–13); Ian Carter's account of "opacity respect" in I. Carter, "Respect and the Basis of Equality," *Ethics* 121, no. 3 (2011): 538–71; and Waldron's own notion of "sortal" status – see Waldron, *Dignity, Rank, and Rights*.

"transcendentally" – as philosophically derived elaborations of our own self-conception as responsible agents capable of practical reasoning.

Apart from skirting the problem of "trait-racism," this Kantian framework has at least three other things going for it. First, it accords well with the traditional view that human dignity is a profound, inner, substrate of moral personality, always present though concealed behind agents' highly varied observable characteristics. Second, it does not depend on any clearly religious or theological premises, and so promises a purely secular basis for critical reflection. And third, it recognizes persons as bearers of dignity independently of the cultures, social practices, and conventional moralities into which they are socialized. In attributing inherent dignity to persons *as such*, it at least purports to define a universal standard guiding moral and political judgment.

These advantages notwithstanding, I doubt that this Kantian framework can rescue B-dignity as a useful category for social and political criticism. As I will now try to show, interpreting human dignity in this mode simply mystifies the concept, miring it in metaphysical and quasi-religious assumptions. Such interpretations moreover cannot capture, and in some cases actually conflict with, assumptions about human dignity that are crucial to our ordinary sense of its social and political importance. We shall see in Chapter 6 that not even Kant's own view can accommodate B-dignity in any pure form, although, as I will go on to claim, his own rather more complex position is independently problematic in a way that puts further pressure on the traditional idea of an "inherent" inner dignity.

Latent Religiosity

If the fixed, invariant and inalienable feature constituting B-dignity is derived *neither* from agents' socially constituted ethical consciousness *nor* from any empirically discernible traits, it inevitably takes on a very mysterious character. Does introspective or "transcendental" reflection on our implicit practical commitments confirm us in the possession of such a feature and enable us to understand exactly how it can guide political judgment? Even if we grant that it discloses some very general notion along these lines, one might still worry that the resulting conception of dignity is too ineffable (literally "unutterable") to improve on more overtly religious understandings of an immaterial soul.

Many defenders of human dignity, of course, happily grant that it *is* an essentially religious idea, and that no secular philosophical outlook can adequately recognize and protect it. John Milbank, for example, has argued that secular ethical doctrines, especially that of modern liberalism, are systematically unable to explain why torture is an affront to human dignity. "A person should not be tortured," he tells us, "because of her intrinsic value, because she resides in the image of God. . . . Torture may often be carried out by religions, but only genuine religion, not liberalism, can promise a rationale to stop torture."[3] I take it that most dignitarian humanists would regard this conclusion, if true, as very bad news. They have aspired to a mode of political criticism that is accessible to all members of society, theist and atheist alike. But if dignitarian arguments are sound only insofar as they rely on religious assumptions, they won't meet this standard of general accessibility.

Now, as stated, Milbank's position is plainly too strong. Set alongside the numerous abuses perpetrated by churches and other theist institutions over the centuries, his unequivocal condemnation of "liberalism," and indeed all other secular worldviews, for incubating the will to torture almost certainly applies a double-standard. More generally, our reasons to object to torture are massively overdetermined, and so even if he is right that no secular account of *dignity* can adequately motivate opposition to it, there remain any number of nondignitarian grounds for repudiating it.

Still, as long as we are talking only about B-dignity, I suspect Milbank is right that we are dealing here with an essentially religious idea. The reason for this is not the thought that "equal dignity" presupposes some divinity whose overawing greatness trivializes human differences, nor the more familiar assertion that the authority of morality necessarily presupposes some sort of divine-command theory of ethics, nor even the claim that any concept of "intrinsic worth" must presuppose some notion of a "divine spark" within every soul. The real reason to doubt that B-dignity can ever be purged of religious content is that a dignity that survives even in persons responsible for, or victims of, abject humiliation seems cognizable only from a standpoint of superhuman charity and love.

The problem is this. To be consistent with any secular outlook, a dignitarian critical morality centered on B-dignity must show that the point of view within which a person's dignity comes to conscious attention is intelligibly *human* rather than divine. Can this be true if it is construed as B-dignity? To be conscious of some quality comprising B-dignity inherent in persons, we must discern in them (and ourselves) an inner dignity that cannot be altered by anything that they (or we) do or suffer. On this view, Christ enduring the torments of the cross and monsters like Hitler and Stalin can come to my attention as bearers of a dignity that has remained unchanged since their birth, despite their subsequent moral careers, and they can do so from within a *human* point of view, that is, one available to anyone.

The current banality of talk about an unalterable dignity inherent in each of us may lead one to underestimate the strangeness and radicalism of such claims. Stoicism is often ridiculed for suggesting that even those tortured on the rack can retain their dignity (and with it the happiness that consists in tranquil imperturbability of soul). But not even Stoics maintained that this dignity is completely invulnerable, for they allowed that we can maim it by our

---

[3] J. Milbank, "The Gift of Ruling," *New Blackfriars* 85, no. 996 (2004): 236.

own poor choices – in particular by identifying ourselves excessively with endeavors or goals whose outcomes lie beyond our control. Stoic dignity is inherent yet vulnerable and therefore by my lights more closely approximates A-Dignity than B-Dignity. Views that genuinely instantiate B-Dignity must not permit even our own delinquency to taint it. To invoke Stephen Darwall's useful language, we must be able to *recognize* B-dignity in Hitler and Stalin despite our *appraisal* of their depravity.

However, while I don't question the logical coherence of this distinction between recognition-respect and appraisal-respect, I doubt that there is any intelligibly *human* standpoint from within which Hitler and Stalin can command our attention as bearers of an inherent dignity that remains unaltered in the face of their deeds. They can do so, it would seem, only from a standpoint of superhuman sympathy and charity. To occupy such a standpoint, I must be able to penetrate the all-too-human mist of pathos, pity, embarrassment, disgust, anger, outrage, indignation, schadenfreude, vengefulness, hatred, and so on, and recognize in such people an inherent value that outshines the impression of utter unworthiness they vividly refract. Perhaps you are a better person than I, but I'm afraid that such "purity of heart" is far beyond my capabilities.

Notice that the problem here is not that I cannot consciously form the general idea of some fixed, inalienable, property or feature inherent in persons and then attribute it to all human beings. That is done easily enough, but it is simply an act of the imagination, not a conscious disposition to engage with any actual person. Mentally attributing something to a person is not the same as having an overriding reason to respect them because I am rightly conscious of their concretely *possessing* it. As the old philosophical joke goes:

PHILOSOPHER	"If you call a tail a leg, how many legs does a donkey have?"
HAPLESS INTERLOCUTOR	"5"
PHILOSOPHER	"Ha! No, 4, because calling a tail a leg doesn't make it a leg."

The joke is more irritating than funny, but it makes an important point. B-dignity purports to be a feature that persons actually possess and to which one can react, not merely something I impute to them in my imagination. As we saw in Chapter 4, "concrete possession" doesn't have to be understood in a strictly physical, spatial, or empirically verifiable, sense. When we excerpt Bach's *Goldberg Aria* in consciousness and notice the grace and dignity that will forever inhere in it, we are not *imagining* these qualities, even though they have no empirically specifiable location. Rather, we are conscious of the piece's actual character and responding to it with awe and wonder. The question is whether, when I contemplate Stalin – the real man and his actual deeds – I can wholeheartedly discern in him the sort of quality that B-dignity purports to be: not only a fixed and immutable feature but also one that should override my immediate feelings of revulsion, contempt, and indignation and allow me to affirm his life as possessing enduring worth.

Of course, there may be independent reasons not to indulge those feelings and treat him with respect nonetheless. Perhaps, for example, our society has internalized a rule or principle under which all persons, regardless of their behavior or characteristics, are entitled to certain forms of treatment in the name of human dignity (a fair trial, humane confinement, charitable understanding of their historical context, etc.). No doubt those who speak of the inherent, unchanging, dignity of all persons often have something like this possibility in mind – that of a society choosing to confer human dignity automatically on all its members as a requirement of decency and justice. Yet, if one thinks clearly about it, such a view actually abandons the idea of B-dignity. For, instead of reacting to a preexisting, inherent, dignity possessed by the person, society here decides to dignify all of its members equally, even those it judges unworthy, in the name of humane consideration. Attractive as it is, this approach assumes that agents enjoy dignity only to the extent that society bestows it on them; but then it obviously dispenses with any notion of an inherent fixed, dignity that precedes and mandates such a response. That line of thought actually points away from B-dignity and toward the notions of C-Dignity considered in Chapter 7 and other views considered later.

The Introspective Argument for B-Dignity

Perhaps, though, all this misses the point: if B-dignity is an *inner* possession, we shouldn't seek it in others (least of all in exemplars of abject suffering and wickedness), but rather – as Kant suggested – through introspective self-contemplation. A common suggestion along these lines is that attending to our own purposes and values automatically commits us to a self-conception that includes an inherent, unchanging, moral dignity. Gewirth's attempt to ground human rights on a doctrine of inherent, undamageable, personal dignity takes this route. He declares: "Every human agent must attribute worth to his purposes . . . [because he] regards his purposes as good according to whatever criteria enter into his purposes." From this assumption of "agent-estimated worth" Gewirth infers that an agent must see him or herself as the "source" of this worth: "they are *his* purposes, and they are worth attaining because *he* is worth sustaining and fulfilling, so that he has what for him is a justified sense of his own worth." The conclusion is that the "generic purposiveness" of rational action, just as such, "underlies the ascription of inherent dignity to all agents" (including oneself).[4]

---

[4] Gewirth, *Self-Fulfillment*, pp. 168–69. This is what Sangiovanni has helpfully labeled the Kantian regress argument. Sangiovanni, *Humanity without Dignity*. Sangiovanni primarily addresses Korsgaard's version of the argument. See C. Korsgaard, *The Sources of*

I see no reason to doubt that our consciousness of ourselves as having values *at all* implies a general entitlement to be considered as a moral patient with interests that others must take into account. But it is one thing to say that persons have basic practical significance for that reason, a claim that, for example, no utilitarian need deny and that can be expressed without any recourse to the language of dignity, and another to say that attending to our valuings and purposive commitments from the inside confirms us in the possession of a stable and unalterable worth on the model of B-dignity. The latter claim cannot survive a realistic confrontation with the unsettling fragility of judgments about our worth mediated through inward contemplation of our values and aspirations. It is a truism that in engaging in actions and projects I presume them to be worthwhile. But it is also a truism that this presumption is subject to later rebuttal. In the first blush of commitment and aspiration, we may experience the speculative quality of human activity as benign, even exhilarating. Over time, however, we often come to see its darker side: our existential bets don't always pay off. Some discover themselves to be habitually lousy gamblers, often when it is too late to make a difference.

Major depression frequently presents as an intensely felt judgment that one's chosen endeavors have proven vain and pointless on reflection, or that the activities to which society has expected one to devote enormous amounts of energy and time were actually a waste of one's life and potential. Unfortunately, one sometimes has *good reason* to reach such conclusions: it may simply be *true* that one has spent precious life time on relationships, careers, aspirations, and projects that were not worth the trouble; worse still, we may become rightly conscious of how our own blunders and assigned roles have made life unnecessarily difficult for others. Whether or not this is our fault (perhaps we were warned), such uncomfortable facts force us to reckon with the possibility that we are complicit in our own abasement. Despair may sometimes be the only honest response. This puts fatal pressure on Gewirth's claim that attending to the way we attribute value to our purposes and pursuits should automatically induce the "justified sense of . . . worth" that he believes "dignity" names. In at least some cases, it induces the self-indictment characteristic of depression: at the limit, it may lead one to consider suicide, and it is hard to see in *that* prospect a propitious metaphor for invulnerable human dignity and worth.

One might reply that depression is an aberrant case, posing no real threat to Gewirth's position. Depression, after all, invites a clinical perspective: it is

---

Normativity (Cambridge: Cambridge University Press, 1996). A similar argument is hinted at in L. Lomasky, *Persons, Rights and the Moral Community* (Oxford: Oxford University Press, 1987) and also in Dworkin, *Justice for Hedgehogs*, p. 204. Gewirth's use of the word "purposiveness" foreshadows Arthur Ripstein's use of that term in Arthur Ripstein, *Force and Freedom: Kant's Legal and Political Philosophy* (Cambridge, MA: Harvard University Press, 2009).

a mental disorder, somewhere along the continuum of insanity, and therefore a nonrational phenomenon. One might therefore think that those who reflect on their projects and purposes, even when they have gone badly awry, and fail to immediately affirm their B-dignity are in the grip of false consciousness. But, apart from its spectacular begging of the question, such a response looks psychologically naïve. Freud was much nearer the mark when he suggested that depressive self-accusation "must surely be right in some way and . . . describe[. . .] something that is as it seems to" the sufferer. He went on to say that those in the throes of clinical depression have "a keener eye for the truth than other people who are not melancholic," adding, mordantly, that "we only wonder why a man has to be ill before he can be accessible to a truth of this kind."[5]

Clearly, not everything about depression is rational, as Freud would have been the first to concede. Still, the despair and damaged self-worth that partly constitute it is sometimes the only truthful response to inside reflection on one's valuings and their vicissitudes. If so, it is hard to believe that reflexive attention of that kind automatically discloses a stable and unchanging worth or dignity within. In the end, honest internal contemplation of one's own life and how it is panning out are too unstable to sustain consciousness of B-dignity without indulging fantasy. And, as I pointed out in Chapter 3, fantasy, self-delusion, and wishful thinking are hard to reconcile with the ordinary connotations of dignity. If dignity requires anything, it requires a candid and courageous refusal of delusion. Ruskin said: "To be deceived is perhaps as incompatible with human dignity as to be whipped."[6]

Here it is worth recalling the characteristic obsession of honor cultures – a major source for our inherited concepts of dignity – with truth-telling and trustworthiness: the honorable person is always true to their word; those who engage in deceit dishonor themselves; "giving the lie" is a standard occasion for a duel: "To 'give the lie' to someone was to announce that their appearance differed from their true nature – to proclaim as false their projection of themselves."[7] The problem with the introspective argument for B-dignity is that it seems to work only by requiring agents *either* to deceive themselves about their worth in an analogous way, *or* to reach judgments that conflict with the assumption that everyone has equal dignity.

---

[5] S. Freud, "Mourning and Melancholia," *The Standard Edition of the Complete Psychological Works of Sigmund Freud* 14 (1914–1916): 245, 246. Here Freud anticipates the view that is today often labelled "depressive realism." For discussion of the latter, see Jon Elster, *Alchemies of the Mind: Rationality and the Emotions* (Cambridge: Cambridge University Press, 1999), p. 300.

[6] E. T. Cook and A. Wedderburn, eds., *The Works of John Ruskin* (London: George Allen, 1905), vol. 17, p. 255.

[7] Kenneth S. Greenberg, "The Nose, the Lie, and the Duel in the Antebellum South," *The American Historical Review* 95, no. 1 (1990): 57, 63.

At first glance, the metaphor of an inherent B-dignity, possessed immutably by all persons, seems to capture the connotations of solidity, adamance, and robustness implicit in our ordinary notion of human dignity. The introspective argument for B-dignity thus seeks to reassure us that standing behind our strivings, however well or ill-conceived, lies some immovable fixed point on which we can always securely hang the worth and importance of our lives. Yet the pitiless self-scrutiny for which dignity itself calls must often cast a light too harsh for such self-affirmation to withstand. The implication is that our ordinary concept of human dignity precisely forbids us from thinking of it as automatically guaranteed in the manner of B-dignity, for such thinking is inevitably dishonest and untrustworthy in many cases, and to that extent dishonoring. At a minimum, a dignified existence requires that agents at least be able to affirm their worth without lying to themselves.

The Empty Charisma of B-Dignity

Even if none of these objections go through, traditional views confront a still more serious challenge – that of explaining why one should *care* about B-dignity, how it can be a source of overriding, unconditional reasons for anyone to *mind* that social practices treat people in certain ways. If something is invulnerable, immutable, and guaranteed in advance, then nothing anyone can do can have any real effect on it: how it is importantly at risk in the treatment it receives, why certain actions are required or prohibited for its sake, become completely unclear. Conversely, insofar as human dignity is a fragile, vulnerable, quality, it is easier to understand how its (presumed) unconditional importance is not merely an idle conceptual truth – what Marx called an "internal, dumb generality" defining an abstract "genus" – but something that directly engages practical attention in the form of urgent, non-overridable, expectations.

To be sure, one cannot legislate against saying that, for example, slavery is an unconscionable social practice because slaveholders must fail to properly appreciate the constraints imposed by their slaves' inherent dignity. Such claims make no clear philosophical mistake. But equally it is unclear that they can do any significant philosophical *work*. If slaves already possess their dignity whole and entire, and nothing a slave-owning society does can take it away, it is hard to see how an appeal to human dignity can figure in a non-question begging criticism of the institution of slavery. It may of course serve as a powerful rhetorical intensifier, but dignitarian humanists have rightly aspired to something more: an explanation of *why* practices like slavery are adamantly objectionable, not merely a decorous way of repeating *that* they are.

Nor is this merely an arcane philosophical point. For all Milbank's protestations about "true religion" being the only safe harbor for human dignity, we cannot ignore the inconvenient historical fact that when "true religion" and its institutional avatars were in charge, they presided over social worlds in which brutality, intolerance and persecution, sexism, racism, sexual repression, and slavery were not only completely routine but also often actively encouraged by those officially committed to recognizing the immaculate *imago dei* in all souls. If B-dignity, in its religious form, is so good as a basis for social critique, why did its historical adherents miss so much of the systematic dehumanization going on around them? Is it just an accident that these abuses were not only accepted, but hardly even noticed as such, during a time when regnant theist ideologies assured all mankind that their dignity is eternally guaranteed by God and that nothing anyone can do can ever take it away? No doubt the Enlightenment thinkers had their own blindspots, but their critique of traditional theism on this point seems entirely well-taken. While metaphorically excerpting human dignity as a fixed and unchanging feature possessed self-sufficiently by each person is conceptually possible, it carries the unacceptable implication of isolating it so thoroughly from the world that it can no longer enter into any definite relations with it. B-dignity becomes a shimmering, atemporal, abstraction floating above the transactions of ordinary human existence. In no interesting sense can it really be *at stake* in anything that happens to anyone.

Worse, once insulated from concrete human relations and projected as a timeless datum, claims made on its behalf become virtually unverifiable. We have seen that the presence of B-dignity cannot depend on any social facts, nor vary with empirically discernible differences between persons; it may be accessible at all only from a point of view requiring preternatural purity of heart. What then is left to determine exactly what respect for this feature, properly grasped, requires and forbids? How are we to definitively resolve disagreements about whether conduct or practice offends or comports with B-dignity? Is suicide compatible or incompatible with respect for it? Capital punishment? How about redistributive taxation? Affirmative action? Sweatshop labor? Human rights? Beyond uninformative truisms about the indignity of torture, slavery, coercion, and so on, which merely repeat uncontroversial and culturally entrenched norms about wrongdoing, fine-grained answers to these questions become virtually incorrigible when advanced in the name of B-dignity.

The persistent tendency to construe human dignity in these terms, I believe, helps explain the vacillation between ambiguity and dogmatism to which traditional dignitarian discourse characteristically gives rise. Conceived as a guardian of B-dignity, the judge presiding over the tribunal of human dignity purports to represent a feature of persons that is so occult that claims made on its behalf are either truistic or almost impossible to authenticate on any publicly accessible basis. This renders her court effectively mute. She can, as it were, speak only in riddles that those who revere her are left to decrypt for themselves. It is as if the attorneys present must simultaneously represent litigants *and* speak for the judge purporting to arbitrate between them. Plainly, however, such a tribunal is not merely a lousy court, but no court at all.

Indeed, it is in many ways more like a church, cultivating reverence for an ineffable mystery that can be represented in physical form only in self-appointed intercessors and sacraments. B-dignity here takes on a charismatic quality, one that its protagonists in the world – not accidently often priests – inherit insofar as they are recognized as authoritative interpreters of its demands, which as we noted in Chapter 3, carry presumptively adamant force. We can expect, therefore, that trusting in B-dignity must inevitably transmute into allegiance to specific persons, institutions, traditions of thought, constitutional documents, or social movements that present themselves as gifted with something akin to prophetic insight into its meaning.

The charisma attaching to "human dignity" under the aspect of B-dignity certainly helps explain why dignitarian idioms have proven powerful agents of political and social mobilization. But rather than enhancing the critical potential of dignitarian ideals, it mystifies them behind attitudes of credulous discipleship. In this mode, incantations of "Respect for human dignity" tend to subvert serious, granular, inquiry into the concrete, often unacknowledged, ways that entrenched practices diminish and enhance the worth of lives. They instead promote the idolatrous veneration of the particular texts, authors, traditions, and social movements (e.g., the Bible, Kant, "liberalism," the "republic" and its constituent power, the "nation," the vanguard party) that step forward in public and intellectual discourse and claim the authority to determine its content. Yet I submit that the more we fetishize these self-annointed interpreters of "human dignity," the less we understand about why it should matter and how it is concretely at stake in peoples' lives.

6

The Inner Ocean

[F]rom our capacity for internal lawgiving and from the (natural) man feeling himself compelled to revere the (moral) man within his own person, at the same time there comes *exaltation* and the highest self-esteem, the feeling of his inner worth (*valor*), in terms of which he is above any price (*pretium*) and possesses an inalienable dignity (*dignitas interna*), which instills in him respect for himself (*reverentia*). Immanuel Kant[1]

Do the arguments advanced in Chapter 5, if sound, refute Kant's account of dignity? Not really: here it is important to distinguish Kant's own position from theories that, while claiming a *Kantian* provenance, often adapt or depart from it in important ways. Although self-described "Kantians" often carelessly assume that Kant's position is committed to B-dignity, a close inspection of his actual views reveals that he did not construe moral dignity in exactly these terms. This chapter explains how Kant's own doctrine departs from that commitment; it goes on to argue, however, that the resulting hybrid only generates a new doubt about traditional understandings of human dignity.

The Warfare He Has Taught You[2]

What is most striking about the self-consciousness induced within Kant's framework of practical reasoning is that it is precisely *not* of a self whose worth (moral dignity) is fixed and predetermined. The metaphors by which Kant renders dignity and moral worth represent it, not as primitive unity, but rather as a complex and dynamic set of internal relations among at least five aspects of the self. From within Kantian practical reason, I recognize the ("noumenal") "I" that commands obedience to the moral law; the ("empirical") "me" who is continually tempted into disobedience and whose "conceits" must be "struck down"; the retrospective "me" that reflects on my moral career

---

[1] Immanuel Kant, *The Metaphysics of Morals*, ed. Lara Denis, trans. Mary J. Gregor (Cambridge: Cambridge University Press, 2007), p. 230.

[2] I take this phrase from a Christian hymn ("Faith of the Fathers") by T. A. Lacey: The Cross of Christ who bought you; Who leads you forth in this new age With long-enduring hearts to wage The warfare he has taught you.

and humbly assesses whether I am "worthy of happiness"; the "me" that other agents encounter and are supposed to treat with respect; and the "me" that encompasses all of these, the site at which they interact antagonistically to constitute human – as opposed to "holy" – agency. Dignity as Kant construes it is certainly something I can be said to "possess," but what I thereby "possess" is a roiling deliberative battlefield, not a stable fixed point. The various elements that constitute it certainly don't fall together to form an untroubled whole.

To the extent that Kantian agency displays any structural integrity, it is sustained through effortful tensions among these internally differentiated subcomponents, of which powerful moral emotions such as awe, fear, intimidation, frustration, and a tenuous sense of elevation are symptoms. Kantian moral dignity is an unsettled relation like a dissonant chord that never resolves or achieves completeness and equipoise as it would if it were the locus of an effortless "holy will." Since, on his view, all human agents share in this predicament, Kant sometimes identifies it with our common "humanity," but this isn't because he thinks its locus is essentially collective or even social. Kant's references to "humanity" in this context rather draw attention to something his theory regards as integral to the human condition: what Rawls would later call the "separateness of persons." This is the fact that the practical standpoint is radically individualized and hence that the system of practical reasoning and judgment is intelligible only from within the unique perspectives of different agents seeking to live autonomously. On Kant's account, "respect for the dignity" of the person is the appreciation of that uniqueness, which is owed to oneself and to other autonomous persons, and which is (he supposes) compelled by introspection from within one's own standpoint.

In quantum mechanics, the properties (location, spin, momentum, etc.) of particles (e.g., individual photons constituting a beam of light) are considered indeterminate. However, when observers attempt to measure the properties of specific particles, they not only reveal some of the relevant information but in so doing also irreversibly alter the character of the beam, so that its constituents cease to behave in a wave-like manner and crystallize as definite particles following a determinate path through space and time. Although the analogy is far from perfect, this feature of quantum mechanics may afford an approximate metaphor for the way in which Kant implicitly understands the complex self-relations just described.

Suppose we think of particular actions performed by an agent over the course of their conscious life as affording momentary measures of their moral worth, akin to measurements of a photon's position in a light-beam made by a physicist at a particular instant. Yet these short-lived moments of moral determinacy are just that; individuated episodes in a continuous flow (a life of conscious self-determination) whose overall moral worth, as it were, remains nonzero but indeterminate. Admittedly, the analogy with quantum effects breaks down if pressed any further: for Kant's theory has no counterpart to the "collapse of the wave function" in quantum physics, such that measuring even *one* photon renders a beam of light determinate in a way that it wasn't prior to the act of measurement. On Kant's account, a particular decision made by an agent at a specific time need not determine the moral worth of her whole life once and for all. However, it shares with quantum physics a denial that under all conditions of observation the same thing must be *either* determined *or* indeterminate.

Paradoxical as its implications may be, that denial may shed useful light on a similarly perplexing feature of Kant's theory: its simultaneous endorsement of the claims that

1. individuals' lives are the locus of a dignity or "worth" that can never be destroyed and therefore always constrains others' treatment of it; and that
2. "by a lie a man throws away and as it were annihilates his dignity as a man."[3]

How can Kant think that moral dignity is both indestructible and annihilable?

My suggestion is that, in the Kantian schema, claim 1 refers to whole lives viewed externally (N.B. *not* empirically), yet from within the practical point of view of agents deliberating about how the presence of other rational beings constrains their choices. In my analogy, this standpoint corresponds to that of the physicist observing a beam of light *before* she has attempted to measure the specific properties of any particular photons within it. From within the perspective of practical deliberation, as Kant understands it, the lives of oneself and others are similarly merely possible loci of worth, and nothing anyone else can do to them can either determine their worth precisely or undermine their potential worthiness completely.[4] Our duty is to act in ways consistent with recognizing this potential value in each life – that is, to respect those whose lives they are (not treating them only as "means," as merely manipulable objects subordinate to the will of others). Kant after all describes the Categorical Imperative as a condition of the *possibility* of a "good will," not of its certainty.

Even so, his theory can regard agents' (lack of) success in fulfilling their duties toward others on specific occasions as a determinate measure of those agents' moral worth as it materializes, or fails to materialize, in the relevant actions. For, we can consciously excerpt a particular action from the general flow of conduct constituting an agent's whole life – for example, a lie uttered on a particular occasion. Once we have mentally isolated such an action as a discrete event, Kant's scheme allows a complete, that is, determinate,

---

[3] Kant, *The Metaphysics of Morals*, p. 225.
[4] This idea is related, I believe, to Margalit's thought that respect may be justified by the idea that no human being should be "given up on" because "there is a chance, no matter how small, that she will repent." Margalit, *The Decent Society*, pp. 70–75.

judgment of the moral worth of the agent as revealed in the action under scrutiny. That is, to be conscious of X's culpability for some wrong W, on the Kantian account, is to be conscious that nothing of moral worth can be detected in "X"s performing W at time t. Yet, since that individuated act is but one episode excerpted from the ongoing flow of conduct constituting X's whole conscious life-course, we can still meaningfully speak of Y as a momentary "annihilation" of X's dignity. For in that lapse, at any rate, we can discern no moral worth – no dignity in Kant's sense – at all. Hence claim 2. It is as if we were to rip a single page out of a flick-book and discover that the image wholly lacks some property whose presence nevertheless cannot be decisively ruled out when we watch the animation that appears as we flick through the remaining pages rapidly.

If this is the right way to read him, Kant implicitly recognizes that, to be an effective metaphor for personal *worth* and *value*, human dignity must be an uncertain and relational quality, not the settled and static one postulated in B-dignity. In this sense, I think Joseph Raz is deeply right to identify his own account of the "value of valuers" with Kant's own approach, even though he develops it in a very unKantian manner. For Raz, the ethic of respect for persons assumes that agents are of "value in themselves." One might think that this assumption implies B-dignity, such that the value of persons is a fixed, permanent, form of worth that is "just *there*," in human beings. Yet, Raz explicitly, and quite rightly, rejects any notion of "value autarchy," according to which some things possess a value that can be specifiable independently of their actual or possible interaction with other things that are "beneficial or detrimental" to them. Instead, he insists that even "what is of value in itself must have a life, or a history, that is, ... [be] capable of interacting in meaningful ways with others or with other things, through which it thrives or declines."[5]

This, I submit, is the fundamental reason why the timanthropic outlook presupposed by the idea of B-dignity collapses so readily, as I have been arguing, into empty, mystical formulae with few clear implications for the assessment of social and political practices. If we want to explain how human dignity is at stake in the conduct of life, a concept of dignity that is essentially *lifeless* is unlikely to help us.

Inner and Outer

John Milbank objects, clearly with Kant in mind, that

> to "use" other human beings can sound odious. ... But actually, to treat oneself or another human being as an "end" ... is much more sinisterly

---

[5] J. Raz, *Value, Respect, and Attachment* (Cambridge University Press, 2001), pp. 148–51.

objectifying. For an end is an objective full-stop, without any personal characteristics – unless one is the infinite God – since these can only be displayed in dramatic and narrative terms which always involve still being on the way somewhere and still being a means to that end, employing other means. To see oneself or someone else as an end is to turn a person into a conclusion that is defined by the sublimely blank pages that follow it.[6]

Milbank here echoes Raz's thought that claims about the value of people and their lives can't carry much weight if they are devitalized abstractions only. Yet, as we have seen, while it may apply to crude Kantian theories that truck in an inherent, unchanging, B-dignity, Milbank's objection cannot as it stands reach Kant's own more subtle view. Kant doesn't treat the dignitarian value of the human person as autarchic and immutable, already possessed whole and entire by each individual. Rather, he regards it as a fragile, and never decisively attained, achievement for which individual agents must constantly fight. For Kant, moreover, responsibility for waging that struggle, while ultimately lying with each agent separately, is at least partly shared across the whole community. Unlike a strictly Stoic view, Kant's position implies that agents share responsibility for giving each other the space to preserve their own dignity – hence his absolute proscription of interpersonal coercion, manipulation, exploitation, and commodification, and his authorization of state power to enforce it. To treat persons as mere "means" in any of these ways is to usurp their power to live autonomously, and so agents are under an unconditional duty, subject to legitimate public enforcement, to respect others as ends-in-themselves.

To be sure, the fulfillment of that duty, and its political enforcement, cannot be sufficient for that purpose because in the end, internal self-determination is constitutive of moral dignity as Kant understands it; the effort to coerce agents into achieving it must be inherently self-defeating. Yet a structural background of external respect remains a desideratum for Kant, and its importance in his scheme foreshadows a leading theme in more recent dignitarian humanist thinking. For, a clear implication of his view is that my efforts to maintain self-respect can sometimes be derailed if others systematically violate their duty to respect my autonomy. In other words, it turns out that on Kant's account, others' respect is a condition for my self-respect. In this sense, he accepts that societies that permit agents to coerce, manipulate, exploit, and commodify each other threaten the "social bases of self-respect," to put it in Rawlsian terms.

One difficult question this move must face is how much disrespect from others is enough to preclude my self-respect: none of us is likely to live entirely without being coerced, manipulated, and so on in ways Kant's theory forbids,

6 J. Milbank, "Dignity Rather than Right," *Open Insight* 5, no. 7 (2014): 116.

but few would say that occasional, sporadic violations are sufficient to vitiate their victims' self-respect entirely. This problem about the robustness of self-respect has been underestimated in recent political philosophy, but assuming, for the sake of argument, that a solution is available, Kant can easily deflect the charges I have laid against simple B-dignity views. *Pace* Milbank, Kant's dignity is not lifeless and autarchic.

For all that, however, Kant's own view retains a problematic feature: its essentially *possessive* understanding of human dignity. It is true, as I suggested earlier, that Kant sometimes identifies dignity with the collective category of "humanity," but what defines "humanity" in his sense is the possibility of morally admirable self-possession in each individual member of the species. The inner world of deliberative integrity remains the center of gravity around which Kant's conception of dignity revolves. So, although the integrity of that inner world is in Kant's account too uncertain and unsettled to fit the model of B-dignity, his complex hybrid still resides somewhere in the Northerly row of our organizing typology. However, as I will now claim, so strongly possessive an understanding of human dignity has a serious limitation: it fails to recognize that dignity and indignity have much more to do with the *external* relationships in which agents stand to each other.

Commentators have in my view overlooked this deficiency because they have been understandably mesmerized by an apparent strength of a possessive, inward-looking, construal of human dignity: its deep resonance with the psychological phenomenology of such familiar archetypes of humiliation and indignity as rape, torture, persecution, and genocide. Overwhelmed by violence, pain, contempt, and cruelty, their victims find themselves bystanders to the implosion of their inner world. Denying that such indignities usually effect such inward trauma would be fatuous. However, this point implies that we should construe human dignity as an inner quality of self-possession only if we *equate* indignity and its characteristic psychic impact on victims. Yet, on reflection, such an equation is misguided; we have to separate the external *fact* of indignity from its inward psychological effects. Once we understand why, the limitations of any narrowly possessive understanding of dignity will become clear.

Recent research on pain has emphasized how its character and severity can vary with the conscious narratives that agents suffering it attach to their experience of it. Daniel Carr and his colleagues, for example, find that soldiers with gunshot wounds do not experience the resulting pain as intensely as do victims of crime suffering similar injuries.[7] This appears to be because soldiers

---

[7] Daniel B. Carr, J. D. Loeser, and D. D. Morris, *Narrative, Pain, and Suffering* (Seattle: IASP Press, 2005). The point has long been emphasized by one of the leaders in modern pain research, Patrick Wall. See his *Pain: The Science of Suffering* (New York: Columbia University Press, 2000), especially Chapter 1.

often have available to them a narrative that puts their pain in a positive light (heroism, a sense of duty done, hopes of being transported off the battlefield, etc.), whereas crime victims normally experience their injuries as part of an aversive narrative (interruption of plans, anxiety about health costs, resentment of the perpetrator, etc.). If this is true of even physical pain, it must surely apply all the more to those forms of psychological trauma experienced by victims of such indignities as rape, assault, torture, and so on – which (notoriously) endure long after the triggering events themselves. This carries dual implications: first, that the relation between the trauma and any indignities that induce it is one of symptom to cause; and second, that the precise character of a victim's traumatic symptoms will normally depend on her conscious interpretation of the triggering events *as* an indignity.

Yet if so, the indignity itself cannot be identified with, or reduced to, those later introspective symptoms, but must rather be prior to and independent of them. And this fits with common sense: a naturally occurring rockfall and a torturous interrogation may both induce similar injuries, physical pain, and a sense of shock in their victims; but while both may be psychologically traumatic for that reason, the experiential quality of the trauma in the two cases will differ because the element of humiliation and indignity present in the interrogation is absent in the rockfall. Hence very different narratives will, indeed *should*, color the victims' respective experiences of otherwise comparable physical bombardment.

Yet, even as these narratives must condition the victims' conscious absorption of what befalls them in each case, the difference between them doesn't depend in the first instance on anything that can be localized to an agent's internal attitudes. The source of that difference rather lies in the contrasting character of the external circumstances constituting the two encounters – most crucially, the fact that an interrogation is a transaction between human beings, and not merely a ballistic collision. As Jean Améry wrote of his own experience of torture and interrogation at the hands of the Gestapo, under such circumstances one's "fellow man" becomes a "counter-man."[8] Only the development of such an interpersonal relation can introduce humiliation and indignity.[9]

This crucial argument implies that although the introspective ramifications of indignity are distinctive and vitally important, they are parasitic on something more fundamental still – its external, relational, character. Another consideration further supports this implication. Although the forms of trauma associated with humiliating abuse and indignity will tend to have an elective affinity, their intensity typically varies with the psychological sensitivities of different victims.

[8] Jean Améry, *At the Mind's Limits: Contemplations by a Survivor on Auschwitz and Its Realities* (Bloomington, IN: Indiana University Press, 1980), p. 28.
[9] Margalit, *A Decent Society*, p. 10.

Imagine two victims of the same Gestapo interrogator who, let us assume, always tortures following an identical procedure; suppose that one copes more effectively with the psychological aftermath than the other. We would not conclude from the fact that one victim is in this sense more "traumatized" than the other that the former has suffered the greater indignity or was any the less humiliated. To the contrary, we would and should say that both suffered the same humiliation and indignity. But if our diagnosis of an indignity is the same in both cases, variation in its psychological reception must be a secondary consideration. The implication is that dignity and indignity – at least the kinds that matter for political judgment – consist in outward, rather than inward, relations and their modalities. They are possible states of human relationships, not things individuals may more or less securely possess.[10]

Kateb on Human Uniqueness

On reflection, the "externality" of dignity and indignity we have just uncovered is the tip of the iceberg. Take virtually any ordinary archetype of dignity and indignity, and one will find some essential reference to agents' relations to something outside them. This should not surprise us given the deep roots of dignitarian consciousness in notions of honor, which invariably presuppose some audience of observers. A couple of examples will reinforce the point.

Consider the dishonor of long-term unemployment. Moshe Halbertal has rightly emphasized that becoming superfluous[11] is a threat to one's dignity as ordinarily understood, and this is surely why unemployment, indignity, and humiliation are so naturally associated. The inability to find a job, a socially valued role, is to entertain the possibility that one's life is nugatory; after all, we talk of those who lose their jobs as being "made redundant," "losers," "good-for-nothings," and so on. It is the stigma of uselessness that the unemployed fear most, but again it is the actual social defeat it represents that makes that fear reasonable. Though it may trigger various psychological disorders, such humiliation is not an internal attitude, but something that external circumstances achieve. Our deep aversion to it presupposes a rational desire to stand in a different relation to one's fellows, that is, *not* to be useless, of no apparent value to anyone. Such relations are not fundamentally psychological.

The point is limited not only to cases of dishonor, humiliation, and other *privations* of dignity; it applies just as much to human activity that ennobles, honors, and dignifies those who engage in it. This is what Margalit aptly calls

---

[10] This claim will be partly qualified later in Chapter 14; but I will maintain that all the conceptions of dignity that are primarily relevant in political argument involve interpersonal, rather than intrapersonal relations.

[11] M. Halbertal, "Three Concepts of Dignity" (Dewey Lecture delivered at the University of Chicago Law School, January 1, 2015). Audio file available at https://soundcloud.com /uchicagolaw/moshe-halbertal-three-concepts-of-human-dignity.

our "reflected glory":[12] Beethoven struggling on through deafness to embrace Schiller's "millions" with a "kiss to all the world"; Martin Luther King sharing his "dream" for an inclusive America; Newton standing on the shoulders of giants and peering like a "boy on a sea-shore . . . into the great ocean of truth"; scientists and civil servants astonishing themselves and everyone else by putting a man on the moon; the ordinary heroism of a man daring a tank to run him down in Tienanmen Square; the "ardent tears of noble men" moistening the graves of those who strove to "accomplish the most for humanity." The grandeur of these exploits exemplifies and enhances human dignity, but we would miss their dignitarian import completely by localizing them to anyone's inward psychological dispositions. They all concern outward achievement, aspiration, defiance, and so on and the sense of pride they engender in an appreciative audience. Albeit not as gravely as torture or genocide, efforts to limit or stifle this reflected glory are to the detriment of our common dignity.

George Kateb is one of the few contemporary dignitarians to take this more outward-looking aspect of human dignity seriously.[13] He associates it with what he calls the "greatness, the stature, of the human species," as exemplified in our ingenuity in solving problems; our establishment of professions and crafts dedicated to the enhancement of life; scientific discoveries that answer to our relentless curiosity and inquisitiveness; the proliferating diversity of our cultural forms; our capacity for aesthetic and artistic achievement; our ability to form and fulfill enduring commitments to friends, family, and others; our propensity to challenge and perfect the remarkable array of talents and abilities distributed across the human population; the courageous deeds and acts of heroism we find both in world history and ordinary life, and so on.

But having recognized this vitally important external dimension of human dignity, Kateb tries to reconcile it with a traditional possessive understanding of it. As we shall see, this creates insoluble difficulties. I conclude my case against traditional construals of "inherent" dignity by explaining where Kateb goes wrong.

Kateb's strategy appeals to an alleged isomorphism between "dignity of every human individual and the dignity of the human species as a whole." He regards both as referring to an absolute, incommensurable, kind of standing rooted in an "existential" identity proper to each: "human dignity," he writes, "in its concern with status and stature has to do with the proper recognition of the identity of every human being and the identity of the human species."[14] In this regard, "all individuals are equal; no other species

---

[12] Margalit, *The Decent Society*, pp. 58–61.
[13] Kateb, *Human Dignity*. See also Martha Nussbaum, *Women and Human Development: The Capabilities Approach* (Cambridge: Cambridge University Press, 2008), pp. 72–73.
[14] Ibid., pp. 12–13.

is equal to humanity."[15] Kateb's insistence on the "existential" idiom of
identity reflects his effort to preserve the traditional assumption that dignity
is somehow inherent in its bearers. Both the human species and individual
persons possess it: it is an essential aspect of who and what they are.

Kateb sometimes explains this symmetry in terms of the "uniqueness" of
individuals and the human species:

> In the idea of human dignity to recognize oneself as sharing in a common
> humanity with every other human being is the primordial component of
> individual identity. Its positive center, however, is belief in one's unique-
> ness together with the uniqueness of every human being. Analogously, the
> dignity of the human species lies in its uniqueness in a world of species.
> I am what no one else is, . . . we human beings belong to a species that is
> what no other species is.[16]

Kateb cannot expect this appeal to "uniqueness" to get us very far, however, for
by itself it is either redundant or insufficient in this context. It is redundant in
that "identity" presupposes it. Unless there is more than one human species,
identifying a group of organisms under that heading is already to say that they
share in the uniqueness of humanity. One could say the same about any other
species, from worms to weasels, and indeed about many inanimate items
(moons, clouds, valleys, snowflakes, etc.). Every blizzard is unique, and so
(we are told) are the geometries of every one of their constituent snowflakes,
but so what? Do blizzards and snowflakes then have their own dignity?

Uniqueness is also insufficient because it is false that attending to individual
uniqueness precludes the abuse and disrespect with which dignitarians are
typically concerned. That is the lesson of Orwell's "Room 101," in *1984,* where
the tortured are forced to confront what they *specifically* fear most (in Winston
Smith's case, the fear of being eaten alive by rats). Certainly, dehumanization is
often accomplished by stripping victims of any distinguishing characteristics,
visibly reducing them to a subhuman herd, or otherwise erasing their individuality. But humiliating indignity can also be very pointedly targeted at
a victim's uniqueness, as in the mocking sign placed over the crucified Jesus:
"And set up over his head his accusation written, THIS IS JESUS THE KING
OF THE JEWS."

Clearly, then, Kateb's understanding of "human stature" cannot be based
solely on the notion of "uniqueness," but rather on the particular characteristics in virtue of which he believes *human* uniqueness and its worth consists.
Accordingly, he offers a list of "commendable" characteristics that make us
"the highest species on earth – so far."[17] His list is a familiar Judeo-Christian
litany: we are not slaves of nature and instinct, but partly "nonnatural," in that

---

[15] Ibid., p. 6.
[16] Ibid., p. 17.
[17] Ibid.

we enjoy some freedom to defy both and adopt our own purposes, changing "the terms on which life is given." That independence is, on Kateb's view, partly a gift of language, a uniquely human capacity that in turn creates the "inner ocean" of introspection and purposiveness, allows us to form general ideas, judge in relation to evaluative standards, and engage in mutual criticism. Not only the greatest human achievements but also our ability to appreciate them for what they are reflect these "commendable" capacities.

Kateb must be correct that these attributes are somehow implicated in human dignity. But what does any of this have to do with his fundamental existential tenet that respect for dignity involves "recognizing what a person is?" Kateb appears to be conflating a claim about the *identity* of the individual and the species with a claim about their *worth* – what makes them "commendable." The conflation is particularly clear in the following passage:

> Human dignity is an existential value; value or worthiness is imputed to the identity of the person or the species. . . . The truth of personal identity is at stake when any individual is treated as if he or she is not a human being like any other, and therefore treated as more or less than human. The truth of identity is also at stake when a person is treated as if he or she is just one more human being in a species, and not, instead, a unique individual who is irreplaceable and not exchangeable for another. These two notions . . . [of] commonness and distinctiveness . . . cooperate in constituting the idea of equal individual status.[18]

These remarks are perplexing. If it is a "truth" that agents' identity automatically confirms them in the possession of dignity and worth, then it is not clear in what sense it can be "at stake" in the treatment they receive. As Kateb implicitly concedes in this passage, the existential "truth" of our identity means that at worst we can only be treated *as if* we are commodities, objects, less than human, and so on. But to the extent that our inherent dignity is existentially guaranteed in virtue of our identity as human, we can never actually *be* any of these things, whatever anyone does to us. Kateb sometimes speaks of an "existential loss" that accompanies indignity. Again, however, since in his view such losses can neither remove anyone's dignity nor be reduced to harms or utilitarian costs, one wonders what exactly they are losses *of.*

This is not of course to deny that how we are actually treated is indeed "at stake." But everyone accepts this – including utilitarians, virtue-theorists, and dignity-skeptics. The question is how the ontological or existential truths Kateb is citing illuminate the practical question of how we should treat each other. Kateb might reply that the appropriateness of what we do to people depends on who they are. Fair enough, but if the relevant identity-claim amounts to nothing more than that each human being is a unique member

---

[18] Ibid., p. 10.

of a unique species, it seems pretty trivial. The same could be said of a worm. The precept "Human beings should treat each other as human beings" is hardly informative. Any interesting version of dignitarian humanism would need to say and do rather more than this – for example, to explain why human beings are not exchangeable while unique commodities (think of an invaluable Rembrandt self-portrait) are.

Perhaps sensing this, Kateb sometimes hints at a slightly different argument. He says, for example, that we must "encourage the perception that each person's common human traits and attributes, in their individualized presence, makes that person uniquely precious." This suggests that, for Kateb, the acknowledgement that human beings possess the existential trait of inherent dignity is *not* automatic and hence that its presence is uncertain and contested. After all, if the bare identification of a human being already makes their value manifest beyond all reasonable dispute, its "perception" would need no such "encouragement." So perhaps Kateb is suggesting that, whatever it is about human beings that convinces *him* that they possess dignity, it isn't self-evident to everyone. We can obviously agree that it isn't sufficient to convince racists, chauvinists, rapists, architects of genocide, and so on, that they should refrain from dehumanizing their victims. This might explain one sense in which the "truth of personal identity is at stake" when such abuse occurs: vigilant assertion, and reassertion, of the existential truth that each person uniquely exemplifies human dignity is needed because otherwise the false claims of racists and other oppressors would go uncontested.

Various other features of Kateb's text suggest that he has something like this in mind. Consider his lengthy discussion of Nietzsche's claim that exploitation, slavery, and degradation of the many is – as it has often been historically – "a necessary condition for the pursuit of great achievements" by an élite few.[19] Kateb takes this claim seriously because he worries that all too often human societies indulge the Orwellian conceit that some are "more equal than others." Indeed, Kateb concedes that people are in fact highly unequal in their talents and abilities, and hence that some will embody "human stature" more fully than others. He worries, too, that capitalism and free societies more generally must unleash ambitions – to dominate, to predate, to win – that can threaten confidence in an inherent, absolute, worth in all individuals. All of these phenomena, Kateb seems to be saying, involve agents indulging false beliefs about the relative importance, status, and worth of different people, with the result that they fail to respect human beings as they should. He concludes that the primary object of the dignitarian humanist critic is to advocate a mode of liberal democratic constitutionalism that limits "human stature" by making "human

---

[19] Ibid., pp. 174–98.

rights count for more than any ambition for greatness."[20] The equal dignity of the individual thus trumps the dignity of the species, which in practice tends to be the preserve of a privileged few.

But this alternative line of argument is also unsatisfying in at least three main ways. For one thing, the concerns animating it aren't really existential ones, to do with the "truth of identity," but are about common belief, suspect motives, and ideological illusion. That is, what is now "at stake" in this version of the argument is not the truth that each possesses human dignity, but the social entrenchment of various distorted beliefs and problematically hierarchical attitudes. I agree that this is the right place to look for diagnoses of human indignity, and the reconstruction of dignitarian humanism I offer later accordingly gives it a large role. But these phenomena concern the formation of socially valid knowledge, not ones likely to be illuminated by a focus on existential identity-claims.

Second, any suggestion that the presence of inherent human dignity is uncertain and contestable must threaten Kateb's confident assumption that we can simply take it as an existential "truth." Kateb faces a dilemma here: *either* he insists that it is a self-evident datum, which leads back to the original argument and its problems; *or* he allows that claims about inherent or equal dignity can be reasonably disputed (e.g., in marginal cases). The latter option however conjures the specter of trait-racism again. Indeed, Kateb occasionally lapses into something very close to it: at one point, he says that "degraded human beings . . . lose their identity as human beings . . . [and] . . . no longer manifest the reasons for which incomparable dignity is ascribed to human beings." Shortly thereafter, he asserts that describing human beings who are in fact degraded by abusive conditions (genocide, forced starvation, torture, etc.) as less than human (as he has just done) "would justify the treatment inflicted on them."[21] These unfortunate passages illustrate the dangers of combining an existential approach with a concession that real dehumanization can actually occur. To my mind, the safer line is to make that concession but insist that nothing can ever justify dehumanizing anyone. But this would require breaking completely with the assumption that the respect required by the value of human dignity is conditioned on any existential identity-claims.[22]

---

[20] Ibid., p. 192.

[21] Ibid., pp. 20–21.

[22] Kateb's tendency to argue this way is particularly puzzling given his hostility to "efforts . . . to give groups the same existential weight or dignity as individuals and the species." If dignity attaches to individuals and species in virtue of their respective identities, denying that nations, universities, trades unions, cultures, can have their own dignities seems arbitrary. Kateb is suspicious of such attachments to intermediate identities on the grounds that "if a person thinks of him or herself first as a member of a group, that person has defined identity as affiliation, and not as first being oneself" (p. 11) Yet his

Finally, we should note that this alternative argument has largely lost touch with the effort to theorize human dignity in terms of species-greatness and its outward manifestation. Insofar as activity attesting to "human stature" carries political import on Kateb's view, it is almost always as a *threat* to the equal dignity of the individual. Rather than integrating the dignity of humanity and the dignity of the individual, then, Kateb places them at odds. His decision to prioritize the latter over the former is understandable, but set in the context of his existential view of each, it encourages something like the same inward turn we found earlier in Kant. The cause of human dignity becomes primarily a personal struggle to maintain self-respect and confidence in one's worth in the face of external threats.

But there is something self-defeating in this withdrawal to an inner citadel. Cocooned within their inner oceans, and unsure of their share in the reflected glory of humankind (perhaps they are unemployed and see their lives as useless), Kateb's individuals are left to seek their value in their bare humanity and uniqueness. Here, human dignity is forced back onto a narcissistic, self-referential, formula that is bound to be unsatisfying, even demoralizing. Perhaps this explains the whiff of panicky despair that Kateb's book occasionally betrays:

> We begin thinking about the human dignity of individuals, their equal status, when we impute to every person this thought: I have a life to live; it is my life and no one else's; it is my only life, let me live it. I exist and no one can take my place; I exist and though I do not owe my existence to fate or other superhuman necessity, I am not nothing. ... In some moods, I fantasize that everything that has so far happened in the world was needed to bring about my particular existence, and that my existence is therefore a necessary outcome of innumerable interlocking causal chains, although I know that the same could be said of all other persons and creatures. Anyway, I am not nothing, even if or even though I go to nothing at the end. I am not nothing, even if in my life I amount to nothing out of the ordinary.[23]

position, as I understand it, is that individuals *should* think of themselves first as members of at least one group – the high-statured species "humanity." To be consistent, Kateb must think that this is the only form of group-identity that one can embrace while remaining true to oneself. But I see no reason to believe this. Certainly people who define themselves as Germans, Princeton alums, white supremacists, and so on, rarely believe that such self-identification competes with authenticity to themselves: quite the opposite. Perhaps that belief is always false consciousness except in the special case of sharing in human identity, but that is a very strong claim. I agree with Kateb that the assertion of group-identity threatens freedom and dignity (as white-supremacism indicates), but to my mind the right response is to doggedly insist that human dignity has nothing to do with "identity." Dignitarian humanism is better off refusing to play the game of "identity-politics."

[23] Kateb, *Human Dignity*, pp. 18–19.

I find it remarkable that someone could write this passage on *behalf* of human dignity. Its sentiment – "leave me alone so that I can be not nothing" – certainly captures something of the late modern *zeitgeist*. Yet its defensive tone is oddly off-key in a book defending human dignity: the words have the character of those spoken by someone trying to hide something of which they are ashamed.

7

Passport-Dignity

The various different construals of individual dignity discussed in Chapters 5 and 6 share a common feature. They all interpret dignity possessively, as rooted *within* the individual person – whether in the form of an existential attribute, an identity, an "inherent worth," or a bundle of important capacities (rationality, autonomy, ability to pursue projects, etc.). The implicit conception is gravitational, with the overriding force of dignitarian considerations emanating from something localized to individuals considered *as such*. We saw that despite its endorsement of a relational view of dignity, even Kant's theory shares something of this centripetal character. For although he theorized moral dignity as the management of a struggle between antagonists, Kant internalized that conflict to the self. Hence, in Kant's view, the struggle for dignity and self-respect is finally an intimate one, played out within agents' deliberative self-consciousness.

The conclusion reached in Chapter 6 was that none of these localized conceptions of human dignity is of much critical import in political reflection. The strong implication is therefore that human dignity is ill-conceived as an individualized possession: we need to construe it intersubjectively. Even if sound, this conclusion is not however sufficient to refute all conventional dignitarian views, because some of them preserve the traditional assumption that dignity is a fixed and unchanging quality while dropping the suggestion that it is straightforwardly inherent in persons. These views look to the southeasterly quadrant of our typology and embrace dignity in mode C. Can conceptions in this neighborhood step in to rescue traditional reactive construals of dignity and respect? This chapter tries to show that the argument is No: in the end, C-Dignity fares no better than B-dignity as a basis for critical reflection on politics, although for slightly different reasons.

Second-Personal Authority and the Kingdom of Ends

Chapter 4 associated C-dignity with Rawls's theory, and we can think of his contractualist turn as motivated, in part, by an implicit recognition that B-dignity won't do as a basis for political criticism. After all, if respectful treatment is dictated by the inherent worth possessed by persons, we wouldn't need contractualist procedures to tell us what respect for persons specifically requires; once the inherent attribute of dignity has been properly recognized, it would remain only to read off our duties to respect it, and then directly assess the legitimacy of social arrangements by reference to them. Rawls, however, explicitly rejected such an approach, for he denied that the idea "of the inherent worth of persons" is sufficiently clear and uncontroversial to justify interesting political conclusions by itself. "It is precisely these ideas," he wrote, "that call for interpretation".[1] His initiation of a new form of contractualism in political philosophy was thus motivated by the need to settle reasonable disagreements about the implications of such ideas for the justice of social and political cooperation. He accordingly set out to "construct" an account in which dignitarian commitments acquire a more "definite" and commonly affirmable meaning.

Even so, a commitment to equal dignity figures more deeply in the sort of contractualism that Rawls launched than in its immediate philosophical competitors: utilitarianism and perfectionism. To the extent that they find any use in the concept of dignity, the latter treat it as a subordinate, downstream, ethical commitment too vague to have any critical import until interpreted in the light of a higher, independent, standard – either the utility principle or some substantive virtue-ethical "conception of the good life."[2] Yet dignitarian assumptions are not straightforwardly "downstream" of Rawls's contractualism in this way; as I noted in Chapter 1, they are present at its very fountainhead.

In Rawls's own account, most obviously, contractees' absolute right to veto social principles they can "reasonably reject" is meant to correct the infamous dignitarian deficit in classical utilitarianism: the fact that its calculus could recommend sacrificing or exploiting the few to the welfare of the many. That contractualist veto is also supposed to capture Rawls's insistence that the "social bases of self-respect" constitute "the most important" social primary good; and he plainly presumed that social relations that violate an expectation of equal respect for agents' dignity and independence erode these "social bases." To this extent, Rawls's contractualism represents a procedural rendition of Ronald Dworkin's formula of "equal concern and respect."

Dworkin himself quite explicitly tied that principle to a Kantian understanding of dignity, and many others have certainly understood the contractualist endeavor in strongly dignitarian terms. The most sophisticated recent account along these lines has been elaborated by Stephen Darwall.[3] He associates

---

[1] Rawls, *A Theory of Justice (Revised)*, p. 513.

[2] Hence MacIntyre's suggestion in *After Virtue* that Kantian and neoKantian attempts to ground political judgment on principles of respect for human dignity alone are, along with other Enlightenment conceits, "doomed to fail," because they do without the guidance of a theory of the human good.

[3] Darwall, *The Second-Person Standpoint*.

contractualism with what he calls the "second-personal standpoint" – the point of view from which agents can legitimately demand that others comply with putatively authoritative norms and expectations. As Darwall's work has helped us understand, that point of view orbits around a conception of the equal dignity of persons that exemplifies C-Dignity: it is changeless and cannot be taken away, yet ambient as a relation that defines a community of persons with equal authority to demand that they be treated with respect. Despite its relational character, Darwall's model remains a reactive one in that it construes respect as the proper response to persons' pre-constituted dignity. The relations of mutual respect that constitute the human community *confer* on each member dignitarian standing. According to Darwall, the ordinary moral psychology of indignation and resentment attests to our tacit commitment to respect for the second-personal dignity of each.

Darwall thinks of this conception as a "foundation for contractualism" because it effectively postulates a supreme assembly of self-legislating agents (something like a Kantian "kingdom of ends") with final authority to determine the legitimacy of any particular positive moralities or institutional practices with which agents in the world might find themselves expected to comply. Each actual person is represented permanently by an idealized counterpart with an equal voice in that assembly.[4] These idealized legislators stand in a fixed relation of mutual accountability to all other members. Each wields a veto power that all recognize. The assembly is permanently in session. Its composition remains the same at all times and under all historical conditions. What *do* change, of course, are the myriad structures of social, political and cultural power to which actual people find themselves subject. Broadly speaking, contractualist thought-experiments of the sort envisaged by Rawls, Darwall, and others aspire to lay bare the idealized deliberations of this permanent supreme assembly as it passes critical judgment on legitimacy of these varying modes of worldly control. Some forms of social and political power will survive scrutiny at its bar; those that fail ought to be eliminated or reformed.

The Critique of C-Dignity

The specific relationship between contractualism in political philosophy and dignitarian ideals will be more easily addressed with the "revisionist"

---

[4] Gerald Gaus, *The Order of Public Reason: A Theory of Freedom and Morality in a Diverse and Bounded World* (Cambridge: Cambridge University Press, 2010), p. 26. It should be said that Gaus thinks of his view as weaker than Darwall's and that he stops short of identifying this idealized status as "free and equal" persons with "human dignity," a concept from which he seems to want to distance himself. Since I will be arguing that status concepts don't really cut it as representations of human dignity, Gaus's caution on this point is grist for my mill.

conception of human dignity reconstructed in the latter half of this book fully in view. Accordingly, I postpone discussion of these matters. Here, however, I want to focus on the adequacy of the underlying conception of dignity (C-dignity) that informs, not only contractualism, but many related political arguments.

Recall an overarching contention of this book: that the dignitarian humanist project in political philosophy is best understood, and is most compelling, as a search for a genuinely *timanthropic* basis for critical reflection on politics. That is, it asserts as a basic outer limit of legitimacy the requirement that the worth of people is duly recognized, supported, protected, and realized, by the major social institutions and practices that dictate the terms on which they lead their lives. Does C-dignity provide an adequate format for specifying that requirement? I think the answer to this question is No.

My general reason for drawing that conclusion is that C-dignity, both conceptually and as represented in the writings of political philosophers who adopt it, is essentially a formalistic status. As I will try to show, the *status* metaphors around which this conception of dignity revolve yield a very impoverished account of the timanthropic dimension of dignitarian humanism. To do justice to that dimension, I contend, we must distinguish between the status of persons or citizens and the value and worth of lives.

Contemporary moral and political philosophy have conflated these ideas to such a point that the terms "status" and "worth" are now used almost interchangeably. A Google Scholar search on the phrase "status and worth" produces over 1600 hits. The prevalence of this elision is due to three considerations. The first is simply the pervasive influence of Kantian and contractualist theories on recent philosophical writing itself; these theories, as we have seen, tend to equate the two. Second, the word "dignity" straddles both senses: in ordinary use, the concept of "dignity" can refer *either* to social and official status (think of the term "dignitary" in the context of international diplomacy, for example) *or* to significations of worth and worthiness (built into the etymology of the word itself, and exposed in the German translation "Würde").

Third, judgments about worth and status are frequently interconnected in specific contexts and so can be difficult to disentangle. For example, judgments about relative importance, inferiority, and worthiness are very often cited as reasons for assigning people differential status. Conversely, once status-orders are in place (whether vertical and hierarchical or horizontal and egalitarian), and especially once they become common knowledge, people inevitably evaluate themselves and each other in their light. That is one reason why low status can often cause individuals to develop what Adler famously baptized as an "inferiority complex." Punishment is another social practice in which the two overlap, for punishment is at once a public demotion (a status-modification) and a disgrace, vividly communicating society's active disapproval of offenders.

Still, worth and status aren't equivalent. The contrast between them is not that between categorical and scalar dimensions of assessment: something can be judged categorically unworthy or "worthless" just as status can be all-or-nothing. Conversely, people can rank more or less highly within some status hierarchy and be judged more or less worthy in relation to some standard of value.

The real contrast, rather, lies in this: status-metaphors characteristically classify items according to a formal rule or procedure. Their usual function is to put things in their proper places, by sorting them into various formal categories. Of course, classifying people into various categories may imply (various sorts of) evaluations, but it doesn't have to do so, and clearly valuing need not be a form of classification (to report one's love for a person is to say something about how one values them but it is not, thank goodness, to *categorize* them). Indeed, status-metaphors and value-metaphors often move in opposite directions. For example, to be the "champion" is to achieve a certain status (supremacy) in relation to the tournament and other competitors; but champions can be worthy or unworthy victors. For that reason, I deny the widely held assumption that having "status as a person" and "worth as a human being" are equivalent despite the Kantian tendency to equate them. The fact that we are both persons certainly implies that we have the same status, but it does not imply that we are equally worthy, nor that personality itself instantiates any sort of worth.

Consider in this regard Darwall's "second-personal dignity" – virtually the paradigmatic form of C-Dignity. In our capacity as beings with "second-personal" standing, we enjoy the authority to address imperatives to others like, "don't treat me merely as a means," and to demand compliance with them. Wrongdoing reflects a failure to hear these commands, to interpret them properly, or to show due regard for them. Insubordination thereby becomes the dominant metaphor for violations of human dignity. Disrespect for the primordial authority all agents enjoy in virtue of membership of a speech-community that presupposes the mutual accountability of persons. Insubordination, equal standing to command, disobedience, equal accountability, and so on, are fundamentally status-concepts. Darwall's second-personal standpoint is, in other words, constructed around metaphors under which all persons are classified as wielding an equal "second-personal competence."

I have no quarrel here with Darwall's contention that the "moral point of view" presupposes the second-personal competence of anyone capable of practical reasoning. The question is whether, for the purposes of political judgment, the status-metaphors populating the "second-personal standpoint" can adequately render the sense in which people and their lives have a worth to which public life should be sensitive. To bring such timanthropic concerns into view, these formalistic metaphors must somehow make contact with phenomena like humiliation, abasement, devaluation, dehumanization, and so on. It is these phenomena, after all, that most urgently engage our sense that agents' value is somehow at stake in social, economic, and political life. I submit, however, that on reflection these categories of C-dignity are just as remote from the concrete transactions on which our social worth likely depends as the unworldly metaphors of B-dignity we rejected earlier.

Dignity as "second-personal authority" is an essentially juridical idea. We might call it "passport-dignity," for it construes human dignity fundamentally as a de jure entitlement to demand things of others. To recognize someone as a rational agent bearing "second-personal authority" is equivalent to their producing a passport requiring certain forms of treatment. The passport of C-dignity moreover never expires and is valid under all circumstances. People can ignore it, but it cannot be mislaid or renounced. The only remaining question is whether others (people or institutions) properly respect the status of passport-holders and act accordingly.

Passport-conceptions of dignity produce a very peculiar diagnosis of the timanthropic defects of slavery, torture, rape, and other archetypes of human devaluation. Was slavery an affront to human dignity and worth primarily because slaveholders *disobeyed* their slaves? Is the humiliating indignity of rape really nothing more than the *insubordination* of rapists? Should we understand the disrespect of torture as a species of *mutiny*? The peculiarity of these formulae highlights the wide gap between the timanthropic discourse of worth, value, degradation, debasement, and humiliation and the juridical idiom of status, authority, command, accountability, prerogative, and sovereignty. Surely the more plausible line for a timanthropic approach is to focus, not on the inalienable, de jure, authority of victims over their abusers, but on agents' *power* (or lack of it) to elicit the concrete forms of respectful attention on which the maintenance of human dignity depends. But this line requires the postulation of a dignity that is subject to change; it requires us, in other words, to abandon the easterly column of our typology (B-dignity and C-dignity) and look west to A-dignity and D-dignity.

Retributive Punishment

Jean Hampton's account of retributivism, which as I noted earlier incorporates C-dignity, illustrates this problem very clearly.[5] Hampton understands crime in timanthropic terms: it represents for her an attack on the worth of its victims. Yet, to explain its timanthropic features, and the need for a penal

---

[5] Hampton and Murphy, *Forgiveness and Mercy*; J. Hampton, "Correcting Harms versus Righting Wrongs, " *UCLA Law Review* 39, 1992: 1659–1702.

response, she appeals to a Kantian notion of C-dignity as equal status. She therefore denies that anything offenders or the law can do ever actually diminishes a person's dignity or worth in the relevant sense. After all, if their dignity finally consists in their wielding a legitimate authority to command others' actions, those who defy those commands no more undermine their authority than does anyone who disobeys an authoritative instruction. Soldiers who ignore the orders of a commanding officer, or citizens who refuse to comply with a police officer's instruction to "pull over," do not automatically call the relevant authority into question: they merely flout it.[6]

To be sure, sufficiently endemic insubordination within some practice of authority threatens the de facto right of the relevant superiors to obedience. But Hampton, Darwall, and other Kantians think of dignity as a form of de jure authority. Even the erosion of its de facto authority (effected, e.g., by schemes of positive morality or law, like those of Jim Crow or apartheid, that systematically violate the rights of racial groups) cannot negate the de jure authority of persons to command the respect of others. For Hampton, Darwall, and many other, the de jure authority that constitutes the dignity of the person cannot be abrogated. But if so, what is left to Hampton, without resorting to utilitarian calculations of costs and benefits, to ground judgments about why society must punish offenders?

Only one line of advance seems to remain, and this is exactly the direction in which she moves. For although the sort of dignity that she takes to matter cannot be taken away or destroyed, one can still gauge how well private agents and public institutions understand, and comply with, the authoritative constraints on their choices commanded by the dignity of persons. And we can interpret their actual conduct as a *sign* of whether, and how far, they do understand and are guided by these constraints. Adopting this focus shifts attention away from any actual harms suffered by victims of crime or punishment, and onto the question of whether citizens or legal institutions (fail to) express their *apprehension* of personal dignity and its implications. Thus Hampton contends that retributive punishment is "designed to represent the *truth* (sic) about . . . [the offender's] . . . value relative to others." This, she tells us, involves a "commitment to asserting moral truth in the face of its denial. . . . It symbolizes the correct relative value of wrongdoer and victim." Hampton analyzes wrongdoing, conversely, as conduct that expresses an incorrect view of the relative worth of these two parties: "By victimizing me, the wrongdoer has declared himself elevated with respect to me, acting as a superior who is

---

[6] That Hampton implicitly equates wrongdoing with insubordination is suggested strongly by her use of the phrase "flouting value" to characterize wrongs. However, while speaking of "value" as something that can be "flouted" clearly abuses ordinary language, one is less likely to notice the oddness of such formulae if the special technical assumptions of Kant's theory lead one to presume that the value of persons is equivalent to a kind of authority that they wield. Hampton, "Correcting Harms versus Righting Wrongs," 1674.

permitted to use me for his purposes. A false moral claim has been made. Moral reality has been denied."[7]

It is important to stress that for Hampton this is not to say that the relevant "moral reality" has *changed*.[8] For, on her view, that moral reality refers to the relation of equal dignity in which agents stand to each other. She presumes that dignitarian relation to be intact throughout, issuing standing commands that offenders flout. What changes when agents engage in wrongdoing or legal authorities punish is the degree to which true and false beliefs about relative status are expressed. The wrongness of crimes and the rightness of punishments are on her view to be understood in terms of their expressive content. Offenses against persons are injuries or wrongs because they assert falsehoods. The purpose of punishment, on this account, is to "correct" such false beliefs by "convey[ing] defeat."[9]

Yet if we already *know*, by hypothesis, that criminals flout the authority of their victims, why is such symbolic correction necessary? Hampton vacillates between saying that punishment merely "conveys" and "symbolizes" defeat and maintaining that it actually inflicts it. When trying to highlight the "communicative" credentials of her view, and to downplay any threat to the dignity of those punished, Hampton emphasizes the merely expressive significance of harsh treatment. For, if legitimate punishments merely "symbolize" defeat, they won't actually accomplish diminishment, humiliation, or indignity themselves. But when she is trying to explain why punishment is required, Hampton slips into a different idiom. Thus she defines punishment as the "experience of defeat at the hands of the victim (either directly or indirectly through a legal authority)."[10] But to experience defeat, one presumably must actually *be* defeated. This requires punishment to accomplish something more than the communication of a message.

The same dilemma surfaces in Darwall's explanation of the special significance of the "moral relation" of "mutual respect": "Wrongs violate that relation; they fail adequately to recognize the dignity of persons and so call it into question. They therefore warrant a reciprocally recognizing response that seeks to reestablish mutual respect, demanding it of the violator in a way that simultaneously bestows it on him."[11]

It sounds right to say that punishment seeks to reestablish a mutual respect and a dignity that offenders undermine. But in what sense is it really undermined if wrongdoing merely "calls into question" a belief about the dignity of the victim that we ex hypothesi know to be true?

---

[7] Hampton and Murphy, *Forgiveness and Mercy*, p. 125.
[8] Ibid., p. 137.
[9] Ibid., p. 126.
[10] Ibid., p. 126.
[11] Darwall, *The Second-Person Standpoint*, p. 302.

To be sure, we can imagine circumstances in which the de facto acceptance of the belief that people should not be raped, beaten, tortured, or abused weakens: think of cases in which anarchy, toxic vendettas, or war induce systematic brutalization. But in settled civil societies that belief is not seriously in doubt. We certainly have reasons to worry if the incidence of (say) rape and sexual assault spikes. But not, I think, because it calls our belief that rape or sexual violence attract adamant opposition into question. It is not as if our reserves of indignation and resentment on behalf of victims deplete as violations become more prevalent; often it will (and should) have just the opposite effect, stimulating calls for more vigorous enforcement. And even when controversy arises about what should count as a violation (illustrated by current disputes about how to define rape and sexual assault), the appropriate way to deal with it is to *argue* that our beliefs about the relevant forms of abuse need to change. It would remain to explain why, apart from deterrent benefits, harsh treatment or violence against offenders is either an effective or necessary way to inculcate or reinforce such beliefs. Hart was right to say that this suggestion rests

> on a strange amalgam of ideas: it represents as a value to be pursued at the cost of human suffering the bare expression of moral condemnation. . . . The normal way in which moral condemnation is expressed is by *words*, and it is not clear, if denunciation is really what is required, why a solemn public statement of disapproval would not be the most "appropriate" or "emphatic" means of expressing this. Why should a denunciation take the form of punishment?[12]

Waldron on Hate-Speech

Jeremy Waldron's dignity-based defense of hate speech prohibitions provides another illustration of the problems faced by proponents of C-dignity. I take no position here on the advisability or permissibility of such prohibitions; my point is only that Waldron's argument cannot work as long as it is framed in terms of C-dignity, because in that case it would encounter the same problem we have uncovered in Hampton's case for retributivism. Roughly, his argument is that hate speech, especially if it denies the claim that members of certain groups are worthy of the equal dignity they enjoy as citizens of liberal societies, threatens their "assurance" that they are members "in good standing":

> The assurance offers a confirmation of their membership: they, too, are members of society in good standing; they have what it takes to interact on a straightforward basis with others around here, in public, on the streets,

---

[12] H. L. A. Hart, *Law, Liberty, and Morality* (Stanford, CA: Stanford University Press, 1963), p. 66.

in the shops, in business, and to be treated – along with every one else – as proper objects of society's protection and concern. This basic social standing, I call their dignity.[13]

Waldron compares a social culture in which agents enjoy such an assurance to a clean, unpolluted, environment, in which public goods like fresh air and water are reliably provided. It is important, he argues, or at least it is permissible, for societies to take a stand against speech (especially written or visually blatant) that denies that members of the targeted group are worthy of that status because it protects the public good of dignitarian assurance from analogous contamination.

Waldron says:

> Philosophically, we may say that dignity is inherent in the human person – and so it is. But as a social and legal status, it has to be established, upheld, maintained, and vindicated by society and the law, and this . . . is something in which we are all required to play a part. At the very least, we are required in our public dealings with one another to refrain from acting in a way that is calculated to undermine the dignity of other people.[14]

The clear tenor of this passage is that B-dignity (though Waldron clearly believes in such a thing) cannot ground hate-speech regulations; Waldron's case turns on the need to preserve a socially actualized relation of equal dignity. One might then think that it depends on the postulation of C-dignity. But if so, the question we posed to Hampton and Darwall now resurfaces: why is "vindication" necessary if the relevant status-relations are already presupposed and effectively enforced in the form of legal protections against force, fraud, and theft? Waldron's argument for hate-speech prohibitions is not addressed to societies in which a commitment to uphold the status and rights of equal citizens is somehow culturally or politically half-hearted. It is addressed to basically decent liberal societies in which the criminal law already enforces strong prohibitions on the forms of abuse and mistreatment that hate-speech may intimate but not actually inflict. However, if it is not a utilitarian anxiety about whether the law reliably delivers the public good of security, any unease experienced by the targets of hate-speech doesn't seem by itself to be enough to undermine their sense of assurance that society is committed to their protection. After all, Waldron is at pains to say that such unease wouldn't justify hate-speech regulation if it were no more than mere "offense," or "hurt feelings." For his argument to get off the ground, hate speech must be shown to *change* the dignitarian standing of its victims.

My point here is not that Waldron cannot show this. It is rather that to do so he would have to assert that the required relations of equal standing are

---

[13] Waldron, *The Harm in Hate Speech*, p. 5.
[14] Ibid., p. 60.

somehow vulnerable. Making that move, however, requires that one renounce C-dignity, which although relational and socially ambient, remains immutable. If the concept of dignity is to be of any use in explaining why retributive punishment or hate speech restrictions are necessary to vindicate human dignity, we have to think of it, not as a status or authority that never expires, but rather as a mutable, vulnerable, property that requires definite social protection. That would bring the timanthropic implications of crime and other forms of abuse back into the foreground where they belong. Plainly, however, C-dignity cannot capture this dimension, because it refers to an irrevocable social relation.

Ideology?

A further, though related, problem about C-dignity deserves mention in conclusion. The juridical, status-related, character of C-dignity also lends some credence to the Marxian charge that dignitarian humanism is little more than an ideological reflection of the liberal capitalist order. Interpreted in mode C, as we have seen, dignity tends to be identified with an authority, attaching equally to all individuals, to prohibit others from trespassing into a domain over which each exercises personal sovereignty. On this view, to decide whether or not social and political arrangements answer adequately to the value of human dignity, we need consider only how far the reigning balance of public and private power mimics a fixed relation of formal equality between persons conceived abstractly as independent, mutually accountable, agents.

It is easy enough to understand why those for whom the modern "liberal" contrast between "homme" and "citoyen" is axiomatic and who regularly confront each other in the marketplace as independent actors free to accept or reject proposed terms of co-operation, would find all this to be so much common sense. But their likely receptivity to it can surely only be the beginning of critical reflection, not its resolution. The tendency among recent political theorists to cite in this context "our" commitment to a "liberal tradition," or "our" socialization into practices of liberal democratic citizenship is wholly question-begging. In Chapter 2, we noted that the "liberal" credentials of a political view carry no probative value whatsoever. To be sure, dignitarian considerations may give us an independent reason to approve of some or all "liberal democratic" practices, but they cannot perform that role if those considerations are already identified with the "liberal" position under scrutiny. If liberalism (however defined) is in the dock, we cannot appoint liberalism to sit on the bench. That would be akin to telling atheists that they have a reason to love God because God has commanded them to do so. Anyway, is it true that "we" are pre-committed to "liberalism?" How do "we" know this about ourselves? Who is this "we?"

More generally, a model of political criticism that is confined to this juridical format will have trouble acknowledging that the satisfaction of important dignitarian desiderata might consist in something *other than* the relation between (1) a particular, institutionally structured, balance of public and private authority and (2) an ideal pattern of status equality (C-dignity) pertaining among abstract persons. Why, as Marx (and many others in the later tradition of critical theory, broadly understood, have) asked, restrict the scope of critical attention in this way? One reason to widen our field of vision, less clearly grasped by Marx himself, is the timanthropic dimension that dignitarian ideals bring into view. Intuitively it is the *value* of human beings, not their abstract status or authority, that should really matter from a dignitarian point of view.

Here it is worth briefly mentioning Arthur Ripstein's elegant exposition of Kant's political and legal theory in *Force and Freedom*.[15] Ripstein argues that the Kantian Doctrine of Right centers on a "right to Dignity, understood as a right to independent purposiveness."[16] Understood in this context, "dignity" is a summary term for a kind of rightful sovereignty that represents "each person's purposiveness" as ideally reconciled with the purposiveness of all other persons in a relation of "equal freedom." As Ripstein would surely want to say, the term "dignity" is being deployed here in a special technical sense. It would be unfair to read him as claiming that it captures the wider connotations of the concept "human dignity" as it is used in political discourse today. Still, we should notice just how narrow that sense is.

As Ripstein is at pains to emphasize, its normative significance in the Kantian theory is disconnected from the aim of preventing harm. It also has nothing to do with enhancing anyone's power to achieve their ends, or to lead good lives. Success and achievement are irrelevant. Everyone's life could be a miserable failure judged by their own goals (or indeed by any other standard), and they might be led in ways that utterly degrade cultural life, but this would not in any way count against the claim that their dignity as purposive beings has been properly protected in public law. Agents could face regular humiliation, various forms of structural oppression, racism, sexism, degradation, and so on, but none of this impinges on dignity as a right to purposiveness. Eager to rebut the charge that the Kantian theory of Right indulges "applied ethics," Ripstein also severs the connection most commentators draw between it and Kant's complex understandings of individual worth. Hence neither the moral psychology of resentment and indignation, nor the idea that human lives should be valued for their own sakes, figures at all in the account. At least within the theory of Right, the only thing that matters for its own sake is an abstract relation of equal freedom, and the approximation in the

---

[15] Ripstein, *Force and Freedom*.
[16] Ibid., p. 330.

empirical world of a timeless formal balance between public and private authority. Like other forms of C-dignity, this is a dignity that centers around reciprocal expectations of *compliance*.

Ripstein's elaboration of this juridical conception of dignity, and of Kant's views, is very impressive. Yet, precisely because it seems so tightly locked *within* that narrowly juristic frame, it tells against assigning C-dignity any broader critical significance. In elegantly reconstructing legal practices that presuppose what I have called here passport-dignity, Ripstein describes the inner clockwork of one of the major *objects* of political criticism: the modern institution of the "rule of law." But to generalize it and suggest that it helps us to step outside that system and introduce critical distance on it strikes me as misplaced. That would be to flirt with an uncritical, ideologically credulous picture of the late modern political predicament, in which dignity assumes the form of an overawing state, charged with coercively guaranteeing a formal relation of abstract equality, that then leaves civil society to determine our timanthropic fate as if our dignity and worth cannot be threatened by anything that occurs therein.

The Starry Heavens

If sound, the arguments in Chapters 5, 6, and 7 carry a hard lesson: traditional construals of "human dignity" are deficient in the very capacity that has led many to invest their political hopes in it. The dignitarian turn in recent political philosophy was officially motivated on the timanthropic ground that utilitarianism, and other views that purportedly discount respect and "human dignity," cannot take the value of persons and their lives seriously. The upshot of the argument so far, however, is that a similar charge can be laid against traditional dignitarian positions. As we have seen, these traditional views tend to take one of two general forms: either they treat the dignity of the person as an immutable, self-sufficient, and ultimately lifeless, quality set apart from the world; or they equate personal *worth/value* with fixed, inalienable, relations of personal *status* that resemble legalistic and juridical models except in that they are supposed to subsist among human beings *as such* and not on some merely conventional or parochial basis. Neither alternative can adequately explain how the worth of persons is urgently at stake, either in the critical assessment of political practice, or in the practices themselves. The reason for this lies in an assumption that both variants of the traditional account share: that human dignity is a fixed and unchanging quality.

In a way, this conclusion should come as no surprise: Chapter 3 noted that our ordinary sense that valued items have urgent or adamant importance tends to presuppose their vulnerability, and hence their transitory quality. When there is no chance that something, even something we regard as valuable, can, for example, be damaged, destroyed, diminished, protected, secured, or improved, it becomes much harder to explain how and why it should figure prominently in practical judgment. No doubt the "starry heavens above" elicit "ever-increasing wonder and awe," but equally they are hardly objects of urgent practical concern. They aren't going anywhere, they don't need us to take care of them, and they are awesome in large part because they are utterly impervious even to our existence, let alone our actions and social practices. If the awe inspired by the "moral law within" is of the same order, it is unlikely to be able to explain the adamant political importance of any associated concept of human dignity.

If dignitarian humanism could only take a traditional form, the argument of this book could end here with dignity-skeptics winning a decisive victory. However, our typology opens space for an alternative account centered on the westerly categories of A- and D-dignity. The balance of this book is devoted to developing the possibility of a "revisionist" account of human dignity along these lines, and seeing how far it can go.

PART III

A Revisionist Approach

8

Dignity-Revisionism: Challenges and Opportunities

The second half of this book attempts to reconstruct an alternative account of human dignity and to evaluate how far its critical credentials in political reflection can be vindicated. The account I will offer is revisionary in that it drops any presumption that human dignity is a preset value standing apart from the transactions and routines of everyday life. It aims to liberate the central dignitarian intuition that all lives matter, and should be valued accordingly, from the two traditionalist mainstays rejected in earlier chapters: on the one hand, the assumption that human dignity is immutably possessed by persons; and on the other, that it consists in an idealized relation of equality defining a kind of dignitarian *kallipolis* like Kant's "kingdom of ends." Instead, the revisionist proposes that human dignity is a transient, vulnerable, and socially extended quality whose emergence depends on the character of concrete, organized, interaction under actually existing regimes. The idea is to open space for a new kind of dignitarian political criticism, one that assesses social practices, institutional routines, and forms of life, by asking whether they align with, promote, or undermine the conditions under which a dignified human existence can be secured for all.

Stated so generally, that ambition may seem familiar enough. However, pursuing it while doing without standard assumptions about individuals' "inherent worth," or about equal relations among independent "ends-in-themselves," turns out to require a theoretical apparatus that departs quite radically from contemporary orthodoxy. So, like a pair of new boots, pinching uncomfortably when first put on, the arguments developed here will chafe against intuitions that have become second-nature in the recent philosophical literature. Having worn these arguments in, I have found unsuspected force in them, but I warn readers to expect a strong initial resistance. I will try hard to anticipate and disarm their likely doubts, especially by anchoring my proposal in understandings of dignity that are perfectly familiar in ordinary use. On first acquaintance, however, my approach is bound to seem counterintuitive, even heretical.

This may, of course, be because it is simply confused and foredoomed. To those who suspect that it is, I enter two pleas: that exploring unconventional lines of argument can be instructive even if in the end we find the resulting position problematic; and that sometimes, as I believe *is* the case here, it can nudge reflection into unexpectedly fertile territory and open new possibilities. In any event, that is the spirit in which I proceed here. In the nature of the enterprise, the ensuing discussion is exploratory rather than definitive, an overture to others to assist in developing it further, and correcting my own likely missteps, should they see anything in it.

Before embarking on any of this, however, an important clarification is in order. Although I offer a heterodox theorization of human dignity, at least in relation to received academic wisdom, it is important to stress that I aim to leave the standard *motives* for investing in dignitarian ideas in political argument intact. That is, I seek to preserve:

- The dignity/price distinction, and the corresponding aversion to thinking of the worth of persons and lives on a commodifying, or objectifying, model;
- The assumption that the claims of human dignity make adamant demands of human association and therefore fundamentally condition our understanding of freedom, justice, and all other important political ideals and social values;
- The anti-utilitarian, non-welfarist, orientation of dignitarian humanism; and
- The thought that in dedicating itself to securing and maintaining human dignity as far as it can, society acts only *for the sake* of its individual members, and refuses to subordinate them to some impersonal abstraction or idol.

Chapter 3 reviewed these standard grounds for embracing a dignitarian humanist approach to political criticism. Not only do I make no attempt to dislodge or question them, I will assume that my revisionist approach stands or falls to the extent that it answers to them. So, although I propose a radical change in our thinking about the phenomenology of human dignity, my assumptions about why it matters in the evaluation of political forms are quite conventional.

The account I will develop turns from the conceptions of dignity located on the Eastern flank of our typology and toward the Westerly ones of D-dignity and A-dignity. This chapter begins my elaboration of that account by exploring both the likely advantages and seeming disadvantages of this shift of focus. Chapter 9 begins the long process of reconstructing a dignitarian humanism that might exploit these advantages while overcoming the challenges it appears to confront.

Performative Accounts of Dignity

The most immediate effect, and (I will suggest) advantage, of turning to the Westerly column to reconstruct dignitarian humanism for political criticism is that it would reverse the traditional relation between respect and dignity. As we have seen, traditional accounts understand that relation *reactively*, such that appropriate respect is commanded by a preexisting, unchanging, dignity – a form of personal value or mutual status that entitles its bearers to various types and levels of respect. The alternative I will explore (and in some measure defend) later in the chapter asserts instead that *human* dignity (the sort that primarily bears on political judgment) depends on respect. The general idea is that the actual performance of respect imparts worth to people and their lives, and hence that "human dignity" is somehow constituted by, or results from, these imparted forms of value.[1] Conversely, when such respect is absent, or when people are greeted with active disrespect, their lives are devalued in a way that diminishes or tarnishes "human dignity." This revisionist model construes the relation between respect and human dignity as *performative* rather than reactive. It regards human dignity as a fragile social achievement that is fortified or set back according as respect or disrespect, and the forms of personal worth they impart or withdraw, circulate within a form of life. Exactly what this might mean remains to be worked out. Clearly, however, our westerly concepts of dignity at least make room for a proposal along these lines, because they construe it as a varying rather than fixed quality.

One might think that ordinary language immediately short-circuits this proposal. Don't we virtually always speak of dignity as a preexisting quality in persons that gives others a reason to respect them? To invert that relation, one might think, is to swim strongly against the tide of ordinary use. However, I wager that such expressions as "dignity commands respect" or "one ought not to disrespect a person's worth," are far more common within technical and scholastic idioms (e.g., of theology or Kantian ethics) than in the ordinary language of moral complaint and exhortation. On reflection, what we would usually say is not that a person's *dignity* commands our respect, but rather that *they* command our respect. At first hearing, this way of putting it sounds hairsplitting. Yet it is nonetheless implicit in the familiar and natural thought that when someone or something leads us to treat it "with respect" we thereby "dignify" them or it. (For example: "I won't dignify that question with a response.") Why would I seek to – *can* I, even? – dignify something whose dignity is settled in advance and not subject to change?

---

[1] In an earlier work (e.g., Colin Bird, "Dignity as a Moral Concept," *Social Philosophy and Policy* 30, no. 1–2 (2013): 150–76), I described such a view as one in which dignity was "conferred" on persons as a result of their receiving respect. I now think this choice of words was a mistake; it tends to reinforce the more formalistic, status-based, conceptions of human dignity that I rejected in Chapter 7 and now think we should be trying to get away from. The language of "impartation" and "imbuing" comports better with a view that captures the sense in which human dignity represents the *worth* of human beings and their lives.

Consider the question (raised pointedly by Michael Rosen) of why we should respect corpses.[2] Many would say that dignity somehow bears on the answer, in part because the material welfare of the deceased is obscurely related to any need to respect their lifeless bodies. Yet if dignity *is* involved in the explanation, it is difficult to believe that this can be due to corpses' possessing some inherent, unchanging, property of dignity that persists beyond death. Corpses lack all of the attributes in which at least B-dignity standardly consists: they are devoid of consciousness, personality, agency, rationality, the capacity to pursue projects, and so on. Even on theist views, the "soul" that bears God's creative hand has already "left" the body: all that is left is the "dust to which you will return." Corpses are also frequently objects of disgust, pity, and horror as well as eloquent symbols of our materiality and subjection to the forces of nature. These suggest the absence of dignity rather than its presence. If corpses have any dignitarian profile at all, then, it would seem to result from the way in which we treat them – indeed Rosen himself uses the familiar language of treating them "with dignity." Why, after all, should we bother to place a deceased person's ashes in an elegant urn, or carry carved coffins in stately procession, if not because we find the effort to impart a certain dignity to their remains worth making?

More generally, in displaying public respect for a completed life, memorial services accord the dead a certain dignity; conversely, the closing scene in the film *Amadeus,* in which Mozart's body, wrapped in sackcloth, is tossed thoughtlessly into a mass grave like rubbish, and then splashed with lime to prevent disease,[3] surely refracts indignity. If dignitarian metaphors help capture how these different transactions respectively elevate and demean the lives in question, they are unlikely to be ones centered around traditional notions of dignity as an unchanging, inherent, possession or a fixed status. They would, rather, be ones in the orbit of what I am calling D-dignity, sensitive to the importance of peoples' lives "abroad," in their ramifications for, impact on, and contribution to, other lives. If this is a plausible way to think about the (in) dignity of the dead, why not think that it can work for the (in)dignity of the living as well?

Until now, we have lacked any very clear theoretical apparatus for thinking about respect and dignity in this performative way. But while, for this and other reasons, the possibility that respect and disrespect can somehow alter the

---

[2] M. Rosen, *Dignity: Its History and Meaning* (Cambridge, MA: Harvard University Press, 2012), pp. 131–33. Moshe Halbertal mentions that some societies "appoint" mourners to attend funerals of those who die friendless and estranged. M. Halbertal, "Three Concepts of Dignity" (Dewey Lecture delivered at the University of Chicago Law School, January 1, 2015). Audio file available at https://soundcloud.com/uchicagolaw/moshe-halbertal-three -concepts-of-human-dignity.

[3] My understanding is that the events depicted in the film are not historically accurate; the actual circumstances of Mozart's death are shrouded in mystery.

dignitarian value of their targets may at first sound strange, it has long been entertained by theorists of love. Comparisons with love are anyway instructive in this context because, like respect, love is certainly a timanthropic emotion; both crucially involve dispositions to engage with others for their sakes. Indeed, in this regard, love and respect are siblings, both somehow holding the value of their targets in view, albeit in distinctive ways. Accordingly, relevant contrasts between them will be important to the arguments elaborated below. The relevant point now is that, at least since Nygren, theorists of love have acknowledged that love can imbue its targets with a worth and significance that they would not have otherwise have carried.[4] This possibility anticipates, in the arena of love, the performative move I want to consider in that of respect and dignity.

Not that love, in any of its forms, can *only* be construed performatively. Reactive construals of love are certainly available, and sometimes tempt those who connect it with dignity. David Velleman, for example, has maintained that respect and love are "the required minimum and optional maximum responses to one and the same value" – the inherent dignity of another.[5] Still, reactive accounts of love are not the only game in town.[6] If, as Nygren and others have thought, the relation between love and personal worth can be performative rather than reactive, we have every reason to consider a parallel possibility in the case of respect and dignity.

To adopt a performative view of either love or respect is not to claim that these affects are in *no* sense responses to their intentional objects. No sane, nonsolipsistic account of these attitudes can afford to deny that they develop in response to encounters with, or at least information about, their targets; after all, agents cannot love or respect someone or something *before* any acquaintance with them. As we noted earlier, even if, as in the case of a memorial service, the participants *dignify* the deceased by publicly offering tokens of respect, they are still responding to her life. It is not as if they spontaneously

---

[4] See, for example, Irving Singer, *The Philosophy of Love: A Partial Summing Up* (Cambridge, MA: MIT Press, 2009).

[5] D. Velleman, "Love as a Moral Emotion," *Ethics* 109, no. 2 (1999): 366.

[6] They also face serious challenges – especially in explaining love's particularity: If dignity grounds love, and we all possess dignity inherently, why do we not love everyone? Velleman offers an interesting answer to this question, but his strongly Kantian, and explicitly moralized, depiction of love has proven very controversial. Insofar as we construe love as responding to a beloved's "value" at all, surely we very rarely, if ever, think of it as elicited by a consciousness of their "dignity." What does it even mean to love someone for their dignity? Try that line on a date and see how far it gets you. We say (at least when it is welcome) that another's love "touches" us, but can one attach clear meaning to the idea that we are touched on behalf of our dignity, or that it is our dignity that is itself touched? While the beloved person is certainly the intentional object of another's love, whatever it is about them that engenders their love from others, or that is touched by it, is unlikely to be some aspect of their dignity.

decide to have a funeral just for the sake of it, select readings, speakers, and hymns, and so on and then wait for someone to die so that they can execute their plan.

So, a performative approach doesn't question the obvious truth that affects like love and respect involve "reactive attitudes" in Strawson's general sense. The difference turns on a more subtle issue about when and how timanthropic considerations enter the story. Reactive versions of dignitarian humanism presume that "human dignity" names a timanthropic circumstance already in place before any concrete interaction between agents occurs. That is, whether construed as an inherent, unchanging, worth possessed by all individual agents (B-dignity), or as a fixed relation of equal status or importance that pertains among all humans *as such* (C-dignity), "human dignity" surfaces in reactive accounts as a set of constraints, perpetually in force, conditioning the proper treatment of others in virtue of their preset timanthropic profile. Critical judgments about the adequacy of different social practices then turn on their tendency to guarantee or promote conduct that answers to those dignitarian constraints.

On a performative construal, human dignity is not a form of personal value or worth that preexists any actual interaction with others, but one that appears on the scene only when, and to the extent that, the affective repercussions of agents' mutual encounters involve respect of a relevant kind or kinds. So understood, the notion of persons' bearing dignitarian worth has no meaning independently of how they are in fact treated, and of the affects that actually motivate that treatment.

Again, it is important to not to make this suggestion appear more radical than it is. A performative view of dignity does not imply that persons or their lives cannot ever be said to be valuable, important, or to be of worth, and so on, apart from their actual interactions with others. Our notions of value are vastly diverse; persons or lives can be worthy in any number of ways. A performative account of dignity need not say that these timanthropic dimensions all obey the same logic, nor deny that many have a reactive structure.[7] For example, that you are talented, brave, honest, or otherwise virtuous is both something that can make you "good value," a "hero," a "brick," or simply a "good egg," and a reason to respond to you in certain ways and not others – offering you the job, recommending you for a medal, trusting or befriending you, and so on. None of this need contradict a performative understanding of dignity, for the latter is committed only to the claim that, whatever is true of other ways in which persons and lives bear value and supply reasons for treating them in particular ways, that named by "human dignity" is not one given in advance of actual engagement with others, but rather varies with its affective mood.

---

[7] I am grateful to Nick Wolterstorff for helping me appreciate the importance of clarifying this point.

In such an account, dignity would relate to respect as "dearness" does to love. One cannot be "dear" (clearly implying augmentation in value)[8] until someone relates to you in a particular affective mode. To be sure, people are presumably lovable in virtue of various valuable qualities, but someone cannot normally be lovable because they are already dear. Rather, they become dear *because* they are loved. Similarly, even if respect is triggered or warranted in the first instance by an appreciation for someone's virtues, impressiveness, intimidating qualities, and so on, dignity may refer to a value that can arrive only later, imparted by patterns of respect subsequently shown by others. After love comes dearness; after respect comes dignity.

Sources of Resistance

Three connected problems, each implying a related set of objections, confront the effort to develop an account along these lines, and partly explain why this way of thinking about human dignity has hitherto gone largely unexplored.

First, the suggestion that human dignity is subject to some kind of variation is admittedly puzzling and can easily be made to look silly. Is the idea that it is composed of some fund of dignitarian "value" that can be spent, used up, added to, or subtracted from such that assaults on dignity somehow diminish its overall amount in some measurable degree? Should we aim for a dignitarian metric under which agents are assigned an indignity "score" according as they are raped, tortured, exploited, abused, or oppressed? Some indeed talk of human dignity in something like this way: witness the efforts of the self-described "Global Dignity & Humiliation Mapping and Assessment Initiative"[9] to devise a "Dignity Index." Such proposals are however difficult to take seriously as a basis for political criticism and likely derive such plausibility as they possess from being disguised forms of welfarist assessment. Dismissing this sort of thing as laughably crude is easy enough; offering a more sophisticated explanation of how human dignity is subject to damage or enhancement is a lot harder.

A second reason why the possibility of a performative account of human dignity not been taken up may be an incipient fear of relativism. The idea that human dignity is the *result* and not the *ground* of respect suggests that it is merely an artifice or convention hostage to contingent exercises of social power. But then it is hard to see how it can be an independent standard by which to judge and criticize social practices; it would seem rather to be their creature. As Alan Donagan has complained, in the course of critical commentary on Nietzsche,

---

[8] As in, "buy cheap, sell dear."

[9] www.humiliationstudies.org/research/assessment.php. See also for a suggestion of a "Dignity Scale" https://blog.politics.ox.ac.uk/11986-2/.

if according honor to things creates value, then in themselves the things honored have no value. . . . In a society Nietzsche would consider healthy, what passes for value is created by the masters, as Louis XIV multiplied distinctions of rank at the court of Versailles. Yet the masters *find* value nowhere. The honors they confer, being grounded on nothing but arbitrary will, can be upheld only by force.[10]

The worry here, I take it, is that if one analyzes human dignity on these Nietzschean terms, it starts to look like an "arbitrary" social construction. Yet the normal office of "social constructionist" arguments in political philosophy is to puncture the image of stability, naturalness, and legitimacy that conventional norms and beliefs tend to project: the point of suggesting that gender, say, is "socially constructed," is to weaken our attachment to complacent "patriarchal" assumptions. But if we apply such acid to "human dignity," it, too, may start to look like the *object* of social criticism, not a basis on which it can introduce valid critical distance on existing practice, still less one that can identify those features of it that should be adamantly rejected. Something like this worry, I suspect, informs Clarence Thomas's insistence in his dissenting opinion in *Obergefell* v. *Hodges* that governments (and, by extension, any contingent complex of entrenched power) cannot confer or withdraw human dignity. As he put it:

> Slaves did not lose their dignity (any more than they lost their humanity) because the government allowed them to be enslaved. Those held in internment camps did not lose their dignity because the government confined them. . . . The government cannot bestow dignity, and it cannot take it away.[11]

Commodification

A third likely source of resistance to a performative approach recalls the deeply appealing Kantian distinction between "dignity" and "price." The circulation of goods and services on the market, in which they acquire commensurable though often shifting, exchange-values, provides one model for thinking about how the value of items can alter as a result of the attitudes agents take to them. Most people, however, are strongly averse to thinking about the value of human beings on that model. Hobbes's notorious claim that "the 'value' or 'worth' of a man is, as of all other things, his price"[12] has attracted widespread condemnation. As I suggest later in the chapter, Hobbes's view is more subtle

---

[10] A. Donagan, *The Theory of Morality* (Chicago: University of Chicago Press, 1977), p. 241.

[11] *Obergefell* v. *Hodges*, 576 US – (2015) (Thomas, C. dissenting), 17 CNFER.

[12] T. Hobbes, *Leviathan: With Selected Variants from the Latin Edition of 1668*, ed. Edwin Curley (Indianapolis: Hackett Publishing Company, 1994), p. 51.

than it appears at first sight, but if he is proposing to reduce human dignity completely to something like exchange-value, we are surely right to reject it.

Those who insist that persons and their lives bear an inviolable worth named "human dignity" are then often motivated by a quite reasonable desire to insulate the value of persons and their lives completely from the shifting sands of market valuation. Whatever else might be said against traditional understandings of dignity, they at least preserve the strong conviction that slavery, human trafficking, the buying and selling of babies, and so on, should be unconditionally restricted – "blocked exchanges," as Walzer has called them. One might worry that entertaining performative accounts of dignity puts all of this into question, threatening the price/dignity distinction itself, and rendering the value of persons and their lives problematically negotiable. On the one hand, a performative approach may seem incapable of vindicating the adamant significance of human dignity against the vicissitudes of social exchange. On the other, it arguably underestimates the importance of insisting that agents' basic standing as "equals" must not vary with the outcomes of economic, social, and other interaction, but be respected constantly.

Here, it is worth stressing that although earlier chapters have stressed the "possessive" character of traditional construals of human dignity, the most plausible traditionalist accounts rightly refuse to characterize the dignity of persons in proprietary terms, as if it were an alienable asset or resource. This is surely a strength of the traditional account. Kant underlined this point very clearly, explicitly rejecting the equation of personal dignity and self-ownership made by more recent libertarians like Robert Nozick. For Kant, to bear moral dignity is precisely *not* to possess an alienable resource that can in principle be traded off for a price. It is to possess something that, unlike property, one is *not* free to "use and abuse" but that rather commands unconditional respect from everyone, including the agent himself or herself.[13] Martin Luther King, who was certainly a dignitarian, expressed the thought thus: "Property is intended to serve life, and no matter how much we surround it with rights and respect, it has no personal being. It is part of the earth man walks on. It is not man."[14]

The implication is that any legitimate scheme of commercial exchange is itself bounded by, and serves, a deeper human attribute – dignity – that is neither marketable nor alienable. That implication is strictly incompatible with the self-ownership thesis, since the latter (as Nozick was prepared to concede) would permit voluntary slavery – which surely commodifies persons, and is therefore difficult to reconcile with any commitment to human dignity. Even revisionists should want to preserve this very attractive feature of dignitarian

---

[13] See on this Samuel Freeman, "Illiberal Libertarians: Why Libertarianism Is Not a Liberal View," *Philosophy & Public Affairs* 30, no. 2 (2001): 105–51 and Bird, *The Myth of Liberal Individualism*.

[14] Martin Luther King, *The Trumpet of Conscience* (Boston: Beacon Press, 2010), pp. 56–57.

humanism. But again, many will ask: why tinker with the traditional account if it already includes this anti-commodifying proviso?

Dignity among the *eloi*?

Daunting as these three sources of resistance are, they need not lead one to despair, as significant intuitions support an alternative view. Some of these were hinted at in the criticisms of traditional understandings of dignity set out earlier, and I conclude this chapter with a short fable intended to capture the dividends that a successful theorization of a revisionist account might yield. The fable asks us to imagine a world in which key desiderata implicit in a traditional dignitarian framework are fully met, but in which human dignity in any ordinary sense will nonetheless strike us as tenuous or incompletely realized.

Imagine a world populated by beings akin to H. G. Wells's "*eloi*" in the *Time Machine,* with the following difference: rather than having to rely on a subterranean class of cannibalistic "*morlocks*," our *eloi* are served by a self-sustaining robotic infrastructure established by earlier generations that automatically provides for their basic nutritional and medical needs. Beyond this guaranteed supply of necessities, the *eloi* are able to enjoy the "surplus value" afforded by resources in their natural environment. Assume, then, that a rudimentary free market in this "surplus value" has developed among the *eloi*: they own, produce, buy, and sell other valued objects (flowers, pottery, furniture, clothes, blankets, tents, jewelry, simple conveniences, horticultural tools, candy, etc.) and, for an appropriate price, they are willing to supply each other services that are in demand. The prices of these goods and services are determined by a competitive market, presided over by a minimal state that enforces what we would think of as classical liberal property rights under the rule of law. In fact, however, little coercive enforcement is needed: our *eloi* are temperamentally conformist and have been socialized to believe that all human beings universally possess an "inherent human worth" or "dignity" that requires that they respect their fellows' right to live, and dispose of their property, as they please. For that reason, theft, assault and fraud are rare: the *eloi* largely "mind their own business." Their way of life is mostly peaceful, and, at least in relation to their actual needs and wants, prosperous.

Suppose, however, that our *eloi* are (much as Wells depicts them) effete, immature, dim, lazy, cowardly, and profoundly limited in their outlook. The goods and services they exchange tend to be generic; little initiative, pride or imagination goes into their production. The reigning ethos is half-hearted, ungenerous, and graceless: "you get what you pay for, nothing more, nothing less" is a favorite *eloian* proverb. Their voluntary cooperation supports a cultural life, but it is one that is narcissistic, philistine, and relentlessly *kitsch*. The arts are no longer appreciated or practiced in any sophisticated form:

soppy romances have crowded out the great novel; twee garden gnomes, rather than graceful Rodins, decorate their public buildings; slapstick pantomimes have put paid to Verdi, Bach, and Shakespeare. Scientific research and intellectual curiosity have atrophied because few have the patience for, or see much point in, them. Whether as consumers or producers, the *eloi* spend much of their time and energy on pointless, trivial, activities: croquet is their national sport ("Trivia quizzes" in winter); they engage in diverse saccharine religious rituals drenched in fantasy and sentimentality; enjoying a nice cupcake defines the upper end of their hedonic range; and they express themselves in relationships and associations that are convivial but completely superficial. When they are not moved to gratify some pressing desire, they are often bored and restless. Their sense of humor is infantile and scatological; neither nobility of endeavor nor tragedy mean much to them.

Many *eloi* feel a vague sense of dissatisfaction with their existence, but lacking any acquaintance with more fulfilling forms of life, and with limited linguistic resources to articulate alternatives, they are unable to put their finger on exactly what is missing. They are not, however, wholly unreflective, nor do they lack any ethical sensibility. When they think about their terms of existence, what strikes them most is the opacity of sentient experience to outside observers, and the idiosyncrasy and uniqueness of the point of view from which each must live their life. They are fond of quoting *Pink Floyd:* "all you see and all you touch is all your life will ever be," and they interpret this to mean that such satisfaction as is available to them can only be attained and realized "from the inside." Given the rather narrow bandwidth of their preferences, the *eloi* are mostly (to use Charles Taylor's terms) "simple weighers" rather than "strong evaluators." Introspective depth and uniqueness are however perpendicular, largely independent, dimensions. So their superficiality doesn't prevent the *eloi* from noticing the systematic idiosyncrasy of their tastes and interests. Accordingly, they develop a keen and jealous sense of their individuality and resent behavior that limits the innocent pursuit of their personal tastes.

The *eloi* are therefore not psychopaths who lack any sense of right and wrong; they recognize a principle of respect for the freedom of each to live as they wish, and become indignant when anyone interferes with the voluntary choices of others, or otherwise seeks to limit or impugn others' uniqueness. They greet these infractions with invocations of the inherent worth of each *eloi* and their concomitant right to do as they please. The idea that they are "self-authenticating sources of valid claims" in Rawls's sense is perfectly accessible to them. They accordingly take great exception to behavior from others implying that their own standards of authentication are misguided. We can well imagine such accusations being a source of social conflict and unrest among the *eloi,* setting off sporadic bouts of petulance, squabbling, sulking, ostracism, and even violence (often involving croquet mallets). They have something of the same rudimentary sense of "glory" and personal honor that Hobbes thought would move individuals even in an anarchic, pre-conventional, "state-of-nature."

The *eloi* can reasonably say that their society is just, peaceable, and stable. But can they claim with any credibility that human dignity is alive and well in their way of life? Since they have internalized and take some pride in their embrace of dignitarian ideals, the *eloi* will likely be reluctant to admit that their society is scant in human dignity. They might point out that, for the most part, their society recognizes the inherent dignity of each of its members and does a decent job of meeting the minimal expectations entailed by that recognition. They may insist that human dignity is "alive" among them in that they live and let live, and that disrespect reliably elicits resentment and indignation. And surely the *eloi* would be partly right to believe that, since cruelty, torture, persecution, and other indignities are rare rather than rampant in their society, they successfully meet at least some basic conditions for a dignified human existence.

Still, this is pretty thin gruel in relation to ordinary dignitarian intuitions, and I defy anyone to maintain that *eloian* society epitomizes human dignity in any rich form. Stanley Fish once complained that "[T]he thing about respect is that it doesn't cost you anything; its generosity is barely skin-deep and is in fact a form of condescension: I respect you; now don't bother me." Fish's complaint about such "a withdrawal from ... any strong, insistent form" of ethical commitment was directed against "liberal" norms of respect for religious diversity;[15] as such, it was certainly unfair, but applied to our *eloi* it pretty clearly hits the mark. Although they respect each other, and resent disrespect, their sense of what respect and human dignity require is shallow and undemanding. *Eloian* respect comes cheap: it amounts to little more than the adolescent demand to "let me be."

More broadly, too much of what Kateb rightly cites as incidents of human dignity is missing among the *eloi*: a spirit of exploration and adventure; determined collaboration and ingenuity in solving common problems; the exercise of intellectual, creative, and rational capabilities; honest, courageous, and emotionally mature reckoning with the challenges of life, and so on. Rawls glosses J. S. Mill as holding that "our sense of dignity is tied ... to our recognition that some ways of life are admirable and worthy of our nature, while others are beneath us and unfitting."[16] Yet the *eloi* lack a sense of dignity in this sense. The *eloi* have little patience for Mill's "higher pleasures"; their society is akin to Socrates's "City of Pigs." In Wells's novel, the sophisticated

---

[15] Stanley Fish, "A Cartoon in 3 Dimensions: Our Faith in Letting It All Hang Out," *New York Times*, 2006, www.nytimes.com/2006/02/12/opinion/12fish.html.

[16] John Rawls and S. Freeman, *Lectures on the History of Political Philosophy* (Cambridge, MA: Belknap Press of Harvard University Press, 2007), p. 265.

scientific and artistic culture the *eloi* inherited from their forebears lies in shreds on the floor of a vast abandoned museum – the derelict "Palace of Green Porcelain." It is not for nothing that his time-traveler dubs the world of the *eloi* a "sunset of mankind."

This adaptation of Wells's story about the *eloi* underlines how much of our intuitive concern for human dignity reflects, not its possessive, individualized, character, but rather its communal, socially extended aspect. This suggests that the revisionist approach proposed here, in which human dignity is taken to be an ambient, but varying, social quality is on the right track. In missing the forest of human (in)dignity for its trees, the *eloi* also inflict on themselves the indignity of self-delusion: it seems to be a requirement of human dignity that its bearers are able to recognize it clearly, but the *eloi* fail that test. If so, properly informed dignitarian social criticism may itself be an important aspect of human dignity, and replacing traditional understandings of it with a revisionist alternative might help us view our forms of life through a sharper, more honest mirror.

9

Commercial and Human Economies

This chapter introduces several general ideas from which I propose to reconstruct an account of human dignity that I hope can answer to the challenges and opportunities described in previous chapters. All of them concern the similarities and differences between the social exchanges that determine market value or "price" and those that one might implicate in human dignity understood (as I am proposing) as a socially emergent quality. Although related, they can be grouped under three headings:

(1) A logical point about the "price/dignity" distinction with an unexpected Hobbesian provenance;
(2) The idea that the affective responses people elicit from each other within the cyclical routines of social life convey information about how their lives are esteemed or valued; and
(3) The claim that (2) is the locus of an "economy," where that term includes, but has a much broader reference than, the model of a commercial market.

These three ideas form the raw materials from which I will try to theorize a new conception of dignity and respect. This chapter seeks to motivate them seriatim.

Hobbes on "Public Worth"

Consider the notorious passage in *Leviathan* where Hobbes appears to equate the "worth" of persons with their "price." Kantian critics today cite this passage as damning evidence that Hobbes subscribed to an objectionable "instrumentalist" theory of human worth.[1] Closer inspection reveals that a more subtle (and charitable) reading is available. For Hobbes evidently found it important to *distinguish* persons' "price" (i.e., what their services, talents, assets, abilities, time, energy, labor, etc. are worth when offered on the market) from the independent sort of *"public worth"* (emphasis mine) that he labels "dignity." Hobbes's understanding of "public worth" plainly reflects the traditional view of secular authority as the "fount of honor," fixing the relative dignities of

[1] Hampton and Murphy, *Forgiveness and Mercy*, p. 46.

different social groups from above. If one takes this on board, however, Hobbes's remarks precisely *contrast* those cases in which a person's "value" or "worth" consists in their "price," from those in which a sovereign state authoritatively confers public standing and dignity upon them. So understood, they more plausibly anticipate, rather than deny, Kant's later distinction between price and dignity, both because they suggest that "public worth" is achieved by a distinct social mechanism, and because that mechanism is constituted by practices of authoritative law-giving.

In suggesting that both "price" or economic value (on the one hand) and "dignity" or "public worth" (on the other) are variables determined by independent processes, Hobbes implicitly recognizes an important logical point: there is no necessary or automatic inference from:

(a) the price of things and the dignity of persons are qualitatively distinct modes of value;

  to

(b) "human dignity" cannot be altered (diminished, augmented, or damaged) by anything that happens to the people who bear, or share it.

The invalidity of this inference reminds us that a traditional, reactive, understanding of human dignity need not be the only available option for those who wish to retain the distinction between dignity and price. (a) entails merely that whether or not the value of lives is a variable quality, dignitarian variation is not well-construed on the model of price determination on a market. One could accept the underlying intuition yet still believe that the worth of persons and lives is determined independently in the course of ordinary social and political interaction. Such a view would accept that, like the prices of goods and services in the economy, the value of persons and lives somehow varies as they participate in routines of mutual circulation. However, it would deny that market valuation, in which commodities acquire a commensurable money-value informing agents of the advisability of sales and purchases, properly models the timanthropic dynamics involved and can explain the significance of "human dignity" within them.

Although Hobbes's account opens this possibility up, it cannot by itself take us much further. Like the later Kantian views that are derived from it, Hobbes's view encourages the sort of juridical and status-centric construal of dignity we have already criticized. As argued in earlier chapters, insofar as human dignity is merely a matter of formal allocation of status by a recognized authority, its relation to the timanthropic impetus informing the recent dignitarian turn in political philosophy becomes unclear. In Hobbes, dignity ("public worth") is conferred by an official authority concerned fundamentally with the practical imperative of securing order and peace, and does not appear to reflect the state's independent "respect" for its citizens. If Hobbes's citizens are to respect the "public worth" of their compatriots, they are to do so by respecting the authority of the state to determine it. But, at least on a standard reading, Hobbes's view denies that "public worth" emerges from any respect flowing from sovereign to subject, or directly from subject to subject. Respect on his view only flows upward, from subject to sovereign; any lateral, mutual, respect among citizens depends on their first respecting state authority. The thought, central to the account I want to offer, that human dignity is constituted by independently expressed attitudes of respect for people and their lives, finds no place in Hobbes's view. To reconstruct the idea that human dignity requires antecedent respect, and can be threatened by disrespect, then, we must move beyond Hobbes's formalistic understanding of dignity as "public worth," created simply by political *fiat* and respect for the privileges of sovereignty. This brings me to the second of the three points framing this chapter.

Affective Catallaxy

Hobbes's contemporary Pufendorf remarked:

> Esteem is the value which is set upon persons in common life, according to which they may be equaled or compared with others, and be rated higher or lower than those they are compared with. For there is a near affinity between the two most noble branches of moral quantity, esteem and price. The first is considered in persons; the second in things: because as the one is the rate of persons in common life, so the other is of things. And as the chief reason why a price was set upon things, was, that when they were to be exchanged or removed from one person to another, they might be the better compared with one another; so the end intended by esteem, is, that we may be able to form a comparison between men, by setting, as it were a value upon them, and, in consequence, establish a becoming order and distance between them, whenever they should happen to be united.[2]

According to Pufendorf, in the course of economic and social exchange both goods and persons acquire comparative "worth," but the logic by which these comparisons develop in the two arenas is in some respects analogous, while in others incongruent. Prices result from the circulation of goods in commercial exchange and express relative economic value, through a monetary standard of equivalence. In Pufendorf's scheme the analogous currency in the social case is that of esteem, which he implicitly contrasts with money. As agents move through the social world, they come to possess, acquire, or lose a worth or value according as esteem and disesteem flow between them.

In making this claim, Pufendorf in effect advances a timanthropic hypothesis – a proposal about how the value of persons is determined in the course of social interaction. In the above passage, that hypothesis is presented in a very

---

[2] S. Pufendorf, *The Law of Nature and Nations* (Oxford: L. Lichfield, 1703), p. 799.

sketchy way, but it is at least clear that (as with economics) it has both an empirical and a normative aspect. On the one hand, it ventures an account of how persons are in fact valued, and of how their social value is actually represented in (for example) their class position or rank. On the other, it clearly assumes that the social exchanges involved can go well or badly: they have certain important purposes and they presuppose standards of correctness. A similar suggestion has recently been more explicitly advanced by Brennan and Pettit, in an important book devoted to the exploration of what they term the "economy of esteem," which they regard as independent of and irreducible to either commerce or politics.[3]

Although these and other writers[4] are clearly gesturing in the right direction, "esteem" is too imprecise a notion to be a helpful metaphor for rendering any specifically dignitarian concerns. Not only does it potentially conflate forms of social valuation that should be distinguished, "esteem" contrasts with other attitudes that mediate our recognition that persons bear value or worth. Brennan and Pettit suggest at one point that the study of the "economy of esteem" might be labeled "kudonomics."[5] "Kudos" however represents only a particular form of personal value, as indeed, they explicitly acknowledge. The idea that the recognition of human dignity is a matter of "kudos," in particular, or of how we "esteem" them more generally, sounds strange. Distinctive evaluative modes – specifically respect – are more pertinent.

Still, these writers all tacitly assume that when persons do (or don't) elicit certain emotional dispositions – like esteem, love, or respect – the resulting treatment can succeed in imparting certain kinds of value to them and their lives (or fail to do so). In effect, they postulate an affective "catallaxy" that parallels the relations of commercial exchange we associate with markets in goods and services. I introduce the term "catallaxy" because it is a term that some economists, especially those friendly to free markets, have recommended as an alternative to that of an "economy."[6] As Hayek noted, the term has its root in a Greek verb *katallattein,* whose meanings include "not only 'to exchange' but also 'to admit into the community' and 'change from enemy

---

[3] Brennan and Pettit, *The Economy of Esteem.*

[4] Luc Boltanski and L. Thévenot, *On Justification: Economies of Worth.* Princeton Studies in Cultural Sociology (Princeton, NJ: Princeton University Press, 2006).

[5] Brennan and Pettit, *The Economy of Esteem,* p. 2.

[6] In 1964, James Buchanan proposed "that we cease to talk about 'economics'. ... Were it possible to wipe the slate clean, I should recommend that we take up a wholly different term such as 'catallactics' or 'symbiotics'. ... the market is not ... a *means* toward the accomplishment of anything. It is, instead, the institutional embodiment of the voluntary exchange processes that are entered into by individuals in their several capacities. That is all there is to it." James M. Buchanan, "What Should Economists Do?" *Southern Economic Journal* 30, no. 3 (1963): 217.

into a friend.'"[7] It therefore connotes reconciliation, reciprocal accommodation, and (as Buchanan suggested)[8] "symbiotic" adaptation within dynamic interaction.

Like other economists who have used it, Hayek appropriates the term exclusively to "describe the order brought about by the mutual adjustment of many individual economies in the market. A catallaxy is thus the special kind of spontaneous order produced by the market through people acting within the rules of the law of property, tort, and contract." A priori, however, the analytical idea of a "catallaxy" need not be restricted only to a commercial context. As its connotations of friendship and enmity imply, it seems no less applicable to affective interactions. This suggestion forms a cornerstone of the performative approach to dignity developed here. For it opens space for a theory of affective repercussion in which the emotional impact of persons upon each other, according as it involves modes of respect and disrespect, has the enhancement or diminishment of human dignity as its emergent product.

In a formal sense, the application of such a performative account of human dignity would resemble economists' efforts to model fluctuations in market value, inflation and deflation, shifting ratios of exchange, the significance of the money supply, conditions of equilibrium, and so on, by understanding how preferences, supply, and demand, as expressed in the marketplace, affect each other. For, it would postulate that human dignity is a function of certain dimensions along which the value of persons and lives can vary, and that the structure of these variations is determined by the attitudes and treatment agents actually elicit from others in formal and informal social interchange. Yet, quite obviously, such a theory would need to have a very different substantive focus. To preserve the central contrast between dignity and price, it must explain dignitarian variation as not merely formally analogous to economic valuation, but also as having its own distinct logic. Rather than quantifying anything like economic costs and benefits, its chief concern would be to specify the timanthropic implications of patterns of interaction, particularly those that are organized or endemic, identifying those that should attract adamant opposition because they somehow damage or threaten human dignity.

Here, it is worth emphasizing that the timanthropic words we often use to mark injustice and oppression (e.g., humiliation, rejection, debasement, dehumanization, subordination) are typically achievement words, presumably referring to ways in which the worth of the victims relative to others can alter. Offhand, it seems quite reasonable to say that victims of slavery, racial discrimination, and other forms of domination are worth less than other

---

[7] Friedrich A. von Hayek, *Law, Legislation and Liberty: A New Statement of the Liberal Principles of Justice and Political Economy* (London: Routledge, 2012).

[8] James M. Buchanan, "What Should Economists Do?" p. 213.

people in their societies because of the way they command respect or contempt from significant others. The phrase, "life was cheap," is after all a natural and frequently used description of profoundly oppressive or brutalized circumstances.

Or consider gangsters who talk of "wasting" people – an ordinary language expression that repays close attention. When they speak of a murder in these terms, they do more than merely report a killing. Their concept of "wasting" adds a vital performative element: it refers to the action of transforming a human being into trash. Describing a successful "hit" as a transaction in which the victim was treated merely "as if" they are expendable would clearly be too weak. For it misses the performance of devastation – the accomplished fact that their lives *were* disposed of as refuse. It also leaves out the swaggering conceit of the thug who will gladly "rub out"[9] anyone standing in their way. The statement, "yeah, I wasted him," is not mere spin, nor does it misdescribe. To the contrary, it very aptly captures the sense in which the hit *rendered* the victim expendable as well as the perpetrator's implicit glorying in their successful devaluation of another human being.

For a defender of dignity-traditionalism like Clarence Thomas, of course, the idea that humiliation, violence, or contempt could effect any such devaluation is anathema. According to him, nothing – not even slavery – can strip anyone of their basic dignity as a human being. Yet surely proponents of a performative approach can counter, with some force, that it is precisely because slavery degrades, diminishes, humiliates, and devalues its victims, that it comes at the cost of human dignity. At any rate, this response strikes me as more plausible than saying that slaveholders, and the wider regime that supported them, simply failed to notice and to respond properly to the inherent dignity of slaves, as if it was there all along. Reducing slavery to a mere error in practical deliberation in this way massively underdescribes the oppression involved and preserves the common sense intuition that, if anything erases human dignity, it is slavery. Those who theorize slavery in terms of "social death" are much nearer the mark,[10] but to endorse a theory in that neighborhood requires one to concede that the worth of peoples' lives can vary with the sort of respect they command or fail to command, at least insofar as "social death" implies devaluation. It seems a short step to the conclusion that "dignity" names the sort of worth that is at stake.

I see no reason to think that allowing dignity to alter in this way threatens the price/dignity distinction. Although earning or forfeiting the respect, affection, or goodwill of one's peers correspond to changes in one's relation to

---

[9] Another performative, here implying something like "rendering someone a nullity"; the term "nullity" is from a Latin word whose meanings include "to despise."

[10] O. Patterson, *Slavery and Social Death: A Comparative Study*, 1st edition (Cambridge, MA: Harvard University Press, 1982).

them, we cannot express these transformations in quantitative terms, still less in the idiom of price. To think otherwise is to make a category mistake: for affects like love and respect cannot be bought or sold, nor assigned an exchange-value. To be authentic, they must be elicited spontaneously and wholeheartedly. They cannot be intentionally given or traded, because conceiving of them as voluntarily contrived attitudes transforms them into mere simulacra. Feigned love is no love at all; showing respect cannot be a mere show of respect.

In *The Economy of Esteem*, Brennan and Pettit recognize this complication and propose some complex apparatus for assimilating the exchange of "esteem services" to the circulation of goods on a market nonetheless. This allows them to analyze the "economy of esteem" in the terms provided by standard neoclassical models in economics. Whether or not their account succeeds for esteem, however, attempting to comprehend the affective phenomena of love, respect, or dignity along similar lines is misguided. Whatever it exactly is, respect isn't a "service" that is "supplied" in exchange for something else, and its appropriateness is not expressible in terms of a price or quantifiable ratio. Thinking otherwise would indeed threaten the vital contrast between the dignity of persons and the price of things. The conclusion to draw from the premise that dignity can vary is then precisely *not* that dignity has its price; rather, it is that the variation to which it is subject follows a logic quite distinct from, and irreducible to, anything like that of commodity exchange.

This point finds further support in the writings of anthropologist David Graeber, who has drawn an important distinction between "human," as opposed to "commercial," economies. Like their commercial counterparts, "human economies" in Graeber's sense involve currencies of exchange. The relevant "social currencies," he argues, are however rarely

> used to buy and sell anything at all. Instead they are used to create, maintain, and otherwise reorganize relations between people: to arrange marriages, establish the paternity of children, head off feuds, console mourners at funerals, seek forgiveness in the case of crimes, negotiate treaties, acquire followers. ... [Such] "human economies" ... are economic systems primarily concerned not with the accumulation of wealth, but with the creation, destruction, and rearranging of human beings.[11]

Graeber emphasizes that the logic of "human economies" invariably presupposes that persons and their lives cannot be commodified, even as they sometimes use persons *as* currency. Here, Graeber leans on Philippe Rospabé's argument that "social currencies," even when apparently used to "purchase" persons (e.g., "bridewealth" paid by a suitor's family to the family of a woman with whom his marriage is to be arranged), are actually best

---

[11] Graeber, *Debt*, p. 158.

understood as "an acknowledgment that one is asking for something so uniquely valuable that payment of any sort would be impossible". As Rospabé and Graeber describe the case of an arranged marriage, for example, "bridewealth" acknowledges the invaluable, priceless, character of the continuance of a blood-line, and of the bride herself. In the analogous case of "wergeld," in which "social currencies" are offered to secure forgiveness for an injury, or to defuse a feud, the purpose of the payment is to acknowledge a debt to those willing to forgive, at whose pleasure any peaceable ongoing interaction is ultimately hostage. These are ways of recognizing "life-debts" that cannot, in principle, be paid off.

Graeber is careful to deny that noncommercial "human" economies "are necessarily in any way more humane" than commercial ones ("some," he says, "are quite humane; others extraordinarily brutal"). In adding this rider, he indicates that viewing social and political life as a kind of "human economy" automatically brings a timanthropic perspective into view.[12] Such economies are after all constituted by processes through which, as they circulate through the routines of everyday interaction, people and their lives are subject to constant evaluation and reevaluation in terms of recognized "social currencies." If there is any area in which we mind deeply how we matter, surely it is this. The characteristic intensity of these cares is hard to explain if how we matter cannot be affected by the outcomes of these iterating processes of mutual exchange.

Incongruity and Ideology

The foregoing remarks already anticipate the third and last of the main ideas advanced in this chapter: that, to explain why the distinction between dignity and price matters for political criticism, we need not construe it in terms of a contrast between economic and non-economic forms of valuation; we might alternatively *broaden* our concept of the "economic" so that the valuation of commercial goods and that of human lives reflect the operation of two quite different albeit analogous economies.

Attempting to *maintain* the price/dignity distinction by enlarging, rather than narrowing, the boundaries of the "economic" is bound to seem initially counterintuitive. Nothing I have said so far is likely to convince a skeptic who sees no clear need to expand the application of the term "economy" beyond its currently accepted use, which restricts it to the domain of commercial exchange. No doubt, such a skeptic might say, social analysts can pun on words like "economics," "currency," and "catallaxy," but why bother? What is the theoretical payoff in doing so? However, two arguments, one conceptual

---

[12] Graeber himself references the importance of the Greek etymology of "timi" in my categorization of the "timanthropic": see ibid., p. 176.

and the other more circumstantial, together provide a stronger rationale for this move, and also offer hints on how to make it effectively.

The conceptual point is that there is something strange about suggesting that the valuation of things and that of people can be entirely unlike each other. Modern thinking about "valuation," especially its most socially relevant forms, has quite rightly become ever more impatient with the assumption that it is a response to some independent, self-subsisting "value" intrinsic to evaluated items. To many, that assumption seems problematically metaphysical and at any rate difficult to explain. It is much easier to construe value as consisting in a *relation* between a valuer and something they evaluate, not as an independent feature of objects to which valuation responds.

Neoclassical economists in particular pride themselves on having escaped the assumption (made for example in theories of "just price") that economic value is somehow "inherent" in goods independently of the attitudes of those interested in them. A central insight of the "marginalist revolution" in economics is after all that economic value is not like this, but is rather projected onto objects by agents in the light of their "subjective" preferences. Quite often, modern economists regard this as an instance of a much more general truth: that the notion of anything having intrinsic "value" apart from the attitudes of some interested observer is strictly speaking meaningless. As Gossen, an important forerunner of the marginalist approach put it in the early nineteenth century, "according to my views of the external world, there exists nothing to which so-called absolute value may be attributed. This is contrary to what is now assumed more or less explicitly by economists, for whom every object is conceived as having some definite inherent value."

Yet defenders of free market capitalism tempted by this agent-relative understanding of value often speak about the dignity and worth of the individual in terms that are very difficult to reconcile with it. Like Nozick, they see free markets and the open society as circumscribed by absolute dignitarian "side-constraints" that protect a value "beyond all price." They are apt to insist that the dignity of free, autonomous persons – guaranteed by the "rule of law" in the form of rights against force, fraud, and theft – *is* somehow inherent in them, and in that sense is absolute rather than relative.

The deep tension between these warring axiologies surfaces even in as subtle a defender of commercial society as Hayek. He contends that "individual freedom" must "be accepted as a value in itself, as a principle that must be respected without our asking whether the consequences in the particular instance will be beneficial. We shall not achieve the results we want if we do not accept it as a creed or presumption so strong that no considerations of expediency can be allowed to limit it."[13] Yet we must remember that Hayek is also a marginalist committed (like von Mises, Menger, and Gossen before him)

---

[13] Hayek, *The Constitution of Liberty*, p. 129.

to a purely "subjectivist" conception of value. He thus embraces the relational, imputed, quality of market "value" while refusing it when it comes to claims about the importance of individual autonomy. He understands commercial value as a psychologically and socially determined *effect* while treating the value of autonomous lives as an independent, absolute, constant (a "value in itself") standing behind the relevant value-determining processes.

At the very least, contrasting price and dignity in these terms looks rather incongruous and ad hoc: if the notion of "inherent value" is so naïve in the context of economic goods, why should it remain serviceable as an account of how people and lives bear worth? Whether this is a stable position is unclear, and one may well suspect that its incongruous quality betrays the presence of ideology in the views of those who adopt it. After all, what business does a defender of the free market who denies, with Gossen and the marginalists, that anything possesses "absolute value" in itself, have declaring that autonomous individuals are in fact bearers of just such an inherent worth? Perhaps the dignity of the individual is the one exception to the general truth that talk of inherent value is meaningless. But how convenient that this single exception just happens to require unconditional respect for exactly the individual rights commercial capitalism needs to function! The Marxian accusation that a dignitarian humanism of absolute property rights is simply an ideological creature of the capitalist order seems quite plausible here.

The incongruity created by trying to have it both ways (socially imputed value for objects, "absolute" value for people) not only raises concerns about ideological credulity. It also relates closely to the objections I leveled at traditional conceptions of B-dignity in Chapter 4. Consider Christine Korsgaard's version of what Sangiovanni has aptly called the "Kantian regress" argument. Her argument is very similar to Gewirth's attempt to ground inherent dignity that we considered and rejected in Chapter 5; not surprisingly, therefore, Sangiovanni's criticisms of it closely track my earlier objections to Gewirth. In any case, much like Gewirth, Korsgaard contends that we can reason backwards from our de facto "practical identities," and the commitments, purposes and values they imply, to a judgment about the worth of the human agents who endorse and pursue them. Yet, like Gossen and the neoclassical economists, Korsgaard's Kant accepts the "relativity of value to human desires and interests." As she glosses Kant,

> when we make a choice we must regard its object as good. His point is . . . [that] being human we must endorse our impulses before we can act on them. Kant asked what it is that makes these objects good, and, rejecting one form of [axiological] realism, he decided that the goodness was not in the objects themselves. Were it not for our desires and inclinations, we would not find their objects good. Kant saw that we take things to be important because they are important to us and he concluded that we must therefore take ourselves to be important. In this way, the value of

> humanity itself is implicit in every human choice. If normative skepticism
> is to be avoided – if there is any such thing as a reason for action – then
> humanity as the source of all reasons and values must be valued for its
> own sake.[14]

As Korsgaard has conceded in her more recent work, no argument of this sort
can establish that anything has value "in itself," if by this one means a value that
is wholly independent of the attitudes of some valuer. Fairly obviously,
Korsgaard's premise that "goodness" or value is not self-sufficiently *in* the
things we value, but rather reflects something about someone's attitudinal
relation to it, precisely *rules out* the possibility that human beings, after all,
do have value in themselves. Accordingly, Korsgaard now grants that "the
condition of all value need not be taken to be valuable itself." She has come to
recognize that if valuing is prior to value (that we should "explain value in
terms of valuing, rather than the reverse," as she puts it), then at best her
Kantian argument for the value of humanity must be construed as showing
that we must "set a value on" our being human.[15] But this, I submit, makes my
suggestion that we should broaden our notion of the "economic" to include the
timanthropic domain look not just plausible but unavoidable.

For suppose one both agrees with Gossen, the marginalists, and the later
Korsgaard, that "nothing" inherently possesses "absolute value," and accepts
that human dignity names a form of value that attaches to people and lives
(rather than commercial goods and services). The natural implication is
neither that "dignity" is, after all, a kind of "absolute value" innate in human
beings, nor that there must be a commercial market in people that assigns
dignitarian value to them in the manner of the price system. Rather, it is that
human dignity is a socially constituted value whose determination proceeds
according to a distinctive, noncommercial, logic. It is just this alternative that
my revisionist approach takes seriously and seeks to elaborate. Its leading
contention is that human dignity depends on the way we, together, "set
value" on each other. The inference that the relevant processes are therefore
the locus of an "economy" then becomes straightforward. What is an economy
if not some scheme of cooperation whose participants set varying values on
what circulates within it?

Oikonomia

This brings me to the second, more circumstantial, reason to find the language
of economics apt in this context. The etymology and historical use of the word
"economy" licenses a much broader application of that term than is usual

---

[14] Korsgaard and O'Neill, *The Sources of Normativity*, p. 122.

[15] Christine Korsgaard, "Valuing our Humanity," forthcoming, www.people.fas.harvard.edu/
~korsgaar/CMK.Valuing.Our.Humanity.pdf.

today. As is well known, it is derived from a Greek word – "oikos" (οἶκος) – that connotes a shared place of habitation and what it contains – not only its physical endowment (e.g., household property) but also its members, united as a family, estate, or homestead. On this traditional understanding, *oikonomia* (understood as a kind of craft) refers to the proper management or "handling" of inhabited dwellings, homes, and their assets. An *oikos* is thus the locus of a form of "stewardship," oriented toward maintaining the schemes of mutual assistance involved, and ensuring that the other needs its members understand them to serve are fulfilled.[16]

To this general formula we can add two further provisos to which self-consciously economic analysis has across history virtually always subscribed. First, unlike states, corporations or other "organizations," *oikoi* are not generally consciously designed or instituted, but are rather spontaneously arising forms of co-operation that emerge apart from anyone's intentions. Second, *oikoi* sustain themselves through iterating processes of circulation, reciprocity, and exchange regulated by commonly shared currencies of comparative valuation. These currencies are used, for example, to value assets, determine what forms of reciprocation are due, to make judgments of proportionality, gradation, relevance, and urgency, to settle the rank and relative status of different members, and so on.

Clearly, "markets" qualify as *oikoi* in this extended sense, and so I am not claiming that modern economics has in any sense misappropriated the general notion of *oikonomia*. The point, rather, is that it does not follow that anything analyzable as an *oikos* must be a market or market-like, governed by a logic of preference, supply, and demand in the context of competition over scarce goods. Any spontaneously arising scheme of cooperation whose sustenance and flourishing requires the continuous circulation of goods, people, and services, that are accordingly valued according to some commonly understood standards, can in principle be analyzed as an *oikos*.

Some – notably free market economists like Buchanan and Hayek – disavow this attempt to link markets and the classical notion of *oikonomia*. They recommend replacing "economy"/ "economics" with the (already mentioned) terms "catallaxy"/ "catallactics." Their worry is that the connotations carried by "*oikonomia*" encourage the assumption that the economy, like a particular

---

[16] There is a rich and deep Christian tradition of thinking about "oikonomia" as the manifestation of God's interaction in the world, and also of the church's superintendence of devotional life. As the Roman Catholic Catechism has it: "The Fathers of the Church distinguish between theology (*theologia*) and economy (*oikonomia*). 'Theology' refers to the mystery of God's inmost life within the Blessed Trinity and 'economy' to all the works by which God reveals himself and communicates his life." For further discussion of the role of *oikonomia* in modern political thought, see Giorgio Agamben, (transl. L. Chiesa and M. Mandarini)*The Kingdom and the Glory: For a Theological Genealogy of Economy and Government* (Stanford, CA: Stanford University Press, 2011).

household or dwelling, is a closed system with discrete goals of its own that call for superintendence by planners responsible for the *oikos* as a whole. Buchanan in particular maintains that Lionel Robbins's definition of economics as concerned with "the allocation of scarce means among alternative or competing ends"[17] is tacitly committed to something like that understanding. The Robbins formula, Buchanan complains, implies that the economy *as such* must choose for itself alternative means for the pursuit of *its* ends. But, like Hayek, he insists that the market is an open-ended "catallaxy" with no ends of its own: "it is a setting, an arena, in which we, as economists, ... observe men attempting to accomplish their own purposes."

Less turns on this point than Hayek and Buchanan think, however, and I propose to concede it. So, when I use the terms "oikos" or "economy" in the context of dignity and respect, I don't intend to mark out anything that has a closed set of ends or goals. However, it does not follow from the claim that some *oikos* is an open-ended catallaxy that one cannot attribute to it a characteristic sphere of concern. For *oikoi*, like emotions, can have "intentionality," that is, something they are "about." When we speak of "affairs of the heart," for example, we refer to that aspect of human life falling under "love." Neither love (considered as an emotion), nor its external manifestation in "affairs of the heart," refer to anything that has a goal; but they share a characteristic intentionality.

Buchanan clearly accepts this general point, although he doesn't use the idiom of intentionality. For, having denied that "market economies" have their own goals, he goes on to maintain, not only that they are but one instance of several social systems "that can be brought under the framework of a voluntaristic exchange process," but also that politics is another.[18] This requires him to distinguish the "economic" from the "political." And he does so in terms of their respective sphere of concern, or (as I would put it) their intentionality: economics, Buchanan says, is "about" voluntary cooperation among individuals seeking to pursue their private, material, ends; politics is "about" reconciling authority, public decision-making, the presence of "leaders and followers," the right to use coercion, principal-agent relationships, and so on, with the voluntary consent of all members of society.

So without having to identify them with any specific set of aims or goals, one can still demarcate *oikoi* in terms of their ideal-typical intentionality. The idea, then, is to reinterpret the price/dignity distinction as one between two different

[17] This is Buchanan's formulation (Buchanan, "What Should Economists Do?" 214), not Robbins's own, which reads: "A Science that studies human behavior as a relationship between limited resources and unlimited wants which have alternative uses."

[18] Ibid., 220. This of course what Buchanan and Tullock did in *The Calculus of Consent*. J. E. Buchanan and G. Tullock, *The Calculus of Consent: Logical Foundations of Constitutional Democracy*. The Collected Works of James M. Buchanan, vol. 3 (Indianapolis: Liberty Fund, 1999).

economies, each with their own sphere of concern. Something like that idea is already implicit in Graeber's contrast between commercial and human economies. Suggestive as it is, however, Graeber's contrast can't get us very far. It merely negatively defines "human" economies as those whose logic is non-commercial, but neither clarifies the character of distinctively commercial *oikoi* nor offers any more granular subdivision of their "human" counterparts. So, to make headway in understanding the particular *oikos* on which I claim human dignity depends, we need to elaborate its intentionality in some more focused way. For help in this endeavor I turn to Marx.

10

Marx on Value and Valorization

The revisionist account of human dignity elaborated here is modeled loosely on the value-theory that Marx developed to analyze capitalism and its "intentionality" (in the sense described at the end of Chapter 9). The object of this chapter is to describe relevant aspects of that theory and motivate my claim that dignitarians can and should emulate it. I stress that using Marx's analysis as a prototype in this manner does not require his general account of capitalism to be sound. Although I do in fact believe that Marx's approach is on the right lines, for present purposes nothing turns on that truth of that belief. Even if it gives a poor account of commodity-value, I contend that Marx's analysis can still provide a useful template for explaining how "human dignity" can represent the value and people and their lives without having to rely on the traditionalist assumptions rejected in the first half of this book. It exemplifies the right *kind* of analysis, one that dignity-revisionists can fruitfully appropriate for their own purposes. Later, I explain more fully why I think Marx's approach is propitious in this regard. I begin, however, with a brief outline of Marx's value-theory.[1]

Marx on Commodity-Value

I take that theory to analyze the system of commercial exchange along three connected dimensions, each of which I will consider in turn: (1) as a scheme with a distinctive sphere of concern, what we can call "market intentionality;" (2) in terms of the forms of value that are recognized by participants; and (3) as centered around common media of exchange through which those forms of value are socially expressed and recognized.

(1) *Market intentionality*: Marx differentiates "modes of production" as they commandeer human labor to satisfy perceived material needs. So viewed, any

---

[1] I am going to present my reading of Marx dogmatically, and prescind from hermeneutic disputes about what he really meant. No doubt my reading of his view is open to dispute, but at the least it is a reasonable and coherent reading, and since I am only using the resulting account as a model for use in a quite different context, it would not matter for my argument here if Marx's actual views differed from the interpretation given here.

oikonomia automatically encases a very general form of intentionality, because for Marx "human labor," as opposed to mere "animal energy," presupposes some conscious purpose – an aim, an unfulfilled need, a problem to be solved or alleviated, a design or instrument to be improved, and so on. Hence his famous comparison of human labor with the work of "spiders and bees:" "what distinguishes the worst architect from the best of bees is that the architect builds the cell in his mind before he constructs it in wax." The *Grundrisse* puts it more poetically: "Labour is the living, form-giving fire; it is the transitoriness of things, their temporality, as their formation by living time."[2] All activity involving human labor, on Marx's account, must be understood as an effort to consciously shape something otherwise formless.

As is well-known, however, Marx claimed that as productive cooperation becomes ever more complex, it passes through distinct historical phases, each marked by characteristic relations of economic power and control. These patterns of control, which though resulting from deployments of human labor, emerge without any conscious design. Yet they are not, Marx held, *neutral* with respect to the needs recognized by agents inhabiting the resulting economic formations, and toward which their productive efforts are directed. Rather, they actively shape how those needs present themselves, at first in concrete productive activity and eventually in conscious beliefs that become widely accepted – what Marx calls "ideologies" – about what needs are important and worth meeting (understandings of human well-being), and about how those who successfully contribute to their satisfaction are appropri-ately rewarded (notions of justice, fairness, what is "due," etc. in remuner-ation). Each successive "mode of production" thus represents, on Marx's view, a particular way in which the very general, indeterminate, intentionality of human labor assumes a definite communal form, at both material and ideo-logical levels.

The later Marx's account of capitalism aims to decode the characteristic structures of commercial society in these terms. It purports to diagnose how distinctively capitalist relations of production constitute and limit the mobil-ization of human labor toward meeting needs that are themselves partly creatures of those same, historically specific, relations. His critical object is to establish the indifference of the capitalist system to humans' real interests, forcing participants instead to serve *its* needs. Market intentionality, for Marx, is then organized around the needs of an impersonal abstraction, and hence displays a fetishistic and dominating character.

(2) *Forms of value*: Marx depicts capitalist societies as *oikonomies* or catallaxies populated by independent ("free") holders of economic assets whose economic cooperation centers on the emergent and self-reproducing (yet he also believes

---

[2] Marx, *Grundrisse*, p. 361.

ultimately unstable) system of commodity-exchange. Accordingly, the commodity and the senses in which it bears "value" for participants in that system assume central significance in Marx's account; his aim is to show that, once properly understood, the determination of commodity-value under capitalism betrays its oppressive character.

He acknowledges that, viewed in one way, a commodity must be a product of human labor that satisfies some human need. As such, commodities bear "use-value," and in that sense represent the "intentionality" of labor: at some level, their existence and consumption indicate that someone has concretely exerted labor to serve another's need. Yet, neither use-value nor the "concrete labor" that actually produces it can explain the central precondition of a market economy – that commodities are equated so that they exchange at quantifiable rates ("exchange-value"), approximated and publicized as money prices. The reason for this is that the needs conferring use-value on commodities are too heterogeneous to serve as a basis for commensuration. In order for commodities to become quantifiably comparable, they must all share some common characteristic such that the economic value of one commodity can be expressed as "worth" a certain amount of another. Having excluded "use-values" as the basis for these ratios of exchange, Marx finds that there is only one quality, common to all commodities, left to serve in this capacity: human labor. To properly understand a capitalist economy, then, one must show how it transforms human labor into a measurable quantity expressed in ratios of exchange.

Since the notion of labor presupposed in the practice of commodity-exchange cannot be that of "concrete labor" (as heterogeneous and unquantifiable as the use-values it serves), Marx concludes that some other modality of labor must be implicated in it. This Marx calls "abstract labor," a form that is measurable as a uniform average such that any one of its products can be assigned an exchange-value in relation to the universe of all such products. That notion of labor was already implicit in the classical political economy that he wished to reject, and Marx was prepared to grant that "Political Economy, has indeed analysed, however incompletely, value and its magnitude, and has discovered what lies beneath these forms."[3] Yet, although he followed Smith and Ricardo in suggesting that commodity-value is determined by the average quantum of "socially necessary labor time" required for the production of given commodities, he regarded that insight as begging a vital question. It cannot explain "why labor is represented by the value of its product and labor time by the magnitude of that value."[4] By failing to ask that question, Marx contends, the classical political economists were unable

---

[3] Karl Marx, *Capital: Volume 1: A Critique of Political Economy*, trans. Ben Fowkes (London: Penguin, 1976), pp. 173–74.
[4] Ibid., p. 174.

to see that, under capitalism, the "process of production has mastery over man, instead of being controlled by him." Marx's thinking on this point is far from clear; to decode it, we must consider the third dimension of his account.

3. *Common media of exchange*: Money – the "universal equivalent" – represents, for Marx, the immediate form in which the exchange-value of commodities is publicly represented; when one commodity is exchanged for a money price, its relative value becomes an object of common knowledge. That is, it is only after purchases have been completed that "abstract labor" can assume any definite, publicly identifiable, form as value. Until then, such value and the "abstract labor" it represents is, as Marx says, "phantom-like":[5] it "exists in these commodities in a latent state, so to speak, and becomes evident only in the course of their exchange."[6]

Marx's reputation as a proponent of "the labor theory of value" – a phrase he never used – has led many to assume that he is committed to thinking that the "true value" of a commodity is a function of the (average) hours of labor embodied in it. Read this way, Marx is arguing that the labor that goes into the production of a commodity is somehow incorporated into it in measurable amounts, like air pumped into a balloon. Just as variation in the sizes of different balloons is a function of the amount of air inflating each, so (given a crude labor theory) the "real" economic value of commodities varies according to the quantity of labor each contains. On this view, exchange-value becomes an inherent property of the commodity itself, constituted in advance of any market transactions in which they are bought or sold, and hence an independent standard of value that one might then expect prices to approximate. That this is precisely *not* what Marx intends is shown by his caustic dismissal of the view, which he associates with his "vulgar" political economist interlocutors, that the economic value of commodities "forms a part of them as objects." Marx counters derisively that "so far no chemist has ever discovered exchange-value either in a pearl or a diamond."[7]

Marx's actual position is more or less the reverse of this one. It is not, for him, that "abstract labor" creates economic worth independent of actual market outcomes, like a gas injected by individual laborers into objects that inflates or deflates their inherent value.[8] Rather, his view is that economic value comes first, in exchanges consummated on the market and representable in the

---

[5] Ibid., p. 128.

[6] Karl Marx, *Contribution to the Critique of Political Economy* (London: Lawrence and Wishart, 1975), p. 286.

[7] Marx, *Capital Vol. 1*, p. 177.

[8] This is a good thing, given the strong reasons to doubt the relevance of this crude "labor theory of value" to Marx's criticisms of capitalism. See especially: G. A. Cohen, "The Labor

universal equivalent of money. The resulting exchange-value is then the form in which human labor is represented and economically realized under capitalist conditions. But it "crystallizes" in these essentially social transactions as "abstract labor," a uniformly measurable quantity that, though only latent prior to exchange rather, acquires reality in completed exchanges as the controlling principle of market intentionality. As Michael Heinrich has underlined, Marx therefore characterizes "abstract labor" as a "*real* abstraction." The abstraction involved is not a purely *mental* phenomenon like formulating in thought the abstract concept "tree." Rather, as Heinrich puts it: "it is an abstraction that is carried out in the actual behavior of humans, regardless of whether they are aware of it."[9] The "crystallization" of an abstract notion of human labor in a commercial economy represents, for Marx, the subjugation/ alienation of human activity to an impersonal and rationally unguided communal process. What counts in that process are not the real needs and interests of human beings, but rather those of the system itself, which accordingly produces its own system of signals and metaphors mediating common awareness of what bears comparative value (prices, exchange-values, interest rates, etc.), or so Marx contends.

In a seminal article to which my reading of Marx is much indebted, Diane Elson also points out that, for Marx, the link between "abstract labor" and commodity-value is not straightforwardly causal.[10] A causal interpretation is again suggested by those who read Marx as committed to a crude "labor theory of value." On such a theory, exchange-value is treated as a dependent variable whose quantity is causally determined by the independent variable of "socially necessary [abstract] labor time." Marx does indeed use the language of "determination" in this context, but, in viewing capitalism as a system that "determines," or "realizes," "abstract labor" as "exchange-value," Marx was not venturing a causal hypothesis purporting to explain and predict variations in economic value over time – rates of exchange, prices, and so on.[11] Nor did he wish to deny that market competition, supply, and demand cause prices to vary around some average. Rather, he sought to understand how, under capitalist conditions, human labor materializes as something that can *have* a socially

Theory of Value and the Concept of Exploitation," *Philosophy & Public Affairs* 8, no. 4 (1979): 338–60.

[9] M. Heinrich, *An Introduction to the Three Volumes of Karl Marx's Capital* (New York: Monthly Review Press, 2012).

[10] D. Elson, "The Value Theory of Labor," in *Value: The Representation of Labour in Capitalism*, Radical Thinkers, ed. Diane Elson (London: Verso, 2015).

[11] Murray Milgate and Shannon C. Stimson, *After Adam Smith: A Century of Transformation in Politics and Political Economy* (Princeton, NJ: Princeton University Press, 2009), p. 263. See also, David Harvey, "Marx's Refusal of the Labor Theory of Value," http://davidharvey.org/wp-content/uploads/2018/03/MARX%E2%80% 99S_REFUSAL_OF_THE_LTV.pdf.

recognizable, average value in the first place. So when he speaks of social "determination," his interest is in explaining how something "indeterminate" – human labor, which can take indefinitely many forms under different historical circumstances – acquires under capitalist conditions the particular form of quanta of "abstract labor."

Elson rightly draws attention to Marx's consistent use of *chemical* metaphors in this context. Market exchange is, for him, like an ongoing chemical reaction in which something goes from a state of latency (or as he sometimes puts it, of "secrecy") into a definite, measurable, form, "crystallizing" as ratios of "exchange value." The sense in which "steam," "clouds," blocks of ice, liquid water, condensation, and so on are latent forms of H_2O, each of which emerges under specific circumstances, provides an approximate metaphor for what Marx has in mind. Just as H_2O will assume the "form" of ice under certain definite atmospheric pressures and temperatures, so "labor" takes on the specific character of "exchange-value," only given the particular social relations distinctive of commercial capitalism. These forms are for Marx symptoms of an impersonal system of communal provision that commandeers agents for its own purposes, unguided by any enlightened account of real human needs. The rational mobilization of human effort for mutual service is disrupted by the appearance of an interloper: the abstract idol of Capital, which now demands that we serve *it* and its needs, and not each other's.

A Digression on Hayek

I stress again that my argument here does not require acceptance of either this general analysis of capitalism or Marx's critical judgment that it is an irrational system of domination. All that is necessary is that the *structure* of Marx's argument be appreciated. I will later explain why that structure promises dividends for dignitarian humanism. However, since my invocation of Marx is bound to strike some – especially libertarians and defenders of free markets – as tendentious, it's worth mentioning that I find remarkably little in the foregoing summary of Marx's account with which as sophisticated a defender of capitalism as Hayek need disagree. Of course, there *are* significant differences between the two thinkers, most obviously in their estimation of capitalism, but in my view the similarities in their theoretical frameworks have been greatly underestimated. Since Hayek's arguments will figure prominently later in the book, I would like to briefly address this point now.

I have already mentioned one reason why commentators exaggerate the distance between these two thinkers: the tendency to pin a crude "substantialist" version of the "labor theory of value" on Marx. Under that interpretation, Marx's view unquestionably differs radically from Hayek's. Yet we have seen that Marx's value-theory cannot be so easily caricatured. If one reads him as I have, Marx accepts Hayek's view that "rules of equivalence (or 'values')"[12] emerge spontaneously from, and then internally guide, the process of market exchange itself.

It is true that Marx interprets the resulting "values" as telling us something about the character of the capitalist "labor process" in a way that Hayek finds unnecessary. Yet it must be stressed that, as I read Marx, market determination of prices and exchange-value comes first: *this* is the basic social fact – the fact of commodity-capitalism – that conditions the character of human labor under capitalism, not the other way round. That is, as he explicitly says, it is not that goods and services exchange in certain ratios because, quite independently of actual market competition, they already *are,* or can be recognized *as,* "the material integuments of homogenous human labor." His point is just "the reverse . . . : by equating their different products to each other in exchange as values, they equate their different kinds of labor."[13]

This means that well before any questions about the significance of labor in economic theory arise, Marx and Hayek can agree on several key points:

(a) The decisions and rational plans of agents entering the market are guided by signals (changes in prices, interest rates, etc.) that emerge as a result of their own competitive interaction. In Hayek, this is obvious. But it is implicit also in Marx's view. He says, for example, that once commodity-exchange is fully entrenched, it acquires "a sufficient extension and importance to allow useful things to be produced for the purpose of exchange, so that *their character as values has already to be taken into consideration during production*" (emphasis added).[14] In other words, in making decisions about production and investment, market agents not only do but also (given the logic of the system) *must* reckon by exchange-values and prices. An established market system is in a sense self-referential: it automatically produces a scheme of value concepts that structures the choices participants make within it.

(b) These agents are rationally compelled by the logic of competition to respond to those signals in ways that others can roughly predict and anticipate. Marx expresses this by saying that they experience that logic as akin to a "regulative law of nature" like "gravity;"[15] Hayek by pointing out that the "inducements" automatically provided by free competition "make . . . individuals do . . . [generally] desirable things without anyone having to tell them what to do."[16] Notice then that Hayek recognizes that not being coerced to do something required for the well-functioning of

---

[12] F. A. Hayek, "The Use of Knowledge in Society," *The American Economic Review* 35, no. 4 (1945): 519–30, 525.

[13] Marx, *Capital Vol. 1I*, p. 166.

[14] Ibid.

[15] Ibid., p. 168.

[16] Hayek, "Use of Knowledge," 527.

the economic system is compatible with being compelled – "made to" – to do it by the logic of that larger system. This is of course a fundamental Marxian tenet. Marx would not only have accepted but also enthusiastically endorsed Hayek's claim that "the fact that competition forces all those whose income depends on the market to imitate . . . improvements [made by competitors] is of course one of the major reasons for the disinclination to compete. Competition represents a kind of impersonal coercion that will cause many individuals to change their behavior."[17]

(c) Agents who are thus compelled to behave in a coordinated fashion do so without any conscious intention to bring about the relevant coordination. Thus Marx says that agents who trade commodities accomplish together the "reduction" of otherwise incommensurable productive labor to an abstract, quantitatively measurable form, "without being aware" that this is what they do. Hayek's version: "people guided by . . . [the price system] . . . usually do not know why they are made to do what they do," where "what they do" refers to the coordination they bring about together.

(d) The coordination that is thereby unwittingly achieved reconciles the entire economic system as a "totality." This is a familiar Marxian theme. Given this, I see no reason to think he would have dissented much from Hayek's claim that "[t]he *whole acts as one market*, [emphasis added] not because any of its members survey the whole field, but because their limited individual fields of vision sufficiently overlap so that through many intermediaries the relevant information is communicated to all."[18] Although Marx regarded capitalism as a similar "whole," he never implied that all the important details about its actual elaboration is "given to anyone in its totality."[19]

Consider, in the light of these surprising points of continuity, Hayek's observation that prices "attach[] to each scarce resource a numerical index which cannot be derived from a property possessed by that particular thing, but which reflects, or in which is condensed, its significance in view of the whole means-ends structure."[20] It is only when we get to the penultimate word of this sentence that we can find anything that departs from Marx's story. For the reference to a "means-ends structure" betrays Hayek's marginalism, which brings utility and "use-value" into the picture in a way Marx could not have recognized. As is well-known, marginal utility analysis enabled "neo-classical"

---

[17] Friedrich Hayek, "Competition as a Discovery Mechanism," *Quarterly Journal of Austrian Economics* 5, no. 3 (2002): 19 (Translated from a lecture originally given in German at the University of Kiel in 1968.).

[18] Hayek, "Use of Knowledge," 526.

[19] Ibid., 520.

[20] Ibid., 525.

economics to break the connection postulated in classical political economy between the theory of economic value and assumptions about how labor is spent in production. Since Hayek is steeped in the marginalist tradition, he presumes that everything interesting that there is to say about the character of market competition can be stated without reference to labor; he therefore simply ignores it. Marx, however, was engaging with classical economists, and so for him labor was central not peripheral.

This undoubtedly *is* a major difference between Marx and Hayek, and moreover one that bears on their starkly opposed evaluations of market society. Yet even here, one must be careful to avoid overstating their differences. Hayek's famous arguments – more about which later – about how market competition uses information most efficiently presuppose marginalist analysis. To this extent, we can say that his positive assessment of free markets stems from a strongly non-Marxian theoretical framework. But it should be remembered that in mobilizing marginalist analysis for this apologetic purpose, Hayek was no more interested in causal explanations of actually observed changes in commodity-prices than was Marx. Like Marx's analysis, Hayek's informational argument rather purports to characterize something about the intentionality of market competition that bears on judgments about its overall value. Hayek's claim is that once we see that the "price system" is "about" the efficient acquisition of knowledge indispensable to rational economic planning, we have a good reason to prefer free markets over the alternative of "central planning." In contrast, Marx wants to say that once we see that free markets are "about" exploiting labor to serve the needs of an idol, and not real human needs, we ought to be deeply suspicious of them.

Quite obviously, these represent very different perspectives on the value of free market capitalism, and their respective plausibility is beyond the scope of this book. But are they mutually exclusive? That is not obvious. Marx of course was unacquainted with Hayek's argument. But suppose he granted its contention that, in a broadly utilitarian sense, markets use information far more efficiently than any central planner. Since Marx had little interest in state planning, certainly in the Paretian form to which Hayek was responding, that contention seems entirely beside his main point. Moreover, the claim that markets use information better than state planners does not contradict Marx's allegation that they are endemically exploitative and oppressive. Since Hayek is largely silent about labor, domination in the workplace, exploitation, and so on, it is hard to think that his objections to central planning, insightful as they are, can themselves decide whether that allegation is sound.

The Determination of Dignitarian Value

If Marx's theory of value was an effort to anatomize capitalist commodity-exchange, the performative account of human dignity that I wish to develop applies a parallel kind of analysis to the valuation of people and their lives as they cycle through the routines of everyday social existence. The hope is that by theorizing the mutual encounters constituting those routines, and especially the affective mood characterizing distinctive patterns of treatment, we can illuminate the dynamics on which, by hypothesis, the emergence, protection, and realization of human dignity depend.

Although it is not one that Marx made himself, this move is not wholly without a Marxian license. A brief footnote to the first volume of *Capital* reads:

> In a certain sense, a man is in the same situation as a commodity. As he neither enters into the world in possession of a mirror, nor as a Fichtean philosopher who can say "I am I," a man first sees and recognizes himself in another man. Peter only relates to himself as a man through his relation to another man, Paul, in whom he recognizes his likeness.[21]

Sadly, Marx never pursued this thought, still less in connection with an account of human dignity. The reasons for, and consequences of, his neglecting this possibility are instructive.

Part of the explanation must be Marx's remarkable disinterest in the emotions, which are, I maintain, integral to concepts of dignity and indignity. Although he clearly regarded affective impulses as a crucial aspect of human action, his social theory assigns no systematic explanatory role to patterns of emotional response, perhaps because he took them to be prime objects of ideological recruitment.

Apart from some suggestive parodies of Kant in his early writings, the concept of dignity equally plays little role in his mature theory. Two factors likely explain this. First, like any thinker in the nineteenth-century German philosophical tradition, Marx could hardly fail to associate claims about the "dignity of humanity" with the strongly moralizing approach of Kantian ethics that he reviled. We noted in Chapter 2 how association might tempt one to dismiss secular dignitarian thought as so much bourgeois ideology. Second, Marx was well aware of the theological evocations of dignitarian idioms, and the more general connotations of piety carried by concepts of respect, awe, worship, and reverence. When set against his diagnosis of religious consciousness as a manifestation of impotence, these theological overtones may explain Marx's evident desire to purge any explicitly dignitarian commitments from his social theory.

Yet, on reflection, that desire is both rather incongruous and also, I contend, symptomatic of a critical deficiency in his account. It is incongruous given Marx's repeated complaints that capitalism dehumanizes, degrades, brutalizes, and "mutilates" human beings. Their natural implication is that capitalism undermines human dignity, fixating on the forms of value emphasized in

---

[21] Marx, *Capital Vol. 1*, p. 144 (fn. 19).

market exchange while devaluing the lives of those forced to serve its needs. Yet Marx's anxieties about the language of dignity, and his materialist leanings more generally, led him to shy away from this line. In his most uncompromisingly "materialist" moments, Marx's attitude to these phenomena of degradation in fact resembles that of doctors toward the pain or discomfort associated with disease: while such symptoms are part of what makes having a disease bad, and can be useful in motivating the patient to seek medical assistance, they are not integral to diagnosing or treating their underlying condition.

Yet Marx could instead have seen these timanthropic deficits as *constitutive* of the irrational quality of capitalist social relations, not mere symptoms but the disease itself. His refusal to entertain that possibility introduces a frustrating timanthropic inarticulacy to his account. His frequent remarks about the dehumanizing, brutalizing effects of capitalism are thereby orphaned within his larger theory, coming across merely as supplementary insinuations tacked on for rhetorical or mobilizing effect. Ever since, his audience has been confused about how these emotional, and often strongly moralized, outbursts fit with the pose of scientific detachment he is otherwise at pains to strike. All of this contributes to a sense of incompleteness in Marx's account of capitalism; one that left his followers without much guidance about how to conceive a form of life in which social exchange does *not* brutalize, degrade, humiliate, "forsake," "fragment," or otherwise diminish people, "mutilating" their humanity.

Marx was rightly suspicious of utopian blueprints,[22] and this may explain his reluctance to confront these issues head on. Yet he would not have needed to build a castle in the air to develop a theory of dignitarian determination to parallel his very astute analysis of economic value in *Capital*. If human beings are, in their own sphere, in a situation akin to that of commodities in the realm of exchange, somehow needing each other to express their respective value, he had every reason to develop an account of how their social value is, or can be, expressed in the affective mood in which their lives are received by significant others. A developed theoretical account of human exchange would have allowed him to deploy a conception of timanthropic adequacy as a counterweight to the commodifying pathologies of commercial societies, integrating complaints about degradation and indignity at the ground level of his diagnosis, and giving us some hints about how lives would and should be valued under conditions of genuine freedom.

---

[22] Though I would stress that it is the *blueprint* part, not the utopianism, that is objectionable. In general, I am sympathetic to David Estlund's defense of "utopian" political philosophy, though Marx himself might have been less so. See David M. Estlund, *Utopophobia: On the Limits (If Any) of Political Philosophy* (Princeton, NJ: Princeton University Press, 2020).

Allergic to anything that smacks of moralism, however, Marx missed this opportunity, leaving his followers to fall back into a familiar positivist groove, in which "morality" (the nonempirical, the ideological, idealizing superstructures, categorical imperatives, etc.) is opposed to prudence (empirically conditioned, explanatory, materially basic, hypothetical imperatives, etc.). As long as the contrast between dignity and price is framed around that opposition, an alternative to the traditional dignitarian mainstays criticized in this book is likely to elude us.

Why Marx?

Three features of Marx's value-theory nonetheless offer vital hints about how dignity-revisionism can escape this bind, even as it also deviates from the Marxian original.

α. Value as a social relation: Like the revisionist version of dignitarian humanism proposed here, Marx's account rejects the assumption that his target notion of commodity-value can be properly understood as an intrinsic feature of particular commodities. Despite being widely misunderstood on this score, he quite explicitly treats value, and the "abstract labor" it represents, *not* "as a ready-made pre-requisite but" rather as "an emerging result."[23] Commodity-value is thus for Marx an inherently relational phenomenon,[24] and his aim is to decipher the characteristic social relations that stand behind it.

My revisionist approach similarly refuses to construe "human dignity" as a kind of inherent worth possessed self-sufficiently by individual persons, instead interpreting it as a variety of D-dignity, ambient in social relations.

One important difference from Marx's theory deserves mention, however. Although, as a formal matter, a performative account would designate "human dignity" as a "real abstraction" in the sense Marx attaches to the categories of "abstract labor" and "Capital," it would reverse the *valence* carried by that designation. In Marx, the manner in which, under capitalism, labor becomes a quantifiable abstraction whose value is "realized" in actual economic exchange is a reason to find capitalist modes of production deeply problematic. He believed that, once we expose the extraction of "surplus value" by capital to view, the oppressive, fetishistic character of common life structured around an abstract, yet socially realized, form of human labor becomes apparent. For, on the one hand, the realization of "abstract labor" constitutes the exchange-value of the commodity "labor-power," fixing it at or near the level of a subsistence wage; on the other hand, it simultaneously measures the rate at which surplus

---

[23] Marx, *Contribution to the Critique of Political Economy*, p. 287.
[24] Value for Marx emerges only in relations, whether it be the relation between a commodity and some need that it meets ("use-value"), or a relation between the relative value of commodities that is financially expressible.

value is available to owners of the means of production in a position to lengthen the working day (moreover creating systemic incentives for them to do so). Marx's objection, then, is that the practice of commodity-exchange conjures into life an abstraction that materializes in a concrete social form as the oppressive exploitation of one group by another.

Whether or not one accepts that analysis, one might be tempted to think that it turns on the premise that realized abstractions are in themselves problematic. But that is not so: "X is a 'real abstraction'" and "X is bad" are logically independent propositions, and Marx's objection doesn't assume that capitalism is bad just *because* it transforms abstractions into social realities. What does the work in his argument, plausibly or implausibly, is rather a claim about the substantive character of the specific "abstraction" that capitalism realizes – a mode of common valuation that can only be lived out in irrational fetishism, oppression, and class domination. Since its intended target is capitalism, not the generic phenomenon of "real abstraction," nothing in his account implies that "real abstractions" cannot be good. And, on reflection, surely many of the best things in life exemplify that possibility. In some sense, "fun," "comedy," "poetry," "music," are all abstractions latent in the human condition that cannot exist in any meaningful form except in concretely realized interaction – a camping trip, a well-told joke, a vital literary tradition, an actual performance of a masterpiece symphony, and so on. Real abstractions then need not only have negative valence. My suggestion is that we think of human dignity as another case in point, theorize it as such, and attempt to gauge its implications for political criticism.

β. *Value and power:* An important aim of Marx's analysis of commodity-value is to decipher the relations that develop between commodities as underlying power relations between the agents participating in their exchange. Capitalism, for Marx, represents a particular mode in which control over social reproduction is exercised. In some ways anticipating Foucault, he sees these relations of power as agentless, latent within social structures that are despotic even in the absence of a despot. The capacity of Marx's approach to render the social relations in which "value" of various kinds is recognized and socially expressed legible as modes of power and control is a second feature that performative accounts of dignity can emulate to their advantage.

To see the importance of this translation of value into power, recall the earlier point that traditional construals are prone to treat dignity as akin to a passport, or at least what it represents – a juridical incident of personality entitling its bearers to respectful treatment upon demand. Under such a construal, basic indignities like rape, torture, and slavery are implicitly coded as species of insubordination – a refusal to acknowledge and comply with victims' legitimate demands to be left to themselves. But where a traditional account is thereby led to fixate, perversely, on the perpetrators' *disobedience,* a performative approach puts the emphasis where it belongs: on their victims' *powerlessness.* Like Marx's view, then, it implicates practices of valuation in the relations of power that pertain between agents who organize their lives around them. Rather than stressing the *authority* agents wield over each other in virtue of a preexisting status or dignity, a performative account would emphasize the *power* agents have (or lack) to affect others in ways that elicit dignity-imparting patterns of respect.

To illustrate, African-American slaves in the nineteenth century systematically lacked the power to induce the rest of American society to accord them even very basic forms of respect. Racist beliefs about their purported inferiority or subhuman standing were of course an important aspect of their oppression; they played a crucial role in identifying the targeted population and shoring up the institution of slavery. But the indignity suffered by the slaves did not primarily consist in the entrenchment of such beliefs. Since they are all, without exception, patently false, those beliefs have to be considered ex post facto ideological rationalizations of an independently existing practice of domination. They were accepted not for any epistemically respectable reason but because they helped the powerful to disregard their consciences.

In any case, the basic indignity of slavery would not have altered had other racial or ethnic prejudices led a different population to be targeted (suppose, for example, the slave trade had not been supplied mainly from colonized Africa, but from some other region or demographic group). It consisted more fundamentally in the fact that, for whatever reason, slaves systematically lacked the power to wrest respect from those occupying positions of social control. Beyond their own social group, they were generally incapable of eliciting anything but a very different repertoire of affects – hostility, violent antagonism, pity, contempt, hatred, mistrust, indifference, rapacity, arrogance, self-glorification, the *libido dominandi,* and so on. Some of those operative affects were expressed in informal ways that the institutional infrastructure of their society permitted or encouraged; others were baked into the very bedrock of its institutional architecture.

Such institutions, and more informal systems of social norms, afford humanly constructed conduits through which certain interpersonal attitudes are emphasized and sedimented as routine. Their reproduction also often requires other attitudes to be suppressed and disposes agents against acting on them. Dominant practices may or may not reliably incubate attitudes and treatment that pay respect to people and their lives. When certain groups are unable to elicit such respect in the course of their interaction with a society's major social institutions, they lack a vital social power: the ability to compel those who operate those institutions to pay them significant heed. Such social impotence is humiliating. Unable to command such attention in any coordinated, effective form, oppressed groups like slaves in the American South find themselves forsaken.

The general phenomenon is beautifully captured in Dickens's *Hard Times* by the mill worker Stephen Blackpool, addressing his employer Mr. Bounderby:

> Look round town – so rich as 'tis – . . . and look how the mills is awlus a goin, and how they never works us no nigher to ony dis'ant object – ceptin awlus, Death. Look how you considers of us, and writes of us, and talks of us, and goes up wi' yor deputations to Secretaries o' State 'bout us, and how yo are awlus right, and how we are awlus wrong . . . Sir, I canna, . . ., tell the genelman what will better aw this – . . . but I can tell him what I know will never do 't. . . . Agreeing fur to mak one side unnat'rally awlus and for ever right, and toother side unnat'rally awlus and for ever wrong, will never, never do 't . . . they will be as one, and yo will be as another, wi' a black unpassable world betwixt yo. . . . Not drawin nigh to fok, wi' kindness and patience an' cheery ways, that so draws nigh to one another in their monny troubles, and so cherishes one another in their distresses wi' what they need themseln. . . . Most o' aw, rating 'em as so much Power, and reg'latin 'em as if they was figures in a soom, or machines: wi'out loves and likens, wi'out memories and inclinations, wi'out souls to weary and souls to hope – when aw goes quiet, draggin on wi' 'em as if they'd nowt o' th' kind, and when aw goes onquiet, reproachin 'em for their want o' sitch humanly feelins in their dealins wi' yo – this will never do 't.[25]

The indignity of this sort of disempowerment and social defeat cannot be well-captured in a traditional view that denies that human dignity can ever suffer damage or be tarnished. To draw attention to how the valuation of lives and power relations are intertwined in the career of human dignity, one needs metaphors that permit indignity to actually occur in the world, to be something that can really befall a community and its members.

To be sure, a traditional, reactive, approach need not deny that the treatment meted out to Blackpool, or African-American slaves, might be wrongful or otherwise objectionable insofar as it fails to respect agents' inherent dignity. Yet, while they can acknowledge that such mistreatment will have real effects (harm, injury, trauma, loss of security, etc.), these accounts cannot really say that such mistreatment alters victims' worth. They offer only a fixed standard of personal worth by which to measure the adequacy of actions and forms of conduct that (fail to) respond to it. But to focus narrowly on "conduct" in this way misses the indignity actually effected by the power relations among the parties. It is not just a matter of *fault* relative to some expectation of behavior, but of the "black unpassable world" that opens between people when some of

---

[25] Charles Dickens, *Hard Times* (London: Bradbury and Evans, 1854), p. 179.

them systematically lack the power to get others to attend respectfully to their lives and struggles. It is in this space "betwixt" and "abroad among" people that human dignity lives or dies, or so I want to suggest.

χ. *Value as valorization:* Stanley Benn rightly observed that

> "value" is a philosopher's abstraction. Though in everyday conversation we commonly talk about "setting a high value upon" or "giving good value for" something, we rarely have occasion to talk about "a value" as such, and if we speak of a person's "values" we are borrowing rather self-consciously from the kind of quasi-technical vocabulary that philosophers have constructed for talking about problems in moral philosophy.[26]

One reason why philosophers indulge this "quasi-technical" language is the fear that natural evaluative language is too unsettled, contested, and unstable to anchor "serious" intellectual reflection. This urge should however be resisted, particularly with respect to our timanthropic idioms – those that express the senses in which people and lives bear value. Rather than seeing these everyday idioms as shot through with fudging equivocations to be eliminated in favor of clearer-cut theoretical formulae, we do better to see the fluidity of natural language as an opportunity for careful fieldwork into how timanthropic and other evaluative concerns actually manifest in ordinary interaction. Although he was less explicit about this than one might have wished, Marx's analysis of commodity-value is in line with this approach. At least as I read him, he sees the concepts of economic "value" that characteristically emerge under capitalist conditions as socially valid metaphors whose analysis can shed critical light on the form of life that incubates them. One underappreciated aspect of his account, which is particularly important for our purposes, is his understanding of the modes in which "value" can be "realized" or go "unrealized."

Ordinary use allows value to be "realized" in any number of ways, but it is possible to draw a broad distinction between a teleological and a more informational sense in which it can occur. Sometimes, that is, "value-realization" is a matter of "fruition" over time: here, it refers to some potential value being conceived, gestating, and then ultimately completing itself. Marx certainly often thinks of "value-realization" in this teleological way: in capitalist production, after all, commodities are first designed with some human need in mind, then actually manufactured for sale through an organized labor process, and finally "realized" as "use-values" in the buyer's consumption.

However, a second, subtler, sense of "value-realization" is more pertinent for this book. In this more informational sense, value is "realized" insofar as anyone at a particular moment can verify that something has a certain value according to a commonly recognized metric. The relevant metaphorical

---

[26] S. Benn, *A Theory of Freedom* (Cambridge: Cambridge University Press, 2009), p. 65.

contrast here is not between value that is (now) consummated as opposed to (previously) embryonic or undeveloped, but between values that are *definite* rather than *notional*. Prior to an auction, for example, the precise economic worth of a painting is unknown. Of course, we can make rough estimates, but not until the moment the auctioneer's hammer falls does its economic value become a definite object of common knowledge (at least until it is sold on again). Not only are we all then in a position to know what sum the buyer must hand over to the auction house to walk away with the painting, but also each knows that everyone else knows as well (or can find out). When Marx speaks of capitalism realizing value in a distinctive manner, this phenomenon – the materialization of definite economic values as common knowledge across a social group – is often what he has in mind. This is value-realization as "social validation" ("*Geltungsverhältnis*") or "valorization." The issue here, as Marx often puts it, is what "counts" for a given community as worth more rather than less.

One very obvious difference between the circulation of people in social and political intercourse and the exchange of commodities on a market is that commodities do not *care* how they are socially valorized. People, of course, not only *do*, but have entirely legitimate reasons to, care about how the reactions of significant others make their social worth manifest. I take it that part of Marx's point in attributing to capitalism a "fetishism of com- modities" was to emphasize the irrational quality of a form of life in which the process by which *things* are valorized ("*Venuertungsprozess*") rules imperiously over the relations between people. Implicit in that complaint, though completely undertheorized by Marx, is the assumption that the valorization of *lives* ought to not to be submerged by the valorization of *things* in this manner.

Like others made by those at the wrong end of social domination, Blackpool's complaint to Bounderby is, I submit, about human valorization in this sense: the fact that he and his fellow workers lack the power to elicit respectful attention from those in control broadcasts information about how little they count for in their shared *oikos*. Their inability to matter thereby becomes accessible as common knowledge. That circumstance constitutes a humiliating indignity, a massive and endemic social defeat. Jean Améry was onto this same point when he spoke of the "social reality" of the "wall of rejection that arose before" central European Jews like him in the 1930s and 1940s. In the face of such rejection, he found statements like "I am a human being and as such I have my dignity, no matter what you do or say!" to be naïve, "an empty academic game, or madness."[27] They are so, in his view, because one must recognize that the "verdict of the social group is a given reality." In his context, that verdict was that, as a Jew, he was a "dead man on leave, someone

---

[27] Améry, *At the Mind's Limits*, p. 89.

to be murdered, who only by chance was not yet where he properly belonged."[28]

To bring the discussion full circle, we can now see that, although it is precisely such a predicament that Rawls feared utilitarianism might permit (albeit on grounds different from those that menaced Améry's life), something like a nontraditional, performative account of human dignity is required to make sense of his basic objection. The immutable dignity and worth postulated by traditional theories, after all, does not require valorization; it is settled in advance, and cannot be abolished. Under such a construal, Rawls's prediction that in a "public utilitarian society" agents "will find it more difficult to be confident of their own worth" makes little sense.

This is not because a dignitarian worth that shines on untarnished whatever disrespect and abuse agents suffer cannot serve as a standard by which to criticize the conduct of the perpetrators. It plainly can. The problem is that it cannot at the same time explain why social arrangements that would allow a human life to be deemed dispensable under some conditions (whether as a result of institutionalized utilitarianism, endemic racism, systematic oppression, etc.) should make it the case that lives are worth less than they might otherwise be. To explain how disrespect actually threatens agents' confidence in their dignity and social worth, one must show how it can transform a human being into something like Améry's "dead man on leave," who is "not worthy of love and thus also not of life ... [whose] sole right, ... sole duty [is] to disappear from the face of the earth."[29] Only then can Rawls's radical thought that, under some conditions, social arrangements can undermine the worth of some of their members become plausible. Whether a theoretically credible explanation along these lines is available to dignitarian humanists remains to be seen; that it would be concerned with the dynamics of timanthropic valorization, however, seems a safe bet.

Valorization Schemes

To help specify this crucial notion of "valorization," I conclude this chapter with a more precise conceptualization. I stress that I am not now trying to construe Marx's own use of that term, but to offer a more general account that can subsume his.

What I will call a "valorization scheme" must have all three of the following features:

A. It must afford metrics or criteria by which a set of items are compared in terms of some *currency of valuation*. Such a metric may be quantitative,

---

[28] Ibid., p. 86.
[29] Ibid.

admitting of comparison along some cardinal scale of more and less, but it need not be.[30] Some may grade items ordinally, and others may be non-scalar but hierarchical or categorical, ordering them by criteria of legitimacy, appropriateness, priority, urgency, importance, relevance, precedence, and so on. But whatever their structure, these criteria constitute media of *evaluation,* not merely the bases for formal classifications. In applying them, agents do more than simply categorize items, they compare them according to their relative value, worth, or importance.

B. The currency of valuation must be socialized within a speech community, such that it is both mutually recognized and in practical use as a medium of common judgment. Valorization schemes thus require some publicly recognizable system of signs, symbols, and tokens that communicate information about how someone or something is or should be valued given some practical context. Insofar as such a system is available, valorization judgments are publicly corrigible: members of a community can settle disagreements about whether something or someone has been valued correctly by applying the relevant criteria. They can in principle know that, and when, it has been used incorrectly, and they can agree, at least roughly, on the value of one item relative to another in terms of the scheme's currency.

C. It must operate on items that are already recognized as bearers of value, not in the sense of having quantity (numerical values), but in that they are variously understood as good or bad, matters of normative concern, something that agents can have reasons to care about, and so on. I therefore stipulate that valorization involves *higher-order valuation,* operating on items that are already valuable in other normative dimensions. Valorization schemes thus apply to matters that are independently objects of human interest but then orient judgment to some particular aspect of their value bearing on some putatively legitimate communal purpose. They do this by abstracting from, or excluding, other dimensions of valuation as not pertinent to certifying certain value-judgments judgments as socially valid.

A schema that satisfies some but not all of these conditions won't be sufficient for "valorization" in my sense to be possible. For example, systems of weights and measures (imperial, metric, avoirdupois, 24-hour clock, etc.)

---

[30] As Parfit noted, cardinal valuations need not be precise. Derek Parfit, *On What Matters,* vol. 2 (Oxford: Oxford University Press, 2013), pp. 555–59: "Suppose that someone asks whether Einstein or Bach was a greater genius, or had greater achievements. We may think this is a pointless question, since we cannot possibly compare the greatness of scientists and composers. But this response would be a mistake. Einstein was clearly a greater genius than any untalented fifth-rate composer, and Bach was clearly a greater genius than any incompetent fifth-rate scientist" (p. 558).

satisfy features A and B, but not C. That is, they constitute metrics that are in common use (on cereal boxes, road signs, timetables), but they order things that are not independently understood as *normative* values: the time of day, or the length of a piece of wood, are quantities, and we often *care* about what they are, but they do not automatically constitute anything of normative concern. The elaborate system of principles and priority rules described in Rawls's *Theory of Justice* satisfy features A and C: they order things that should matter to any community (e.g., social primary goods) by priority and urgency. However, as they are not actually in common use, they are not yet a valorization scheme as I propose to use that category (although if his ideal society became a reality, they would). The practice of assigning people names satisfies features B and C: they operate on something independently valuable (people!) and the relevant rules are in common use such that we can all tell who is and isn't Colin Bird. By themselves, however, the names we give people don't assign them any sort of relative value, so they don't satisfy feature A (though I suppose that some naming schemes, inasmuch as they encode information, for example, about rank, nobility, and social importance (Lord John, Lady Alice, etc.), may sometimes implicate feature A).

Marx implicitly treated capitalist commodity-exchange as a scheme of valorization that satisfies all three of these conditions. Feature A, because it involves a quantitative system of financial commensuration by which commodities acquire a proportional exchange-value relative to each other. It satisfies feature B, because that system is in common use within capitalist social forms, such that it affords a "socially valid" point of view from which agents can agree whether an exchange is fair, worth it, an opportunity for profit, and so on. That point of view in turn informs their decision-making, allowing agents to anticipate the likely behavior of others. It satisfies feature C, because what the valorization scheme values – commodities – are already independently valuable (they have use-values of various heterogeneous kinds).

Neoclassical economics understands "marginal rates of exchange" in much the same way; it theorizes marginal utility as the key dimension of comparison around which commercial valuation revolves. In doing so, it abstracts from other possible dimensions of valuation – most obviously, it excludes "total utility" from counting toward the determination of economic value (the failure to make that exclusion, marginalists argue, caused classical economists like Smith to be misled by the famous "water-diamonds" paradox). But it accepts, more or less explicitly, that prices institute common knowledge.[31] Not

---

[31] Michael Chwe provides an interesting illustration of prices as "common knowledge" generators. He notes that when the Sadat régime in Egypt raised the price of bread in 1977, it sparked social unrest and some riots. To reduce the risk of unrest, the government subsequently decreased the size of loaves. As he notes "These tactics are more than just a matter of individual deception: each person could notice that their loaf was smaller . . . but be unsure about how many other people noticed. Changing the size of loaves . . . is not

surprisingly, then, we find in the work of Hayek's unjustly neglected pupil G. L. S. Shackle an exemplary description of market valuation as a valorization scheme in my intended sense, although of course he doesn't use my technical term:

> Though valuation is in origin the personal and private act of the individual mind, yet it becomes through the device of the market a public and objective fact upon which every individual, at least in regard to goods for immediate consumption, agrees. This is achieved by the power of exchange to adjust each person's supply of this commodity and his supply of that other commodity until the market valuation of one in terms of the other is the same as his own marginal relative estimation of the two goods. When all the individual valuations have been adjusted to that market valuation which reflects and is itself determined by them all, the public prices of goods have been established as public and objective facts to which all relevant conduct will in its own interest conform. Prices, given this public authority and validity, enable collections of the most diverse objects to be measured in a single dimension and treated as representing a scalar quantity.[32]

As figures as politically diverse as Marx and Hayek all recognize, more or less implicitly, studying valorization schemes can in principle tell us something about the intentionality of the social forms that use them, although in any particular case analysts may canvass competing theories purporting to elucidate it. Alternative theories may show the same scheme in a negative or positive light, as Marx's and Hayek's respective accounts of commercial capitalism well illustrate. If Marx is correct, elaborating how "Capital" valorizes itself through commodity-exchange lays bare the oppressive and exploitative character of capitalism. If Hayek is right, once we understand how the "price system" both uses and conveys otherwise inaccessible information about shifting economic circumstances, we come to appreciate how that valorization scheme serves agents seeking to make rational decisions about how to promote their material interests. Despite their starkly different assessments of capitalism, both impute to it a spontaneously arising schema affording a common point of view from which socially valid judgments of value are possible and corrigible.

Two last points about "valorization." First, in this context, it is important not to confuse social validation and finality. Valorization schemes in my intended sense need not, and probably mostly do not, yield "once and for all" judgments of value. In the economic case, for example, the same commodity may be bought and sold many times for different prices; there is no final, "all

---

the same public event as raising its price." Michael Suk-Young Chwe, *Rational Ritual: Culture, Coordination, and Common Knowledge* (Princeton, NJ: Princeton University Press, 2001), p. 11.

[32] George Shackle, *Epistemics and Economics: A Critique of Economic Doctrines* (Cambridge: Cambridge University Press, 1972), p. 9.

things considered," price. But each time it is exchanged, the "price system" values the commodity at a rate that counts as its socially valid economic value at that moment. Of course, some goods and services are one-off, and are economically valued in a single exchange. But this need not be true.

Second, I underline the implication of feature C, that, because valorization schemes are higher-order modes of valuation, they invariably *abstract* from other ways in, and points of view from, which items might be found valuable or less valuable, rendering the latter irrelevant for the purposes of certain social judgments. Valorization schemes thus address a major problem about our consciousness of value: that modes of valuation are protean and superabundant, and that without some simplifying heuristics to direct our necessarily selective attention, practical judgment would simply be overloaded by the unmanageable profusion of values claiming our allegiance.[33]

---

[33] Much modern philosophy, and social thought more generally, has wasted time on the question: "how can anything have value?" This tendency is particularly encouraged by positivism, which suggests that the world is constituted only by inert "facts," and that our "values" must therefore be flimsy and tenuous, perhaps merely illusory projections of "subjective" feelings. This suggestion that "normativity" is somehow insecure is the counterpart in practical reflection of the epistemological problematic Descartes introduced when he tried to vindicate knowledge of the external world by asking: what if *nothing* is as it appears? Ever since, practical reflection on morality, politics, and society has been stalked by the nihilist anxiety that the normative judgment is systematically questionable because nothing has any real value or meaning.

As it lost faith in an omnipotent deity Who had, for centuries before, been assumed to be the source of all goodness, modernity was bound to be a sucker for nihilism. But nihilism about value is not, I think, a problem human beings have ever really had. The real challenge facing practical, evaluative, reflection is close to the opposite. Nihilism implies that there is a dearth of warranted value-judgments, as if real goodness and badness are like chemicals found only under highly unusual conditions or substances with very short half-lives. But in general agents have no trouble judging agony and suffering to be bad, preferring justice to injustice, resenting oppression, desiring freedom, grieving lost loves, joying in new life, admiring heroes, condemning tyrants, and so on. If moral and political arguments are notoriously hard to settle, it is not because the reasonableness of any of this is seriously in question. The problem is exactly the reverse: the superabundance, not the dearth, of sound reasons for evaluative judgments and of valid perspectives from which to recognize them. What I am calling valorization schemes help us navigate this problem of superabundance, though as Marx suggests with respect to capitalism, their cure may be worse than the disease.

11

Love and Respect: Attentional Currencies

Our effort to improve on the traditional dignitarian accounts rejected in earlier chapters has led us to hypothesize that the circulation of people within the routines of associational life might be interpreted as a distinctive timanthropic economy on whose well-functioning the emergence and protection of human dignity depends. It is one thing, of course, to hypothesize that the timanthropic intentionality of actual human interaction might be so conceived, and quite another to specify that hypothesis in a theoretically satisfying and realistic way for the purposes of political criticism. Chapters 12 and 13 address themselves to this task.

Chapter 10 emphasized the likely importance in this context of socially embedded "valorization schemes." I argued there that such schemes make available accepted currencies by which the relative worth of different items can be plotted along commonly intelligible dimensions. As I suggested at the conclusion of Chapter 10, decoding the operation of such valorization schemes can in principle tell us something about the intentionality of the social formations that use them.

My claim is that timanthropic affects like respect and love, which both involve being oriented toward another human being "for their sake," can be thought of in this way. As people cycle through the organized routines of social life, they set the terms on which lives are valorized in relation to each other. Love and respect, in other words, are attentional currencies rendering the relative worth of their objects – in this case people – socially legible. Insofar as this is the case, the central claim of dignity-revisionism might be vindicated: that as respect and disrespect flow between agents and lend their interaction a distinctive character, human dignity is variously protected, promoted, endangered, and suppressed. To begin to defend that contention, therefore, this chapter and Chapter 12 analyze some relevant features of love and respect. I stress that love is relevant here only for the purpose of comparison, not because I believe that it bears particularly on the determination of human dignity. To the contrary, I will interpret human dignity as depending exclusively on respect. However, as we shall see, comparing the timanthropic implications of love and respect can still help clarify exactly how respect and disrespect constitute dignity and indignity, understood as socially ambient, variable qualities.

Labors of Love

We noted in Chapter 8 that neither love nor respect can be bought and sold. Still, respect can be *paid*, as ordinary language attests. This suggests that there is some currency of payment. What is that currency? The question is crucial because answering it helps to elaborate the main contention of a performative understanding of respect and dignity: that the payment of respect in some way maps the worth of the respected. I will argue that, in both love and respect, *attention* functions as a timanthropic currency.

Although I have suggested that love is not paid, attention is recruited in both love and respect. My point, then, is not that love does not involve the payment of attention (though, tellingly, it is more natural to speak of lovers *giving* each other attention rather than *paying* it). Rather, it is that in love it is only the attention that is paid, not the love. However, in respect, the attention paid *is* the respect, and its character as payment, cost, burden, and so on is at least partly constitutive of the attitude itself. We see this very clearly in Kant's use of the German word "achtung" to describe respect, for that word straddles the English words "respect" and "attention."

The ordinary language phrase a "labor of love" provides some further useful clues on this front. When one describes a project as a "labor of love," one suggests that the work involved was so pleasurable and absorbing that any negative connotations of the word "labor" (drudgery, monotony, suffering, sacrifice) become irrelevant. Alfred Wainwright described his "pictorial guide" to the mountains of the English Lake District, the most successful rendition of a whole landscape in the pages of a book I have ever encountered, as an extended love letter. The pains he took in composing his love letter were heroic: for thirteen years, during which he held a full-time job as an accountant, he wandered the mountains and valleys in sun, rain, wind, and snow, relying almost exclusively on public transportation. Wainwright's text and images are entirely in his own hand – not a single printed letter or photograph appears in any of its seven volumes. Yet it is plain that he regarded his Herculean labors as overcompensated by the joy of discovering and recollecting something dear to him.

Why does the metaphor a "labor of respect" fall flat? Not, I think, because it makes no sense to think of labor as a token of respect. To the contrary, it is precisely because our consciousness of respect already includes some notion of a burden imposed upon the respecter that the metaphor lacks the drama of paradox played out in the phrase "labor of love." Any labor required by respect is *labor*, pure and simple. Unlike the lover, the respecter is not required to deny the burdensome quality of their efforts on behalf of the respected; its character as work is in no way qualified or transcended because it is undertaken in the name of respect.

Importantly, the point here is not one about the presence or absence of compulsion. The Lakeland landscape clearly compelled Wainwright. He was driven to explore it, to spend time in its presence, to agitate for its preservation, and to preserve his memories of it. Love is surely often compulsive in this way – that is why we speak of lovers as captivated. What distinguishes the compulsion of love from that of respect is that the lover delights in her compulsion. This doesn't mean that one always delights in the presence of a beloved; those one loves can often be a royal pain. Even Wainwright must have cursed the hills on gray days of rain, blisters, mud, unrelenting gradients, and bitter cold. But, in the context of love, such cursing must be the exception rather than the rule.

The compulsion of respect is however essentially joyless and often accepted reluctantly. Respect is readily grudging; love cannot so easily be. For Kant, notoriously, that reluctance is in fact the locus of respect's unique status as a moral incentive. When Schiller mocked him for taking this line, his target was the oddness of Kant's suggestion that one is morally purer to the extent one ignores not only some of one's inclinations, but all of them. Whatever one thinks of the resulting account of moral motivation, Kant's account radicalizes the standard contrast between love as an emotion of attraction and unification and respect as one of repulsion and differentiation. For that identification depicts respect as more aggressively intrusive than a simple analogy with a physical force like magnetism might suggest. Since, in a way explored more fully below, love and respect are sustained by conscious attitudes, they operate in part through the agency of the respecter, not through some external force holding things apart or pulling them closer. If their mutual respect keeps agents at a distance, then, it is because they consciously observe certain boundaries in defiance of strong inclinations to breach them. Tellingly, Kant uses the metaphor of *exaction*, connoting extraction and even extortion, to capture this inclination-frustrating quality. The resulting sense in which respect reaches into, and in some ways invades, an agent's mind and commands her to do what she may not wish is, I believe, broadly loyal to our ordinary understanding of respect, regardless of the plausibility of Kant's wider ethical position.

If this is right, then love and respect do not really differ in that one, but not the other, operates in some measure from "inside" the agent concerned. Both do this, and both moreover involve internal submission to a certain sort of control from an outside source (the objects of their love and respect). The chief difference is rather that in respect one submits at a certain cost to oneself and therefore typically in the face of some internal resistance. In love, on the other hand, one accepts the compulsion of the various affects triggered by the object of one's love, not as something that imposes an unwelcome cost, but rather as a life-enhancing boon. Again, that is why respect is "paid" and often commanded, whereas love can neither be paid nor commanded.

This offers a first important hint about our central hypothesis that how people are valorized depends, in part, on their power to command certain kinds of affective attention. For it suggests that, at least in the case of respect, agents pay an attentional cost that in some sense subsidizes the value of the respected. We might think of that payment as a measure of how respected lives matter in a way that disrespect threatens. If it can be made good, this suggestion could explain how, when generalized and refracted through public institutions and dominant social routines, affects like respect determine how people and their lives gain and lose relative worth along socially recognized dimensions. On this proposal, respect is an attentional currency whose payment conveys information about how agents who (don't) receive it bear value in their form of life.

Currencies and Comparisons

The metaphor of currency is partly financial and physical. On the former side, it connotes a standard by which otherwise incommensurable items admit of evaluative comparison, giving some account of what they are worth in relation to each other (in the way that demand and "willingness to pay" afford a measure of value in standard economics). On the latter side, it recruits images of liquid flow, volume, intensity, and so forth. Our interest in the currency metaphor concerns how it might serve in the former capacity, conveying information about the relative value persons acquire in the course of their mutual engagement. A natural possibility to pursue, then, is to try to explain this in terms of the latter, as a function of the volume, intensity, or amount of attention persons receive.

However, this initially tempting suggestion is a nonstarter. It isn't that we are never well-conscious of affective attitudes as streams of psychological arousal or energy. "Waves" of pain, pleasure, guilt, remorse, depression, excitement, joy, despair, disappointment, desire, grief, and yearning are surely common enough, as is our sense that some are larger or more intense than others. The problem is rather that these physical metaphors seem quite ill-adapted to the context of attention. They tend to conceal, rather than explain, how the "payment" of attention to X might serve as a standard of value, such that X's receiving it somehow determines X's worth.

For one thing, attention is too episodic to make sense as any kind of flow; there are no "waves" of attention, let alone of greater or lesser intensity. This may be why it makes sense to speak of attention as *paid*, but not as "*spent*," as if it were a force or a stock that can be used up at differential rates. Metaphors of closeness, distance, excerption, direction of glance, magnification, focus, and the absence of distraction are more apposite in this context.

Moreover, following Goffman, "disattention" is often an important element of respect as ordinarily understood.[1] Paying too much attention to others – staring at them, prying into their personal business, constantly interfering in and attempting to control them, and so on – is archetypically disrespectful. The

---

[1] Goffman, *Relations in Public*, pp. 249, 385.

same applies to friendship and love, which become cloying, and shade into obsession, if the parties become unduly fixated on each other. Hence Coleridge's injunction to "reverence the individuality of your friends!" Conversely, torturous abuse is often marked by a very focused attention on the victim, but if anything involves contempt and hostility, surely it is torture. This suggests that one's significance in the eyes of those who respect or love one cannot be a simple linear function of the "amount" of attention they pay, if the notion of quanta of attention even makes sense. The notion of an Aristotelian "mean" seems more appropriate here – we want to be noticed, regarded, taken seriously, but neither overlooked, ignored, discounted, nor gawked at, fawned over, "checked out," fixated on, and so on .

So I doubt that we can capture our target idea that aspects of a person's worth are determined by how agents attend affectively to them simply in terms of mere degrees of attention. What will presumably matter, rather, is the quality of attention that agents engaging with objects and persons bring to their interaction with them: in giving respectful or loving attention to X, one treats X as valuable in relevant ways; that one does not pay that sort of attention to Y indicates that one doesn't take Y to be valuable in the same way. Here, one could reasonably think that the presence or absence of a certain sort of attention tells us something about the relative worth of X and Y, at least in the eyes of the agents who love/despise or respect/disrespect them. If I love X and not Y, for example, then the way I attend to X implies (in some sense) that she possesses greater worth to me than Y. In this way, the respectful or loving quality of the attention agents pay/give each other affords a basis for at least some judgments of comparative worth. To see more clearly why it is appropriate to speak of "currency" or "standard of value" in this context, it will be useful first to consider some important commonalities between love and respect. Chapter 12 completes my account by discussing their differences.

Dispositional Emotions

Both love and respect are fundamentally "dispositional" affects in two senses. First, they are not primarily "occurrent" emotions, although their expression may depend on the latter.[2] Occurrent emotions are usually constituted by some kind of somatic arousal like trembling, a "startle" response, weeping, blushing, and so on. The visceral terror I feel when I come upon a black widow in my basement exemplifies an occurrent emotion. In contrast, a dispositional emotion is a settled propensity, like arachnophobia, to feel certain emotions toward something whether or not one is currently experiencing their characteristic symptoms.

---

[2] Gaus, *Value and Justification: The Foundations of Liberal Theory* (Cambridge: Cambridge University Press, 1990) pp. 109–12.

I have difficulty thinking that respect ever presents as a momentary psycho-logical occurrence in the way "joy" or "surprise" does. Such ordinary notions as "love at first sight" may suggest that it is easier to conceive of love as an occurrent emotion. Yet, on reflection, even here the idiom of disposition seems far more natural. It is not just that "love at first sight" has something of the character of an urban myth. If the phrase captures a real phenomenon at all, surely it refers less to a discrete period of arousal (weeping, giggling, seething, etc.) than to a sudden realization, like a *Gestalt* switch, that one is now disposed toward another person in a new and intense way. In any case, notoriously, the people we love do not command warm, fond feelings continu-ously. Sometimes we feel only hostility, hatred, and exasperation toward them. Still, that you currently cannot stand the sight of your spouse doesn't automat-ically tell against your loving them. More generally, it is usually physiologically impossible to experience occurrent emotions continuously – they quickly exhaust themselves and are inevitably replaced or overridden by others in the flux of experience. To construe the dignitarian humanist expectation of mutual respect (or the parallel Christian principle of agapeic neighbor-love) as demanding that agents be constantly in the grip of particular occurrent emotions would therefore be very uncharitable.

We do better, then, to think of it as requiring only that agents be disposed to certain affective responses when circumstances call for them. Complicated questions arise at this point about who is responsible, and in what way, for cultivating these dispositions; we can at least say, however, that the "delibera-tive" stance presupposed in much moral philosophy, which focuses on cases in which individual agents are culpable for specific choices they make, is unlikely to be in point. Agents generally lack the sort of individual control over their emotional responses necessary for that deliberative model to be applicable.

The idea is particularly implausible in the case of occurrent emotions – I hardly *choose* to feel terror upon stumbling on a cobra, or to be furious about a colleague's tactless condescension. Yet, on reflection, the same holds true for dispositional emotions as well. People do not choose to fall in love, still less deliberate about doing so (hence the aptness of the metaphor of "falling," which is rarely a voluntary act). Those disposed toward special respect for particular people (e.g., those with great integrity or a deep religious faith) have not generally weighed up their merits, as if assigning an academic grade, and then resolved to "award" them their respect. Usually, rather, their respect for someone emerges gradually, but spontaneously, from being struck by them in the course of repeated encounters; it then entrenches itself as a settled dispos-ition to hold them in high regard (which may later be shaken in the light of further experience). Rarely can one pinpoint specific moments at which one's respect or love for a person began or ceased.

Clearly, such dispositions are often creatures of individual habit, tempera-ment, and quirks of personality. When that is so, there will be some pressure to deny that they can have much relevance to political criticism; they concern, one might object, the fine texture of private relations, too idiosyncratic, variegated or trivial to bear on judgments about the large-scale institutional practices of public life. This objection raises an important difficulty and is surely right up to a point; obviously, the political theorist cannot afford to get lost in the minute detail of day-to-day affective repercussion. Still, we should remember the feminist slogan that "the personal is the political," and especially the connected point that social, official, or cultural roles (employer, lender, husband, mediator, judge, etc.) characteristically require and instill certain dispositional orientations in those who occupy them. Arguably, for example, part of what it is to be "noble" in the ancien régime sense is to be disposed toward contempt for the ignoble. If so, one could think that this is precisely one of the ways in which ancien régime was an affront to human dignity: its fundamental structures, and the affective dispositions they cultivated, valorized the poor, the unprivileged, the peasantry, and so on, as worthy only of a contempt that its targets were powerless to overcome.[3]

Action Tendencies as Tokens

The second way in which love and respect are dispositional has to do with a feature they share with virtually all emotions: they presuppose "action-tendencies." Loving and respecting are things we do as well as merely feel; they characterize, not only introspectable emotional attitudes, but affective modes that materialize in typical conduct. This feature leads Raz to deny that respect is any sort of emotion, but merely a form of treatment.[4] Although Raz goes too far in suggesting that its emotional resonances are merely contingent and dispensable elements of respect, he is correct to notice that respect is as much a form of treatment as it is an affect. The same is true of love.

The point here is not just that love and respect often function as verbs and not merely as the names of distinct feelings. Fear and hope, after all, can also function as verbs, and one can also "joy in" or "enjoy" events. Quite generally, too, we speak of agents "emoting" in various ways. These generic verbal uses,

---

[3] '[T]he splendor of [the nobility's] homes, the pomp of their receptions, have something impersonal about them, something not unlike the grandeur of churches and of liturgy, something which is *ad maiorem gentis gloriam* . . .; when [nobles] treat someone badly, . . . it is not so much their personality sinning as their class affirming itself. *Fata crescunt.* For instance, Don Fabrizio has protected and educated his nephew Tancredi. . . . You say that he did it because the young man is a noble too, and that he wouldn't have lifted a finger for anyone else. That's true, but why should he lift a finger if sincerely, in the deep roots of his heart, he considers all 'others' to be botched attempts, china figurines come misshapen from the potter's hands and not worth putting to the test of fire?' Di Lampedusa, Giuseppi, *The Leopard* (New York: Knopf, 2013), p. 168

[4] Raz, *Value, Respect, and Attachment*, p. 138.

however, typically refer only to the behavioral expression of various feelings (laughing, smiling, yelling, chanting, stamping, hurling plates across the room, etc.). The focus here is on observable symptoms of some episodic emotional reaction. Yet when we think of people as lovers or as respecters, however, we also think of them as disposed toward certain sorts of conscious action. These action-tendencies, when realized, condition the parties' mutual engagement. They constitute the *performance* of love and respect.

For example, respecting authority is more than just habitual obedience. It involves decisions to follow commands for the reason that one recognizes their source as an authority. One who ignores authoritative commands invites complaints of disrespect; and the complaint is both that she fails to be moved by certain attitudes and that she therefore fails to recognize something and act accordingly. In such complaints the conduct and internal dispositions of antinomian individuals are inseparable.

Love is similar. When an intimate relationship runs into trouble, the parties sometimes report that they "do not know how to love each other." Such declarations of despair don't deny the presence of loving feelings; indeed, they are often most poignant in cases where the parties are quite genuinely fond of each other. The problem being reported, rather, is that despite their mutual affection, the parties have encountered difficulty in living it out in a stable, sustainable way. They find themselves unable to answer the invitation such feelings issue – to associate for each other's sake.

Relevant here, too, are the spatial connotations of both love and respect, which tend to locate the relative positions of respecter and respected, lover and beloved, within some metaphorically projected social space. Consider "AIDS does not respect borders," "drivers generally respect the speed limit around here," or "the cease-fire was respected by both sides." In these phrases, respect refers to some property of external conformity to a boundary, rule, or expect-ation, and can often be identified without any reference to attitudes, intentions, and dispositions whether imputed or real. Respect in this spatial sense subsists merely in the maintenance of a certain distance, the preservation of limits, and the avoidance of contamination or interference. Conversely, love is associated with binding things together and the erasure of boundaries. Hence the earlier mentioned contrast between love as an attractive, unifying force, and respect as one that preserves distance between respecter and respected. So, although the affective content of love and respect cannot be wished away, love and respect are much more than emotions in any narrow sense: they form a more complex category of affectively charged "relatings" for which we lack any simple English word.

Consider the metaphorical phrase: "fear gripped the land." The metaphor is useful shorthand for the fact that many individuals in some society at a particular time were emotionally aroused in a similar way. However, one cannot analyze claims about a "respectful community" or a "loving family" in this way, and this is not because respect and love are somehow experienced by "communities," "families" as collective subjects. The point is rather that the respectful or loving quality of these relationships turns ultimately on the character of serial interactions among participants. The fundamental unit of analysis standing behind all this is not first-personal emotional experience but rather the ongoing encounter. Love and respect, whether as affects, modes of action, or as their social effects, fundamentally condition the lived history of concrete interaction, not simply what agents caught up in them experience from the inside. Hence the deep plausibility of Kolodny's view that love is a way of valuing a relation; the same also applies, I believe, to respect.[5]

An analogy with musical modes is helpful here. Music that is written in a minor or a major key, or in the Lydian, Dorian, Myxolydian, or Phrygian mode, will have a distinctive character for that reason. That character will, of course, be indefinite. Just as no two loving relationships are exactly alike, two pieces can be very different despite being composed in the same mode. For all that, the modal idiom of a piece will have a discernible effect on how it sounds; all pentatonic music, for example, shares an immediately recognizable family resemblance. Moreover, musical character doesn't inhere in the notes taken separately, but (as Debussy pointed out) in their sequential relations. Similarly, the affective/evaluative modes of love and respect are legible only in the historical development of personal interactions.

I submit that love and respect have the performative capacity postulated by my revisionist account of human dignity in virtue of this micro -Hegelian structure. Just as the modal idiom in which a motet is composed will shape its musical persona, so the affective modes of love and respect will impart a particular quality to ongoing encounters displaying them. According to the hypothesis I wish to explore, then, iterated interaction among persons who respect each other imparts a certain quality to their association; on a revisionist account, dignity names that quality. Disrespect and contempt threaten it.

Helpful as it is, the analogy with musical modes breaks down at two points. On the one hand, to compose a piece of music is not to organize relations between people, but simply to arrange abstract pitches and timbres in a serial order. On the other hand, the mode in which music is composed obviously doesn't reflect the *notes'* mutual attitudes; it is simply a set of harmonic rules that the composer follows in structuring the piece. Affective modes like love and respect differ on both counts. They reflect conscious dispositions to attend to each other, thereby conditioning the terms on which their mutual engagement proceeds. There is also no "composer" standing behind the social performances conducted under these affective modes. The place taken by the composer in the musical case is here distributed among the performers

---

[5] Niko Kolodny, "Love as Valuing a Relationship," *The Philosophical Review* 112, no. 2 (2003): 135–89.

themselves – the agents who do the loving and respecting. Still, like composers observing a harmonic mode, in avowing or attributing to each other emotional dispositions like love and respect, such agents follow scripts given by common understandings of what these emotional complexes are like.

These scripts are certainly far less settled and more open-ended than musical modes. As they attend to others with love and respect, agents cannot appeal to anything akin to a formalized manual of harmony to highlight lapses or incongruities. And, without a composer who has provided an explicit score for performers of respect and love to follow, agents who engage with each other in these affective modes must negotiate uncertainly between the roles of innovators and enforcers of various inchoate expectations. Partly for that reason, what can and cannot count as a token of respect or love is moreover highly culturally inflected; that is why outsiders unfamiliar with cultural norms accepted within a particular community can invite complaints of disrespect even though they are doing their best to show respect as they have been socialized to recognize it.

Yet the affective modes of love and respect are not so elastic as to be completely unadjudicable, even across cultures. Leaving aside exceptions due to Poe's "imp of the perverse" (e.g., sado-masochism), we can safely exclude ridicule, acts of cruelty, violent assault, rape, and spitting in peoples' faces as standard tokens of either love or respect. Because they often record relevant differences, the emotional metaphors familiar in ordinary use also expose clear contrasts between these affective dispositions. Agents cannot "fall madly in respect with each other," passionately "make respect" to each other, or easily "burn" with respect; I don't address people as "honey," "babe," or "cutie-pie," if I want to express my respect for them. But all of these metaphors make perfect sense in the context of love. Conversely, we would not qualify our criticisms of others by saying "with all due love," or insist that "the state show equal concern and love for its citizens," and Shakespeare's Timon would never have spoken of the "icy precepts" of love (as he does of respect).[6]

The loose, open-ended, scripts associated with these and other affective metaphors thus create expectations of those who profess love and respect, guide agents' understanding of what it is to attend to someone in a loving or respectful spirit, and open recognized lines of mutual criticism. In so doing, they provide agents with markers to gauge whether they matter to others as they (have been led to) hope. That agents carefully monitor all this for information about how they figure in others' concerns is a commonplace. Our amour-propre is highly sensitive to that information, though that of

---

[6] For further discussion of the relation between culturally common and divergent elements of dignitarian concepts, see Meir Dan-Cohen, "Defending Dignity," in *Harmful Thoughts: Essays on Law, Self, and Morality* (Princeton, NJ: Princeton University Press, 2002), pp. 163–66.

course is not to say that the inferences drawn are especially accurate; this is notoriously an area in which vanity, conceit, pride, self-doubt, exaggeration, narcissism, catastrophizing, invidious comparison, wishful thinking, and so on, are rife. Given the inaccessibility of others' private thoughts and feelings, guesswork is often the order of the day. Yet we are constantly interpreting others' responses to us, and the ways they treat us as a result, as evidence of how we matter. Our shared understandings of such emotions as love and respect constitute a common language for articulating, (in)felicitously communicating, and assessing these interpretations.

Imprecise as they inevitably are, these interpretations are nonetheless in principle about something real rather than imagined: our actual emotional impact on others. Affective modes like love and respect have evolved as hermeneutic frameworks on which to hang our consciousness of how, de facto, we count in our social relations. The analogy with commodity-exchange is again instructive here. Prices are, as both Marx and Hayek thought, "social constructions" in that they can't be explained as approximations of some inherent or natural value that commodities or services bear independently of human attitudes. Rather, they emerge spontaneously from commerce itself, and reflect the interacting desires, needs, and preferences that stimulate it. The resulting price system enables us to converge in judgments about economic value, but the latter are not figments of our collective imagination just because the valorization scheme that makes them possible is a social contrivance.

Consider "bankruptcy," which is a concept intelligible only in the light of the scheme of economic valorization regnant in market societies. In allowing us to recognize the unbridgeable discrepancy between a person's assets and liabilities, and to calculate the exact magnitude of the shortfall, that scheme determines who counts for us as "bankrupt." Yet, even though such judgments rest on a framework that is as "socially constructed" as anything, it obviously doesn't follow that someone's going bankrupt is somehow make-believe, like a bad dream that can simply be shrugged off. It is not as if the bankrupt can pay off their creditors by photocopying banknotes: the operative valorization scheme won't recognize them as valid. The example illustrates how those enmeshed in a valorization scheme can sometimes find themselves in a situation akin to checkmate,[7] except that bankruptcy is no game. The bankrupt has no further moves available, but he can't just abandon the game-board and go for a drink: others – bailiffs, collection-agencies, attorneys, courts, – will soon intervene.

The affective modes of love and respect similarly put the catallactic intersection of our lives under the control of accepted valorization schemes. They enable anyone to judge the quality and import of the attention I actually receive

---

[7] It is worth noting here that Améry, in his moving discussion of suicide and its motives, speaks of the "échec" of social rejection, ruin, and death.

(or don't) from those with whom I interact, according to the shared expectations built into our consciousness of love and respect. Consider the suitor whose fervent love is unrequited and then very decisively rebuffed by his beloved. His avowal and her disavowal of love bear information about their actual relation to each other. Whether or not the transaction is witnessed or occurs in the unobserved secrecy of an apartment, its significance is transparent to anyone who knows the facts. What makes this possible is an implicit comprehension of the scripts defining the affective mode of love.

Information and Valorization

Clearly, such affective modes recruit consciousness in a way that more basic occurrent emotions like fear or disgust need not. But the senses in which love and respect are "conscious" emotions, and the way they accordingly communicate information, need to be carefully understood. It isn't just that they are "emotions of which we can be conscious," for that is true of most emotions. For example, I can be conscious of the fact that I was on some occasion terrified, and I can use metaphors current in ordinary use to convey the quality of the emotional states involved. For example, I might report that "I was petrified." Here, the well-recognized metaphor of "being turned to stone" is propitious because it succinctly captures some of the characteristic physiological symptoms of visceral terror: hence its connotations of paralysis, feeling "stone-cold" and hence trembling, and so on. Yet this doesn't make "petrification" itself a "conscious" reaction: usually it will be purely reflexive, and occur without any deliberation. That is why animals lacking language or any capacity for conscious introspection can still be said to be fearful or disgusted.

But except perhaps in very rudimentary forms, love and respect presuppose introspective self-awareness from the start and are not available to sentient animals lacking language. When a speaker says that they love or respect someone, they avow that they are disposed to attend to them in a distinctive manner. Such avowals do more than just report or describe a past state of arousal like "terror": they directly condition the speaker's relation to someone else, informing listeners of how their encounters with another dispose, and perhaps commit, them to treat those others in particular ways. In this sense, we cannot love or respect, nor attribute these emotions to agents, without presuming that they qualify how an agent is consciously entangled with something beyond themselves. In this sense, the modes of love and respect are like affective lenses focusing our awareness of what (or who) matters to us and how.

Love and respect are also not unique in the capacity to convey information. Jesse Prinz[8] has shown that even basic, nonconscious, emotions can do this.

[8] Jesse J. Prinz, *Gut Reactions: A Perceptual Theory of Emotion* (Oxford: Oxford University Press, 2006).

Since fear almost certainly evolved as a response to percepts typical of events that threaten an animal's safety, Prinz argues, we can speak of the emotion having the function of "stimulating evasive action when danger is near." In that sense, fearful arousal conveys valuable information about an animal's situation, yet without requiring any high-level introspection. A zebra may feel fear upon seeing the shadow of a prowling lion; its subsequent flight may save its life, but it would be misleading to describe this by saying that "it occurred to the zebra that it was in danger, and it decided to run away." Human emotional response also often lacks this conscious element while still conveying information.

Since even very basic emotions like fear often have observable symptoms (e.g., fleeing), in principle they can also convey information to interested parties nearby without any conscious mediation. Hence the contagion to which many such emotions are subject: once a single member of a herd flinches and then runs, the whole herd is alerted to a potential danger and may flee en masse. But the word "contagion" is appropriate here precisely because we are dealing with largely nonconscious, automatic, responses. Conscious emotions like love or respect are not normally contagious in this way; my observing you avowing your love for X won't automatically induce me to feel any affection for X (perhaps I despise him). Plainly, however, such avowals, and other tokens of love and respect, still broadcast information to observers, and may in turn trigger other emotions in them (e.g., given your avowed feelings for X, I may now pity you for falling in love with that bastard).

The way these affective modes condition agents' interactions with each other therefore refracts timanthropic content: the respectful or love-imbued character of their catallactic adjustment informs both those directly involved, and in principle detached observers, how parties value, and count for, each other. Difficult questions arise here about how agents who are differently situated can access such information: those who *avow* feelings of love and respect obviously have a different perspective on the relevant relationships from those who may hear (or wish for) their avowals; love and respect can manifest themselves independent of explicit avowals, sometimes in ways that the agents involved refuse to acknowledge; often the question of whether they are or not present, in what form, and to what degree, is very uncertain; and assessing the sincerity of avowals is rarely straightforward. I discuss some of these complications in a moment.

The immediately pertinent point is that we can now think of love and respect, and the rich repertoire of emotional metaphors that has developed to express and characterize them, as media of valorization in the sense sought by a performative account of human dignity. Their attribution, avowal, and outward performance attest to agents' (lack of) power to elicit distinctive forms of attention from others. They can and do, I therefore argue, function as attentional currencies, offering publicly available, albeit often rough and ready, measures of how lives are, or are not, valued. When rendered in the attentional currency of respect, these consciously mediated affective repercussions form the rudiments of human dignity, or so I propose.

Investment and Detachment

I conclude this chapter by discussing several important symmetries and asymmetries between the standpoints of different parties who engage with each other through these affective modes. These require careful elaboration and will become important later. Let those whose respect or love is at stake be *relevant agents*, and anyone else in a position to recognize those agents' love or respect be an *observer*.

Distinguish further between *invested* and *detached parties*, such that the former have, and the latter lack, a personal stake in a relevant agent's respect or love. I stress that I do *not* here intend the contrast between:

(a) agents who have *some* reason to care about whether, and how, love or respect are (not) shown by some relevant agent; and
(b) those who lack *any* such reason.

In my view, (b) is not a serious possibility. All else equal, anyone should welcome the presence of respect and love. Prima facie, they enhance human relations, and contempt and hatred damage them, if anything does. The reasons to acknowledge this do not evaporate in the absence of any personal interest in the fate of those involved. For example, the organized contempt of a genocide or a pogrom clearly warrants indignation regardless of any personal tie to the victims.

As I am defining them, then, invested parties are those whose attitudes to the presence or absence of love or respect reflects their partiality toward (or against) specific individuals or groups. Those targeted for liquidation in a genocide, for example, are invested parties; presumably they have a strong personal stake in their own survival. Invested parties need not, however, be concerned only on their own behalf: I remain an invested party if my concern about mounting racial abuse is motivated by a fear that my daughter or others in a group I care about are likely targets. Those who object to such abuse in the absence of any personal interest in the victims however do so from a standpoint of detachment in my sense.[9] So understood, investment and detachment are clearly not exclusive. In practice people's actual attitudes will often reflect both and in such cases it may be impossible to disentangle the respective roles played by each.

---

[9] See on this Kristen Renwick Monroe, *The Heart of Altruism: Perceptions of a Common Humanity* (Princeton, NJ: Princeton University Press, 1996).

Still, it is important to distinguish the two stances analytically, because otherwise one may overlook the important point that those who tolerate or support abusive practices need *not* be invested parties. Consider racial abuse. In the main, racists are indeed invested parties, in that their conduct or attitudes reflect their own definite animus toward targeted groups. However, acquiescence, and even active participation, in racist practices can reflect a detached acceptance of ideologies and beliefs. Of course, the relevant beliefs will be spurious, and their affirmation in practice difficult to distinguish from naked racial antipathy. Yet, in principle, agents can acquire and act on them independently of any strong personal investment. Such agents certainly betray stupidity, ignorance, complacency, epistemic irresponsibility, ideological illusion, and any combination of these and other cognitive distortions, but they need not exemplify a lack of detachment as I intend that term.

The Nazi's "Final Solution" is a case in point, for it almost certainly relied on the assistance of some parties who were in this sense detached. The very term "final solution" gets at this very disturbing feature of what occurred, for it implies that the project was simply a technocratic fix for an engineering problem, mere pest control, and not motivated by any personal feelings toward the victims. This isn't to deny the crucial role of the committed (often rabid) anti-Semites in Germany and German-occupied territories who initiated and prosecuted the whole effort. But for these strongly invested parties, the holocaust would certainly never have happened. Even so, I doubt that anti-Semitic attitudes can alone explain the vast mobilization of resources implicated in the holocaust. Securing the complicity of the many detached parties who participated or acquiesced in it required something more: the inhibition of ordinary conscience.

The lazy indulgence of bullshit eugenic "science," the disabling of standard modes of legal control, cowardly deference to authority in the name of civic or military duty, all played their roles in desensitizing participants to the completely uncontroversial reasons to oppose genocide on principle. Although no special tie to those threatened by genocide is required to appreciate these agent-neutral reasons, it unfortunately does *not* follow that a stance of detachment is sufficient to ensure that agents won't lose sight of them. "Turning a blind eye" or "burying one's head in the sand" can be done with complete dispassion.

Given the above classification, we can safely assume that relevant agents will usually be invested parties, at least in that they will presumably care about whom and how *they* respect and love (though I suppose this does not entail that they will inevitably acknowledge that special reason – some people are Frankfurtian "wantons" about love). But observers can be invested or detached.

By default, all observers, whether detached or invested, are in an epistemically symmetrical position. In principle, those with a personal stake in the love or respect of a relevant agent are in no stronger or weaker an epistemic position than are detached bystanders to reach defensible judgments about how individuals matter in the eyes of (dis)respecting or (non)loving others. There is no general reason to suppose that, for example, one who is in love with P and who therefore hopes fervently that P also loves them is better placed to determine whether P really does love them than a detached observer who has no personal stake in P's love.

This symmetry is merely prima facie, and will rarely be perfectly realized in actual instances. For example, as a result of private interaction, an invested party may acquire special insight into a relevant agent's true feelings. This is often the case when a suitor's love is requited and blossoms into a close relationship in which confidences are kept (a character in Iris Murdoch's *The Sea, The Sea* at one point astutely notes that "marriages are secret places"). Equally, however, agents may sometimes shield their true feelings from invested parties and confide them only to detached others – for example, priests or therapists. Invested parties are of course also notoriously prone to wishful thinking, particularly in the context of love. In principle, however, the debunking significance of such factors is neither more nor less accessible to invested observers than to detached ones.

Whether these symmetries are fully or incompletely realized, moreover, is not merely a matter of differential access to pertinent psychological facts. For one's ability to verify that a relevant agent does or doesn't respect or love someone depends also on beliefs about what love and respect are like. These conscious beliefs are corrigible. If an observer has a distorted understanding of love, for example, such that he thinks of it as a Freudian "drive" (to use an example from Velleman), he is hindered in his ability to certify that a relevant agent loves another person. He may think that evidence of her overwhelming physical attraction to another person is sufficient to determine that she is in love. But other observers can discredit his judgment by pointing out that it confuses love and sexual attraction. Again, all else equal, no observer (whether an interested party or not) is in any stronger or weaker position than another to show that someone's attribution of respect or love is defective in such ways. The relevant criteria and information are in principle public, accessible to anyone.

However, a systematic asymmetry does exist between relevant agents and observers, for lovers' or respecters' consciousness of their own love or respect is a matter of self-knowledge, which implies some sort of privileged access. The epistemic privilege of self-knowing lovers or respecters is moreover not merely a function of their more immediate acquaintance with their internal feelings. It is as important that these are *their* feelings to avow or disavow. Relevant agents are responsible for the characterization of their own emotional attitudes in a way that observers are not; the latter aren't expected to stand by them in the same way. As Richard Moran and others have suggested, the privilege of self-knowledge involves the capacity to make certain things true of oneself by avowing them.[10] Of course, agents' judgments will be informed by at least some of the same evidence about their feelings as is available to observers. However, one who says, "I love you" is not merely describing her internal feelings, a first-personal equivalent of "she loves him." In making this declaration, she avows her love and takes on certain commitments. It is in that sense a commissive speech act, not a mere report.[11]

These symmetries and asymmetries introduce complexity into discourse about respect and love. Whether they are interested parties or not, observers must count as evidence in favor of (or against) attributing respect and love to those agents *both* psychological data *and* relevant agents' (dis)avowals. In regard to the latter, observers owe relevant agents a certain deference, a presumption of sincerity. Even so, that presumption can sometimes be overridden by an accumulation of evidence that the relevant agent is insincere, unreliable, or manipulative in their avowals. If I avow that I love or respect you, and then manifestly ignore you and your legitimate interests; am always visibly disgusted by your presence; invariably express open contempt for you; or betray some discrediting ulterior motive for avowing respect or love (flattery, brown-nosing, etc.), anyone should doubt that my avowals are sincere.

In the end, then, we are all answerable to each other for the tokens of love and respect we actually offer in relation to our professed dispositions toward those we claim to love or respect. This is so in something like the sense in which we are answerable for debts incurred, contracts signed, and promises made in commercial contexts, despite the fundamentally different logic by which such accountability is apportioned in the two cases.

---

[10] R. Moran, *Authority and Estrangement: An Essay on Self-Knowledge* (Princeton, NJ: Princeton University Press, 2012).

[11] Of course, like other speech-acts, such a commissive may be, on an Austinian account, infelicitous and fail to come off.

12

Attentional Precedence

Even one convinced by the arguments of Chapter 11 might still find my use of "currency" metaphors in the context of respect stretched. Chapter 9 characterized "valorization" as a mode of relative valuation, and our ordinary (financial) understanding of currency similarly connotes a basis for evaluative *comparison*. However, one might reasonably complain that nothing I have said so far really entitles me to the claim that love and respect have any comparative element. Perhaps the affective modes of love and respect are, as I have argued, frameworks whose operation tells us something about how people matter to significant others, but it remains to show that they can inform us about how people matter *relative* to one another.

That further suggestion of course also faces resistance from a traditional, Kantian, direction. For traditionalists, after all, the force of the price/dignity distinction derives from the insistence that people and their lives bear a worth that is "incomparable," and "admits of no equivalent." To respect them in their dignity is to respond to people as "ends-in-themselves," not "in comparison with others." Proponents of this traditional view might allow that there are some forms of respect that have a comparative element. But these, they will say, are cases of what Darwall calls "appraisal-respect" – the kind commanded by particularly impressive, virtuous, or admirable individuals; the respect that human dignity attracts instead exemplifies Darwall's contrasting category of "moral recognition-respect," to which all persons are unconditionally entitled. As Darwall himself puts it: "if all persons as such should be treated equally, there can be no degrees of recognition respect for them, although one may be a greater or lesser respecter of persons."

Ultimately, of course, this line of thinking is only as good as the traditional accounts of human dignity on which it rests. The first half of this book criticized such accounts. But even if my objections to those accounts go through, it remains to explain the sense in which respect can serve as a currency of relative worth. The traditional view may have fatal problems of its own, but its proponents might still be right that the sort of respect implicated in our concept of human dignity is fundamentally noncomparative.

This chapter attempts to answer this challenge. I therefore begin by present-ing, and endorsing, an account of respect offered by a defender of the trad-itional view.

Second-Order Affects

David Velleman, whose Kantian theory of love remains the state of the art as far as dignitarian humanist thinking on this subject is concerned, has rightly noted that love and respect are both second-order emotions.[1] Self-disgust provides a paradigm example of a second-order emotion. Suppose you find yourself experiencing schadenfreude – delight at someone else's misfortune; your subsequent self-disgust is a second-order emotion in that it embodies an attitude to your prior emotional response. Respect and love, Velleman argues, similarly make sense only as affective attitudes that qualify some prior emo-tional disposition. He speaks of love and respect primarily as second-order motives rather than as emotions but, given my wide characterization of them as affective modes, I assume that his labeling makes no substantive difference.

Velleman argues, plausibly, that agents are naturally and normally affected by two motives, each straddling both a psychological sense (involving causes) and a normative one (involving sensitivity to reasons). The first is that of self-love, the propensity to care about one's own welfare and interests. The second, which Velleman refers to as one of emotional self-protection, is a bit less straightforward, but can be clarified by considering Nietzsche's and Bernard Williams's claim that it would be psychologically unbearable to be emotionally vulnerable to all the suffering in the world. For both Nietzsche and Williams, it is a condition for our being able to proceed in life that we are in this way insulated from each other's torments (and also from their joys, which if they are apparently far greater than ours can inspire intolerable feelings of envy and of "FOMO" – "fear of missing out"). This natural apathy toward others' pleasure and pain, aided by the opacity of one mind to another, is a blessing that liberates us to concentrate on our own concerns.

Velleman describes respect and love as second-order emotions in that they "arrest" these two reflexive orientations. Respect, for Velleman, arrests our self-love, our natural partiality to our own good. It is a second-order emotion of repudiation, and what it repudiates is an unqualified attachment to our own well-being. The resulting "decentering"[2] opens agents to the claims of others as worthy to preempt their self-concern.[3]

---

[1] Velleman, "Love," 338–74.

[2] I take this term from Gaus, who follows Piaget. See Gaus, *Value and Justification*, pp. 199ff.

[3] That is one reason why, I believe, the affective content of respect is linked to feelings of intimidation and shame (here I am adding to Velleman's account, though the thought is clearly implicit in Kant). Respect leads us to see others' claims as trumping those to which we are attached on our own behalves. It thereby often involves what Silvan Tomkins

Velleman sees love, contrastingly, as a second-order emotion that disables our normal affective invulnerability toward others. Whereas respect is a second-order emotion of repudiation, then, love is a second-order emotion of acceptance. To love a person, in other words, is to be affected emotionally by them in a way that we embrace and affirm. In this way, it "arrests" our natural emotional invulnerability to them.

Note that saying that love and respect condition preexisting emotional dispositions isn't to say that their targets are simply those dispositions themselves. Earlier, I illustrated the general notion of a second-order emotion by citing the case of a person who reacts to their own schadenfreude with self-disgust. Here, the emotion of self-disgust is triggered by the recognition of a prior emotion: joy in another's suffering. Yet, the real target of such self-disgust is not the joy, but the agent themselves. Their schadenfreude reveals an unwelcome truth about their own character, and their disgust is hence a self-evaluation. As Velleman would agree, the same point applies to love and respect, except that these are other-regarding, rather than self-regarding, emotions. Their target is the people who evoke them and the character of their relation to those moved by them. In this sense, as we saw in Chapter 11, respect and love both involve the valuation of their objects.

I accept all of this, but resist Velleman's traditionalist interpretation of it. In Chapter 8, I questioned his view that personal dignity is relevant to the emotion of love, but the focus here is Velleman's account of respect. Since he accepts the Kantian view that dignity is a "self-standing," incomparable value that inheres in each individual, he is compelled to interpret the second-order affect of respect as responding to that intrinsic worth. The performative account of dignity developed here obviously rejects that interpretation, but care is needed in pinpointing exactly where it parts company from Velleman.

For reasons also enumerated in Chapter 8, dignity-revisionists need not deny that respect responds to people; claiming that love and respect for people are not first triggered by the presence of those people, as if it could somehow preexist any acquaintance with them, would be silly. In any case, Velleman's account of these emotions rightly presupposes the reverse sequence: someone or something initially comes to the attention of the agent concerned, and this *then* elicits the latter's love or respect. So, since I intend to follow Velleman's basic analysis of respect as a second-order affect that "arrests" self-concern, my revisionist account incorporates that presupposition.

Yet, and this is the crucial point, there is a difference between saying of an emotion that:

rightly saw as the rudimentary feature of shame: the "incomplete interruption of interest." S. Tomkins, *Affect, Imagery, Consciousness Vol. II: The Negative Affects*, pp. 118–84. For, one who respects others may not cease to want what she must forgo in order to properly respect them. The resulting feeling of rightful self-frustration is the beginning of shame.

(a) it responds to people; and
(b) it responds to their dignity.

A performative account rejects (b) but accepts (a). It replaces (b) with the claim:

(c) human dignity – understood as a variety of D-dignity, socially ambient, and transient – emerges insofar as agents respond to each other with respect.

It also endorses (c)'s converse:

(d) human dignity is threatened insofar as agents respond to each other with disrespect.

In what follows, I will not only try to show that Velleman's account of respect as a second-order emotion is compatible with (a), (c), and (d), I will also argue that it entails that the forms of respect involved in (c) and (d) typically *do* imply comparative evaluations of people and their lives. If I am right about this, my claim that the affective mode of respect can reasonably be understood as a currency of valorization should fall into place.

Comparison and Hierarchy

Although the assumption that respect (at least "recognition-respect") for others, and perhaps also love, involves attending to their worth in a noncomparative way is a commonplace in the philosophical literature, it is virtually impossible to reconcile with the ordinary uses of these concepts.[4] One way to highlight this in the case of respect recalls a point emphasized in Chapter 3: the profound historical link between the discourse of respect and dignity and hierarchical forms of life and practical reflection. To be conscious of the respect due to one's superiors, social betters, and so on, is surely to make comparative judgments about the relative importance of different people. To be sure, modernity has seen a sustained campaign to purge hierarchical discrimination in the name of equality. Yet its traces still pervade contemporary dignitarian thinking, even in its most avowedly egalitarian modes. That is why dignitarians like Waldron, Finnis, and Kateb, all of whom connect dignity and human equality, so frequently resort to idioms of "rank," "status," and "stature." However, speaking of an absolute, inherent, nonrelative "rank" or "stature" makes no sense at all. These categories depend on implicit comparisons with others ranked hierarchically above or below.

To be sure, members of these categories need not be ranked relative to each other. Even so, this horizontal, intra-rank, equality presupposes an implicit

---

[4] Surely it is rather difficult to explain what it is for you to love someone without suggesting that they somehow matter more to you than others. What accounts for the ubiquity of jealousy and envy in affairs of the heart if not the presence of social comparison?

background of vertical comparison. Suppose that, as Waldron argues, we should "level up" everyone, so that all human beings share in the same rank. This results in the idea of a "single-status" community, but the comparative element in the argument doesn't simply disappear. It rather gravitates to the relation between that "sortal" community and other beings that count for more or less (Angels, animals). Again, tacitly invoking an altitudinal metaphor, Dworkin famously speaks of the members of such a "single-status" community inhabiting an "egalitarian plateau." Not surprisingly, we denizens of these Olympian uplands find in the metaphor of "height" a natural way to characterize our attitudes to particular individuals who command greater respect than the bare minimum commanded by anyone who has attained the plateau. Like particularly prominent peaks in a mountain range that compel our attention before their shadowed foothills, we speak of the eminence and preeminence of those whom we more and less highly respect. And when we reproach those of whom we profoundly disapprove, we find them "beneath contempt." These judgments are hard to describe as noncomparative.

Similar vertical comparisons are ubiquitous in Kant's various discussions of respect and dignity. For example:

> In the system of nature, man (homo phaenomenon . . .) is a being of slight importance and shares with the rest of the animals, as offspring of the earth, an ordinary value (*pretium vulgare*). . . . But man regarded as a *person*, that is, as the subject of a morally practical reason, is exalted above any price; for as a person (homo noumenon) he is not to be valued merely as a means to the ends of others, or even to his own ends, but as an end in himself, that is, he possesses a dignity (an absolute inner worth) whereby he exacts respect for himself from all other rational beings in the world. He can measure himself with every other being of his kind, and can value himself on a footing of equality with them.

This passage hovers uneasily between the claim that dignity is noncomparative ("an absolute inner worth") and the claim that respect involves "an exact comparison of ourselves," whereby we feel the "highest self-esteem" and can "measure" our equal value with others. But if dignity is incomparable, what business does Kant have using superlatives ("highest self-esteem"), referencing "measures" of equivalence, and trading on the vertical metaphor of "exaltation"? What can it possibly mean to say that persons are "exalted above all price" if not that they have comparatively higher worth than, for example, animals, commodities, and mere objects?

The natural answer is to follow Waldron's line: relative to *each other*, individuals are equivalent and so are owed the same treatment; yet their equivalence consists in their sharing an "exalted" "stature" compared to greater and lesser beings. It is this "exaltedness" that lends the imperative of respect its overriding urgency in the Kantian scheme: mere worms can still be members of a "sortal," single-status community, but as such they are equivalently dispensable, equally fit for little more than fish-bait. As Kant says: "one who makes himself a worm cannot complain afterwards if people step on him."

Yet on this view, the practical import of equality within a rank derives from a prior judgment about the relative significance of that rank. I am owed the same respect as you, but we know that our respective dignity has equivalent urgency because the class to which we belong is more important than others to which it compares. But if so, then it is misleading to say that dignity "admits of no equivalent" and is beyond all comparison.

Anderson's Mode-Hierarchy Proposal

Elizabeth Anderson has offered an ingenious argument that might explain how, despite the points just made, dignitarians can have it both ways after all. She maintains that the evaluative attitudes of "respect," "awe," and "honor" characteristically accord their objects "higher worth" even as they presume them to have "incomparable" value. Having introduced that formulation, she is immediately (and rightly) perplexed by it, noting that the claim that "some goods are incomparably higher in worth than others" has an "air of paradox surrounding" it. As she puts it: "in the same breath, one denies that two goods can be compared and goes on to compare them."[5] She nonetheless maintains that this is a coherent position.

I stress that in seeking to reconcile these seemingly contradictory claims, Anderson is not trying to explain how agents can make *any* comparative value-judgments without applying some monistic standard of commensuration like that canvassed by consequentialists. By the time she confronts the paradox of the "incomparably comparable," Anderson has already established that even though evaluative comparison cannot be reduced to a master metric like aggregate welfare, "pragmatic" judgments of comparative value are routinely and quite reasonably made in ordinary life.[6] I fully endorse her conclusion on that larger point. The difficulty with which we – and Anderson – are now concerned arises after one concedes that comparative dimensions of evaluation are irreducibly heterogeneous. The question is: how can we say, as we sometimes do, that some values are comparable and incomparable at the same time? As Anderson says, tacitly referencing the price/dignity distinction,

> people often speak of some goods as incomparably higher in worth than others. Money, commodities, conveniences, luxuries and sensual pleasures represent paradigmatic lower goods. They are seen not simply as less

[5] E. Anderson, *Value in Ethics and Economics* (Cambridge, MA: Harvard University Press, 1995), p. 70. See also Ruth Chang, "The Possibility of Parity," *Ethics* 112, no. 4 (July 1, 2002): 659–88; Ruth Chang, *Making Comparisons Count* (London: Routledge, 2015).

[6] Anderson, *Value in Ethics and Economics*, pp. 47–64.

valuable, but as not even comparable on the same high scales as those on which paradigmatic higher goods such as human life, friendship, freedom and human rights are measured.[7]

Anderson is right that we often make such claims, but that doesn't mean that they make sense. I don't think they do. Saying, for example, that people and their lives are "incomparable in intrinsic worth" because they exemplify "higher" goods strikes me as incoherent. Intuitively, our confidence that they have such "higher" worth implies a comparison with goods of "lower" value; but then surely we have abandoned the pretense that their value is incomparable.

Anderson thinks otherwise. To dispel the apparent paradox of the "incomparably comparable" she proposes that "[o]ne good is of incomparably higher worth than another if it is worthy of a higher mode of valuation than another . . . one way of valuing something is higher than another if the things concerning it make deeper, qualitatively more significant demands on the attitudes, deliberations and actions of the valuer."[8] This proposal implies that different affective/evaluative modes (love, respect, utility, etc.) are themselves hierarchically arrayed within the structure of practical reasoning. Read in Anderson's terms, then, an idolator or fetishist misapplies a "higher" mode of valuation ("reverence" or respect) to an object than it deserves. Slave-owners, conversely, perpetuate a degrading social practice in that they value their slaves as mere commodities, engaging with people through a "lower" mode of valuation (utility, self-interest, etc.) than is appropriate.

Consider the statement: "a slave, unlike a gentleman, is fit only to be bought and sold for his utility." This may at first *look* like a judgment comparing the relative worth of slaves and gentlemen, but Anderson's point (I take it) is that this appearance is misleading. We should instead parse the statement as two quite independent judgments, one of which is appropriate (about gentlemen) and the other inappropriate (about slaves), but which don't together constitute any sort of evaluative comparison between the two groups. The speaker is simply reporting his disposition to value slaves in the mode of "utility" or "price" and his disposition to accord a gentleman "respect and reverence." Anderson of course thinks that this toggling between modes is arbitrary and unwarranted, but her point is that its inappropriateness needn't reflect any comparative evaluation of slaves and gentlemen. The only relevant consideration is the speaker's refusal to recognize that the slave is worthy to be engaged with in the "high" affective mode of respect. This, Anderson could say, has nothing to do with the way he engages with anyone other than the slave. It would remain inappropriate even if he treated everyone, including other gentlemen, as badly as he does slaves. Viewed in this light, his unwarranted

---

[7] Ibid., p. 66.
[8] Ibid., p. 70.

response to the slave is just an error in practical reasoning, like selecting a hammer to turn a screw, or a screwdriver to pound in a nail. Such incompetent carpentry implies nothing about the relative worth of nails and screws, though it does allow us to criticize the carpenter's poor choice of tools.

Ingenious as it is, Anderson's solution is unsatisfying, for at least three reasons. First, it isn't clear what it means to say (or how we know) that some evaluative modes are "higher" or "lower" than others. Anderson alludes to the property of "making deeper, qualitatively more significant demands," but as it stands this is not very helpful. One wonders whether one could explain the relevant sense of "qualitative significance" without referring to some independent story about why some things matter more than others. That would reintroduce comparison by the back door; the sense in which the values under discussion are "incomparable" would again come under pressure.

Second, once one implies that some mode of judgment itself admits of qualitative comparison as "higher" or "lower," it becomes difficult to deny that selecting one rather than another as an appropriate way to engage with a person or object implies something about the latter's relative worth. To return to the earlier analogy, hammers and screwdrivers are not more or less worthy in the pantheon of tools; they just have different functions. So, quite obviously, using a hammer rather than a screwdriver doesn't imply that a nail is somehow more worthy of the hammer's attention than a screw. But suppose we think of a Stradivarius as a superior instrument than some cheap, clapped out, fiddle. If we then ask what music is and isn't worthy to be played on each (e.g., "Whistling Dixie" or a Bach partita), our answers will likely imply some judgment of the comparative worth of different sorts of music.

Third, and most important, it is misleading to suggest, to use the earlier example, that slave owners are merely toggling back and forth between two completely insulated evaluative modes – that of respect and that of utility – in their dealings with gentlemen and slaves. Putting it that way implies that there is no sense in which the slave owners engage with their slaves through the evaluative mode of respect. But if that were so, how could we say, as we ordinarily should, that the most offensive features of master-slave relations consist in the disrespect and contempt of masters toward those they enslave?

Anderson's view implies that slave owners, as it were, *reserve* the evaluative mode of respect entirely for their engagement with non-slaves, and engage with slaves *only* as commodities with utility. That they do commodify slaves is of course not in question, but the point is that ordinarily we would say that this constitutes a kind of contempt for them. But we can say this only insofar as they *are* attending to their slaves in the evaluative mode of respect – otherwise how can we interpret their treatment of them as disrespectful? To be able to charge them with disrespect and contempt, and not only with simony (buying and selling things that shouldn't be for sale), we have to assume that they engage with both slaves and others in the affective mode of respect.

Intra-Mode Comparison

This last objection points toward a better way of thinking about the comparative implications of affects like love and respect. Rather than following Anderson's suggestion that such modes are themselves ranked hierarchically in relation to each other, we might instead say that the relevant comparisons occur *within* them. On this view, to engage with something within a certain affective/evaluative mode is to make internal comparisons about how they are worthy of relevant sorts attention compared to other things. To love something is at least to put it into comparison with other loves and things one doesn't love. To respect something is automatically to compare it with other objects of one's respect and disrespect. But the question of how the mode of respect is itself hierarchically ranked in relation to that of love does not arise. Although in this sense the two modes are incomparable, I doubt that this can rescue the claim love and respect imply dispositions to engage with something or someone as having "incomparable" worth. These affects just *are* dispositions to compare their objects as mattering more and less in particular dimensions.

This view preserves Anderson's intuition that to engage with something within a particular evaluative mode is to implicitly judge them as worthy or unworthy objects of the relevant affective attention – whether love, or respect, or trust, and so on. But it abandons her effort to retain the idea of "incomparable worth" in the context of these dispositions.

An account along these lines can handle the cases of idolatry or commodification better than Anderson's mode-hierarchy view. The problem with the idolator is not that, in venerating his chosen idols, he is selecting an inappropriately "high" mode of valuation given the inherent character of the relevant objects. Rather it is that, from within the affective mode of reverence and worship, he reveres that object too highly as compared with others falling within the relevant frame of judgment. He fixates on graven images, the performance of rituals, outward conformity with "biblical morality," and so on, but in paying these superficialities most of his attention, God himself – the proper object of reverence – is demoted to lesser significance in the idolator's attitudes.

Similarly, the timanthropic defect involved in slavery would not be remedied by asking slave owners to engage with their slaves through the affective mode of respect as opposed to that of mere utility. This they already do. The problem is not that the affective mode of respect gets "switched off" in the master-slave relation. Rather, it is that it is already "switched on" but operating in an arbitrary, distorted, fashion (like a composer trying to observe a harmonic mode but failing to flatten or sharpen pitches as it requires). That the masters and other "respectable" members of their society accord each other regard and social importance attests to their dispositions to be affected by some people in a way that elicits their respectful attention. The problem is that their disposition operates selectively, so that other human beings (slaves) lack the same power to trigger it in them. This discrepancy institutionalizes a comparative evaluation of people, in this case by social class: members of some classes matter more than others in the eyes of socially dominant groups. This opens the way to interpreting these discrepancies as reflecting the operation of a scheme of comparative valorization.

Precedence and Proximity

I have suggested that each of our two target timanthropic affects – love and respect – affords an evaluative mode within which judgments of comparative worth are made. How then should we characterize the relevant dimensions of comparison involved in each? I think ordinary language gives a pretty clear answer to this question, one that we have already anticipated by noting the deep connection between our concept of respect and a vertical dimension of height. Crucially, this vertical emphasis is absent in our ordinary metaphors of love: madness, yes; closeness, yes; depth, yes; but "I love you 'highly,'" or "I have the highest love for him" just don't ring true.

To see why these altitudinal metaphors work for respect but not love, recall that both of these affective modes involve dispositions to attend to, and then treat, their objects in certain ways. Now, attention and time are limited; at any given moment, one can attend and respond only to so many things and frequently those things compete for our attention. My suggestion is that the metaphor of height is involved in our consciousness of respect because that affective disposition is centrally concerned with a distinctive way of managing these conflicts. I maintain that the "altitude" of respect is a function of how we are disposed to accord something (what I shall call) attentional precedence.

The notion of attentional precedence presupposes some sort of conflict between possible objects of attention, and implies a disposition to resolve those conflicts by putting them in order of priority or urgency. Here, it is worth noting the close links between rank and temporal notions of *precedence*. Consider an eighteenth-century gentleman who has internalized the hierarchical norms of the ancien régime: a peasant and a lady cross his path at exactly the same moment. Following the conventions of the day, the lady clearly outranks the peasant, and so he will attend first to her. I submit that the *timing* of his actions – responding to the lady *before* the peasant – matters more for characterizing the internal comparisons involved in respect than the specific tokens of respect the gentleman might select (bowing, genuflecting, laying his coat before her, etc.). That is, the lady's power to dictate others' physical behavior is less important than her power to get them to give her presence priority over that of others. In this way, the conventions of respect in the ancien régime, by expecting that some people command more immediate attention than others, comprise a schema of comparative valorization.

Insofar as these conventions are followed and reproduced, the aristocracy will de facto, and not just de jure, count for more than peasants.

The relevant "more than" relation has nothing to do with a mode of valuation like price or exchange-value, in which items stand in a quantitatively expressible ratio. Rather, it involves saying that some people are worthy to be attended to before others. Metaphors of height capture the effect of doing this: those deemed worthy of more urgent respect are elevated over those considered later (if at all); those whose presence or claims are deemed non-urgent, trivial, or ignored entirely are in effect demoted in significance. The contempt suffered by the latter reflects their being "brought low." Attentional priority materializes as hierarchy.

In this sense, I think Waldron is entirely correct to see a systematic relationship between respect, dignity, and rank.[9] Our concept of respect has evolved far beyond its origins in hierarchical social practices and has now become a psychological category used to describe a very broad set of individual dispositions. Yet it retains, at its core, a concern with priority, preemption, relative urgency, and precedence. Its tendency is always to compare its objects along some such dimension of relative attentional importance. It is in this dimension that respect, and the form of attention it recruits, is *paid*.

To my mind, the fact that we do not speak of "high" love indicates that any comparative evaluations involved in love are not matters of attentional precedence. One might doubt this on the grounds that to love a person surely is to be disposed to attend to them before those whom I do not love. There is obviously a sense in which this is true: the special significance my children, parents, friends, and intimate partners hold for me entails that they loom larger in my circle of concerns than do other people. And certainly, I routinely give far more attention to them than others. But again, it is not the quantum, but the quality, of attention involved that differentiates love and respect. As I have suggested, the notions of priority and precedence, central to the disposition of respect, apply when one is conscious that something must yield to something else. This feature is absent in the case of love.

In attaching great significance to those whom I love, I am not, nor should I be, conscious of resolving a conflict in anyone's or something's favor. To love a person is not to see them as the victors in a competition for my attention. Much as Velleman says, it is rather to be affected such that one finds oneself emotionally vulnerable to them in a way in which one delights. Love represents the welcome intrusion of a care for someone or something beyond oneself, such that one is disposed to integrate them into the central animating concerns of one's life.

The leading metaphors for the resulting forms of mutual adjustment are thus not those of altitude, rank, of up and down, inferiority and superiority,

---

[9] Waldron, *Dignity, Rank, and Rights.*

and so on, but rather those of lateral inclusion and incorporation. It is thus not comparative precedence that is central in love, but comparative closeness, nearness, and distance. But in both cases one is comparing people to each other, (on the one hand) as more or less distant, and (on the other) as commanding greater or lesser attentional precedence in various contexts.

That is not to say that the sort of attentional precedence implicated in respect is obviated by or somehow transcended in love. I may have to choose between acting for the sake of my daughter or for the sake of her brother. In the moment, the needs of one may have to yield to the other. The presence of mutual love changes the character of relationships in a fundamental way, but it cannot abolish attentional conflicts that arise routinely in ordinary life. To respect well those whom I love, I may need to reckon first with the more immediately urgent needs of one of the parties. I also may come to have higher respect for the moral character of one person whom I love than I do for another. And I may, if my judgment falters, inadvertently (and sometimes even quite deliberately) disrespect those I love by failing to give due attentional precedence to their claims.

The fact that these conflicts must be resolved against the background of love means merely that our judgments about how to do so will be freighted with greater personal significance. It may call for some modification in the manner in which we respect the relevant parties. And that underlines an important point: these modes of valuation (along with others – trust, hope, utility, etc.) coexist side by side and indeed claim some right to condition and control each other. This is particularly true of love and respect, given the second-order character that Velleman rightly ascribes to them. Both love and respect involve dispositions to suppress other affects (self-concern, deference, detachment). This mutual conditioning can create the illusion of some independent evaluative dimension within which love and respect are hierarchically ranked relative to each other. I suspect this is what lends Anderson's "mode-hierarchy" proposal a residual plausibility. But, at least on the account I am offering, there is no such independent medium of valuation, only the complex interaction of mutually referential second-order affects, each of which recruits attention in ways that determine how some matter compared to others.

Recognition-Respect as Comparative

The start of this chapter referenced Stephen Darwall's famous distinction between "two kinds" of respect, and some may suspect that I am overlooking the noncomparative quality of what he calls "recognition-respect." I deny, however, that recognition-respect is noncomparative. While Darwall's distinction is both real and important, it does not entail that appraisal-respect is comparative while recognition-respect is not. The reason for this is that the dimension of attentional precedence identified here and the interpersonal comparisons it automatically implies play a role in both.

Consider a speaker who reports their "high" appraisal-respect for an expert, a person's achievements, or someone's character. It is true that such cases need not be ones, like that of the lady and the peasant, requiring a decision about what to do; they are therefore distinct from situations calling for recognition-respect, in which agents deliberate about how to treat someone. Equally, however, appraisal-respect must involve more than just the appraisals on which it is based. I award a student an A+ because I rate her performance outstanding; I regard Tiger Woods as one of the most accomplished golfers ever to have played; I admire Barack Obama more than Donald Trump. These are certainly all appraisals, and they may ground appraisal-respect, but no element of respect is yet present; in making them, I have done nothing more than evaluate people in relation to some standard of merit. What is missing is the disposition to pay these people greater and lesser attention *given* our appraisals of them.

For example, if I say that I respect A's expertise on some subject more "highly" than B's, because I appraise it as greater than B's, the implication is that across cases in which they give conflicting advice, my tendency is to let A's judgments preempt B's, or to defer to A's *before* B's. One who says that they have high "appraisal-respect" for C's character is not just saying that they admire C but that they are disposed to (as we say) "have more time for them" than less accomplished others. Conversely, I might report my vanishingly low appraisal-respect for D by saying "I have no time for D – he's a total shit." It is instructive to reflect on what is implicit in such claims. I parse them thus: if D were competing for my attention with E, I would be disposed to attend to E first because whoever/whatever it is, E is unlikely to be as unworthy of my time and attention as excrement. Notice, too, that it is because time and attention are scarce resources that "having time for someone" in these formulae implicitly connotes payment, a willingness to forfeit something of value to oneself.

The attentional precedence recruited in appraisal-respect therefore plainly involves an element of comparative valuation. To see why this is also true of recognition-respect, albeit in a different way, note that appraisal-respect typically presupposes the presence of at least three parties, two (or more) of whom are implicitly compared to each other by the respecter. That is, in appraisal-respect, there is usually at least: (1) the respecter, (2) someone the respecter is disposed to give a certain degree of attentional precedence because of their appraisal of them, and (3) someone else whom the respecter is implicitly disposed to give greater, equivalent, or lesser attention because they appraise them more or less highly. In these cases of appraisal-respect, the comparative quality of the judgments is plain to see, because the respecter's disposition toward one person stands alongside her disposition toward another.

This comparative element is obscured, but not eliminated, in the contrasting case of recognition-respect. Since recognition-respect requires only two parties – the respecter and the respected – it looks at first glance as if it cannot be comparing the latter to anyone else. Darwall says that our entitlement to basic recognition-respect is the entitlement "to have other persons take seriously and weigh appropriately the fact that they are persons in deliberating about what to do." Darwall is certainly correct that notion of "degrees" of respect is not in point here. If all persons *as such* are owed such respect, the only relevant question appears to be whether others give them that respect or don't. Your entitlement to my recognition-respect would remain even if you are the only other person in my world.

Yet it simply does not follow from any of this that the targets of recognition-respect are not compared with anyone else, because there is always at least one other party involved, namely the respecter. When we say that recognition-respect requires me to "take seriously and weigh appropriately the fact that you are a person," part of what we mean is that I can't simply ignore your claims just because it would be personally convenient. A disposition to deliberate appropriately about what difference your presence makes to my choices is a disposition to measure the relative urgency of my own interests (my self-concern, desires, plans, and projects) against the claims you make on my attention.

Recall here Velleman's analysis of respect as a second-order emotion which, it should be emphasized, is mainly intended to capture just the sort of unconditional recognition-respect for persons currently under discussion. His telling description of respect as "arresting" motives of self-concern highlights exactly the comparative element I seek to expose, even though it points away from his own interpretation of respect as attunement to an "incomparable" worth inherent in other persons. For Velleman's account reminds us that attentional precedence persists in recognition-respect in the form of preemption.

Insofar as its "arresting" effect kicks in when one agent encounters another, it will at least cause the respecter to consider whether the latter's presence requires any change in his own plans. And, in at least some cases, an agent's self-concern must yield to the other's legitimate claims if they are to respect them: when that is so, the respecter must postpone, modify, or even abandon their original plans in order to treat the respectee appropriately. In consciously adjusting themselves to others on these terms, sometimes forfeiting personal advantage for the sake of another, respecters make implicit judgments about when another person's claims should take precedence over their own. These judgments in effect determine whose demands matter more when they conflict in a specific situation. There is clearly an implicit comparative element in this, which becomes explicit when we describe a person who violates others' entitlements, that is, fails to show them appropriate recognition-respect, as "placing themselves above" the victim (*"who do you think you are?"*). And, as we have seen, recognition-respect often requires, and is shown in, the respecter's willingness to forfeit something of value to them. Where this is the case, paying respect requires a double payment – of attention and of some personal advantage forgone.

Catallaxies of Respect and Disrespect

To be sure, a one-off payment of recognition-respect, or its nonpayment on a particular occasion, won't usually be dispositive of how someone matters in any definitive, once-and-for-all, sense.[10] Yet, insofar as such performances of respect and disrespect actually take place, they become part of the record, indelible events in the life-narratives of those involved. They attest to facts about one agent's actual impact on another in a specific transaction: where things went well, that they counted for something in the eyes of another; where they went wrong, that they failed to count for much, if anything.

Even if (as profound disrespect often does) they involve violence, these catallactic repercussions are not fundamentally Newtonian or ballistic. As we saw in Chapter 11, they are mediated by the conscious attitudes recruited in the particular affective modes involved. As agents trigger (or fail to trigger) the affect of respect ("arrested" self-concern) in others, the resulting encounters make manifest, to both participants and observers, how the relevant parties matter relative to each other. This is so because respect functions in these contexts as a currency of relative valuation, establishing a baseline of expectation and conditioning the terms on which conscious mutual adjustment occurs. Just as financial valorization schemes determine who counts for us as bankrupt, so the respectful and disrespectful quality of agents' conscious mutual adjustment tells us something about how one person counted relative to another in the relevant transactions. Although no single such transaction is likely to make all the difference, in principle any of them can determine something about a person's timanthropic career.

This point can be supported by reflecting on a phenomenon that is otherwise difficult to explain: the sense of shame, humiliation, and even embarrassment that typically attends victims' attitudes to past mistreatment and abuse. On the face of it, this is not what one might expect. Surely it is only the perpetrator who should be ashamed: why should their innocent victims feel shame as well? Of course, one way to account for such reactions is simply to assimilate them to those cases in which a powerful emotion induces an irrational response – as when someone who is perfectly comfortable riding in a car is paralyzed by a fear of flying. On this response, victims have no real

---

[10] As I noted in Chapter 10, valorization need not be once-and-for-all, but an iterating cycle.

reason to feel ashamed and humiliated, but as a psychological matter, the traumatic emotions triggered by abuse will predictably induce these irrational feelings.

Such a response is superficial. Noting that torture "is the most horrible event a human being can retain within himself," Jean Améry observed that "whoever has succumbed to torture can no longer feel at home in the world. The shame of destruction cannot be erased."[11] Or as he more succinctly put it: "whoever was tortured, stays tortured."[12] Primo Levi agreed, quoting the latter remark in *The Drowned and the Saved.* When Levi committed suicide in 1987, Elie Wiesel commented that he had "died in Auschwitz 40 years later." These comments draw attention to an enduring change in victims' perceptions of how they fit into the world. Those perceptions are not plausibly histrionic projections of emotionally unhinged individuals, but rather reflect a deeply disconcerting, yet entirely reasonable, realization about the terms on which they relate to their fellows.

Susan Brison, an American philosopher who was raped and left for dead by an assailant while traveling in France in 1990, similarly claims that we should not focus only on the immediate physical and emotional trauma of violence. She writes:

> That's not all there was to my experience of rape. . . . What's missing is that "aha" moment of realizing *this is what I was warned about since childhood.* What's missing is that realization that *this man hates women* or, at least, doesn't consider them worthy of respect and concern. What's missing is the expressive component of the rape that echoes and amplifies and propagates the sexist messages one has already heard all one's life.
>
> That expressive component of rape is there whether or not the rape is accompanied, as it's so likely to be, by misogynistic sexual slurs. And when it is, it's not the first time one's heard these slurs, but hearing them – whispered or shouted – while being raped gives them increased power to harm, not only during the rape, but also in its aftermath.[13]

The "aha" moment Brison describes refers to an abrupt and searing loss of innocence about one's place in a social world, one that will strike a chord with anyone who has suffered serious abuse. Here, the epistemic connotations of the word innocence are important: to be innocent of something is to lack full cognizance of it and its significance. As Brison suggests, at one level, no woman in our society can be unacquainted with sexism. But when it materializes in the

---

[11] Améry, *At the Mind's Limits*, p. 40.

[12] Ibid., p. 34.

[13] Susan J. Brison, "Why Rape is not 'Sex without Consent,'" unpublished manuscript presented to a conference at the University of Virginia, April 2016, on "Yes, No and Beyond: Consent and Coercion in the Sexual Sphere." I am grateful to Susan for granting me permission to use this passage.

form of direct, violent, abuse, victims are viscerally confronted with the forms of power and domination latent in sexist conditions. Such abuse harshly exposes a truth about how such conditions conserve dispositions to devalue other human beings; the victim becomes, in effect, the medium in which that truth is demonstrated.

Améry captured this revelatory quality when he claimed that the "knowledge" that the tortured acquire from their experience is "that of a great amazement and a foreignness in the world that cannot be compensated by any subsequent communication. Amazed, the tortured person experienced that in this world there can be the other as absolute sovereign, and sovereignty revealed itself as the power to inflict suffering and destroy." As the perpetrator "boundlessly asserts himself through torture," the victim learns "that a living person can be transformed ... thoroughly into flesh, and by that, while still alive, be partly made into a prey of death."[14] In the evident gratification of another's desires at one's own expense, one comes to matter only as matter. This is a metaphor, to be sure, but it is not mere spin. It loyally captures what the transaction accomplishes: a form of social death.

I also doubt that one can plausibly attribute victims' subsequent sense of shame and humiliation to an "injury to self-respect" that such abuse inflicts. Perhaps influenced by Rawls's thought that "self-respect" has "social bases," many today seem tempted by such a diagnosis. But in the comments cited earlier, Brison, Améry, and Wiesel don't come across as people who have lost their self-respect. They give no indication, for example, that their experiences have left them any less inclined to condemn, resent, denounce, or openly protest against torture, rape, persecution, domestic abuse, and so on. If anything, exactly the opposite is true – their self-respect is quite plainly intact enough to motivate their indignation and active resistance on behalf of other victims, past, present, and future. After all, many of those who have suffered such abuse not only become such activists but also take justifiable pride in being so. Yet it is equally plain that this sort of pride and self-respect does not diminish the enduring sense of humiliation engendered by their experiences.

The reason why shame and humiliation can coexist with even very robust self-respect was suggested already in Chapter 6. Self-respect is a reflexive attitude, a "technique of the self" in which agents refuse to deny the legitimacy of their own claims to rightful treatment or to compromise their inward integrity in other ways. But the humiliating quality of disrespectful abuse is a function of what it accomplishes outwardly – it is in this external sphere that respect and disrespect are performative. Disrespectful abuse need not impair agents' capacity to respect themselves (though it may in fact do so in some cases), but it must expose their powerlessness in relation to the perpetrators, at least in the events constituting the abuse. For, at least if the account developed

---

[14] Améry, *At the Mind's Limits*, pp. 39–40.

here is right, it just *is* such powerlessness. In a way that is accessible to anyone who knows the facts and has the basic concept of respect as attentional precedence, such abuse manifests a victim's inability to activate the arresting, inhibitory affect of respect in the perpetrator. The subjugation and defeat it achieves become stigmata marring the history of the victim's entanglements with other human beings. This, I believe, is the most plausible explanation for the otherwise puzzling sense of shame and humiliation that victims of abuse characteristically report.

We see this in a milder form even in the case of love and its failure. That we normally feel embarrassed when we have to disclose a separation, a divorce, a break-up, or the rebuff of unrequited love, suggests that we have some reason to be embarrassed. I submit that it is the revelation of impotence that explains this: the inability, or loss of the power, to affect another such that they want to (continue to) take us in.[15] What is at stake here is the fuzzy boundary, drawn in different ways in different cultures, that divides friendship, companionship, or intimacy from estrangement, isolation, and ostracism. When people approach that boundary and are pushed away, or cross into it and are then later expelled, the feelings of rejection and humiliation are often profound. But it is neither the inward unpleasantness nor the intensity of these feelings that matter, but the fact that the feelings are themselves warranted in the light of external events. Their warrant derives from our tacit acceptance of love as a mode of personal valorization. The metaphor of being "dumped" makes sense to us in the light of that acceptance, and confessing it to others invariably involves an element of "shameful revelation."[16] While, in the nature of the phenomenon, it is not a *culpable* failure, it is nonetheless a failure to matter. It is a stigma, a blot on the narrative record, exposing damage to a life. The counterpart forms of indignity accomplished by abusive disrespect are both more serious and politically pertinent.

These aspects of respectful or disrespectful transactions will tend to be underemphasized, and even go unnoticed, by dignity-traditionalists intent on recruiting dignitarian categories to account for our ordinary notions of wrongdoing and moral responsibility. As we noted in Chapter 2, to think about dignity and respect from that angle is to involve them in a particular philosophical research program, concerned primarily to explain how individuals are

---

[15] Marx famously said that "if you love without evoking love in return – if through the vital expression of yourself as a loving person you fail to become a loved person, then your love is impotent, it is a misfortune." This formulation is however partly misleading. It suggests that it is the potency of one's love that is on the line. Yet no one wants to be loved for their own love; and the bare fact of Y's love for X is no reason for X to love Y. One hopes, rather, to be loved for who one is, for one's own sake. It is one's *own* potency that is implicated. Whence the humiliating sting of rejection of love.

[16] I take this phrase from Jo Wolff. See Jonathan Wolff, "Fairness, Respect, and the Egalitarian Ethos," *Philosophy & Public Affairs* 27, no. 2 (1998): 97–122.

morally accountable for their voluntary actions. Inquiry along these lines will quite naturally focus on the question of when individuated actions or action-types (coercings, thefts, arrests, punishments, lies, threats, offers, etc.) are justified, permissible, required, obligatory, forbidden, or excused. Yet nothing in the sophisticated and, I believe correct, phenomenologies of recognition-respect suggested by Darwall and Velleman forces one to orient dignitarian humanism in this traditional direction.

Darwall's emphasis on the deliberative element in recognition-respect may seem to suggest otherwise. If recognition-respect is a matter of "deliberating properly" about what to do, one might think, its importance in political judgment can only reflect a concern with the moral probity of individual decision-making. Certainly, deliberative consideration of others' legitimate moral claims is a vital token of respect with great political significance. But this need not be the only way in which the affective mode of respect matters politically, and an important and often overlooked feature of Darwall's own construal of recognition-respect explains why. For, despite his emphasis on deliberation, he is careful not to identify recognition-respect straightforwardly with deliberative propriety; rather, as he rightly says, recognition-respect is a *disposition* to deliberate appropriately about the claims of other parties.

This feature of his view fits readily into the revisionist approach recommended here. Once they appreciate that recognition-respect consists in dispositions to give, or not give, deliberative consideration to others, dignitarian humanists need not focus exclusively, or even primarily, on the justifiability of particular voluntary actions from a moral point of view. They might attach as much, if not greater, importance to two further, and closely related, ways in which the presence or absence of those dispositions might condition political relationships.

One is that different agents, either (or both) because of their personalities or because of their social and political circumstances, may be more and less disposed to give others due consideration – as Darwall acknowledges when he notes that one can be a "greater and lesser respecter of persons." The other is that the same agents may be disposed to deliberate properly about some people but not others. The earlier mentioned case of the gentleman and the slave illustrates that latter possibility. The gentleman is disposed toward his fellow non-slaves such that he recognizes that their legitimate claims limit how he may treat them. Insofar as he and other "respectable" members of society mostly enact that disposition in their dealings with each other, they adjust to each other on a footing of mutual respect. They reliably pay each other respectful heed, are willing to accord attentional precedence to the claims of their fellows over their own, and are prepared to sacrifice something they would otherwise wish to obtain as a token of that respect. However, they are not so disposed toward those they identify as slaves. Those conventionally regarded as fit only for slavery rarely trigger in them the second-order affect of respect; they lack the power to reliably "arrest" the self-concern of the privileged.

No doubt such privations of respect will materialize in specific mistreatment committed by particular agents (acts of cruelty and humiliation; ruthlessly exploitative agreements and coerced cooperation, whether undertaken for commercial advantage or personal gratification; gross lack of consideration; etc.). Judging the moral culpability of those involved, if that is what one is interested in doing, requires one to atomize these forms of disrespect into discrete individual actions. I doubt that one needs the concept of dignity to do this; the wrongness of the relevant acts is uncontroversial and anyway massively overdetermined. Yet, even if one does, it still wouldn't follow that the broader phenomena they represent must be so atomized. They can also be viewed holistically, as endemic to the total social situation in which individuals under particular historical conditions find themselves. Where, as in a slave-owning society, these performances of respect and disrespect are systematically uneven and selective, they permit a more general diagnosis of a whole regime. Such inconsistencies represent an overall pattern of conscious mutual adjustment in which some members of society come to matter comparatively more than others.

I contend that it is only under this wider optic that the concept of human dignity can find its feet as an agent of political criticism. The hard work of the last two chapters has demonstrated that while preserving the sophisticated characterizations of respect offered by Velleman and Darwall, we can begin to think about the emergence and protection of human dignity as depending on these patterns of respectful or disrespectful mutual adjustment. It remains to specify the alternative conception of human dignity toward which this account points, and to see how it might usefully inform critical reflection on politics.

13

Human Dignity

So far, this book has said a great deal about what human dignity is not, or, at any rate, how we *shouldn't* think about it. I have denied that it is helpfully construed as an inherent possession of the person, an inward attribute revealed in conscious introspection, an existential identity or uniqueness, a quasi-juridical status, a form of authority or personal sovereignty, a generic "purposiveness," or an inalienable quality that never changes. If human dignity is none of these things, then what would a more compelling conceptualization of it look like? Is any cogent and politically useful account of human dignity left?

I have yet to give any clear answer to this crucial question. To be sure, several hints have been given along the way. I have said that the needed construal would likely fall somewhere in the neighborhood of D-dignity in our fourfold typology, because the latter combines the idea that human dignity is transient and vulnerable with the assumption that it is ambient in social relations rather than lodged inherently in the person. Chapter 7 suggested that whatever human dignity is, the imaginary *eloian* society I described there lacks it in any rich or vital form. And I have suggested that we think of it as a "real abstraction" in something like the sense that Marx thought that "abstract labor" crystallizes as a ruling principle of economic cooperation in the concrete elaboration of capitalist commodity-exchange. Yet, so stated, these pieces of the puzzle are at best suggestive. The time has come to move beyond these gestures and to elaborate them more precisely. To do this, I start in what may at first seem an incongruous place, and persist a little longer with the analogy I have been drawing between dignitarian humanism and economic modes of analysis.

Hayek on Information

To drop traditional accounts of human dignity in favor of the revisionist approach suggested here is to take a theoretical step formally akin to that Hayek took in rejecting excessively abstract models of a commercial economy. The target of Hayek's critique was the tendency, if anything more prevalent today than when he was writing, for economists to assume that agents interacting on the market already possess all pertinent information about what goods it is worth their while to obtain. He accepted that if one makes that assumption – that the relevant knowledge is simply "given" because market entrants have "perfect information" – one can formalize the operation of competitive markets and logically derive their conditions of equilibrium. Yet Hayek insisted that the "tautological propositions of pure equilibrium analysis as such are not directly applicable to the explanation of social relations."[1] His reason for thinking this is that purely formal analyses give a highly unrealistic, and essentially static, picture of an economy in which all agents are "price takers" – the economist's equivalent of an abstract Kantian "kingdom of ends," in which the value of persons is taken as given and cannot change.

Hayek's complaint against comparably idealized economic models was their inability to take seriously the *dynamic* nature of actual economic cooperation. In order for an economy "to secure the best use of resources known to any of the members of society, for ends whose relative importance only these individuals know,"[2] it must develop a mechanism that allows agents to respond intelligently and rapidly to "changes in particular circumstances of time and place."[3] This he regarded as the main "economic problem";[4] but because purely formal economic models of the economy solve it by stipulation, they cannot in his view offer any real insight into the solution that competitive markets actually afford in practice.

Commentators sometimes represent Hayek's argument on this point as turning on the claim that, because it is dispersed across an unimaginably complex scheme of cooperation, the information needed for rational economic decisions is essentially local. But, while not wrong, this construal is importantly misleading. Despite his reputation as a theorist of "local knowledge," Hayek denied that decentralizing economic decision-making is by itself sufficient to solve the "economic problem," for (as he put it) "the 'man on the spot' cannot decide solely on the basis of his intimate but limited knowledge of the facts of his immediate surroundings." This local knowledge won't give him enough to "fit his decisions into the whole pattern of changes of the larger economic system."[5] Hayek therefore does *not* conceive of economic rationality as inherently local: the important question for him is how economic agents communicate to each other the further, nonlocal, information required to bring about a propitious, system-wide, reconciliation of their constantly shifting plans. Hayek thinks of the economy as a single extended web that continuously reconfigures itself in response to myriad local changes. If the equilibrium of

---

[1] F. A. von Hayek, "Economics and Knowledge," *Economica* 4, no. 13 (1937): 35.
[2] Hayek, "Use of Knowledge," 520.
[3] Ibid., 524.
[4] Ibid.
[5] Ibid., 525.

the whole is to be maintained, however, individuals need information about these changes even when they occur at very distant nodes in the web.

He attributed the practical achievement of this sort of order to the "price system," a shared, yet spontaneously arising, scheme of economic valorization that (in his view) facilitates the efficient coordination of independent commercial activity. The operation of the "price system" makes such an order possible even though the information required to bring it about "is not given to anyone in its totality."[6] According to Hayek, this is because price variations inform agents about pertinent changes in economic circumstances that occur beyond their immediate locales, and of which they would therefore otherwise be unaware. When he described prices as "quantitative indices (or 'values') in which all relevant information is condensed,"[7] the information to which he is referring is precisely *not* local. His point is that the price system permits adaptive coordination *across* locales without central planning, not that such systemic coordination is unnecessary or undesirable.

Hayek's understanding of the "economy of knowledge" may seem a strange place from which to illuminate a conception of human dignity fit to inform critical reflection on politics. Yet my proposal shares several key features of his approach, while also being instructively different; understanding these similarities and differences will therefore help to specify how revisionists might best understand human dignity.

Price and Dignity Revisited

I begin by noting two clear differences, both of which help keep the price/dignity distinction intact. First, Hayek is theorizing something – price – that everyone recognizes is a quantitative dimension of valuation. The valuations made in respect and love, however, cannot be quantified, and while they reflect dynamic interaction, they don't emerge from anything like a commercial market in which items are bought, sold, or traded (see Chapter 8). Still, as Chapter 12 stressed, that doesn't mean that they are noncomparative. If my arguments there are right, love compares people as more and less distant relative to one another, while respect recruits interpersonal comparisons of precedence.

Second, like most defenders of commercial society, Hayek presses his case on behalf of individuals seeking to promote their private interests. Agents after all engage in economic cooperation for mutual advantage; they are motivated only by an expectation that it will advance their respective ends. Prices are important according to Hayek because they provide agents with information they need to plan how best to do that. His famous conclusion that the guidance

[6] Ibid., 520.
[7] Ibid., 525–26.

of the price system must outperform all efforts at "central planning" is thus broadly consequentialist in spirit: it turns on the claim that the price system serves the instrumental needs of private individuals and organizations better than any alternative mode of economic coordination. According to Hayek, competitively determined prices communicate information without which agents cannot efficiently adjust their independent plans, either to each other, or to the changes to which economic cooperation is constantly subject.

Although I have been arguing that tokens of love and respect also serve as informational vectors, apprising agents of their affective impact on each other, both the type of information they convey and the nature of agents' interest in it must differ from anything postulated in Hayek's theory. Most importantly, our interest in love and respect is not plausibly instrumental, certainly not exhaustively so. Agents do, and should, care that others love and respect them, but not only, or mainly, because these attitudes (and any information they convey) are merely "means" for the advancement of their independently chosen ends. They enter at a deeper level into our very conception of what ends are worth pursuing. Love and respect aren't just strategies for getting what we want, but modes of relating to others that we live *for*.

Some social scientists have been tempted to reduce the way such affects actually figure in human life to a kind of cost–benefit analysis; a particularly clear example is the sociological "Exchange Theory" pioneered in the 1950s and 1960s by George Homans and Peter Blau, still quite influential today. Exchange theorists – Blau especially – have certainly offered some astute insights into affects like love and respect.[8] But more often than not, their work serves only to underline the mismatch between the model of commercial exchange and the plane of concern on which love and respect move. Witness the following recent remarks from three proponents of the theory:

> Social Exchange theories all share the basic premise that people tend to initiate, develop, and maintain relationships that are profitable in that the rewards gained from the relationship outweigh the costs. That is, people in relationships have a metaphorical spreadsheet in which relational credits and debits are tabulated, and future profits are forecast. People are satisfied with their relationships when the rewards exceed the costs, and they continue in those relationships where investments lead to projected future profit.[9]

---

[8] George C. Homans, "Social Behavior as Exchange," *American Journal of Sociology* 63, no. 6 (1958): 597–606; Peter Michael Blau, *Exchange and Power in Social Life* (New Brunswick, NJ: Transaction Books, 1986).

[9] T. R. Levine, S. Kim, and M. Ferrara, *Social Exchange, Uncertainty, and Communication Content as Factors Impacting the Relational Outcomes of Betrayal Human Communication.* A Publication of the Pacific and Asian Communication Association. Vol. 13, No. 4, p. 306.

I can only say that I hope (for their sake) that these authors do not actually relate to their friends, spouses, lovers, and children on anything like these terms.

So, although previous chapters have emphasized that respect involves "payments" of attention, our interest in those payments (*pace* the Exchange Theorists) is plainly not well rendered in a consequentialist idiom of instrumental rationality, costs, and benefits. To this extent, theorists like Kateb are correct to think of dignitarian concerns as having an "existential" dimension. Yet, this book has also argued that translating such "existential" concerns into the currently fashionable idiom of "identity" is equally unhelpful. As we noted in Chapters 4 and 6, when combined with a traditional "reactive" understanding of dignity and respect, this translation creates a dilemma. If the locus of dignity is some identity trait that commands due recognition and respect, we need to know what that trait is, and this is where the trouble starts. Wolterstorff and others are right that thinning out these qualifying identity traits so that they are genuinely inclusive tends to denude them of any significant practical force; conversely, construing them more thickly courts a trait-racism that sabotages the dignitarian aspiration to encompass a common humanity.

To better capture what Kateb calls the "existential" aspect of human dignity while resisting any temptation to instrumentalize respect, dignitarian humanists need a quite different approach. It is at this point, I think, that Hayek's "catallactic" framework offers dignity-revisionists some useful help.

I have already alluded to a relevant overlap between them: both dignity-revisionists and Hayek refuse the assumption that the values which their respective theories are concerned are settled and known in advance of social interchange. The first part of this book roundly rejected the traditional conception of dignity as a fixed worth whose immediate recognition calls forth a corresponding respect. The approach of dignity-revisionism is accordingly more Hayekian in spirit. We might say that, just as Hayek denied that market entrants are "price-takers," dignity-revisionists deny that we are "dignity-takers." The revisionist hypothesis is that human dignity is not an antecedent datum, but is rather continuously being *worked out*, and rendered more or less vital, in the course of historical interaction.

On this hypothesis, as Chapter 7 mentioned, respect is to dignity as love is to "dearness." For, it is absurd to suppose that a person's "inherent dearness" precedes and justifies others' love for them. It is rather that their dearness emerges, comes to life, and (alas) sometimes withers, according as others concretely engage with them in a certain spirit over time. The particular "lovable" qualities of a beloved cause their lovers to be affected by them in a characteristic way, triggering the exchange of performances and tokens of love whose significance as such is commonly understood.

Chapters 11 and 12 analyzed respect as a parallel currency by which agents can understand the import of various ways in which others attend to them. Like the signals sent by changing prices in Hayek's conception of economic cooperation, the circulation of commonly recognized tokens of respect and disrespect condition the terms on which agents consciously adjust to one another. They thereby communicate information about the impact of some lives on others, and by extension, about how their lives actually matter within their wider social forms. Viewed from this angle, then, the affective modes of love and respect are closely analogous to the price system as Hayek understood it. Each functions as a valorization scheme with its own logic, furnishing a distinctive point of view from which certain comparative value-judgments can be accredited on a commonly accessible basis. In all of these cases, moreover, that accreditation is not a presupposition, but rather an accomplishment, of actual mutual adjustment that is itself guided by the publicly accepted criteria of valorization implicit in each.

So, the core suggestion is that, in virtue of their recruitment of dispositions of respect, everyday interactive routines transmit socially valid information about how the agents and institutions involved "set value" on people and their lives. To embrace that suggestion is obviously not to assert that anyone's "identity" has an adamant claim on others' attention such that they have legitimate grounds for complaint whenever they judge (on what basis?) that it is not receiving the recognition and respect it is due. Nor does it entail that our interest in respect is instrumental in the way that Hayek takes the value of price information to be. Its main implication is rather that the significance of human dignity somehow reflects our stake in the information relayed in respectful or disrespectful interaction. Broadly: human dignity matters because its presence is a function of how we matter relative to each other, as publicly revealed in performances of respect and disrespect.

Of course, this doesn't yet explain exactly how concrete patterns of respect (or disrespect) constitute (or threaten) human dignity. And the noninstrumental character of our interest in the information communicated in such patterns remains to be clarified. Still, a broadly Hayekian approach at least allows the dignitarian humanist to drop the traditional assumption that human dignity is a preset value standing apart from the transactions of everyday life. It makes room for a construal of human dignity as an uncertain, vulnerable creature of those transactions, much as economic wealth depends for its emergence, maintenance, and expansion on the actual process of commercial exchange itself. At a first approximation, then, one might say that for revisionists human dignity is a form of timanthropic wealth or vitality; the question they wish to ask is how this sort of human wealth is, or is not, realized in social formations patterned by systematic respect or disrespect.

This leaves three outstanding questions for dignity-revisionists:

(a) So then what *is* human dignity, on the revisionist view?
(b) If it is not simply a means facilitating private planning, why is the information I am claiming respect communicates so important from a revisionist point of view?
(c) How do the answers to (a) and (b) explain how human dignity matters for political judgment?

The rest of this chapter proposes a revisionist answer to the first question. Chapters 14 and 15 address (b) and (c).

From Labor to Attention

For all his suspicion of dignitarian ideals, Marx, rather than Hayek, offers better guidance on the first question. Not surprisingly, however, transplanting the relevant Marxian claims into a dignitarian context requires significant modifications. Accordingly, I now follow up the proposal advanced in Chapter 10 that leading elements of Marx's value-theory can be adapted to derive a reformed account of human dignity.

Recall Marx's general thesis that the character of different "modes of production" depends on the way they socialize a completely universal "labour process." He defined that process as

> purposeful activity aimed at the production of use-values. It is an appropriation of what exists in nature for the requirements of man. It is the universal condition for the metabolic interaction between man and nature, the everlasting nature-imposed condition of human existence, and it is therefore independent of every form of that existence, or rather it is common to all forms of society in which human beings live.[10]

However, the "universal labor" to which Marx refers here is completely indeterminate. The particular forms that labor takes, the specific objects to which it is directed, the needs it seeks to fulfill, and (especially) how it is organized socially, depend for him on the historically specific relations of production that prevail in different epochs. As we saw in Chapter 10, Marx claimed that capitalist commodity-exchange accomplishes something that is in no way a necessary feature of human labor *as such* – its susceptibility to being quantitatively equated, so that "every particular kind of useful private labor can be exchanged with, i.e. counts as the equal of, every other kind of useful private labor." This equality "can be arrived at only if ... we reduce" productive effort to "human labor in the abstract."[11] This

---

[10] Marx, *Capital Vol. 1*, p. 290.
[11] Ibid., p. 166.

reduction is, for Marx, a uniquely capitalist achievement, albeit on his view one of doubtful value.

The details of how Marx thought Capital is valorized as "abstract labor" need not detain us. The interest of this Marxian argument for dignity-revisionists lies neither in its descriptive accuracy nor in its plausibility as a diagnosis of capitalism's failings. Indeed, there is no reason at all why they shouldn't accept Hayek's much more flattering portrayal. It is the *form* rather than the content of the Marxian argument that allows us to clarify, by analogy, the contours of a revisionist conception of human dignity. Building on the arguments of the previous chapters, I now elaborate that analogy.

In Marx, we have three terms (using "L" for "labor"):

(L1) The general, "everlasting" condition of a universal "labor process"
(L2) The particular logic of capitalist valorization, and the way it socializes (L1)
(L3) The way (L2) realizes "abstract labor" as the animating principle of commercial cooperation.

Incorporating the analysis of respect and attention from Chapters 11 and 12, I propose that dignity-revisionists similarly distinguish (using "D" for "dignity"):

(D1) the general condition of a self-conscious species whose members *attend* to each other through distinctive affective complexes (love, respect, honor, trust, etc.)
(D2) the specific form of human valorization accomplished (or not) through performances conducted in the affective mode of respect
(D3) the way (D2), as actually recruited in dominant social formations, realizes (or threatens) "human dignity" as a quality of those formations.

Two formal differences between the progression from (D1) to (D3) and Marx's original deserve comment before proceeding. First, as I mentioned in Chapter 10, whereas for Marx (L3) refers to a *defect* of the social phenomena under scrutiny, (D3) is concerned with a putatively desirable property of social relations.

Second, this proposal makes human dignity at once more and less "universal" than the categories implicated in the Marxian argument. It is *more* universal in that (D3) need not be exclusively concerned with any particular historically instantiated mode of life. "Abstract labor" is for Marx an exclusively capitalist creature; but the question posed in (D3) – to what extent does some social formation realize or threaten "human dignity?" – can in principle be addressed to *any* set of social practices, regardless of historical period.

On the other hand, (D1) refers to something *less* obviously "universal" than the "labor process" presupposed in (L1). Marx takes the latter to be imposed by nature. By contrast, in predicating dignity on the recruitment of interpersonal attention (as per (D1)), dignity-revisionism presupposes a level of self-consciousness that is not likely integral to all natural conditions of human existence. To be sure, Marx assumed that all human labor presupposes some awareness of a purpose, but that need not require any rarefied self-consciousness – even a Rousseauean savage can engage in rudimentary labor in Marx's universal sense. The capacity to avow, interpret, and care about, affects like love and respect, however, presupposes both amour-propre, and the development of linguistic capacities sufficient to grasp their meaning and operation.

This dependence on consciousness may seem to weaken the view; certainly Marxians with a strongly "materialist" bent will tend to resist it. Others may worry that to anchor the proposed account of dignity in historically contingent forms of affective consciousness is to build on a swamp. On the other hand, do dignitarians have a choice? I have argued since Chapter 2 that, on any realistic view, dignitarian ideas form an elaborate scheme of metaphors inherited from history and culture. Unless we want to resurrect strongly metaphysical or religious understandings of dignity as rooted somehow in a cosmic order, or as reflecting the relation of a created species to a divine creator, I see no option but to accept this circumstance. Earlier arguments suggest, moreover, that this need not be a damaging concession.

Chapter 3 argued, for example, that acknowledging the historically conditioned *origins* of these metaphors need not prevent one from *applying* them in a more universal way. Furthermore, the account of the affective modes of love and respect canvassed in the preceding pair of chapters is not obviously culturally parochial. To be sure, different cultures may recognize different tokens of love and respect; they may develop distinctive norms surrounding their expression; they may discriminate between their different forms in any number of ways; and their tendency to approve and disapprove of those forms may conflict with attitudes common at other periods and in different societies. Yet, while all of this must complicate efforts to negotiate and apprehend love and respect across cultural spaces, it's unlikely that these affects are culturally or historically idiosyncratic at any deep level. Were they so, we would be unable to interpret, for example, Aristotle, the Christian gospels, Lao Tzu, Chaucer, or Dostoyevsky as wrestling with challenges posed by friendship, honor, love, respect, and so on, that are immediately familiar to us all. Courtly love, chivalric honor, Confucian filial piety, the veneration of saints, genres of irreverent satire, newly developing forms of "polyamory," all recruit modes of respect and love in distinctive, sometimes transgressive, ways; yet these practices are intelligible at all only because our general concepts of these and other affects are sufficiently stable to be able to decode exactly how they do so.

That stability must then be anchored in at least some broadly shared assumptions about the character of these affects. As I have been arguing, dignity-revisionism mobilizes one of these basic assumptions about respect: that it conditions how we consciously attend to others for their own sakes. This, it maintains, is the key to the timanthropic intuition at the heart of dignitarian humanism – that the political importance of human dignity reflects the way the worth of people and their lives is at stake in the dominant routines and institutions of common life. It regards the affective mode of respect, and the conscious mutual adjustments that occur under its aegis, as specifying the form of personal worth involved. This sense of worth can indeed only get a grip after human societies have developed a consciousness of respect, honor, attentional precedence, personal and human dignity, and so on. But Rousseau was not wrong to think that a common affective psychology of amour-propre fuels virtually all forms of civilized life, and can hence serve as a general point of reference for understanding them.

In line with Marx's thought that the value relations typical of capitalist commodity-exchange are ultimately relations of social power, (D2) and (D3) similarly interpret the patterns in which human dignity consists as informing us about agents' de facto power to command certain forms of attention from each other. (D2) specifies the kind of attention involved as that associated with the affective mode of respect, understood in the way proposed in Chapters 11 and 12. That is, human dignity is a function of agents' de facto power to command in significant others attentional precedence. (D3) directs us to consider how pervasive social practices and institutions actually organize that power in particular historical contexts. Dignity-revisionism proposes that, taken together, (D2) and (D3) give human dignity a diagnostic significance in critical reflection on politics. They afford an angle from which we can ask how dominant routines, norms and institutionalized practices socialize (D1) in ways we should approve or regret.

Civility

On the view I am reconstructing, human dignity is neither something given in advance nor an ideal to be approximated or realized in the future. To be sure, the concept of human dignity is, from a revisionist perspective, an abstract metaphor that characterizes a general quality of social relations, but it doesn't for that reason refer to something unreal. To the contrary, although its presence may be more or less vital or tenuous under different circumstances, and individuals' lives denied a share in it, human dignity is a fully present *feature* of some actually existing social arrangements. Again, this parallels the way Marx intended the category "abstract labor." For, on his view, capitalist social relations *make it the case* that human labor is reduced to a quantifiable abstraction, and this is not for him just a philosophical interpretation. Marx's point, valid or not, is that capitalism *actually* transforms (vast numbers of) people into creatures whose lives, labor, vital energy and so on count de facto for little more than units of a uniform, measurable source of "value" that the economic system extracts as it appropriates for its own purposes the "surplus" they create.

Quite apart from any legitimate objections Marx's analysis of capitalism invites, however, "human dignity" has a significant advantage over "abstract labor" as a useful category in social criticism. "Abstract labor" is a technical term of Marx's devising (though he derived it from classical political economy) and is not in general use. Indeed, it is important for Marx that this is the case given his aim of exposing to view hidden aspects of commercial society that would otherwise go unnoticed and that ordinary language is hence unlikely to register.

(Human) dignity, and categories like respect and love, are however *not* technical terms. They carry with them rich and powerful metaphorical connotations familiar in ordinary use. This means that when it comes to recognizing how human dignity is ambient in social relations, we are fortunately not limited to terms provided by a highly esoteric philosophical system like Marx's. We can check our judgments against expectations that already form a part of our ordinary concepts of dignity, respect, and so on. With that in mind, consider some concrete examples that illustrate how well vernacular intuitions about human dignity align with the theoretical analysis suggested here. I will first look at circumstances prodigal in human dignity before turning to ones exemplifying its radical privation.

Consider first the most basic and inoffensive norms of civility that regulate any decent human interaction – what we often call "common courtesy." We shake hands, bow, or give people a cheery nod when we meet. We ask after their well-being ("how's it going?"), make polite requests, openly express gratitude for kindness, and are ready to apologize for any inconvenience caused. We acknowledge others' presence, visibly show them consideration ("is that your seat?"), signal that we aren't inclined to simply ignore them. We pretend not to notice their embarrassing facial tics, their speech impediments, the snot hanging from their nostril, and will inflict some pain on ourselves to try not to laugh. We form orderly queues, don't elbow our way to the front of the line, and gently enforce such expectations without humiliating people. Even when we are desperate to intervene in a conversation, we don't interrupt or shout others down. We try to be diplomatic and measured in criticism and are mortified by lapses in tact. We accept satire and irreverence, but only when it includes self-deprecation and steers clear of contemptuous scorn or incitement.

Most of us take these mundane expectations so much for granted that we scarcely notice how they impart a dignified quality to social life. The sense in which this is so will elude us to the extent that we adopt a moralistic outlook and focus only on individual acts of (in)civility that redound to agents' (dis)credit. Such judgments are of course perfectly legitimate, and indeed an integral aspect of civility itself – part of its "positive morality." Yet, as I have been arguing here, we don't have to view them exclusively from the perspective of captious insiders, intent on finding fault with their fellows. Nor, the Kantian tradition notwithstanding, does that perspective correspond to ordinary assumptions about how dignity is at stake in the maintenance of basic civility.

The notion that respect is "performative," central to dignity-revisionism, can also lead one astray here. For the Austinian focus on performative "speech-acts," might lead one to think that individuated specimens of respectful or disrespectful conduct must be the primary objects of criticism in this context.

The language of "performance" however need not imply this; some performances involve not only *concerted* social action (like many speech-acts), but also iterated routines that become ingrained in social practices. The norms and expectations of civility are a case in point. The dignity we intuitively discern in such routines is more than the sum of the individual actions constituting them. It is localized neither to individuated acts nor to the individuals to whom those acts respond, but manifests directly in the balance, reciprocity, proportion, and even grace of civilized mutual adjustment itself.

To be sure, maintaining such balance and decorum depends on individuals attending to each other in a certain spirit, and this might again lead one to suppose that the deliberative consideration agents give each other in deciding how to act must be the ultimate target of dignitarian concern. But this is not so. Civility requires that agents pay the relevant attention *as a matter of course.* This is a clear case in which Bernard Williams's famous precept about "One thought too many" applies. The dignity achieved in the basic routines of civility would immediately be stultified if the agents involved were engaged in constant self-conscious deliberation about whether they should jump the queue, ridicule someone's stammer, or punch them in the face for personal amusement. It would lend the whole practice of civility an insincere, calculated and forced quality that would precisely denude it of its value.[12] It is important for the vitality of human dignity that we can assume that, most of the time, abuse, cruelty, rape, torture, and so on are actions that it will never even occur to people might be worth considering.

And, in line with the more technical analysis of respect developed in this book, our ability to count on such civility pro forma corresponds to our de facto power to command attentional precedence from others. The dispositions of respect enacted in these routines attest to others' uncalculated willingness to "take trouble," to forfeit something of value to them for our sake. What is at stake is the power to affect others such that they are at least sometimes prepared to put us before themselves. When (see Chapter 10) Dickens has Blackpool complain that, in a class society, one "side" is "unnaturally and always forever right and the other unnaturally always and forever wrong,"

---

[12] Hayek approvingly cites Alfred Whitehead on this point: "It is a profoundly erroneous truism, ... that we should cultivate the habit of thinking what we are doing. The precise opposite is the case. Civilization advances by extending the number of important operations which we can perform without thinking about them." Hayek, "Use of Knowledge," 528.

what is in view is the way radical social imbalance disposes the powerful against taking the voices of the weak seriously.

The distention of social power to which *Hard Times* alludes so well exemplifies indignity in a sense loyal to both ordinary intuition and the more theoretical account developed in this book. For, on a revisionist analysis, such privations of dignity consist in systematic disparities in agents' powers to get others to pay them heed. This is to the detriment of a *human* dignity because there is nothing about any human being that disqualifies them from a reasonable share in these powers. But the presence, absence, or distribution of those powers is a relational circumstance subject to alteration. Contrary to dignity-traditionalism, human dignity construed in these terms is neither an immutable fact about something persons inherently possess nor an idealized relation of abstract equality. It is from start to finish a function of the social relations in which agents *actually* stand to each other in their form of life. As I will argue later, it is the locus of an irreducibly common responsibility.

Exploits and Professions

The case of everyday civility represents a low-intensity context in which human dignity is clearly discernible as an ambient property of social relations. Consider now more high-intensity circumstances in which respectful attention invigorates human dignity in some related but different senses. Think of orchestral musicians straining every sinew, every ounce of concentration and emotional energy, to bring off a superb performance of a masterwork before a rapt audience. Such occasions manifest human dignity in that everyone involved collaborates in a glorious exhibition of human creativity and self-expression. As the last chord fades away and roaring applause breaks out, we are amazed at ourselves and what we can accomplish together. The total event attests to humanity's remarkable capacity for self-inspiration, and intuitively this is an incident of human dignity. It is precisely the disinclination toward this sort of exploit that characterized the *eloi* introduced in Chapter 8. Their conception of human dignity seems limited and impoverished for that reason.

These judgments include elements of self-congratulation and pride – and, no doubt, imply a degree of contempt for the *eloians*. Some may find this disturbing. Yet the achieved splendor of a blistering concert, and that of other comparably ambitious ventures, is dignified precisely insofar as they come about through individual conduct purged of any narrow, preening, self-aggrandizement. What is required to bring human dignity to fruition in such ventures is precisely a respectful humility on the part of all involved. And again, this mobilizes the dispositions of attentional precedence that I have been emphasizing. To stick with the concert example, the musicians must respect the composer's intentions, take the musical integrity of the piece seriously, submit religiously to the conductor's beat, endure hours of tedious practice beforehand, train their fingers, lips, lungs, and vocal chords to make all kinds of unnatural and challenging moves, and so on. The audience must stay still and quiet, despite invariably cramped seating, not be distracted or a source of distraction, and so on.[13] Without active dispositions to pay such often onerous attention selflessly and generously, the power to realize human dignity in the form of such ennobling exploits must diminish.

The *eloians* represent a "sunset of mankind" because they have allowed that power to atrophy. But their problem is not one that can be meaningfully ascribed to the failure of individual *eloi* to conduct themselves as they should. As we pointed out in Chapter 8, the *eloi* recognize, and mostly comply with, some undemanding principles of mutual respect. That basic moral sensibility is far from worthless; but nor is it sufficient to make up the dignitarian deficit we notice in their society. The presence or absence of the powers on which human dignity, in this form as in others, depends cannot localized in that way. They are social powers; they can only be husbanded, exploited, or squandered in patterns of cooperation. Hence, any contempt the *eloians* invite on this score is not directed at anyone in particular; its object is an impoverished form of life.

Now consider another high-intensity case – that of doctors and nurses in an emergency situation. Their attention – here again likely taxed at a very high rate – will be primarily directed to the immediate needs of their patients. They must make constant, often very difficult, triage judgments about the relative urgency of different injuries and illnesses. They will often have to perform burdensome, unpleasant, procedures requiring undivided concentration. They may have to swallow their pride to follow rules and orders that best coordinate their various roles. In all of this, they are disposed to attend to themselves *last*. In cases of infectious disease, they incur considerable personal risk.

Ruskin noted that our ordinary sense of what makes professions honorable is the presumption that their practitioners may be called upon to *die* for those they serve: "the soldier's trade," as he rather bluntly put it, "... is not slaying, but being slain." Just as, on "due occasion" the soldier must be prepared to die "rather than leave his post," so the physician, the teacher, and the lawyer must be prepared to do so rather than "leave his post in a plague," "teach falsehood," or "countenance injustice."[14] Although Ruskin was exaggerating a bit, the underlying insight seems to me right. The disposition he is getting at – the willingness to let personal considerations be preempted by others to whom one gives greater attentional precedence – is not categorical devotion to an abstract moral principle. Ruskin is rather revisiting a Platonic insight about crafts, now

---

[13] Although in some cases active audience participation – dancing, showing visible signs of being moved, singing along, and so on, rather than just conforming to the bourgeois norm of the "concert-goer as impassive statue" – can be a form of respect that dignifies the occasion.

[14] John Ruskin, *Unto This Last, and Other Writings* (London: Penguin Books, 1985), pp. 175–76.

transplanted to the modern concept of a profession: that their integrity requires that practitioners accord the legitimate needs and interests of others' precedence over their own.

Although dedication, devotion to duty, the absence of self-servingness, heroism, and so on are in one sense individual virtues, they also have a close intuitive connection with human dignity, as Kateb rightly sees. But it is the dignity of neither the agent nor the patient that is named by that term in this context, still less that of the species *as such*. It is instead a quality that emerges symbiotically when the needs of some automatically activate these virtues in others, thereby causing the latter to attend to the former before themselves in some concrete, coordinated, interactive practice. To live with the assurance that there are institutions, professions, practices, and so on that reliably dispose agents to dedicate themselves to one's needs at some cost to themselves is to know something about what one counts for in one's society. To be worth a stranger's trouble to save, and to enjoy the power to get doctors, nurses, and so on to actually *take* that trouble when the need arises, is to share in an important aspect of human dignity. If one doubts this, consider circumstances in which hospitals reliably turn away dangerously ill patients because of their skin color, nationality, class, criminal record, inability to afford treatment, lack of health insurance, and so on.

Extreme Devalorization

I have described some ways in which human dignity in the revisionist sense is already ambient in routine social practices, and how well-established ordinary intuitions recognize it as such. Many other illustrations could be given. Such examples imply that although human dignity is for revisionists subject to attenuation and augmentation under different historical conditions, the transience they attribute to it is not such that it is in constant peril of disappearing completely from the human scene. To the contrary, our intuitive sense of what human dignity includes depends on its secure presence and regular manifestation in familiar social routines – like those of civility or professional life. Dignitarian metaphors ring true because they resonate with our ordinary acquaintance with these milieux.

So when revisionists describe human dignity as vulnerable and fragile, one must be careful to specify the sense in which this is so. It isn't one continuous thing, but a quality of social relations that shows up in distinctive forms in many different aspects of human life. It is *vulnerable* in the way that careers can be advanced or set back by luck, cultures go through periods of decadence and renewal, or prosperity is liable to economic shocks and bear markets. It is *fragile* in that its emergence in some human activities depends on social performances that are easily disrupted. In such cases, the relevant performances can avoid (what Austin called) "infelicity" only if stringent conditions (sincerity, the delicate coordination of multiple actions, high levels of concentration, etc.) are met. Many things may have to go right for performances to fully "come off," as the concert example illustrates very clearly. A cell-phone ringing at the crucial moment can ruin everything.

Insofar as they think of it as waxing and waning in various dimensions, revisionists might in principle think of human dignity as a value to be promoted in a way that may bear on political judgment. However, the natural orientation of dignitarian political concern is less toward the *promotion* of human dignity than towards its *privation*. The politically urgent cases are ones in which the performances on which human dignity depends fail in particularly serious or systematic ways. As earlier chapters emphasized, the concept of human dignity enters political discourse primarily as a way of marking practices to which we should be adamantly opposed – beyond all possible justification.

Revisionists and traditionalists can agree that the categorically objectionable abuses to which they wish to draw critical attention reflect radically deficient ways of valuing people. But they differ over how to understand the relevant deficiency. Traditionalists see it as a failure to respond to a dignity that is perennially present in all human beings *as such*. They therefore deny that human dignity could be a historical, narrative phenomenon. As one commentator has recently put it, "[t]he principle of human dignity, as a universal affirmation that human beings have the highest value, does not itself have a history, because a universal statement is meant to have limits neither in space nor in time."[15] To be sure, traditionalists allow that there *is* a history of efforts to grasp and apply that principle – a history of greater and lesser compliance with an unchanging expectation. Yet surely it is strange to reduce the protection of human dignity to a mere compliance problem, especially when this supposedly universal principle has conspicuously *not* been affirmed, let alone formulated, in all historical periods – to say nothing of the issue of how we determine what complying with it actually requires.

Revisionists find such efforts to read human dignity out of history fatuous. For them, the indignities that human beings can suffer involve more than a failure, on the part of some responsible agency, to perceive and respond appropriately to an ahistorical *datum*. They instead regard human dignity as ambient in various historically conditioned practices, but subject to actual deformation, even destruction, under oppressive, brutalizing, or degrading conditions. As we have seen, revisionists analyze such conditions as effecting the radical "devalorization" of some human beings relative to others. Such devalorization occurs when human lives lose the power to induce others to accord them the attentional precedence of respect.

---

[15] Mette Lebech, "What Is Human Dignity?," in *Maynooth Philosophical Papers*, ed. Mette Lebech (Maynooth: Maynooth University Press, 2004), pp. 56–69.

Valorization is an ugly word, and "devalorization" is worse. Stylistic draw-
backs notwithstanding, I maintain that on reflection the technical sense in
which revisionists intend these terms offers a far more credible diagnosis of the
gravest human indignities than can more traditional accounts. To see why,
consider the Nazi holocaust, which has become for us *the* standard archetype
for understanding privations of human dignity. The traditionalist view presumes that the perpetrators of the genocide knew, or should have known, that
all human beings are equal in basic dignity, and as such entitled de jure to
unconditional respect, always to be treated as "ends-in-themselves," and so on.
But this presumption, I want to suggest, creates a problem for traditionalist
efforts to diagnose phenomena like the holocaust. Their tendency is to reduce
the indignity of genocide to a vast agglomeration of separate acts of abuse, each
perpetrated by agents who overlooked or discounted the inherent, immutable,
dignity of their victims, and who therefore acted wrongly.

That the holocaust involved culpable wrongdoing on an industrial scale is of
course beyond dispute. These wrongs are of obvious importance from a moral
and legal point of view, and using standard Kantian language (and other
serviceable ethical idioms) to describe them is completely unobjectionable.
Intuitively, however, the difference between (a) genocidal circumstances and
(b) basically civilized or decent societies in which at least some crucial conditions of human dignity are routinely met can't just be a matter of the relative
frequency and concentration of wrongful acts. Murders, rapes, and violent
abuse regularly occur under civilized conditions, but a genocide is surely more
than just an exponentially magnified crime rate, or a sudden massive increase
in culpable wrongdoing. The point (obviously) is not that any number of
murders, rapes, or other violent offenses is acceptable, but rather that there
is a difference in kind, and not merely of degree, between social conditions that
tend to preserve human dignity and those that are absolutely toxic to it. The
problem for dignity-traditionalism is that it seems unable to capture this
difference-in-kind in any clear way. A revisionist account can do better.

As I have said, revisionists claim ((D2) mentioned earlier) that the patterns
in which human dignity consists reflect agents' de facto power to command
certain forms of attention, specifically, the power to command a certain
precedence in others' order of concerns. The question is ((D3)) how, in
particular historical contexts, pervasive social practices and institutions actually organize that power. Consider, from this point of view, the predicament
faced by those transported to Auschwitz, Treblinka, Sobibor, and other extermination camps in the 1940s.

The victims who were seized from their homes, shoved onto trains like
freight, and later separated at gunpoint from their loved ones and marched to
their deaths in gas chambers were stripped of virtually any power to affect
those determining their fates in ways that, under more civilized conditions, we
take for granted. In the treatment they received at the hands of those

controlling their destinies, one can find no trace of their lives or interests counting for anything, except perhaps as posing certain organizational challenges (e.g., how to herd them most efficiently through the assembly line of death; how to encourage their docility by installing dummy shower heads in the gas chambers; how to identify those with enough energy left to be fit for exploitation in running the camp until it was their turn to be exterminated; how to extract valuable resources from their personal effects, clothes, hair, and so on; how to dispose of the bodies at a fast enough rate).

These are the features that primarily shock the dignitarian sensibility of visitors to Auschwitz and of others acquainted with what happened there. Neither the sheer number of casualties nor the concentration of individually culpable acts, though of course terrible enough, can fully account for this: what strikes one most forcibly is a mode of subjugation from which any affects of humane attention have been totally erased. This circumstance constituted a radical social defeat, a social death worse than physical death: we recognize that the victims were utterly forsaken from the moment they were taken, and no longer had any hope of inducing any of the affects (and allied modes of attention and treatment) that enable people to share in human dignity.

To try to capture this phenomenon as a failure to recognize the "inherent dignity" of the victims is to imply that human dignity was there to be recognized all along. I think we must follow revisionists in rejecting that traditionalist implication: certainly, I can discern nothing of human dignity in the routine sequence of events that followed the arrival of the trains at the death camps. But to avoid misunderstanding, it is vitally important to appreciate exactly what this claim does and doesn't entail.

I stress in particular that in denying the presence of human dignity under these circumstances, the revisionist is making a claim only about the character of the social situation in which the victims found themselves and what it accomplished. The essential point is that the presence, absence, and character of human dignity in particular contexts like this one rests entirely on irreducibly social or relational facts. This revisionist commitment has two key implications.

The first is that the question of culpability for specific wrongs committed by those who participated in the holocaust moves on a different plane from that of genocide's character as a radical privation of human dignity. Not that revisionists regard judgments about culpability as any the less important. Their point is that because such judgments must be localized to specific actions, they can't tell us very much about the way human dignity is at stake, for the patterns of power in which it consists can be discerned only at a higher, nonlocal, scale. The revisionist strategy for preserving the difference-in-kind between a genocide and a mere accumulation of wrongs is then to separate two standpoints from which same phenomena can be analyzed; one is a moral or legal one, concerned with local culpability; the other is political, to do with the nonlocal disposition of social power. They maintain that human dignity, and the privations to which it is subject, are legible only in that second, higher-scale, frame of reference. The relationship between these two levels is like that between the shape of individual jigsaw-pieces and the image that is formed when the puzzle is completed. The topology of the pieces is local. The image is nonlocal. Although the jigsaw pieces make up the image, their shapes don't determine it. Similarly, although the holocaust comprised countless wrongful acts, the indignities it effected can be perceived only in larger structural patterns.

The second implication preempts a likely objection; understanding why that objection is misguided will clarify why "valorization" plays an ineliminable role in the revisionist position. The objection is this. Suppose we agree with revisionists that human dignity is determined socially, and that under radically brutalizing conditions like the holocaust, it effectively disappears. Aren't we then committed to saying (absurdly) that the victims were worthless?

Not at all: the reply is that judgments about human dignity reflect *a* dimension in which human beings can gain or lose value relative to each other; but to focus on that dimension need not imply that it is the *only* one in which we can and should attribute worth to them. The parallel with economic value is again useful here: the market values goods and services relative to each other, but that a Rembrandt fetches a certain price at auction doesn't tell us everything – or even anything – about the painting's, for example, artistic, personal, and cultural value. Similarly, there is no reason for revisionists to deny that holocaust victims were, from any number of perspectives, of immense value independent of what happened to them. They were after all individuals with lives to lead, talents to offer, passions to pursue, curiosity to gratify, skills to perfect, virtues to cultivate, judgment to educate, joys to hope for themselves and bring to others, and challenges to overcome. We don't need the concept of dignity to recognize any of this; it is quite obvious and needs no philosophical defense. Like us, they were simply human beings for whom we should care for all these reasons and many more; that is all there is to it.

Yet – and this is the revisionist's key point – while it is certainly necessary, the bare presence of abounding human value in this sense is not sufficient for human dignity to actually reveal itself. If the value and potential of human beings is no more than a mere latency, condemned to remain an abstract and lifeless possibility only, human dignity cannot subsist, or so revisionists claim. And, on their account, that is precisely what the extreme dehumanization of the death camps accomplished: it rendered the manifest worth of the victims *immaterial* to their actual conditions of life; it created a circumstance in which that worth made no difference to the way others attended to, and then actually treated, them. They might as well have been sticks, stones, or rotting trash to be disposed of as rapidly as possible. Their latent abilities, unique potential, all of the things about them that might have enriched human life, and in the end, they themselves, were radically starved of any power to matter. Their value became a lost cause, a hope utterly defeated. This, according to revisionists, is the sense in which the holocaust exemplified an extreme privation of human dignity.

Why use the ungainly term "devalorization" to describe this transformation of legitimate hope into despair and abject defeat? Recall from Chapter 10 that "valorization" is a "second-order" mode of valuation, operating on items that are independently valuable in other dimensions. What I have called "valorization schemes" establish a common point of view from which, for the purposes of social authentication, some evaluations count while others are bracketed as irrelevant. Consider an insolvent business – for example, a restaurant that goes bust. A declaration of insolvency is certainly a kind of value-judgment: it publicly announces economic failure and ruin. Yet such declarations are not true by *fiat*; they are valid or invalid in the light of independent, socially recognized criteria. Insolvency is established in exchange and known by the valorization scheme provided by the market. As far as that scheme is concerned, other evaluations, even if sound, are irrelevant. That the restaurant was wonderful, well-run, beautifully decorated, had a superb view, served excellent food, will be sorely missed, and so on is immaterial. None of these manifest virtues can save it. What determines its solvency is its power to command the interest of enough customers to cover its costs and liabilities. Similarly, if the revisionist view is sound, what counts for human dignity is the power to command attentional precedence from others within socially entrenched routines.

We might say, then, that on the revisionist account, the extreme privation of human dignity we observe under genocidal and similarly desperate conditions is a kind of timanthropic insolvency. The analogy with insolvency is far from perfect and must not be pressed too far, but it at least clarifies a crucial point. "Devalorization" no more changes anyone's value as a human being, still less renders anyone worthless, than a restaurant's going bust establishes that it had no culinary merit. Indeed, devalorization tells us nothing about any one person *as such*, for it is, like dignity and indignity, a nonlocal phenomenon, describing a disposition of human relations. It is a condition in which the value of human beings loses any power to shape the attention and treatment they receive from others. Their real worth no longer makes any impact on their conditions of existence and effectively loses all de facto relevance in their form of life. So, although neither respect nor disrespect can make anyone more or less valuable than they are, they nonetheless harbor a fateful social power. For they can determine whether human worth finds a welcome home or dies, forsaken, in total exile. The circulation of respect in the routines of ordinary civilized life may be banal, but its organized withdrawal is nothing of the kind. As Améry said, "there is no 'banality of evil,' and Hannah Arendt, who wrote about it in her Eichmann book, knew the enemy of mankind only from hearsay, saw him only through the glass cage."[16]

[16] Améry, *At the Mind's Limits*, p. 25.

14

After Respect

> Write me down in the book of life . . . and forsake me not.
>
> *Hourly prayers of St. John Chrysostom*

Chapter 13 fleshed out a revisionist conception of human dignity. It tried to show how well that conception resonates with archetypes of human dignity and indignity familiar in ordinary reflection and political culture. However, a convincing defense of the revisionist approach requires more than this. The revisionist must still explain why human dignity on their construal can usefully inform critical reflection on politics. The diagnosis of the holocaust given at the end of Chapter 13 may have offered some promising hints in that direction, but it is not enough by itself.

One reason for this is that to wield any sharp critical edge, dignitarian humanism must take us beyond truisms about overdetermined atrocities like the holocaust. It must justify at least some more surprising political judgments, or allow us to view social and political practices from a critical angle that is fresh, telling, and otherwise unavailable. The issue of whether, and on what terms, the reformed version of dignitarian humanism developed here can do this forms the topic of Chapter 15. Here, however, I address a more fundamental question standing behind that issue: why think that human dignity as revisionists construe it has any significant critical force in the first place? Why should it matter *at all*?

Two Skeptical Angles

To dramatize these questions, imagine a skeptic who says, "OK, I grant that your revisionist view offers a hitherto unexplored, intriguing, and doubtless legitimate way of thinking about human dignity. As such, it may indeed be of some interest to novelists, film-makers, cultural commentators, trade journalists, and philosophy professors offering upper-level seminars; but beyond these arenas of private speculation, it has no significant claim on public attention."

One direction from which dignity-revisionism comes under skeptical pressure of this sort is a utilitarian one, and here it is worth remembering that classical utilitarianism remains the main interlocutor against which all forms of dignitarian humanism define themselves. For all of its other problems, utilitarianism at least has a ready response to the kind of skepticism just expressed. Pain, suffering, pleasure, and welfare are not theoretical abstractions. That vast numbers of people currently endure unnecessary suffering that could be prevented by comparatively inexpensive institutional reforms is not just an interesting aperçu to be discussed at a book club. If anything should command public attention, surely it is this. To offer classical utilitarianism serious competition as a vehicle of critical reflection on politics, then, dignitarian humanists must be able to explain why human dignity, as they understand it, has comparable, if not greater, political urgency. Why think that my revisionist conception of human dignity can help provide that explanation? Isn't it just too recherché to displace more urgent welfarist considerations?

I will address this first, utilitarian, line of resistance in Chapter 15. Here, I focus on a second direction from which skepticism about dignity-revisionism is likely to arise, of more immediate concern because it will tempt many card-carrying dignitarians already hostile to utilitarianism. The worry is this.

If, as revisionists claim, human dignity is not attached in any definite way to individuals, and consists only in a nonlocal pattern of social relations, doesn't it become much harder to explain how it matters, and can be a source of politically urgent reasons? I have repeatedly taken traditionalists like Clarence Thomas to task for denying that slavery and other patterns of oppression can take anyone's dignity away; this, I have complained, makes it very difficult to understand why dignity explains why we should *mind* slavery, oppression, and other abuses. But if, as revisionists claim, human dignity is not possessed by the person, but a nonlocal relation in which individuals stand to one another, then they don't seem able to say that, for example, enslaving people takes it away *either*. It is one thing to conceive of "human dignity" as a fragile social property, but another to explain why something that seems to float so mysteriously above individual lives should be of overriding concern.

This challenge is all the more pointed given the philosophical rebellion against utilitarianism that motivated recent dignitarian humanism in the first place. As I stressed in Chapter 3, Rawls and other dignitarians effectively charge utilitarianism with idolatry: in claiming that "aggregate welfare" is the ultimate standard of political judgment, it regards an impersonal collective abstraction as worth valuing for its own sake. Revisionists construe human dignity as a "real abstraction" in Marx's sense; but insofar as it consists in an abstract social relation, the claim that it matters in its own right seems to invite the same critique dignitarians have aimed at utilitarianism. After all, even Marx shared this worry: for in drawing attention to the way capitalism conjures into social existence the alienating specter of "abstract labor," his aim was precisely to expose it as a "vampire" from which agents need to be emancipated.

So, it is all very well to say that some "real abstractions" are good, an objector might then say, but we must remember that this is what the most pernicious collectivists always claim. They "justify" their predations in the name of some social, impersonal, good, transcending the lives of individuals that allegedly matters for its own sake. In imbuing a nonlocal relation with adamant, overriding importance, dignity-revisionism courts the same danger. Recalcitrant individuals who refuse to adjust themselves to the required relational patterns must become, in effect, enemies of human dignity. The "party of humanity" must then bring them into line, force them to be free, and so on, and we find ourselves back on the road to serfdom. Dignity-revisionism is fated to betray the larger dignitarian humanist enterprise.

This "dignity-collectivism objection," as I will call it, is the starting point for most of the discussion in this chapter. Considering its implications will allow us to further elaborate some important aspects – and I believe strengths – of the dignity-revisionist proposal. At the end of the chapter, however, I will look separately at a related but distinct issue raised by the remarks above. For quite apart from whether the view defended here courts collectivism, one might also think that it is important to be able to claim that oppression, injustice, abuse, and so on can (as we often ordinarily say) "strip" individuals of *their* dignity. But since dignity-revisionism denies that human dignity is possessed by individuals *as such*, it seems to rule out such a claim. The chapter ends by addressing this subsidiary challenge, which fortunately can also be defused.

The Dignity-Collectivism Objection

The intuition standing behind the main, dignity-collectivism, strand of the objection has been well stated by Christopher McCrudden. He claims that dignitarians are committed to the following thesis: "The intrinsic worth of the individual requires that we think that the state should exist for the sake of the individual human being, not *vice versa*."[1]

To express a comprehensive anti-collectivism, however, McCrudden's statement needs to be strengthened. We must replace the word "state" with something like "any and all collective structures, impersonal systems, cultures, nations, traditions, institutions, and so on that purport to have value, goals, needs, interests, welfare, projects, plans, reproductive imperatives, or fates in their own right." For the central anti-collectivist claim is that *none* of these social entities, and not only the "state," should be valued for their own sakes: all of them should be valued only for the sake of the individuals and lives they serve. McCrudden is right that this claim is usually advanced in the name of human dignity; most if not all of our archetypes of indignity involve individuals being

---

[1] C. McCrudden, "Human Dignity and Judicial Interpretation of Human Rights," *The European Journal of International Law* 19, no. 4 (2008): 260.

sacrificed, exploited, or oppressed by agents or organizations claiming to further some collective aim. The "indignity of collectivism" occurs when mere things – abstract collective properties – take precedence over people, who are not mere things. If the dignity-collectivism objection is correct, however, the account of human dignity offered here erects just such an idol and hence falls prey to the very collectivist seductions to which it is officially opposed.

Revisionists can have no quarrel with anything that comes after the word "requires" in the strengthened version of McCrudden's statement. And this gives them at least some initial responses to the objection. For one thing, they can point out that to say that human dignity consists in certain irreducibly social relations need not be to say that it matters for *its* own sake. Recall here the analogy I have occasionally drawn on revisionists' behalf between dignity and "dearness." Part of the force of that analogy is that, as with the revisionist construal of dignity, "dearness" cannot exist apart from a relation of love; only *after* that relation develops does it make sense to say that anyone is "dear." Yet, even if "dearness" requires a nonlocal relation, why should that imply that "dearness" should be valued for *its* own sake? It is still only the parties involved whose value is in view; "dearness" is not an end in itself, but merely attests to people's being valued for their own sakes.

Similarly, if human dignity comes only "after respect," and respect also involves valuing people for their sake, the implication is not that human dignity is valuable for its own sake, but rather that human dignity emerges only when human beings *are* valued for their own sakes. So on the revisionist view, the failure to attend to people for their own sake and a damaged relation of human dignity turn out to be one and the same phenomenon. And this point applies straightforwardly to the revisionist account of the holocaust given at the end of Chapter 13. On that account, the devalorization of holocaust victims consisted precisely in the institutionalization of dispositions to accord precedence to such collective abstractions as "The Reich," "the Aryan race," "following orders for its own sake," and so on, over the needs, interests, and value of those targeted for liquidation. Here, certainly, inhuman abstractions are being valued for their own sakes at the expense of individual lives, but it seems that dignity-revisionism is already very well-attuned to the problem.

Still, these initial responses may seem to miss the point, because they don't really address the crucial divergence between revisionist and traditionalist understandings of human dignity. The distinctiveness of the revisionist proposal lies in its denial that human dignity should be equated with "the intrinsic worth of the individual," to use McCrudden's opening formulation. After all, much of this book has argued that it is a mistake to identify human dignity with a local, "intrinsic," quality or worth inhering in the individual. The outstanding, and most important, issue raised by the dignity-collectivism objection is whether refusing that identification undermines the essential dignitarian commitment to always and only value human beings and their lives for their own sakes.

Valuing People for Their Sake

The successful resolution of this issue plainly turns on how dignitarian humanists should address two very basic questions that frame the rest of the discussion in this book:

(a) What is it to value individuals and their lives "for their own sakes?"
(b) How do we know when individuals and their lives are not being valued "for their own sakes" in a way that attracts *political* concern?

All dignitarians, I take it, accept two general assumptions about these questions. They agree, first, that the importance of (a) reflects the inadequacy of utilitarianism as a basis for critical judgment about politics. The whole thrust of the dignitarian turn initiated by Rawls, the very essence of the price/dignity distinction, is to deny that, from a public point of view, people and their lives matter only instrumentally. At least on the standard dignitarian critique, the problem with utilitarianism is that it allows, indeed may require, individuals to be sacrificed for the sake of the overriding goal of aggregate welfare – something that is not itself human life, but an actuarial tally. Treating people as mere resources (or worse: commodities) in this way is incompatible with valuing individuals and their lives for their own sakes. Dignitarians attach central importance to *respect* because it represents a mode of valuation (among others) that is noninstrumental. When I respect someone, I don't think of them as valuable just as a means to some other more important end; I rather value them for their own sake. The characteristic emphasis on respect in dignitarian humanism therefore reflects a tacit acknowledgment that it needs a good account of (a).

However, and this is the second point on which dignitarians can all agree, although necessary, such an account cannot by itself suffice to answer (b). The reason for this is that agents can legitimately complain that they are not being, or have not been, valued for their own sake in any number of ways that fall outside the scope of political concern. Betrayal, deception, manipulation, disregard, thoughtlessness, selfishness, self-centeredness, scapegoating, derision, venality, ingratitude, cold-heartedness, self-promotion, taunting, pettiness, and so on may all invite legitimate complaint on these grounds, but they are extremely common in daily life. The point is not that the prevalence of such behavior gives any reason to excuse it, but that, intuitively, political criticism cannot be equally concerned with all of it. It is hardly the job of the political theorist to referee complaints of shabby treatment at the hands of friends, intimate partners, colleagues, roommates, petulant neighbors, car salesmen, and so on.

To explain how an expectation that human beings are to be respected for their own sakes becomes a matter of *political* urgency, then, one needs some standard by which to differentiate departures from that expectation that trigger serious public concern from those that are less serious or better negotiated privately. Thus, Nozick pointedly raises the issue posed in (b): "In getting pleasure from seeing an attractive person go by, does one use the other solely as a means? Does someone so use an object of sexual fantasies?" He goes on: "These and related questions raise very interesting issues for moral philosophy; but not, I think, for political philosophy. Political philosophy is concerned only with certain ways that persons may not use others."[2] How then do we determine when failing to be valued for one's own sake becomes a serious enough matter to bear on the legitimacy of large-scale political practices and institutions?

The general *shape* of the dignitarian answer is clear enough: "human dignity" is an adamant sine qua non, and so any activity or practice that cannot be reconciled with a commitment to protecting it triggers political concern. Recall here the point made in Chapter 3, that the adjective "human" in "human dignity" normally functions as an intensifier, selecting within the very large set of actions, practices, transactions, relationships, and so on that involve *some* indignity (intrusive medical exams, being marched off in handcuffs in front of one's friends and colleagues, the "silent treatment" etc.), a subset whose members are so grave that no civilized community could possibly tolerate them. At the margins, we have some fairly uncontroversial intuitions about what kinds of things a plausible dignitarian answer to (b) will include and exclude: genocidal abuse, torture, slavery, will be included; the minor humiliation of a snub won't. But, for their view to be of any theoretical interest, dignitarian humanists must explain how, and on what basis, they propose to draw a principled line in the tougher intermediate cases. What are their criteria?

Notice that, in order to hold their anti-utilitarian line with regard to (a), dignitarians cannot recommend an answer to that question on the grounds that some set of *beliefs* about human dignity would, if inculcated and accepted in the population and/or codified in law, conventions, norms, and so on, tend to reduce human suffering or produce a better outcome overall. For then their view would lose its distinctively dignitarian character and become vulnerable to all the usual Rawlsian objections to rule consequentialism. They must instead derive the boundary that marks out the most serious, politically salient, forms of indignity from *within* some account of what it is to value human beings and their lives for their own sakes.

In Chapter 15, I will argue that dignity-revisionism offers a more propitious basis for making this derivation (i.e., giving an answer to (b)) than

---

[2] Nozick, *Anarchy, State and Utopia*, p. 32.

more traditional accounts. But quite clearly any dignitarian answer to (b), successful or not, will depend on assumptions about how best to answer (a) – the question of what it *is* to value human beings for their own sakes and, more urgently still, what it is to *fail* to value them in this way. The dignity-collectivism objection is troubling, I take it, because it challenges dignity-revisionism at this more fundamental level. For it charges that, having abandoned the idea that human dignity is possessed inherently by the individual, dignity-revisionists cannot really give a good account of what it means to value people for their own sakes. If that objection goes through, we don't really need to consider dignity-revisionist answers to (b), because it will have already disqualified itself from serious consideration on that ground (and, perhaps, as a result unwittingly left open the door to all sorts of collectivist abuse).

However, dignity-revisionism not only has a ready answer to (a), but also one that carries considerable force. Once we appreciate that answer, the outstanding worry raised by the dignity-collectivism objection can be defused. We will see that there is no tension at all between a nonlocal conception of human dignity and the commitment to only and always value people and their lives for their own sakes.

Hopkins on "Sakes"

In their rush to reject what they regard as the utilitarian tendency to subsume the value of persons under instrumental rationality, dignitarians have under-standably looked to Kantian categories to explicate what it means to value human beings for their own sakes. In particular, they have stressed Kant's insistence that agents must be regarded as "ends-in-themselves." My point here is not to argue that this Kantian fixture should be abandoned or that it is a confused idea. However, I want to suggest that, as a guide to what is contained in the idea of valuing human beings for their sakes, it is rather one-sided and potentially misleading. In particular, it can encourage us to think of the kind of "value" at stake in an unduly static and internalizing way. Yet we can, should, and ordinarily do, construe "valuing-for-someone's-own-sake" in richer, more outward-looking, terms.

Consider the following striking remark made by the poet Gerard Manley Hopkins:

> Sake is a word I find it convenient to use. . . . It is the *sake* of "for the sake of," forsake, namesake, keepsake. I mean by it the being a thing has outside itself, as a voice by its echo, a face by its reflection, a body by its shadow, a man by his name, fame, or memory, *and also* that in the thing by virtue of which especially it has this being abroad, and that is some-thing distinctive, marked, specifically or individually speaking, as for a voice and echo clearness; for a reflected image light, brightness; for

a shadow-casting body bulk; for a man genius, great achievements, amiability, and so on.[3]

This comment is quite compatible with the Kantian thought that a person's "sake" reflects something that is both peculiar to them and whose value is noninstrumental. However, Hopkins here talks about "sakes" in a way that emphasizes, in a way that Kantian ethics doesn't, the external manifestation of something's or someone's qualities. The Kantian impulse is to localize someone's sake as far as possible to their personality considered as static, or self-sufficient ("*selbständig*"): it corresponds to their "value-in-themselves," a kind of worth they bear *as such*, appreciable immediately upon excerpting them in thought as independent persons. As Velleman glosses the standard Kantian view, persons are valuable for their own sakes in that they are "self-existent ends" and as such "are the objects of motivating attitudes that regard and value them as they already are."[4]

Hopkins, however, suggests that the unique features in virtue of which something has a "sake" need not be so *immediate*. They can, and sometimes only can, manifest themselves in an external medium; the implication is that the historical, narrative interaction of one thing with something else that it affects can in principle perform this mediating role. As a mountain interacts with the setting sun, its shadow faithfully expresses its bulk. Although speaking of the shadow as revealing the mountain's "sake" admittedly sounds strange, Hopkins nonetheless loyally captures the logic of many sake-idioms in ordinary use. In a "keepsake," for example, I preserve the memory of (say) a past love in some object that manifests something about the beloved – a letter, a lock of hair, a photograph, and so on.

So, whereas Kantian accounts radically localize "sakes" to the immediate properties of things or persons considered "in themselves," Hopkins suggests that "sakes" have an important nonlocal dimension. He clearly presumes that talk of something's "sake" has everything to do with its unique attributes.[5] But he is pointing out that when we speak of things bearing "sakes," we are very often, if not always, thinking about how those attributes reveal themselves through their impact on, or interaction with, something beyond their bearers.[6]

Applying Hopkin's analysis to the case of an agent *valuing* someone or something for their own sake (through, say, the noninstrumental affective

---

[3] G. M. Hopkins, *The Poems of Gerard Manley Hopkins* (Teddington: The Echo Library, 2008), pp. 80–81.

[4] Velleman, "Love," 357, 367.

[5] In his poem "Purcell," Hopkins speaks of the "moonmarks" and "forgèd feature[s]" of Purcell's music as they "throng" on the listener's ear as a reflection of the composer's "sake" – his "own, . . . abrupt self."

[6] Hopkins famously coined the term "inscape" to refer to something's inherent qualities, of something an observer can notice, and perhaps subsequently capture in a poetic metaphor that then refracts its "sake" to listeners.

modes of love or respect) highlights the nonlocal character of the timanthropic valorization involved. Whatever it is about an individual that might be valued for its own sake often requires the love and respect of a valuer to serve as a nonlocal medium to find life and expression; the aspects "by virtue of which" the valued person elicits this response and treatment – that is, evaluatively relevant characteristics – thereby become apparent in the valuer's response.

In one way, the nonlocal character of such engagement recalls Marx's conception of "exchange-value." Marx pointed out, surely correctly, that "I cannot . . . express the [economic] value of linen in linen. 20 yards of linen = 20 yards of linen is not an expression of value." Exchange-value cannot, in other words, be immediate. To specify the exchange-value of one commodity requires that it be related to at least one other commodity that can mediate that value, as in "x commodity A = y commodity B: or x commodity A is worth y commodity B."[7] The parallel with exchange-value may seem risky given my commitment to preserving a clear contrast between dignity and price, but fortunately the concept of valuing something for its own sake stands at an angle to the local/nonlocal distinction.

For, Marxian exchange-value, nonlocal as it is, can have nothing whatever to do with valuing anything "for its sake," at least as I am construing it. As Marx was at pains to stress, exchange-values reflect only the proportional relations *between* the commodities to which they are attached, *not* anything about their specificity or uniqueness (e.g., their use-value to a specific consumer). In Marx's view, to be expressed as a quantifiable financial ratio, relative and equivalent exchange-value require mediation through the commonly recognized medium of money. That is why he concluded that the phenomenon of exchange-value is intelligible only by applying the (he thought) alienating and oppressive idiom of "abstract labor," which he maintained backs that common recognition.

Conversely, if, as Hopkins would analyze it, "valuing X for its sake" *does* express something about the individuality of X, it must be an entirely different mode of valuation. That is good news for the effort to sharply distinguish price and dignity, for it suggests that in "valuing X for its sake," one is not engaging with X in a quantifiably comparable manner. Yet that fundamental difference need not mean that such "valuings-for-something's-sake" are any more *immediate* than Marxian exchange-value; nor, as argued earlier, need this imply that there is no evaluative comparison involved. Moreover, on Marx's analysis, in the system of exchange-value, one *thing* expresses the value of another thing, thereby introducing an "objectifying" mode of valuation that obviously does not involve one commodity consciously engaging with another as valuable for its own sake. To be sure, participants in the economic system who reckon by exchange-values often do so consciously, but in doing so, *they* do not form

[7] Marx, *Capital Vol. 1*, p. 139.

a nonlocal medium expressing those exchange-values. They simply operate (plan, invest, buy, and sell) according to a readymade valorization scheme that independently settles the exchange-value of all commodities relative to each other. When an agent loves or respects another for their own sake, however, her conscious affective responses themselves form the medium through which the relevant value is manifested. Timanthropic valorization of this sort therefore recruits conscious mutual engagement in a way that exchange-value does not.

The resulting conception of "sakes" as individuated but nonlocal also shares something of the logic of "honor," "fame," "notoriety," and reputation, which I argued in Chapter 4 foreshadow an idea of D-dignity. One's honor or reputation are indeed one's own, but they are precisely *not* "self-existent" properties of their bearers, excerpted as separate individuals. They are "abroad" in social relations because they presuppose others whose reactions, in effect, constitute the medium in which one's honor or reputation is impressed. Those reactions do not form a merely passive medium like wax receiving an imprint; they require the active responses of a conscious audience. Without these conscious responses, one cannot enjoy *any* reputation or honor. It follows, moreover, that our ambient reputation and honor must record information about how we and our lives have had an impact on other lives, how we have affected, are affecting, or tend to affect others' conscious dispositions toward us.

Although in this way formally similar to the categories of honor, reputation, and fame, *valuing* someone or something for their sake differs importantly. It implies active engagement with X that is elicited by, and targeted on, X's specific *worth*. My reputation, honor, and fame also convey information about how an audience responds to me, yet whether those responses show me in a good or a bad light is neither here nor there. I can have a bad reputation: infamy is not a lack, but a form, of fame; and some are famous just for being famous. Moreover, my fame and reputation may misrepresent me completely, but as Hopkins insists, "sakes" do have to be true to their bearers. I can be your namesake only if I really have the same name as you, especially if I was named for your sake. The two names must accurately correspond for my name to serve as a medium through which you are remembered. A keepsake must be (or at least I must believe that it is) relevantly connected to some real feature of the person remembered – I can't go to a barbershop, grab a lock of hair off the floor, and simply nominate it as a keepsake of a long-lost friend. As I gloss Hopkins's view, then, my actively valuing you for your sake is for my attention, activity, and treatment to form a medium in which something of your value comes to life in your affective repercussions on me, and in my subsequent conduct.

These considerations align closely with claim, defended by dignity-revisionists, that human dignity – a metaphor purporting to capture a politically relevant dimension in which people and their lives are valued for their own sakes – is constituted by engagement with others in the affective mode of respect. In Chapter 13, I suggested that we recognize it in emergent patterns of mutual affective adjustment whereby one agent's encounter with another triggers payments of respectful attention – a willingness on the part of one agent to forfeit something of value to them for their sake. So, like "honor" and "reputation," it is a socially ambient quality whose presence records information about how human beings who share in it have affected others and conditioned those others' willingness to adjust to them on terms that require them to forgo advantages they would otherwise prefer to enjoy. However, since the affective mode constituting it presupposes that those respected for their own sakes are *worth* the attention and personal sacrifices those disposed to respect them then pay, it reflects something of the targets' value and brings it to life in concrete mutual engagement.

The etymology of the word "sake" highlights another important aspect of the concept, one that is also strongly indicated by what Hopkins says. It originated as a term signifying a cause of dispute or conflict (from the Old English "*sacan*" to "quarrel, fight, claim at law, accuse"; the Old Saxon *sakan* "accuse:" Old High German *sahhan* to "strive, quarrel, rebuke"). In due course, it became a word for a lawsuit and more generally for a "cause," in the sense of "he gave his life for the cause." An important feature of "causes" in this sense is that they presuppose resistance and uncertainty: success is not guaranteed; they must be prosecuted, kept alive, fought for, defended, and vindicated; and sometimes they can be lost. To return to an example from Chapter 13, when a team of doctors, nurses, and attendants battle with great concentration and energy to save an acutely ill patient, his being a cause worth fighting for becomes vividly real here. Although the treatments the doctors administer are instrumentally valuable in relation to the patient's presumptive desire to live, the sense in which the patient's mattering-for-his-own sake is legible in these events is plainly noninstrumental. The emotionally engaged, and largely selfless, payment of attention triggered by the patient's arrival at the emergency room is what strikes us most forcibly in such cases. The medical team drops everything and does whatever it can to save him. Their treatment may be ineffective; but even if the patient does not survive, the effort to save him reveals his life as mattering for its own sake. It makes a material difference to the shape of the patient's biography that he died with others prepared to wholeheartedly forfeit personal convenience for his sake, struggling to keep him alive, and not walking by on the other side, forsaking him completely.

Although he mentions it, Hopkins does not specifically define the word "forsake," which has come up often in what I have said here about indignity. But in the light of the etymology, its natural sense is that of "abandoning a worthy cause." To forsake something is to abandon the fight on its behalf. Something that is completely, or, as I will say, "*radically*," forsaken finds its value helpless and forlorn – stripped of any power to elicit conscious action for its sake. As I suggested in Chapter 13, that looks like a good description of the predicament in which victims of the holocaust found themselves. There appears to be a deep connection between the most serious privations of human dignity and conditions of profound disrespect under which the value of human beings finds no favorable medium to manifest itself in others' respectful attention and is in that sense radically forsaken.

Narrativity and Uptake

To think of what it means to value human beings for their own sakes in these Hopkins-inspired terms is to adopt a narrative perspective that is today rarely taken up in moral and political theory.[8] The tendency in the philosophical literature has been to follow the paradigm in moral philosophy and focus on the way in which agents deliberating about their voluntary choices are constrained by assumptions about the value of other persons who stand to be affected by what one does. The question here is, roughly, how the expectation that we value one another for each other's sakes shapes and constrains our moral duties, obligations, and others' entitlements. In principle, there is no reason to think that good answers to that perfectly reasonable question would turn on an understanding of "acting for someone's sake" that contradicts anything I have extracted from Hopkins.

However, as I have already mentioned several times, focusing on ethical choice *as such* encourages theorists to abstract from the narrative flow of social interaction and consider actions atomically, as excerpted instances of one agent deciding to treat another in this way rather than that. It requires one to consider an action prospectively, as it looks in the moment of decision, from within an agent's "deliberative stance." But especially when thinking about such prospective choices for the purposes of a general theory of ethical decision-making, the others whose "sakes" should be taken into account in personal deliberation will inevitably figure in a rather stylized form. The larger narrative arc of their lives will very rarely be in view in any detailed or informed way. The moral philosopher will have to make do with ciphers like "agents with their own plans,"

---

[8] Two notable recent exceptions are Sharon Krause and Samuel Scheffler: Krause, because her account of the "socially distributed" character of agency, and of "uptake," resonates with what I am arguing here. S. Krause, *Freedom beyond Sovereignty: Reconstructing Liberal Individualism* (Chicago: University of Chicago Press, 2015); Scheffler, because he forcefully argues that "the entire range of phenomena that consists in people's valuing things, in things mattering or being important to them . . . [assumes] that human life itself matters, and that it is an ongoing phenomenon with a history that transcends the history of any individual." S. Scheffler, *Death and the Afterlife* (Oxford: Oxford University Press, 2016), p. 59. Again, the overlap with the position taken here is striking.

"autonomous beings," "project-pursuers," "right-holders," "wielders of second-personal authority," "independent persons sui juris," and so forth. The result is that their "sakes" will tend to take on a very static quality; that, I think, is why the Kantian tendency to localize "sakes" *in* the person comes so naturally to theorists steeped in the tradition of modern moral philosophy or ethics.

Again, the point is not to draw attention to any real inconsistency between such stylizations and the more ordinary sense of a "sake" that Hopkins exposes. It is rather that we can also think about engagement with someone/something for its own sake from a different point of view, and construe the phenomenon in narrative terms. Recall the metaphor of a flick-book I used in the discussion of Kant in Chapter 6. Each page records the disposition of the image at a particular point in the animation, and, together, the pages contain all of the visual information that is animated by the book. But to experience the animation itself, I need more than the immediate information on the pages. Laying them out on a table so that I see them all at once won't do. To bring the animation to life, I must physically manipulate the book so that the pages flash by rapidly. Without that mediating physical engagement, the animation is merely latent.

Considered narratively, as an actual element of biographical interaction with significant others, "being valued for one's sake" is very much like that. It is something that *happens* (or fails to happen) accordingly as one is able to affect others such that they engage with us in particular ways. In other words, whether one's being-valued-for-one's-sake is brought to life – animated, one might say – depends on our affective "uptake," to use Krause's helpful language. The quality and mode of that uptake is a medium through which our value-for-its-own-sake is manifested (or not) in some performative response. It conveys information about how we matter to others and thereby shape our actual biographical trajectory through the routines of social life. The underlying picture is then one in which agents present themselves to each other, sometimes in the course of cooperative activity, sometimes independent of it, setting off affective reactions that direct others' attention and conduct in various ways, and that in turn shape subsequent uptake and interplay. These affective repercussions radiate and propagate outward as agents make an impact on others, are amplified by social roles and institutional expectations, and accordingly trigger certain ways of attending to their lives, emphasizing some, ignoring others, and so on.

In the revisionist account, human dignity serves as a metaphor that picks out a particular class of these repercussions, those coded in ordinary language as respect or disrespect, on which agents depend for their lives coming to matter for their own sakes in a way that is an adamant political desideratum.

Radical Forsakenness

I have been arguing that the philosophical tendency to localize a person's "sake" as an immediately possessed attribute requires one to abstract artificially from the dynamic engagement of human beings with each other for their own sakes. Such engagement has a fundamentally narrative character; it depends on how valuers attend to them over time in a certain affective spirit. Engagement of this kind is important in the ordinary course of events because it renders value that would otherwise remain merely latent vital. Its absence tends to preserve that latency. What I have called "radical forsakenness" effectively transforms that latency into entombment; it seems extensionally equivalent to the sort of extreme dignitarian "devalorization" discussed in Chapter 13. On the revisionist view, radical forsakenness of this kind is a – perhaps *the* – paradigmatic privation of human dignity. But, again, such privations deny human beings a share in a dignity that is essentially nonlocal.

Far from casting doubt on the nonlocal theory of human dignity developed here, then, taking the narrative character of mattering for one's own sake seriously strongly supports it. On that theory, human dignity names, not a local attribute of the individuals whose lives and value are on the line, but a fragile social accomplishment that requires two powers to coincide: on the one hand individuals' ability to elicit in others affective dispositions to engage respectfully with them for their own sakes; and on the other, a concomitant payment of self-sacrificing attention in return. Lives can share in that symbiosis only *after* respect; disrespect, contempt, and indifference, especially if systemic, threaten it. Its emergence attests to a power – an essentially social, nonlocal, power – to bring something of our value to life beyond ourselves by affecting others such that they engage attentively with us for our own sakes. That something is not itself human dignity; it is the value and worth latent in human beings, struggling to valorize itself in the routines of daily life and the way they organize the power to command the attention and respect of one's fellows.

So, revisionists needn't deny that human beings have "intrinsic worth" in that sense; but they deny that the form of value that is in view in human dignity is "autarchic" in the sense rightly rejected by Raz and discussed in Chapter 6. The purpose of introducing the idea of human dignity as they construe it is not to make a claim about any individual in particular, because it is a nonlocal quality; it is to direct critical attention to the external affective conditions under which human beings and their lives actually *are* valued for their own sakes, or at least not utterly forsaken. I see no obvious reason to think that this approach cannot capture anything that proponents of the dignity-collectivism objection might cite as a case of intolerable subordination to some nonhuman idol or impersonal system of domination. This suggests a challenge to proponents of the dignity-collectivism objection: name any sufficiently grave instance of individuals being ground down under the wheels of some collective or impersonal project that does *not* fit the description of radical forsakenness given here.

Consider victims of the slave trade, forcibly transported to an alien world across an ocean, where they find themselves surrounded by powerful others disposed to attend to them only as subhuman, dangerous animals that, when domesticated, disciplined, and put to work, nonetheless have considerable agricultural utility. They are sold, bought, and brutally exploited by others who have no disposition to pay them any attention except as a source of personal profit. To be sure, insofar as their masters regard a slave as an economic opportunity for them, their dispositions realize a conception of his value. But in commandeering the slave's life solely as a tool for their use and personal benefit, the masters (and the form of life that supports their activities) represent his life merely as an object of their contempt. Slaves matter only for the sake of their masters, not for their own sakes. Such radically degrading conditions effect social death in that nothing of a slave's worthiness to be respected for his own sake is discernible in his conditions of life. According as people are valorized as slaves, they find themselves radically forsaken and devalorized as human beings.

Consider some other standard cases: conscripts marched off to slaughter on the fields of Flanders in the name of "national honor"; terrorization of "enemies of the people" undertaken to shore up the "dictatorship of the proletariat"; and "ethnic cleansing" for the sake of "racial purity" or "national unity." The problem with all of these affronts to human dignity seems to me to be precisely that some collective idol is taken to matter for its own sake at the expense of individuals whose lives are accordingly forsaken. If all relevant cases of objectionable collectivist abuse fall under this description, then we don't need a traditional account of dignity to recognize them as indignities that no civilized society should condone.

I again stress that, while it is likely necessary, being forsaken is not sufficient to justify any distinctively *political* objection. As I have said, all dignitarians must concede that there are many ways of suffering indignity and disrespect that don't directly invite political concern, and revisionists are no exception. When someone cold-heartedly breaks off a relationship, refuses to speak to their former companion, and gives no reasons why, they forsake them. No one, revisionists included, thinks such humiliating indignity justifies any political intervention. Still, I do take revisionists to assert that, in seeking to identify the most urgent dignitarian abuses that do attract political concern, this is the right continuum along which to locate them.

Some may resist that last suggestion on the grounds that the small-scale, interpersonal, humiliations of private life are different *in kind* from the sort of radical forsakenness witnessed in human disasters like the holocaust. Doubtless many are; but we should notice that these more intimate humiliations, even as they likely lack direct political import, can completely devastate a person's life in a way that does seem to me continuous with the phenomenon of radical forsakenness. A recent psychological study of ostracism cites the horrifying case of "Lee," whose husband subjected her to the "silent treatment" *for forty years.* During that time, he completely blanked her out, ignored her presence, and refused to engage in any conversation with her. Lee wrote of her experience:

> I wish he would've beaten me instead of giving me the silent treatment, because at least it would have been a response. This has ruined my life. . . . The bottom line is that it's the meanest thing you can do to someone, especially because it doesn't allow you to fight back. I should have never been born.[9]

The language Lee uses to describe her forty years of forsakenness at the hands of her husband is striking. Her talk of a "ruined" life recalls the discussion of economic ruin and insolvency in Chapter 15. What bothers her most is her complete inability to elicit payments of attention from her spouse; he proceeds as if she doesn't exist, entirely unworthy of his consideration. I submit that if one thinks about what it is actually like to confront the prison guard, the torturer, the public official, the implacable bureaucrat, the SS man, who is "just doing their job" in carrying through some worthless collectivist project at one's own expense, one will immediately see the affinity between these instances of political subordination and Lee's predicament. The more concerted, politically organized, versions of this phenomenon trigger a sense of common responsibility for human dignity in a way that Lee's situation doesn't, but in other obvious respects they do seem to be on a continuum.

I have not, it is true, canvassed any clear criterion that would tell us where, on that continuum, the failure to matter for one's sake becomes serious enough to bring the adamant requirements of human dignity in a way that commands political attention. Intuitively, this will be a function of several factors: whether the mistreatment under scrutiny is atypical or occasional, rather than systematically directed at certain classes of human beings for no good reason; whether the agents concerned have available to them other ways of receiving respect that are sufficient for a reasonable share in human dignity; whether, considered as a whole, an agent's biography is so scarred by ostracism, stigmatization, exploitation, and so on that no impartial narrator could relate it except as a story of a complete failure to matter; whether responsibility for valorizing the lives in question in the affective mode of respect naturally falls to private individuals as they negotiate their personal relations, and not to public officials or to formal or informal practices that are in principle open to conscious

---

[9] Kipling D. Williams, *Ostracism: The Power of Silence* (New York: Guilford Press, 2000), p. 20.

modification through communal effort; whether their share in such patterns of respectful attention as do constitute "human dignity" in their society is made problematically conditional on their being asked to suppress, or conceal, wholly innocent aspects of their identity that reflect qualities in which their value-for-their-own sake could in principle find vitality in mutual engagement; whether arbitrary and unjust disparities in agents' access to the conditions for respectful uptake go unnoticed and unaddressed; whether or not agents excluded from a reasonable share in human dignity have recourse to effective legal and political remedies whereby their claim on such a share might be restored, and so on. In Chapter 15, we will see that dignity-revisionism almost certainly offers a better framework for thinking about these issues than do traditional accounts that localize human dignity to the individual. But we don't need that further point in order to rebut the dignity-collectivism objection.

Human Dignity and Personal Dignity

I conclude this chapter by considering another independent reason to resist my nonlocal construal of human dignity. Doesn't that construal conflict with the important ordinary intuition that degrading conditions can deprive victims of *their* dignity? If, as I have been arguing, "human dignity" exemplifies D-dignity, nonlocally ambient in social relations, we no longer seem able to say this. To be sure, the revisionist view allows "human dignity" to change and be damaged, even erased in relation to some populations; but I have emphasized that these alterations are legible only in nonlocal patterns, and not as losses of anything one can localize to an individual.

In response, recall that the westerly column of the typology introduced in Chapter 4 comprises not one, but two, ordinary ways of thinking about dignity:

Human Dignity change→ ↓locus	Transient Vulnerable to Damage/diminishment
Inherent within the person	A
Ambient among persons	D

Both of these forms of dignity are transient – they can diminish or be taken away – and so revisionists are free to refer to both of them in understanding patterns of dignity and indignity in human life. On this basis, they can distinguish between nonlocal "human dignity" (a form of D-dignity) and the local quality of "personal dignity" (a form of A-dignity). When we say that some event or practice "strips" someone of their dignity, it is personal dignity (in mode A) that is at stake. Ordinary use reflects this: to add the adjective "human" to the statement "they stripped me of my dignity" is not only unnecessary; it would also sound odd. Often, the oddness of a formulation from the point of view of ordinary use is a sign that some important distinction is being blurred, and I think that is so here. The strangeness of speaking of "my human dignity" attests to our tacit acceptance that "my" dignity and "human dignity" are distinct. Still, since personal and human dignity must be related in various ways, the revisionist owes us some further explanation as to how.

We saw in Chapter 4 that A-dignity is not an inward quality, but rather consists in features, forms of bearing, and demeanors that are broadly copresent with an individual's physical location. It manifests in the maintenance or diminution of observable qualities and behavior like one's "cool," gait, freedom of movement, grace, physical self-possession, and so on. Responsibility for A-dignity and its maintenance is often the responsibility of its bearer. Donald Trump, a permanent infant, seems temperamentally incapable of maintaining many forms of A-dignity. Grace, sagacity, self-control, even-temperedness, judiciousness, all seem quite beyond him. But his immaturity, petulance, pusillanimity, vulgarity, and incontinence, though they exemplify A-indignity, are to no one's detriment than his own. We are in no sense responsible for them (though perhaps we share a responsibility not to elect such idiots to high office).

Still, many of our standard archetypes of affronts to human dignity, those that revisionists want to analyze in terms of D-dignity, do in fact also disrupt victims' A-dignity. Consider those subjected to torture, forced labor, solitary confinement, humiliation, rape, open ridicule, and so on: they may be disfigured, enfeebled, emaciated, bruised, and bear other stigmata of abuse; they may lose their cool, screaming uncontrollably in ways that compound their visible humiliation; they may be goaded into undignified displays of anger or violence; they may be rendered unfree, physically confined, their activity frustrated. and powers of communication disabled; and they may acquire observable symptoms of exhaustion, anxiety, and nervousness.

In these ways, revisionists can acknowledge that privations of *human* dignity can also take *individuals'* dignity away. This is surely a strength of their view. On the one hand, it allows them to construe personal dignity as something possessed by individuals without identifying it with the sort of occult, invulnerable, inner quality that traditional conceptions of human dignity are prone to indulge. On the other hand, they can say that insofar as it assumes responsibility for protecting human dignity (in the diffused sense of D-dignity), a society will in fact tend to protect individuals from personal indignity of these kinds.

Why then not *reduce* responsibility for the protection of human dignity (as D-dignity) entirely to an expectation that society refrain from organized practices that take away individuals' A-dignity in these ways? The abolition or reform of any shared social practice or institution that systematically strips individuals of the qualities in which their A-dignity consists would, on that view, be sufficient to discharge our common responsibility for human dignity.

This tempting proposal is however misguided.[10] The reason is that damage to A-dignity is neither necessary nor sufficient for some shared social practice to invite adamant disapproval as compromising human dignity. It is not *necessary* because human dignity can be undermined even though no one's A-dignity is observably effaced. Those who confront oppressive, manipulative, or enslaving social conditions need not lose their A-dignity: for example, women whose lives and opportunities are stunted by patriarchy may nonetheless be able to preserve a dignified persona (think of all the Grandes Dames of European literature); systematically deceived people (like the hero of the film *The Truman Show*) may show no discernible signs of personal indignity; and even slaves, if their masters are kind and their own reserves of self-respect robust, may project a quite genuine demeanor of personal dignity.[11]

This book has often suggested that human indignity consists in a kind of "social death" or "social defeat," but such phenomena cannot be completely localized to their effects on victims' self-presentation. They are constituted in social relations – on the revisionist view proposed here, in the affective repercussions of some lives in others. Human dignity, on the revisionist view, depends on how these repercussions work themselves out in social practices, and it is threatened when they evince agents' powerlessness to compel others to attend to them in important ways. The loss of A-dignity is often an aggravating factor in these relational indignities, and can often alert us to their presence. But what they alert us *to* is an independent and in my view more basic dignitarian deficit, one that must ultimately be theorized nonlocally, in terms of D-dignity.

Damage to A-dignity is also not *sufficient* for human dignity to be compromised because it has few if any of the timanthropic implications that I have argued give dignitarian considerations their vital political significance. Here, revisionists can incorporate an intuition that might otherwise only seem available to traditional accounts of human dignity: that visible humiliation, abjection, physical abuse, ill-considered outbursts of exasperation, violence or

---

[10] Sangiovanni recognizes this point; see *Humanity without Dignity*, pp. 24–25.

[11] Here dignity-revisionists can embrace the insight recovered by Quentin Skinner, Philip Pettit, and other defenders of "neo-Roman" conceptions of liberty, that what matters for liberty, and by extension the human dignity that genuine freedom subserves, is the bare existence or absence of certain forms of slavish dependence, not the degree to which oppressors successfully efface the manifestation of personal dignity. Like the dignity-revisionist, the neo-Roman view of liberty is more centrally concerned with the relations of power that leave agents at the mercy of others. And, in a way that is at least consistent with the neo-Roman view, the dignity-revisionist is also particularly concerned with the maintenance of an affective atmosphere disposing agents to respect the independence of free agents. The presence of such an atmosphere comprises a nonlocal precondition of a form of freedom that both dignity-revisionists can and neo-Romans do embrace.

anger, and so, on can't by themselves denude their victims' lives of worth. Lives don't lose value accordingly as the A-dignity of the person leading them falters in these ways. The loss of A-dignity is often a painful and embarrassing experience – and not only for the person who loses it – but our aversion to it doesn't derive from its tendency to impugn anyone's value.

In this sense, revisionists can join with traditionalists in saying that, for example, the undignified demeanor of the starved, exhausted, brutalized, confused, and pathetic figures found wandering about in the abandoned Nazi concentration camps at the end of the war is no reflection on their worth as human beings. However, revisionists will rightly insist that this perfectly sound intuition shouldn't blind us to the possibility that human societies can sometimes be structured in ways that effect devalorization of the sort described here. Social circumstances can leave human lives forsaken; this debases and cheapens the lives led within them to varying degrees, sometimes in ways that are adamantly objectionable. Yet, once again, these forms of human spoliation can no more be detected as properties of individuals taken separately than prices can be understood as inherent features of goods and services. They subsist on common human relations for which we, together, are ultimately responsible.

15

Human Dignity and Political Criticism

Returning to where we began, consider again B. F. Skinner's withering dismissal of the "autonomous . . . inner man, the homunculus, the possessing demon, the man defended by the literatures of freedom and dignity." Like Skinner, this book has urged that we "dispossess" individuals of dignity understood as an innate, occult, inward, quality, or as a fixed juridical status that remains unchanged regardless of how the lives of its bearers actually work out. Yet, where Skinner sought to exorcise dignitarian considerations entirely in order to make room for a program of technocratic social reform, this book has instead tried to reappropriate a revised construal of human dignity as a valid basis for social and political criticism. The revisionist strategy recommended here has accordingly sought to conceptualize human dignity as an external social phenomenon, entrenched (or not) in actual patterns of social interaction, in something like the way that Hobbes and other early theorists of the modern state attempted to construct an account of that institution as the central locus of public concern. Rather than thinking of human dignity as a local property commanding various forms of respect, this book has recast it as a nonlocal state of human relations, constituted by the de facto power to reliably elicit respectful attention from others. On this revisionist account, the focus of dignitarian concern is the actual configuration of that power; its aim is to identify and eliminate those configurations that leave human lives radically forsaken, and to promote conditions in which, as far as possible, they enjoy, and we exercise, the powers on which their mattering for their own sakes depends.

If my effort to rebalance dignity-skepticism and dignity-enthusiasm has succeeded, the next step would be to apply the revisionist account to the various contexts in which one might think human dignity, so construed, is importantly at stake. The ultimate test of dignity-revisionism is whether it can shed interesting critical light in these cases. I hope to pursue that project in future work, and perhaps the arguments of this book might persuade others to do so, too. But I won't attempt to move very far in this direction here. Given the vast range of topics that a concern for human dignity brings into view, doing so would either require several further volumes, or deal so superficially with complex political questions as to bring my approach into immediate disrepute. So rather than strangle dignity-revisionism at birth, I propose instead to pursue a more modest prolegomonic goal: that of explaining what a practice of dignitarian social criticism, conducted in the light of the view recommended here, might look like, and why one might find it worth pursuing. I will try to explain in what senses it is distinctive, and some reasons to think that it improves on other paradigms widely adopted by political theorists today. I begin, however, with some general remarks on the scope and character of political criticism itself.

Common Responsibility

Throughout this book, I have emphasized that, despite their likely many points of intersection, the preoccupations of moral philosophy or "ethics" and those of political criticism differ. I moreover (broadly) agree with contemporary "realist" critics that political judgment is not completely contained within moralizing discourse about "criteria of right action," rights, obligations, duties, the "deliberative stance" from which individuals resolve on voluntary actions, and the grounds on which agents can be held morally (or legally) culpable for their conduct. This is not because, as Machiavellians argue, *ragion di stato* confers on political leaders' latitude to depart from everyday moral expectations, though that may be a defensible position. The reason – one that Machiavelli himself would surely also have accepted – is rather that I take political arguments to be implicitly addressed to a "we" prepared to assume some responsibility for "its" common institutions and practices. To my mind, the primary focus of political criticism is not the question of how individuals are morally accountable for their voluntary actions, nor that of how they should select them, but rather how we, as political associates, should step back and submit the operation of our communal practices to appropriate critical scrutiny. In this weak sense, I take political criticism to be an essentially communist endeavor.

To be sure, these two targets of reflection are bound to be linked in various ways. The moral philosopher's "deliberative stance" is not supposed to be completely idiosyncratic or solipsistic, so whichever "criteria of right action" are worthy to guide, it must be commonly intelligible. Moreover, since "moral" duties are usually other-regarding, any "criterion" purporting to specify them will likely have implications for how agents should understand their political relations, more so in that the character of political communities will depend on how certain moral norms and principles are in fact widely internalized and followed by their members. Still, it is one thing to reflect on the moral probity of individual actions, whether retroactively (in judgments of praise and blame) or prospectively (in deliberation about how to act), and another to ask whether large-scale social and political practices are adequate, in order, worthy of approval, and so on, as opposed to oppressive, perverse, or illegitimate. Critical political inquiry is concerned, rather, with what agents should and shouldn't regard as legitimate objects of common, public concern; establishing that certain defects in communal arrangements are to our common detriment; and how we might together assume collective responsibility for doing something about them.

I stress that presuming that political criticism addresses a common "we" that seeks to step back and reflect on the general adequacy of its shared forms of life is *not* to presuppose a "collectivist" or "statist" view of politics. The modern state presents itself, of course, as the authoritative maker of "we-judgments," but it is precisely such professions that invite critical assessment; the question here is whether apologists for the state like Hobbes are right to say that "we" can and should recognize ourselves in that institution's claim to speak for "us" Those who deny this or otherwise wish to trim back the state's remit are still engaged in political criticism as I am construing it, yet clearly *they* aren't presupposing a "statist" outlook. Perhaps "we" should be cosmopolitans, transnationalists, or even anarchists.[1]

Or consider Hayek's argument against socialism and collectivist economic planning. According to him, the socialist proposal represents a doomed effort to transplant expectations of altruistic concern that evolved in small-scale, face-to-face, societies to the radically different context of large-scale modern economic cooperation. Under the latter conditions, information about agents' real needs and the resources available to meet them is too copious and widely dispersed to permit rational planning by a centralized authority. We do better, according to Hayek, to rely on free market incentives to match needs and powers efficiently.

Whether or not one is persuaded by this argument, its conclusion about the limited possibilities for rational state control over commerce is still addressed to an implicit "we." One way to bring this out is to notice that its upshot is a plea for collective self-restraint. The argument invites "us" to critically examine our motives for supporting centralized management of the economy and purports to reveal that, on reflection, they are hangovers from a bygone epoch that continually tempt us to seek greater public control

---

[1] The revisionist view developed here may, indeed, support not only dignitarian communism (in the weak sense just suggested), but also dignitarian anarchism, a position that seems to me to have a lot going for it. The modern state and its sovereignty, after all, are loci of dignity in our common legal understanding (I once received a speeding ticket in West Virginia that accused me of an offense against the "peace and dignity" of the municipality). But the dignity of the state, or indeed of any institution, is not *human* dignity as revisionists construe it. For reasons articulated in Chapter 14, dignity-revisionism seems well-attuned to the dangers of treating mere institutions, as opposed to people and their lives, as valuable for their own sakes. If human dignity requires us to deny the dignity of sovereignty, so be it.

over the economy than is realistic. Hayek's point is not just, or even mainly, targeted toward those who claim that central economic planning can, after all, work; it is far more addressed to those for whom its failure would constitute a reason to criticize public institutions that attempt it. For Hayek, the assumption that this is a reasonable standard to impose on common institutions is itself irrational, a form of wishful thinking based on misplaced expectations. Yet the irrationality he claims to expose is not one that comes to light when we take up the moral philosopher's "deliberative stance" and apply a putatively correct "criterion of right action" to voluntary decision-making. It arises, rather, when "we" fail to dissociate a psychological attitude that we share in virtue of a common evolutionary inheritance from an institution that is part of our common historical inheritance (the modern state). Succumbing to this confusion is for Hayek a kind of collective irrationality distorting political judgment. Unlike Nozick's Kantian arguments for a minimal state, his argument turns, not on an implicit theory of individual moral responsibility, but on the need to adapt our expectations of common institutions to the radically transformed conditions of modern life.

Whatever the merits of his overall position (I criticize it below), Hayek was, I believe, entirely correct in presuming that critical political judgments of this kind need not presuppose any particular view about how agents ought to deliberate about their voluntary choices. The need for a "criterion of right action" will seem most pressing in contexts – exemplified by "Trolley Problem" cases common in the ethics literature – in which it is genuinely unclear how one should act given various conflicting, but intuitively compelling, considerations. In any pure form, however, such practical dilemmas arise in everyday life quite rarely. Even when agents do encounter them, the resulting sense of deliberative uncertainty doesn't give them any particular reason to question the value of the *political* practices in which they are immersed. As Hayek especially appreciated, most of our "voluntary decisions" anyway concern choices about how best to advance our purposes within the range of discretion left to us by commonly recognized positive moral constraints (institutional, ethical, legal, professional, religious, etc.). The latter already supply "criteria of right action" adequate for most practical purposes, and agents don't usually experience any deep sense of quandary as they voluntarily conform to them.

Yet this does not render critical reflection on the relevant norms and practices any less urgent. To the contrary, recognized institutional expectations and positive norms invite critical scrutiny precisely because, when what one must do to comply with them is quite clear, the general propensity to follow them has a large impact on the overall character of common life. As Marx, the classical utilitarians, and indeed Rawls, understood, the primary concern of the critic is with those positive moralities, institutional structures and practices that shape the terms of human interaction in especially consequential ways. The aim, then, is not to help individuals to decide what to do in the absence of generally accepted or unequivocal criteria, but to put what is settled into question, and to gain some critical distance on conventionally accepted norms and practices.

The search for "criteria of right action" would further that aim only if one thought that judging those norms and practices is itself a special case of choosing morally defensible voluntary actions. But that is plainly false. Critical reflection on politics certainly aims to uncover reasons for judging the practices under scrutiny favorably or unfavorably, but the word "judging" here doesn't name any particular action that we might contemplate performing. When we speak of ourselves as "forming" the judgments about politics to which critical political reflection addresses itself, we aren't referring to a voluntary action like running a red light, accepting a bribe, or returning a guilty verdict. "Forming judgments" of the relevant kind is an indefinite, typically sporadic, and largely non-voluntary, process by which our conscious evaluative attitudes toward our political circumstances evolve and update themselves in the face of argument, criticism, discourse, observation, experience, and our own emotional reactions. Critical reflection on politics is of a piece with this process, trying to make us better conscious of why we hold the particular attitudes we do, and to attune us, as best one can, to the reasons for maintaining, revising, or repudiating, them.

Whatever their cogency or outcome, however, arguments purporting to expose such reasons do not usually canvass candidates for our voluntary assent, as if agents can (as we sometimes misleadingly suggest) choose whether to "buy" them.[2] They aren't addressed to the will, but rather attempt to get its addressees to "see reason" with respect to the value of political arrangements under consideration. That familiar phrase captures the central point: while people can choose to close their eyes and ears (and sometimes do so unconsciously), once they are open they generally cannot choose what they see or hear. Similarly, whether an agent's political attitudes are rationally defensible as opposed to confused, unwarranted, or ideologically deluded is not a function of whether they have somehow *chosen* to endorse them. The question is whether the arguments, discourse, persuasion, rhetoric, evidence, experiences, education, culture, and so on,

---

[2] To be sure, once we are convinced (or have convinced themselves) of the value or disvalue of some political practice, agents may *then* be led to think that "something must be done," and to consider which voluntary actions might constitute an appropriate response (e.g., resigning from a position; joining a political party; disobeying, amending, or repealing a law; standing for office; going on strike; assassinating a leader). But this doesn't mean that the critical judgments that framed this subsequent deliberation were themselves voluntarily chosen.

that have involuntarily shaped their attitudes toward their political situation do or don't reflect the reasons[3] that truly apply to them.[4]

Here it is worth recalling that classical utilitarianism, the chief foil against which dignitarian humanism has historically defined itself, need not be interpreted as an "ethics-first" theory in the sense to which contemporary realists object. The contemporary academic tradition of utilitarian ethics obscures this point, because it often supposes that utilitarians must regard the utility principle as a *moral* imperative directly imposing a duty on persons and institutions to maximize welfare. Yet the classical utilitarianism of Bentham and Mill was not moralistic in this way: its ambition was rather to assess the *rationality* of various normative expectations, positive moral practices, institutional structures, and so on, according as they promote overall material well-being, taking the welfare gains and losses of each affected party into impartial account.

Classical utilitarianism rests ultimately, not on any narrowly moral imperative, but on a more general idea of impartial prudential rationality, informed

[3] I am thinking here mainly of *practical* rather than epistemic or theoretical reasons. "Seeing reason" in the relevant sense is *not* "seeing facts" or becoming newly acquainted with unfamiliar data (though acquiring descriptive beliefs, too, is usually involuntary). Rather, it involves achieving a keener appreciation of the rationality or irrationality of one's attitudes. Successful Socratic interrogation that induces *aporia* does not present the interlocutor with a *choice* about whether to find their attitudes (e.g., to justice, piety, courage) confused and self-contradictory. It directly exposes their incoherence and irrationality.

[4] This isn't to say that seeing the relevant reasons is an unconscious reflex, as when we flinch from a projectile hurled in our direction: appreciating reasons certainly requires conscious reflection. As Parfit writes: "Though we can seldom choose how we respond to our reasons to have particular beliefs and desires, our responses to these reasons are not things that merely happen to us, like . . . our slipping on a banana-skin. Our being rational consists in part in our responding to such reasons or apparent reasons in these non-voluntary ways. We can be asked *why* we believe something, or want something, and we can often give our reasons." Parfit, *On What Matters*, vol. 1, p. 48. Nor is it to deny that avowing, declaring, or committing yourself to normative attitudes and beliefs because you have come to appreciate reasons for them reflects a definite voluntary choice (for these are specific speech acts that one may or may not perform). Nor can we preclude the possibility that agents might simultaneously appreciate roughly equivalent, or incommensurable, reasons for and against holding a certain practical attitude, so that they then enjoy some latitude to choose those with which they wish to identify (Frankfurt's second-order volitions are indeed *volitions*). Nor does the fact that agents often voluntarily comply with (or ignore) expectations they have reasons to reject (or affirm), imply that their appreciation of those reasons is itself voluntary. Such cases of *akrasia*, weakness of the will, need not be analyzed as an inconsistency between voluntary choice and voluntary judgment. Indeed, the standard (and most philosophically interesting) cases of *akrasia* are precisely those in which agents acknowledge that they cannot choose to believe that, for example, smoking is good for them yet somehow still believe that they can rationally choose to smoke. These possibilities all have their place, but none entails that we can or generally do appreciate our practical reasons voluntarily.

by a nonmoralized theory of human welfare and its psychological conditions. When utilitarians argue that social and political practices should be abolished or reformed because, in their current form, they inflict widespread unnecessary suffering on large numbers of human beings, they are not making a judgment about the moral propriety of any particular action. They are rather addressing speakers reflecting on the adequacy of their political arrangements and arguing that it is to the discredit of their community itself that it is willing to tolerate unnecessary human suffering. Such an argument presupposes that the responsibility to avoid unnecessary suffering is shared indivisibly across a community. The existence of such common responsibilities is routinely presupposed in everyday political discourse, as when speakers say that "we" share a responsibility to see that justice is done, to preserve and fortify democratic accountability, to ensure that economic opportunities are fairly distributed, to protect and secure human dignity, and so on. When we draw attention to a failure to fulfill these responsibilities, we are not criticizing particular individuals, on moral grounds, for behaving in ways that are merely to their individual discredit. Rather, we are criticizing our forms of life for deficiencies that are to our collective detriment (as for example Hayek does in his critique of socialist dirigisme). Common responsibilities of this kind are natural objects of political evaluation in that the extent to which they are fulfilled can be a reason to form a judgment on a community *as such*. When a responsibility is in this way indivisible, it becomes a res publica, a matter of common or public concern among those who together are prepared to take some responsibility for their shared form of life.

I take dignitarian humanism to compete with classical utilitarianism, and its other interlocutors, on these terms. Like utilitarians, it aims to submit the practices of common life to standards of rational assessment. And, as I emphasized in Chapter 3, it also shares with utilitarianism the ambition to pursue political criticism of this sort from some standpoint of impartiality, in the light of reasons appreciable by anyone (regardless of their partial interests, propensities, moral or religious outlook, etc.). That is why dignitarians present themselves as speaking from the perspective of a "common humanity." Clearly, however, the dignitarian approach must have a distinctive content and structure, for in any of its forms, it rejects the idea that collective prudence should serve as the ultimate standard by which we judge the adequacy of social and political arrangements. As dignitarians understand it, our common humanity does not consist ultimately in a shared interest in welfare but in something else.

One of Rawls's formulations is particularly germane here: his rejection of the utilitarian idea that "the principle of choice for an association of men [*sic*]is . . . an extension of the principle of choice for one man" such that "[T]he principle of rational prudence [is] applied to an aggregative conception of the welfare of the group." It was this feature of utilitarianism that led Rawls (and Nozick and many others) to complain that its "conflating [of] all persons into one . . . does

not take seriously the distinction between persons."[5] For him and the dignitarian humanists who came after, that feature problematically instrumentalizes
human lives, leaving open the possibility that some individuals' welfare may be
sacrificed in order to reduce overall suffering or maximize happiness. It
smudges the crucial distinction between the inviolable dignity of human
beings and the "price" or instrumental value of objects.

Accordingly, dignitarian humanist political criticism became an effort to
specify a common responsibility to ensure that all human beings matter for
their own sakes, and not merely as "means" to some abstract, impersonal, end
that can be identified with society *as such*. On pain of violating an overriding
responsibility to protect human dignity, any decent and just political order
must ensure that individuals and their lives are respected as "ends-in-
themselves." Our fundamental common responsibility is to guarantee, through
institutionalized cooperation, the basic conditions securing a dignified existence for all. When we criticize social forms from a dignitarian perspective, that
is the primary, adamant desideratum.

Dignity-revisionism shares this ambition, and agrees that common responsibility is not well-construed on the model of society as a single, collective,
agent with a closed set of goals. Nonetheless, it accuses the traditional construals of human dignity criticized in this book as misdescribing that responsibility. It rejects, in particular, the tendency of Kantian theories to blur the
distinction between moral philosophy and ethics (on the one hand) and
political criticism (on the other). The Kantian framework is centrally constructed around an idea of moral accountability – the terms on which agents
are liable to praise and blame for their voluntarily chosen conduct. The
"adamant" quality of dignitarian claims accordingly tends to materialize
within it as an unconditional moral requirement or "side-constraint" for
whose violation agents or institutions can be held culpable. The pervasiveness
of Kantian assumptions has made it difficult for dignitarians to conceive of the
possibility that the adamant requirements of human dignity could apply in
political judgment in any other form.

Yet, just on conceptual grounds, it seems entirely possible that social
arrangements *as such* can threaten human dignity in a way that is adamantly
objectionable whether or not anyone involved is guilty of wrongdoing from
a moral or legal perspective. Consider here Ken Loach's film, *I, Daniel Blake*,
which documents the plight of those caught up in the UK benefits system
under the recent régime of economic "austerity." The film captures very
effectively how agents who encounter others representing organized public
institutions can confront what Loach himself has called "conscious cruelty,"
despite the best intentions of those operating the system. None of the officials
who deal with Daniel Blake in the film can be plausibly charged with improper

---

[5] Rawls, *Theory of Justice*, pp. 23–24.

conduct; they are simply doing what is asked of them; and the rules they enforce are designed with the demands of reciprocity, fairness, and respect in view. They could readily deflect charges that they culpably treat clients of the welfare system merely as "means" in a Kantian sense: they don't perform any actions akin to assault, fraud, or theft either in their character or moral unacceptability. Yet, Blake is clearly humiliated, and many would describe his predicament as an intolerable indignity. His situation closely resembles that of Blackpool in *Hard Times*.

Throughout this book, I have argued that we can and should think of the gravest privations of human dignity (like genocide and slavery) as irreducible to any culpable wrongs committed by those involved. On the revisionist view, human dignity reflects a nonlocal disposition of social power, not a principle that constrains morally appropriate choice. This strikes me as an advantage of the revisionist account as a vehicle for critical reflection on politics. It provides a framework for thinking of the protection of human dignity as a common responsibility with specifically political import, and for at least considering whether, from a dignitarian perspective, arrangements like those confronting Daniel Blake should be acceptable in any civilized society.

Drawing the Line

The question I am posing about the scope of dignitarian *political* responsibility returns us to a loose end left hanging in Chapter 14. The argument there was that even though it understands human dignity as a nonlocal, social relation, dignity-revisionism has just as good an account of why standard cases of extreme subordination (slavery, collectivist oppression, genocide, etc.) represent adamantly objectionable privations of human dignity as do more traditional views. But I promised that I would go on to defend a stronger claim: that the nonlocal account of human dignity developed here gives a *better* framework than dignity-traditionalism for reflecting on how to define the political responsibility to protect human dignity. The issue here is how dignitarians should draw the line between indignities (or "forsakings," "usings," "exploitings," "objectifications," "humiliations," or "treatings" only as "means" – whatever description one prefers) that are serious enough to trigger political concern and those that aren't. Clearly, many such indignities (the minor humiliations of daily existence) aren't plausibly regarded as objects of any sort of common responsibility. So dignitarians need some framework for thinking about when they threaten *human* dignity in ways that no civilized political community should accept. I now turn directly to my contention that the revisionist view is almost certainly more helpful on this score than dignity-traditionalism, and hence offers a better model of dignitarian political criticism.

The first half of this book was devoted to exposing serious problems with traditional conceptions of human dignity, and so a cheap way to defend that contention would simply be to review those earlier objections and leave it there. But I won't do that. This is not only because (it goes without saying) some may not have been convinced by those earlier objections, but also because the issue in view now is importantly independent of the case I made against B-Dignity and C-Dignity. For the most part, the critical arguments I made in Part II of this book targeted the *fixity* of traditionalist dignity. But with my revisionist alternative out on the table, a different issue has now moved into the foreground: the adequacy of *nonlocal* as opposed to *local* understandings of human dignity.

Many will still feel a residual allegiance to the traditionalist claim that, at least in political contexts, human dignity is nothing more than a local property or feature of the individual. They will be strongly inclined to think that, for political purposes, it is sufficient to identify human dignity with some individualized status, entitlement, or right, and will accordingly resist my suggestion that we should construe it in nonlocal or relational terms. As Joel Feinberg famously observed, "what is called 'human dignity' may simply be the recognizable capacity to assert claims. To respect a person, then, or to think of him as possessed of human dignity, simply is to think of him as a potential maker of claims."[6]

So the argument I want to offer now is addressed to those, tempted by Feinberg's observation, who suspect that construing human dignity nonlocally can only confuse us about the overriding importance of the essentially local entitlements that define it. The most visible dignitarian positions in contemporary political discourse certainly lend circumstantial credence to this suspicion, for they very often reinforce the sort of dignity-traditionalism that I am seeking to replace.

Natural Lawyers like John Finnis or Robert George, for example, identify human dignity with the "intrinsic worth" of human life *as such*. Anything that possesses that property locally will come to seem deserving of adamant respect and protection in a way that has clear political relevance – hence the characteristic focus in that tradition on the law's (alleged) legitimate concern with the "life" of the fetus in utero. Similarly, if one is a dignity-traditionalist libertarian like Nozick, one will identify human dignity with a local status or right of individual self-ownership, such that the most urgent political responsibilities are coded as physical aggression against the person, the use of coercive force, and the seizure of legitimately acquired external assets. If one is a dignity-traditionalist of a Dworkinian kind, one will define the most urgent political responsibilities in terms of a principle of "equal concern and respect" that

---

[6] Joel Feinberg and Jan Narveson, "The Nature and Value of Rights," *The Journal of Value Inquiry* 4, no. 4 (December 1, 1970): 252–53.

protects the local status and independence of each person considered as an abstract equal. And so on.

It is true that some traditionalists, like Stephen Darwall and Arthur Ripstein, acknowledge that individual dignity – in the form of what I earlier called "C-dignity" – has a partly nonlocal, relational, character. Yet for all practical purposes their understanding of dignity remains basically possessive and individualized. The reason for this is that relationality figures in these strongly Kantian theories only in a purely formal sense. As Ripstein in particular tirelessly emphasizes, the relevant relations are in Kant's sense purely regulative, noumenal, ideals with no determinate location in time or space. They comprise "a formal system of equal freedom, in which each person's purposiveness is restricted only by the purposiveness of others."[7] Yet, as Ripstein recognizes, actual political and legal regimes must realize that relation in the ordinary spatiotemporal world. So, in practice, Kant's requirement that restrictions on "one person's purposiveness" are legitimate only if enacted exclusively "for the sake ... of freedom" materializes politically as an unconditional demand for respect for "each person's right to be *sui juris*, her own master."[8] Hence it is *my* personal sovereignty and independence that determines in the actual world what it is to act rightly for my sake in the Kantian theory of Right. As Ripstein says, "the relational aspect of right reflects the fact that a wrong is always a wrong against some other person in particular. If I wrong you, ... I wrong you in particular, and you in particular have a complaint against me."[9] So in the end, even these relational accounts preserve the traditionalist assumption that the dignity that matters in politics is possessive and local – it is centered on *my* rights, *my* entitlements, *my* purposiveness, *my* sovereignty, *my* status, and so on.

The Dignity of Ignorance

Given the currency of these views, why then deny that the various locally defined claims (personal sovereignty, our status as abstract equals, our rights as self-owners, etc.) with which they identify human dignity tell us all we need to know about where the political responsibility to protect it begins and ends? Why not just agree that adamant, politically enforced, respect for these local entitlements is necessary and sufficient to specify what political communities must do to ensure that individuals and their lives are valued for their own sakes?

At this point one might expect me to canvass, on behalf of the revisionist view, some alternative positive account defining the common responsibility to

---

[7] Ripstein, *Force and Freedom*, p. 63.
[8] Ibid., p. 64.
[9] Ibid., p. 382.

protect human dignity. But although I will suggest in a moment that the view I have developed in this book does offer some actionable guidance about how to pursue that question, I do not have any fully worked out account up my sleeve. I think anyone, if they are being honest, should admit the same. The better line for the revisionist to take is precisely to make a virtue of *not* claiming to know what, exactly, what an adamant commitment to protecting human dignity requires of a political community. To my mind, the very open-endedness of the revisionist position on this point compares favorably with the confident assertion on the part of dignity-traditionalists that, for political purposes, there is nothing more to human dignity than individual rights, personal sovereignty, equal status, and so on.

For how do they *know* that standing pat on such localized formalisms is sufficient to elaborate a common commitment to protecting human dignity? What makes them so sure that it doesn't actually function as an excuse to divert critical attention away from serious but perhaps unnoticed indignities afflicting social and economic forms? No sensible revisionist would, I take it, want to deny that using the power of the law and the state to uphold individuals' basic rights, civic status, entitlements to security of person and property, and so on is often required to ensure that no human being or group of human beings suffers radical indignity or is forsaken. But that is hardly the issue. What is in question is how, when we take up a critical perspective on our forms of life, we can *know* that such rights and entitlements have dignitarian import (as opposed to just being instrumentally valuable conventions, or legal and moral entitlements that are incidental to it), and verify how far enforcing them is sufficient to discharge a common responsibility to protect human dignity. Which individual rights and entitlements are crucial for human dignity and which peripheral? Are only formal entitlements needed? What about those represented by Daniel Blake, who clearly suffer indignity at the hands of public institutions even though none has wronged them? These matters cannot be settled just by *defining* human dignity in terms of the various individually localized entitlements whose dignitarian significance is under scrutiny. That just begs the question.

As I suggested in Chapter 13, begging the question in that way is formally akin to the mistake Hayek thought that formal models of the economy make when they stipulate that economic values are "given." In urging us to keep an open mind about what is and isn't politically necessary to protect human dignity, the dignity-revisionist is similarly refusing to take "human dignity" as a "given." For, as argued in this book, they see human dignity as a nonlocal, varying, social accomplishment that depends on how human lives are actually valorized in social routines, and hence not simply "given" in some pre-fixed pattern of juridical entitlements. Under different social and political conditions, it can be more and less securely entrenched, and different individuals can enjoy a greater and lesser share in it; the task for the dignitarian social critic is then to *really look*[10] at how actual forms of life are disposed with respect to the realization of, and inclusive access to, a dignified human existence. We should ask, without presuming that we already know the answers, who, under given social, historical, and political conditions, is radically forsaken, in the sense defined in Chapter 14? Who is denied a share in the nonlocal patterns of affective engagement on which the emergence of human dignity depends?

The revisionist does not claim to know how, for the purposes of political judgment, inquiry along these lines will actually pan out. But she does claim that these are the right questions to ask, and that answering them may be able to tell us something about when political grievances that are couched in dignitarian terms have merit and when they don't. The account given here, for example, surely puts pressure on Nozick's claim that redistributive taxation is "on a par with" forced labor, at least from a dignitarian point of view: any suggestion that affluent groups forced to contribute to public provision can credibly claim that their society thereby radically forsakes them, or that they face anything akin to timanthropic "insolvency" of the kind discussed in Chapter 13 is silly. Feinberg regarded the possession of rights as constitutive of dignity in that they protect a capacity to assert claims, thereby allowing us to "'stand up like men,' [and] look others in the eye." Yet, as Nozick's example illustrates, emphasizing that capacity can be a double-edged sword, sometimes enabling privileged groups to rightfully but prematurely block public action needed to ensure that vulnerable social constituencies do not find themselves radically forsaken. It is in this guise that dignitarian arguments invite plausible charges of ideological distraction, protecting suspect social practices from clear-eyed critical scrutiny.

Yet dignity-revisionism offers resources for looking beyond the familiar tendency to inflate complaints made on behalf of particular constituencies into inviolable dignitarian red-lines in a way that allows the "ghostly hand of the present to throttle the future."[11] It directs critical attention away from the bare capacity to assert claims, which is surely only the beginning of critical reflection, and onto the more pertinent question of whether the relevant claims deserve to be upheld as adamant desiderata of human dignity. As Chapter 14 suggested, what ultimately matters for human dignity is not the mere *assertion* of grievances, but their discriminating and appropriate uptake in social and institutional routines that are disposed to respond to individuals with respect rather than disrespect. Many plausible candidates for dignitarian concern along these lines will be familiar: those facing extreme poverty, the homeless, those born into desperate urban slums and ghettos, the long-term

---

[10] This, of course, is Iris Murdoch's language. Iris Murdoch, *The Sovereignty of Good* (London: Routledge, 2006).

[11] R. Geuss, *History and Illusion in Politics* (Cambridge: Cambridge University Press, 2001), p. 154.

unemployed, members of stigmatized groups (racism, sexism, homophobia, xenophobia, etc.), those condemned to the degrading working conditions of the sweatshop, and so on. Others may be less familiar or entirely unexpected: in particular, there is no reason to assume that dispersed individuals who share no recognizable "identity" can't all face a structurally similar circumstance in which the dominant institutions that de facto control their lives have no disposition to attend to them in ways that bring anything of their worth as human beings to light. Why should political criticism discriminate against these individuals just because they aren't united by some "identity" around which a "social movement" is likely to coalesce?

In any case, three other merits of the revisionist approach I have been describing deserve stress. First, it directs critical attention onto phenomena that can in principle be empirically investigated: the politics and affective psychology of respect, contempt, and disrespect; the routines in which agents are immersed; the directions in which institutional, ideological, and cultural attention are in fact oriented; the affective dispositions encouraged or discouraged by the role-moralities of the workplace, the lobby, the civil service, the family, the police, the classroom, and so on. With the revisionist account of dignitarian devalorization to guide them, empirically informed judgments about if, when, and how, the configuration of existing social powers devalues its members' lives in these and other milieux might be defended, and help us consider whether coordinated defensive or offensive action afford suitable remedies. By, in effect, *naturalizing* human dignity, the revisionist account refuses B. F. Skinner's ultimatum: *either* empirically informed utilitarian technocracy *or* alternately unadjudicable and dogmatic appeals to an inscrutable "inner worth" that stands apart from the world.

Second, I have repeatedly stressed throughout this book that an aspect of human dignity is the avoidance of fantasy and delusion; it opposes idolatry, idealizing fantasies, and sham value. A society that "lives in an interminable series of glittering tomorrows, which it discovers to be tinsel when it becomes today"[12] is not being honest with itself; it attends to idols before real human needs whose systematic nonfulfillment may leave some lives radically forsaken. Orienting political criticism toward the honest acknowledgment of such unfulfilled needs is then one way to act for the sake of those whose needs they are. Such critical reflection is itself a mode in which human dignity discloses itself in practical activity. This chimes with our ordinary consciousness of dignitarian concern as implicating truth-telling, wisdom, proportionality, attunement to the social conditions for personal independence, and the exercise of reasoned judgment.

Third, and relatedly, the practice of dignitarian political criticism I have been describing would have an essentially democratic impetus. For

---

[12] Richard Tawney, *Equality* (London: Unwin, 1962), p. 108.

revisionists, the question is whether people in our society are being attended to in ways that allow them to matter for their own sakes, or confront them with the sort of systemic, institutionalized, disrespect that I have argued can "devalorize" their lives. But a society cannot inform itself about this without its members being willing – as Danielle Allen has argued – to "talk to strangers" in a spirit of respect and good will, seeking to appreciate challenges faced by others that might otherwise escape their notice.[13] The ethos for which Allen is calling, however, is precisely not one in which citizens stand on "their" dignity – understood as a locally possessed entitlement to make adamant demands of others on their private behalves. It points, rather, toward a mode of democratic engagement in which citizens are disposed to pay attention to the claims of others for their own sakes. If the argument of this book is right, citizens who do cultivate such delocalizing dispositions will automatically impart a dignified quality to their civic life, at least if they do it reasonably well. For on the revisionist account, human dignity *just is* a nonlocal pattern of dispositions in which agents attend respectfully to each other (in many different social contexts) over time. In this sense, healthy democratic engagement is itself integral to the achievement of human dignity as revisionists understand it.

The classical case for universal suffrage, today called into question by "epistocrats" like Jason Brennan, has often turned on just such claims:

> It is a matter of humiliation for a society, if a large portion of its members be in so degraded and uneducated a state, that they are deemed unworthy of having a voice in the affairs which interest all. The consciousness of the possession of such a voice, like that of property, is a great instrument of moral elevation, and tends to give a man a dignified position in his own and his neighbour's eyes; while the want of such advantages allows him to fall into the lowest depths of degradation.[14]

Critics of universal suffrage like Brennan tend to depict such arguments as merely "expressive" or "semiotic" – little more than "poetry," or "symbolism" that floats frothily on the real substance of politics (the power to coerce, formal rights to property, and the maintenance of economic efficiency).[15] I will later canvass a hypothesis about why Brennan and others are tempted to characterize these issues in "semiotic" terms. But the immediate point is that the characterization itself is implausible.

For what is at stake in universal suffrage is not merely ceremonial, ritualistic, or symbolic, but an absolutely fundamental political power –

---

[13] Danielle S. Allen, *Talking to Strangers: Anxieties of Citizenship since Brown* v. *Board of Education* (Chicago: University of Chicago Press, 2004).

[14] George Drysdale, *The Elements of Social Science* (London: Truelove, 1861).

[15] Jason Brennan, *Against Democracy* (Princeton, NJ: Princeton University Press, 2016), pp. 113ff.

the power to bring grievances and other matters of concern to public attention. As Melissa Schwartzberg has argued recently, that power matters for Hayekian reasons:[16] it is a condition under which political communities can acquire valuable information about how their members are faring that would otherwise elude it. The grievances may or may not have merit, but in order to assess them, we need to at least know what they are and what motivates them.

A. D. Lindsay's unjustly neglected "shoe-pinching" argument makes the essential point:

> [I]f . . . the end of democratic government is to minister to the common life of society, to remove the disharmonies that trouble it, then clearly a knowledge and understanding of that common life is a large part of the knowledge essential to the statesman. But the common life is the life lived by all members of society. It cannot be fully known and appreciated from outside. It can only be known by those who live it. Its disharmonies are suffered and felt by those who live it. It is their shoes that pinch and they only who can tell where they pinch.[17]

Brennan's *Against Democracy* spends pages complaining about how little ordinary democratic voters know about politics. But how much would episto-crats – particularly ones who have already decided that very many citizens are unworthy of the franchise and should be excluded from political power – know about ordinary people and their struggles? Would they be disposed to pay much attention to their grievances?

The problem about epistocracy and the rule of "experts," as Lindsay goes on to say, is that the "experts do not like being told that the shoes they so beautifully made do not fit. They are apt to blame it on the distorted and misshapen toes of the people who have to wear the shoes. Unless there is power behind the expression of grievances, the grievances are apt to be neglected."[18] The power to reliably command the warranted attention of those who control one's terms of existence for one's own sake, because (say) one's conditions of life are unacceptably degrading, is not merely expressive or "semiotic." To the contrary, as I have argued here, it is essential to a reasonable share in human dignity. If our current democratic arrangements still do not guarantee to all citizens enough of that power (surely they don't), the answer is not to denude that power still further by moving in an epistocratic direction but to extend and deepen democracy.

---

[16] Melissa Schwartzberg, "Sheep May Safely Graze: On the Instrumental Justification of Democracy" (unpublished manuscript, available at www.law.nyu.edu/sites/default/files/upload_documents/Colloquium_SchwartzbergSheep.pdf).

[17] A. D. Lindsay, *The Modern Democratic State* (New York: Galaxy, 1962), p. 269.

[18] Ibid., p. 271.

Hayek versus Hayek

Revisionists are thus rightly suspicious of those who suggest, on behalf of a possessive, localized, conception of human dignity, that we can preempt critical inquiry along these lines simply by asking questions like "was anything stolen?," "did anyone culpably wrong anyone?," "was everyone's personal sovereignty respected?," "is this public act of coercion justified?" Again, the point is not to say that these questions are *irrelevant*; certainly, they are unlikely to have no importance at all in any campaign to cooperate politically in protecting human dignity. But how important they are and whether they are sufficient are not *known* in advance; nor can we settle these matters by formal stipulation. In pressing this point, revisionists urge us to become consistent Hayekians, and to extend his general understanding of how human engagement *effects* social valuation beyond the narrow commercial sphere and into the more momentous timanthropic domain.

Of course Hayek himself did not make anything like that move, in part because he said very little about human dignity. But he did say a great deal about the attitude we ought to take to the "*système de principes*" (Constant's term) that he regarded as essential to protecting the individual rights and entitlements of private property and by extension free markets. He thought our attitude to these principles, and the local, individualized, entitlements they confer, should be very much like the attitude dignitarians claim we should take to human dignity – one of adamant commitment. Freedom, he said, must be "accepted as an overriding principle," be "stubbornly adhered to as an ultimate ideal," and added that "there must be no compromise for the sake of material advantages."[19] And, of course, many other libertarians *do* identify all this with dignity: "to restrict the capacity of people to make economic choices or, worse, to treat their economic activities merely as means to the social ends of others, would violate the dignity of such persons."[20] But again, this tends to equate dignity with the local entitlements and individual status possessed by independent individuals in commercial competition, and to assume that we already know that there is nothing, politically speaking, to human dignity but the right to assert such individualized claims.

What makes Hayek – especially as a theorist who stressed the uncertainty and ignorance of our knowledge of what has value – so sure that these localized entitlements are worth such uncompromising allegiance? His own answer is a broadly consequentialist one, and it turns on his arguments about the effective use of information accomplished by the "price system" reviewed in Chapter 13. In his view, the principle of freedom and the disposition to conform adamantly to it protect the operation of the "price system," and thereby serve the interests of efficient economic planning on the part of private individuals and firms. Hayek

[19] Hayek, *The Constitution of Liberty*, pp. 129–30.
[20] John Tomasi, *Free Market Fairness* (Princeton, NJ: Princeton University Press, 2012), p. 98.

offers a "slippery slope" argument against violating those principles; once we make a single exception, we will be tempted to entertain others, and gradually freedom will be "destroyed" by "piecemeal encroachments."[21]

But this argument can hardly satisfy a dignitarian. It amounts to the rule-consequentialist claim that the principle of freedom must be religiously followed because the efficiency of the economic system requires that agents take that attitude to it. Our common responsibility for preserving and conforming to his principle of freedom turns out to be ultimately a responsibility to the market – an abstract, lifeless, *système* – and its requirements. This leaves Hayek vulnerable to a charge of system-idolatry. Indeed, sometimes he talks about the *système's* right to our deference for its own sake in terms that invite objections of exactly the anti-collectivist sort discussed in Chapter 14:

> What we must learn to understand is that human civilization has a life of its own, that all our efforts to improve things must operate within a working whole . . . whose forces we can hope merely to facilitate and assist so far as we understand them. Our attitude ought to be similar to that of the physician toward a living organism: like him, we have to deal with a self-maintaining whole which is kept going by forces which we cannot replace. . . . In all our endeavor at improvement we must always work inside this given whole.[22]

So, for Hayek it turns out that although economic value is not "given," the market system itself, and *its* overriding importance, *is* "given." The problem with this position, other than the odd but telling indulgence of "organicist" and holist tropes in the passage just cited, is that simply taking the market as "given" begs the same question as the dignity-traditionalist: to be able to claim that it always values its members for their own sakes, and never treats them "only as means," needs a political community only enforce the rights of the market. It is not as if the allegation that markets are objectionably exploitative has never occurred to anyone. How do we know, on a Hayekian view, that simply by conforming religiously to the rules of the *système*, we completely fulfill any common responsibility to ensure that no human being is ever unacceptably exploited or otherwise forsaken?

Hayek's reply, I think, would be to say that we don't (and perhaps can't) know this, but that we do know that the only alternative to unbending conformity to the rules of his abstract order must be something worse: a political system that tries to organize social cooperation on the model of "a true economy in which all effort is directed toward a uniform order of objectives."[23] Then (he would say) we are well and truly on the "Road to

---

[21] Hayek, *The Constitution of Liberty*, p. 130.

[22] Ibid., p. 131–32.

[23] This is the free marketeer's version of Rawls's objection, mentioned earlier, that utilitarianism falsely generalizes the "principle of choice for one agent" (i.e., rational prudence) to the case of collective choice.

Serfdom," because individual freedom will be sacrificed to a closed set of ends, whereas a free society will be an open-ended catallaxy.

But, even if one accepts the "Road to Serfdom" argument (which I don't), this book has argued that this is *not* the only alternative. We can instead think of the commercial catallaxy, whose intentionality (if we accept Hayek's view, for the sake of argument) is given by its superior "discovery procedure" for economic worth, as nested within a more fundamental catallaxy: a "human economy" or *oikos* that determines, in the way that dominant social and institutional routines pay or refuse to pay individuals attention, how human beings are valued in their societies. This more important system of mutual adjustment, though also open-ended, and also a site of freedom,[24] exploit and adventure,[25] has its own intentionality: it is a venue in which various

---

[24] The implications of dignity-revisionism for conceptions of freedom and emancipation deserve more elaboration than I can give them here. But it is worth sketching the most obvious points at which it intersects with familiar understandings of political freedom. Dignity-revisionism is plainly attuned to the forms of unfreedom emphasized by theorists of "negative liberty" – interferences, forms of confinement, subjection to coercion, curtailments of freedom of action, and so on – though it will tend to regard these as threatening *personal* dignity as A-dignity. But it is also, and more centrally, sensitive to the ways that disposition of social power can instantiate domination as neo-Romans understand it. Like the neo-Romans, dignity-revisionists can insist that the disposition to attend to others' claims for their sake is too important to be enjoyed at the pleasure of those in a position to activate or withdraw it. The conditions for a dignified and free life are not discretionary, but adamant.

[25] Does dignity-revisionism point in a perfectionist direction? Insofar as "valuing-people-for-their-own-sake" in the revisionist's sense implies engaging with them in ways that allow them to realize aspects of their good, it is certainly compatible with a broadly perfectionist outlook. For revisionists, after all, the struggle for human dignity is the struggle to configure human communities as optimally resonant *acoustics* in which anything that is great, wonderful, and worthy in members of the species can be realized, faithfully recorded, and properly appreciated for its own sake. To push the metaphor a bit, "optimal" here would lie in a mean between acoustics that are excessively "dry" and excessively "live" (as sound engineers say). The former would stifle the echoes of one person's worth before it ever touches the lives of others; the latter would drown their contributions in an indiscriminate cacophony. And nothing in dignity-revisionism would automatically preclude taking the promotion of valuable cultural forms as a common responsibility. On the other hand, as even Raz accepts, "respect" implies dispositions to recognize and preserve something or something's value but stops short of active promotion or participation in its full realization (Raz, *Value, Respect, and Attachment,* pp. 154–55, 164). Furthermore, the kind of "acoustic" in which human dignity can reverberate freely may often depend on private initiative as much as concerted public action. Indeed, it is likely threatened by excessive political intrusion inasmuch as it depends on spontaneous affective uptake. Trying to force the expression of the needed affects and attention, or treating it as a mandatory obligation, dampens its impact by inviting charges of insincerity. More generally, human dignity, as revisionists construe it, does not depend on a teleological claim about the realization of individuals' good or about the cultivation of a healthy relation to self, in contrast to many classical perfectionist theories. Human dignity is, for the revisionist, a matter of individuals' external affective impact on others,

valorization schemes (respect, love, etc.) offer "discovery procedures" that inform us about how social attention is (or is not) directed toward the value of different human lives, and hence how they count, or matter, in their form of life. For that reason, it is also, as I have argued here, where human dignity lives or dies, and where human beings are granted or denied a reasonable share in the social powers on which it depends. Only by understanding these dynamics, and their consequences for agents' ability to lead lives that are valued for their own sakes, the revisionist claims, can we begin to make reasonable judgments about the scope of our common responsibilities for protecting human dignity.

Contractualism and Detachment

Contractualism, as practiced by political philosophers since Rawls, might seem to offer a propitious alternative for ascertaining conditions under which all human beings can access a dignified life and reasonably expect their fellows to share some responsibility for those conditions. Certainly, that has been the intent of many contractualists. Dignity-revisionists are likely to be sympathetic to many of the substantive recommendations of Rawls's original theory. But I want to suggest a general reason to suspect that any contractualist approach will be inferior to dignity-revisionism for determining the scope of any common responsibilities to protect human dignity. The reason is closely related to the points just made, but it requires a little more explanation.

Insofar as they claim to "model" human dignity, most forms of contractualism, and many closely related theories, incorporate it as the idea that parties to the contractualist agreement possess a veto-right that must be respected. Different contractualist theories cash that veto out in contrasting ways: respect for their standing to "reasonably reject"; respect for "second-personal authority"; respect as refusing to assert the authority to demand that others "do what they do not themselves have reason to endorse,"[26] and so on. Many

not one of internal psychological adjustment (though sometimes "personal dignity," as defined in Chapter 14, may be implicated in the latter). One's life doesn't have to *make sense, hang together,* or be *heading in any clear teleological direction,* to inspire respect or, for that matter, love, in virtue of the unique qualities and capabilities it has to offer others' lives. After all, we owe many of the greatest achievements in art, literature, science, exploration, politics, to human beings whose own lives were a complete mess at the time, their mental health marginal, their closest relationships unraveling, their personal conduct shabby, and often without any clear recognition of the significance of their activities from the inside. These external accomplishments partly constitute human dignity, on a revisionist view, but it seems more natural, from a dignitarian standpoint to emphasize how they enable the free development of human capacities and not so much their tendency to realize the telos of any particular person. Liberty and emancipation are more central to the realization of human dignity than is personal self-development and the cultivation of human excellence.

[26] Gaus, *The Order of Public Reason,* p. 19.

noncontractualist theories also incorporate the same idea. Rainer Forst, for example, writes that "humans must be regarded as beings who have an unconditional right to justification, a basic right on which all other basic rights are founded. To possess human dignity means being an equal member in the realm of subjects and authorities of justification," and this again implies a right of veto enjoyed in principle by all.[27] Why do contractualists, and others, attach such fundamental importance to this formal veto – the right to say No – within critical reflection on politics and link it with the idea of dignity?

As we shall see, the answer relates to the distinctions drawn in Chapter 11 between "*observers*" whose concerns about the affective dispositions (love, respect, etc.) of some "*relevant agent*" might be "*detached*" or "*invested*." To be invested is to have some personal, or partial, reason to care that a relevant agent(s) is (are) motivated by love or respect; to be detached is to have a reason, regardless of personal perspective, bias, or partial interest, to care that some relevant agent(s) is (are) paying/giving attention to oneself or others in a respectful/loving spirit. To see the relevance of this distinction in this context, however, we need to go back to Rawls's original repudiation of utilitarianism and its consequences.

For a utilitarian, judgments about whether, and to what extent, we should approve or disapprove of social and political practices carry weight only insofar as they reflect "impartial reasons ... to care equally about everyone's well-being." Utilitarians are of course well aware of agents' propensity to be partial to particular institutions, social groups, and other individuals and, insofar as they tend, when routinized, to promote aggregate welfare, they will endorse them. Yet they insist that partiality must not taint the standpoint from which such utilitarian judgments themselves are reached. Their welfarist algorithm purports to derive its authority from being "no respecter of persons." The ideal utilitarian social critic thus aspires to be a *detached observer* in the sense introduced in Chapter 11; she regards judgments of aggregate welfare as definitive precisely in that any rational agent, regardless of any personal loyalties or partialities, can and should recognize their force, as it were "from the point of view of the Universe."

Under Rawls's influence, many came to worry that, insofar as it regards individuals as nothing more than sites at which aggregable quanta of welfare are experienced, this stance of detachment harbors an implicit contempt for persons and their lives. According to the critics, the obsession with critical detachment renders utilitarianism insensitive to the fact that each of us leads our lives separately, judging, feeling, and acting always from a particular inside perspective, populated by unique combinations of affective propensities, temperamental dispositions, and personal experiences. Hence the utilitarian's readiness to entertain sacrificing some for the sake of the many. This anti-

---

[27] Forst, "The Ground of Critique," 968–69.

utilitarian argument implies (as Gaus has explicitly noted)[28] that any adequate standard of political judgment must precisely be a "respecter of persons" – not in the Kantian sense, but in the early modern sense of *prosopolepsia* mentioned in Chapter 3, connoting, not impartiality, but *partiality*. Gaus's provocative use of that phrase in this context suggests that he and others who reject utilitarianism regard partiality and personality as mutually constitutive: what it is to be a person worthy of respect *just is* to occupy a particular, agent-relative, standpoint; and what it is to respect persons is to uphold as far as possible their prerogative to conduct their lives on their own terms, in the light of what quite reasonably moves *them*, but that others may reasonably reject. The detached, impartial, utilitarian philanthropist fails to respect people in this way: she is a welfarist actuary who treats them as little more than lines in a hedonic budget.

The contractualist remedy, adopted as well by many noncontractualist theories, is to insist that social principles, practices, or institutions can be legitimate only if each of those involved can reasonably affirm them from *within* the system of personal values that guides their personal deliberation about how to live. The *detached* perspective of the impartial utilitarian critic is thus replaced by a view that gives priority to the *invested* perspectives of private agents. Respect becomes the attitude that those private agents can legitimately demand for their own points of view from within those points of view. This broadly contractualist line doesn't wholly abandon the desideratum of "impartiality" in political judgment. But rather than interpret that desideratum as the fruit of a critical observer's detachment from all particular perspectives, it instead conceives it as a shared ("public") stance that any invested party could reasonably affirm from within their own, agent-relative, perspective. Working outward from individuals' private standpoints, exponents of this position propose to "construct" a common point of view from which no reasonable personal perspective is excluded.

A feature of the resulting position, however, is that it subordinates the legitimate concerns of "public reason," and common responsibility more generally, to the approval of invested agents moved by personal, agent-relative, interests. It therefore institutes a kind of private veto circumscribing the legitimate bounds of any common responsibilities. That veto becomes the locus of human dignity, and the source of the respect it commands. Dignity becomes a right to say No to sharing common responsibilities and any burdens (economic or existential) it might impose.

The implication is that, as bearers of "human dignity," persons "live life from the inside"; this "inside-out" perspective on human dignity has accordingly become axiomatic and ubiquitous within the political philosophy of the

---

[28] Gaus, *Value and Justification*, pp. 10–11.

past half-century. Consider, for example, Dworkin's late conceptualization of dignity. He reduces "human dignity" to two principles:

> The first is a principle of self-respect. Each person must take his own life seriously: he must accept that it is a matter of importance that his life be a successful performance rather than a wasted opportunity. The second is a principle of authenticity. Each person has a special, personal responsibility for identifying what counts as success in his own life; he has a personal responsibility to create that life through a coherent narrative or style that he himself endorses.[29]

But notice – and here I *am* returning to some fundamental themes in Part II of this book – that human dignity is here being defined in a completely *inward*, reflexive, way. The influence of Rawls's commitment to the "social bases of self-respect" as "perhaps the most important" primary good is quite clear here.

The burgeoning literature on recognition, even when hostile to Rawls's own approach, often displays this same reflexive character. Thus, Honneth, one of its pioneers, finds it entirely "natural" to suppose that "legal recognition" makes a "type of positive relation-to-self" possible.[30] Tellingly, Honneth approvingly cites Feinberg's understanding of "human dignity" in support,[31] identifying dignitarian concerns with legally recognized rights that enable one to have the "minimal self-respect" necessary to "assert claims" on one's own behalf. Even some defenders of the free market have argued in this way. For example, Tomasi's recent defense of "free-market fairness" turns on the idea that "people respect themselves, in part, because of their genuine achievements. Economic liberties protect this fundamental interest."[32] For Tomasi, then, the dignitarian reason to enlarge market freedoms is that they are crucial bases for agents' self-respect. All of these views implicitly treat the outward circumscription, and preservation, of an inward domain of private self-affirmation ("self-respect," "healthy self-relation," self-esteem etc.) as the chief incident of our common responsibility to protect human dignity.[33]

[29] Dworkin, *Justice for Hedgehogs*, pp. 203–04.
[30] Honneth, *The Struggle for Recognition*, pp. 118–19.
[31] Ibid., p. 120.
[32] Tomasi, *Free Market Fairness*, p. 83.
[33] Richard Tuck has denied that, historically speaking, a notion of personal sovereignty preceded the concept of state sovereignty. Rather, he suggests, the concept of state sovereignty came first, with the modern construction of the "sovereign individual" a derivation from it. His account suggests that the picture of international relations we find in the early modern theorists of the state – especially Grotius and Hobbes – in which independent agencies interact in a space regulated only by very exiguous common expectations became the dominant metaphor for conceptualizing the relations between individual agents interacting in society. Whether or not Tuck's historical thesis is sound, the dignitarian views under discussion here resonate strongly with his characterization of modern thinking about interpersonal relations. This is primarily "passport-dignity," the juridical dignity of border-protection. Common responsibilities for outward interaction

I am not here questioning the importance of self-respect. But it is obvious neither that human dignity just *is* self-respect nor that the common responsibility to protect it reduces to promoting conditions favorable to self-respecting attitudes. Assimilating human dignity and self-respect in this way moreover introduces a very strong constraint on what is allowed to count as a common responsibility. The scope of legitimate common responsibility becomes hostage to a personal veto rightfully exercisable whenever individuals can reasonably claim that their psychological integrity, their "positive relation-to-self," their own sense of their religious or moral identity, is threatened by norms and practices that they are expected to follow. Earlier, I objected to Jason Brennan's tendency to regard dignitarian complaints as merely "semiotic" – to do with symbolic expressions that make people (as he puts it) "feel bad about themselves." If one starts from the assumption that human dignity is ultimately a form of first-personal self-esteem, it is at least understandable why one might characterize dignitarian considerations in that light. Viewed from that angle, the struggle for human dignity amounts to a search for such modes of treatment as can be interpreted as external "messages" or communications supporting inward self-respect. On a revisionist account, however, the struggle for human dignity is not merely communicative in that way – a search for semiotic indicators that allow you to matter to yourself (obviously important though that is). The issue, rather, is how your life matters to others, for its own sake, because it reliably commands their respect. External valorization, not inward self-relations, is the proper object of dignitarian concern.

Agonist Investment

Some political theorists take the refusal of utilitarian detachment one step further. I have in mind those who associate the value of human dignity with an "agonist" politics of identity, self-assertion, and recognition.[34] Dignity matters in politics, from this point of view, because it captures the grandeur of political contestation in a way that a menial utilitarian concern with costs and benefits misses. Standing on one's dignity is here identified with self-vindication in the face of resistance: fighting one's corner, forcing one's valid demands on the attention of a reluctant audience, extorting recognition from unwilling oppressors, disrupting complacent ideologies by directly exemplifying and enacting a conventionally stigmatized mode of living, and so on. These forms of political engagement have great value, and can legitimately claim a dignitarian

---

are to be publicly discharged for the sake of preserving an inward domain of deliberative sovereignty, and of securing inner reflexive dispositions that support it. Richard Tuck, *The Rights of War and Peace: Political Thought and the International Order from Grotius to Kant* (Oxford: Oxford University Press, 2009).

[34] Fukuyama, *Identity*.

character, but it is an open question whether they provide an apt model for political criticism (as opposed to simply being objects of such critical evaluation, or direct modes of political action). What is clear, however, is that the more closely one assimilates political critique to self-assertive contestation of this sort, the less one will think of the critical perspective as a detached one.

Not surprisingly, then, those who today characterize the practice of social criticism in these "agonistic," contestatory, terms tend to deride the aspiration to impartiality in political judgment. These theorists regard political criticism as participating in the existential dialectic of "identity\difference" that for them defines all politics. For them, any determinate political position expresses the will of some individual or group – the interior locus of a first-personal identity (singular or plural) – to define itself in opposition to some third-personal exterior world of "difference." The implication is that, like any form of political engagement, critical reflection on politics must obey the adversarial logic of I/you, us/them, friend/enemy.[35] That hypothesis entails that the political critic must always be an invested party of some kind. The idea that she occupies some privileged standpoint of detached impartiality, above the fray, is a vain delusion, and professions along those lines must be in bad faith.

All of these approaches to political criticism, from the more radical, agonist, account to the gentler, more complaisant, views built on a contractualist agent-centered veto, thus reinforce a central assumption: that the demand for respect finds its primary relevance in political reflection as a demand made from within, or on behalf of, some partial, invested, point of view or "identity." Insofar as dignity figures in these arguments, then, it materializes as an adamant demand that something about who one is commands unconditional respect *as such* (one's status or personal sovereignty, one's "comprehensive views," one's authentic identity etc.).

Getting Ourselves Out of the Way

Dignity-revisionism, I submit, offers a legitimate and attractive way to resist this possessive (and arguably narcissistic, self-absorbed) interpretation of human dignity while rejecting the problematically exploitative impetus of utilitarianism. Here, it is important to separate two aspects of the utilitarian view: on the one hand its aggregating welfarism – the view that what ultimately matters is the sum of Sidgwickian "desirable consciousness" – while on the other hand, its effort to submit political institutions, positive moralities, conventional norms, regnant ideologies, and so on to critical assessment from a third-personal position of impartial detachment.

The first is the source of legitimate dignitarian unease about sacrificing lives to the Baal of "welfare maximization." But the second is well worth keeping;

---

[35] See Chapter 3, note 15.

one should not underestimate the incisiveness of utilitarian social criticism. If we know that some "tradition" (e.g., homophobic taboos), or institution (e.g., slavery), inflicts needless suffering on large numbers of people, are "we" – by hypothesis committed to submitting our form of life to critical scrutiny – at liberty to ignore all that suffering and recommend the status quo regardless? The utilitarian surely has a point in insisting that one should demand very impressive arguments before drawing that conclusion under these conditions; collective asceticism is very difficult to defend. Still, dignitarians must be right that the pursuit of welfare is constrained by a more fundamental expectation that certain ways of using human beings, even if they produce a better outcome overall, are adamantly unacceptable, and that one of our most important common responsibilities is to organize human life so that this never happens.

The revisionist analysis developed in this book, however, allows us to bring respect and human dignity to bear in specifying that common responsibility without abandoning the utilitarians' stance of third-personal impartial detachment. We need not assume that respect and dignity figure in political reflection only as ways to motivate a rightful veto protecting some stance of first-personal investment. This isn't to say that dignity-revisionists must oppose such entitlements, forms of status, rights, personal independence, veto-authority, and so on, only that they don't *identify* human dignity with any such localized claim. Like utilitarians, they maintain that the value of such entitlements is subject to a higher-order, critically detached, criterion. But whereas the utilitarian criterion is a welfarist one, the dignity-revisionist's is informed by the account given in this book.

Instead of looking at the world and asking about the consequences of different social practices, institutions, patterns of legal and moral enforcement and so on, for human welfare, the dignity-revisionist looks at that same world and asks whether human beings are being attended to for their own sakes in ways that allow them a reasonable share in human dignity and that leaves no life "radically forsaken."[36] Where the utilitarian is concerned with "desirable

---

[36] How do these standards relate to expectations of "equality"? This is an important topic for future work, but I take this book to imply: (1) dignity-revisionists refuse to reduce "human dignity" to a principle of respect for persons as "equals" in Dworkin's sense, because that would reinstate the possessive, juridical, status-centered views they wish to escape; (2) however, enforcing legal conventions and other positive norms that define status equality require respect for persons, and so on and are likely important aspects of any common responsibility for protecting human dignity in the revisionist's sense – but as in classical utilitarianism, these are the targets of, not the basis for, dignitarian political criticism; (3) although revisionists are committed to the general presumption that all human beings matter, or that nothing about any particular human individual should affect the force of any relevant dignitarian expectations, this (as Raz has correctly said) is better understood simply as an "affirmation [] of humanism," the idea that all people should count, and not as distinctively egalitarian; and, I think most interestingly (4) the question is as much about the de facto distribution of *power* to affect differently situated

consciousness," the revisionist dignitarian is concerned with the intersecting biographical trajectories of our lives, and how their mutual adjustment involves de facto dispositions to attend to each other in certain ways and not others. If the argument of this book is sound, we already understand the affective mode of respect well enough to be able to accurately recognize patterns of respect that constitute human dignity and patterns of disrespect that affect indignity. These patterns, I have contended, valorize and devalorize human lives; the respect and disrespect that accomplish this involve the exercise of definite social powers, no less real than, for example, "market forces." Revisionists, then, seek to understand not psychological facts about the pleasurable or painful quality of others' experience but historical and social facts about the actual disposition of the power to command attention.

Of course, the complete, detailed, history of the transactions in which that power is exercised "is not given to anyone in its totality." We catch only partial glimpses, from very particular vantage points in the story, and often with very limited ability to certify the character of our affective impact on others, not least because other minds are opaque, sincerity hard to gauge, and attitudes frequently concealed. Agents reflecting on their biographies have available a large range of reasonable interpretations, no one of which may be clearly correct or complete, and all of which register something of the truth. There is no fixed position outside this unfolding flux that affords a synoptic perspective on the whole. The catallaxy is centerless: the individual biographies that constitute it don't sum together into a Hegelian meta-biography of a single collective subject.

Yet the history of the whole ensemble remains unique, following irrevocable, if radically splintered, narrative paths through time. Our interpretive latitude is still bounded by a Dworkinian expectation of "fit":[37] we know that there is a point, impossible to specify precisely, at which biographical, auto-biographical, and historical reflection loses touch with what has actually occurred and flips over into fantasy, self-delusion, and fiction. In principle, there are "facts of the matter" about how attention is socially organized in patterns of respect and disrespect, and hence, if the revisionist is right, "facts of the matter" about how those patterns constitute human dignity and affect indignity.

---

individuals and groups such that they are disposed to respond respectfully to particular agents as it is about the de jure distribution of entitlements to certain kinds of treatment. While (4) brings the issue of *relative* social power into the picture, I am skeptical that dignity-revisionism would require "equality" of power (whatever that would mean). Still, if dignity-revisionism has a distinctively egalitarian character, this is where it would show up, as a commitment to taking seriously disparities of power.

[37] Ronald Dworkin, *Law's Empire* (Cambridge, MA: Belknap Press of Harvard University Press, 1995).

When we discern these patterns, and engage our fellow citizens in democratic discussion about how we might assume responsibility for them, our critical scrutiny *is* directed toward "relevant agents" and the way their attention to each other involves dispositions of respect. But we do so as detached observers, reflecting on the adequacy of our social forms from a common standpoint of human dignity, not as invested plaintiffs pressing personal demands. We are no more viewing it from a standpoint of partisan investment, (asserting demands, standing on our sovereignty, issuing vetos etc.) than is a medical team trying to diagnose and cure a disease for the sake of the patient.

To the utilitarian objection that this narrative emphasis is just too recherché, and that in the end all practical rationality is and should be oriented ultimately toward pain and pleasure, the revisionist responds with a flat denial: the reasons to want human beings to be attended to (loved, respected, engaged with, etc.) for their own sake are independent of, and often more important than, our reasons to hope that they experience "desirable consciousness." It *is* better to have (been) loved and (been) lost than not to have (been) loved at all *even if* the net pain greatly exceeded the pleasure (as it invariably does in this arena). More pertinently, it is possible to imagine forsakenness that is both "radical" in my sense and painless. Had the Nazis administered general anesthetics to holocaust victims before putting them on the trains, so that they experienced nothing of the terrifying journey to the camps and on into oblivion, would the critical significance of their being forsaken simply disappear? No: it would just make an adamantly unacceptable human indignity less painful.

To the dignity-traditionalist objection that human dignity is nothing more than a locally possessed individual right, status, or identity, the revisionist responds that this begs the question, confuses means and ends, and erects formalistic idols that distract attention from what really matters from a human point of view. As Simone Weil put it:

> There is something sacred in every man, but it is not his person. Nor yet is it the human personality. It is this man; no more and no less. . . . It is neither his person, nor the human personality in him, which is sacred to me. It is he. The whole of him. The arms, the eyes, the thoughts, everything . . . . If it were the human personality in him that was sacred to me, I could easily put out his eyes. As a blind man he would be exactly as much a human personality as before . . . . I should have destroyed nothing but his eyes. . . . So far from being his person, what is sacred in a human being is the impersonal in him . . . Gregorian chant, Romanesque architecture, the *Iliad*, the invention of geometry were not, for the people through whom they were brought into being and made available to us, occasions for the manifestation of personality. . . . These things are essentially anonymous.[38]

---

[38] Simone Weil and Siân Miles, *Simone Weil: An Anthology* (New York: Grove Press, 2000), pp. 70–71, 75.

BIBLIOGRAPHY

Agamben, Giorgio, transl. Lorenzo Chiesa, and Matteo Mandarini. 2011. *The Kingdom and the Glory: For a Theological Genealogy of Economy and Government*. Homo Sacer, II, 2. Stanford, CA: Stanford University Press.

Allen, Danielle S. 2004. *Talking to Strangers: Anxieties of Citizenship since Brown v. Board of Education*. Chicago: University of Chicago Press.

Améry, Jean. 1980. *At the Mind's Limits: Contemplations by a Survivor on Auschwitz and Its Realities*. Repr. Bloomington, IN: Indiana University Press.

Anderson, Elizabeth. 2010. *The Imperative of Integration*. Princeton, NJ: Princeton University Press.

　1995. *Value in Ethics and Economics*. Cambridge, MA: Harvard University Press.

Austin, J. L., J. O. Urmson, and G. J. Warnock. 1979. *Philosophical Papers*. Oxford: Oxford University Press.

Austin, John L. and Geoffrey James Warnock. 2010. *Sense and Sensibilia*. London: Oxford University Press.

Bagaric, Mirko and James Allan. 2006. "The Vacuous Concept of Dignity." *Journal of Human Rights* 5 (2): 257–70.

Barak, Aharon. 2015. *Human Dignity: The Constitutional Value and the Constitutional Right*. Cambridge: Cambridge University Press.

Barry, Brian M. 2002. *Culture and Equality: An Egalitarian Critique of Multiculturalism*. Cambridge, MA: Harvard University Press.

Beitz, Charles R. 2013. "Human Dignity in the Theory of Human Rights: Nothing but a Phrase?" *Philosophy & Public Affairs* 41 (3): 259–90.

Benn, Stanley I. 2009. *A Theory of Freedom*. Cambridge: Cambridge University Press.

President's Council on Bioethics. 2008. *Human Dignity and Bioethics: Essays Commissioned by the President's Council on Bioethics*. Washington, DC: U.S. Independent Agencies and Commissions.

Bird, Colin. 2013. "Dignity as a Moral Concept." *Social Philosophy and Policy* 30 (1–2): 150–76.

Blau, Peter Michael. 1986. *Exchange and Power in Social Life*. New Brunswick, NJ: Transaction Books.

Bloch, Ernst. 1995. *The Principle of Hope, Vol. 3*. Translated by Neville Plaice, Stephen Plaice, and Paul Knight. Cambridge, MA: The MIT Press.

Boltanski, Luc and Laurent Thévenot. 2006. *On Justification: Economies of Worth*. Princeton, NJ: Princeton University Press.

Brennan, Geoffrey and Philip Pettit. 2005. *The Economy of Esteem: An Essay on Civil and Political Society*. Oxford: Oxford University Press.

Brennan, Jason. 2016. *Against Democracy*. Princeton, NJ: Princeton University Press.

Buchanan, James M. 1964. "What Should Economists Do?" *Southern Economic Journal* 30 (3): 213.

Buchanan, James M., Gordon Tullock, and James M. Buchanan. 1999. *The Calculus of Consent: Logical Foundations of Constitutional Democracy*. Indianapolis, IN: Liberty Fund.

Butler, Judith. 2009. *Frames of War: When Is Life Grievable?* London: Verso.

Carter, Ian. 2011. "Respect and the Basis of Equality." *Ethics* 121 (3): 538–71.

Chwe, Michael Suk-Young. 2001. *Rational Ritual: Culture, Coordination, and Common Knowledge*. Princeton, NJ: Princeton University Press.

Connolly, William E. 2002. *Identity, Difference: Democratic Negotiations of Political Paradox*. Minneapolis, MN: University of Minnesota Press.

   1993. *The Terms of Political Discourse*. Princeton, NJ: Princeton University Press.

Darby, Derrick and John L. Rury. 2018. *The Color of Mind: Why the Origins of the Achievement Gap Matter for Justice*. Chicago: University of Chicago Press.

Darwall, Stephen. 2009. *The Second-Person Standpoint: Morality, Respect, and Accountability*. Harvard University Press.

   1977. "Two Kinds of Respect." *Ethics* 88 (1): 36–49.

Debes, Remy. 2009. "Dignity's Gauntlet." *Philosophical Perspectives* 23 (1): 45–78.

   2017. *Dignity: A History*. Oxford: Oxford University Press.

Düwell, Marcus, Jens Braarvig, Roger Brownsword, and Dietmar Mieth, eds. 2014. *The Cambridge Handbook of Human Dignity: Interdisciplinary Perspectives*. Cambridge: Cambridge University Press.

Dworkin, Ronald. 2008. *Is Democracy Possible Here? Principles for a New Political Debate*. Princeton, NJ: Princeton University Press.

   2011. *Justice for Hedgehogs*. Cambridge, MA: Belknap Press of Harvard University Press.

   1995. *Law's Empire*. Cambridge, MA: Belknap Press of Harvard University Press.

Eberle, Christopher J. 2002. *Religious Conviction in Liberal Politics*. Cambridge: Cambridge University Press.

Elson, Diane, ed. 2015. *Value: The Representation of Labour in Capitalism*. London: Verso.

Elster, Jon. 1999. *Alchemies of the Mind: Rationality and the Emotions*. Cambridge: Cambridge University Press.

Estlund, David M. 2020. *Utopophobia: On the Limits (If Any) of Political Philosophy*. Princeton, NJ: Princeton University Press.

Feinberg, Joel and Jan Narveson. 1970. "The Nature and Value of Rights." *The Journal of Value Inquiry* 4 (4): 243–60.

Forsyth, Murray. 1987. *Reason and Revolution: The Political Thought of the Abbe Sieyes.* New York, NY: Holmes & Meier.

Frank, Robert H. 1986. *Choosing the Right Pond: Human Behavior and the Quest for Status.* New York, NY: Oxford University Press.

  1999. *Luxury Fever: Why Money Fails to Satisfy in an Era of Excess.* New York, NY: Free Press.

Fukuyama, Francis. 2018. *Identity: The Demand for Dignity and the Politics of Resentment.* New York, NY: Farrar, Straus and Giroux.

Gaita, Raimond. 2000. *A Common Humanity: Thinking about Love and Truth and Justice.* London. New York, NY: Routledge.

Gaus, Gerald. 2012. *The Order of Public Reason: A Theory of Freedom and Morality in a Diverse and Bounded World.* Cambridge: Cambridge University Press.

Gaus, Gerald F. 1990. *Value and Justification: The Foundations of Liberal Theory.* Cambridge: Cambridge University Press.

Geuss, Raymond. 2008. *Philosophy and Real Politics.* Princeton, NJ: Princeton University Press.

Gilabert, Pablo. 2015. "Human Rights, Human Dignity, and Power." In *Philosophical Foundations of Human Rights,* edited by Rowan Cruft, Matthew Liao, and Massimo Renzo, 196–213. Oxford: Oxford University Press.

Gilligan, James. 1997. *Violence: Reflections on a National Epidemic.* New York, NY: Vintage Books.

Goffman, Erving. 1982. *Interaction Ritual: Essays on Face-to-Face Behavior.* New York, NY: Pantheon Books.

  2010. *Relations in Public: Microstudies of the Public Order.* New Brunswick, NJ: Transaction Publishers.

  1986. *Stigma: Notes on the Management of Spoiled Identity.* New York, NY: Simon & Schuster.

Goolam, Nazeem M. I. 2006. "The Cartoon Controversy: A Note on Freedom of Expression, Hate Speech and Blasphemy." *The Comparative and International Law Journal of Southern Africa* 39 (2): 333–50.

Graeber, David. 2014. *Debt: The First 5,000 Years.* Brooklyn: Melville House.

Greenberg, Kenneth S. 1990. "The Nose, the Lie, and the Duel in the Antebellum South." *The American Historical Review* 95 (1): 57.

Griffin, James. 2009. *On Human Rights.* Oxford: Oxford University Press.

Hampton, J. and Jeffrie G. Murphy. 1998. *Forgiveness and Mercy.* Cambridge: Cambridge University Press.

Hampton, Jean. 1991. "Correction Harms versus Righting Wrongs: The Goal of Retribution." *UCLA Law Review* 39: 1659–702.

Hart, H. L. A. 1963. *Law, Liberty, and Morality.* 1 edition. Stanford, CA: Stanford University Press.

1994. *The Concept of Law*. Oxford: Oxford University Press.

Hayek, F. A. 2011. *The Constitution of Liberty: The Definitive Edition*. Edited by Ronald Hamowy. Chicago: University of Chicago Press.

Hayek, F. A. 1937. "Economics and Knowledge." *Economica* 4 (13): 33–54.

Hayek, F. A. 2012. *Law, Legislation and Liberty: A New Statement of the Liberal Principles of Justice and Political Economy*. London: Routledge.

Hobbes, Thomas. 1994. *Leviathan*. Indianapolis, IN: Hackett Publishing Company.

Jaynes, Julian. 2000. *The Origin of Consciousness in the Breakdown of the Bicameral Mind*. New York, NY: Houghton Mifflin.

Kant, Immanuel. 2017. *The Metaphysics of Morals*. Edited by Lara Denis. Translated by Mary J. Gregor. Revised edition. Cambridge Texts in the History of Philosophy. Cambridge: Cambridge University Press.

Kateb, George. 2011. *Human Dignity*. Cambridge, MA: Harvard University Press.

King, Martin Luther, Coretta Scott King, and Marian Wright Edelman. 2010. *The Trumpet of Conscience*. Boston: Beacon Press.

Kolodny, Niko. 2003. "Love as Valuing a Relationship." *The Philosophical Review* 112 (2): 135–89.

Korsgaard, Christine M. and Onora O'Neill. 1996. *The Sources of Normativity*. Cambridge: Cambridge University Press.

Larmore, Charles. 2005. "Respect for Persons." *Hedgehog Review* 7 (2): 66–76.

1999. "The Moral Basis of Political Liberalism." *The Journal of Philosophy* 96 (12): 599–625.

Larmore, Charles E. 1987. *Patterns of Moral Complexity*. Cambridge: Cambridge University Press.

LaVaque-Manty, Mika. 2006. "Dueling for Equality: Masculine Honor and the Modern Politics of Dignity." *Political Theory* 34 (6): 715–40.

Lazari-Radek, Katarzyna de and Peter Singer. 2014. *The Point of View of the Universe: Sidgwick and Contemporary Ethics*. Oxford: Oxford University Press.

Lebron, Christopher J. 2015. *The Color of Our Shame: Race and Justice in Our Time*. Oxford: Oxford University Press.

Leiter, Brian. 2013. *Why Tolerate Religion?* Princeton, NJ: Princeton University Press.

Lovejoy, Arthur. 1961. *Reflections on Human Nature*. Baltimore: Johns Hopkins University Press.

Margalit, Avishai. 1998. *The Decent Society*. Cambridge, MA: Harvard University Press.

Marx, Karl. 1992. *Capital: Volume 1: A Critique of Political Economy*. Translated by Ben Fowkes. London: Penguin Classics.

Grundrisse. Penguin Classics.

Marx, Karl and Friedrich Engels. 1978. *The Marx-Engels Reader*. Edited by Robert C. Tucker. New York, NY: W. W. Norton & Company.

McCrudden, Christopher. 2014. *Understanding Human Dignity*. Oxford: British Academy.

Milgate, Murray and Shannon C. Stimson. 2009. *After Adam Smith: A Century of Transformation in Politics and Political Economy*. Princeton, NJ: Princeton University Press.

Moran, Richard. 2012. *Authority and Estrangement: An Essay on Self-Knowledge*. Princeton, NJ: Princeton University Press.

Moyn, Samuel. 2012. *The Last Utopia: Human Rights in History*. Cambridge, MA: Belknap Press of Harvard University Press.

Murdoch, Iris. 2006. *The Sovereignty of Good. Reprint*. Routledge Classics. London: Routledge.

O'Neill, Barry. 2001. *Honor, Symbols, and War*. Ann Arbor, MI: University of Michigan Press.

Parfit, Derek. 2011. *On What Matters*. Oxford: Oxford University Press.

Patterson, Orlando. 1982. *Slavery and Social Death: A Comparative Study*. Cambridge, MA: Harvard University Press.

Perry, Michael J. 2010. *The Political Morality of Liberal Democracy*. Cambridge University Press.

Prinz, Jesse J. 2006. *Gut Reactions: A Perceptual Theory of Emotion*. Oxford: Oxford University Press.

Quong, Jonathan. 2010. *Liberalism without Perfection*. Oxford University Press.
    2014. "On the Idea of Public Reason." In *A Companion to Rawls*, edited by J. Mandle and D. Reidy, 265–80. Wiley-Blackwell.

Rao, Neomi. 2007. "On the Use and Abuse of Dignity in Constitutional Law." *Columbia Journal of European Law* 14: 201–56.
    2011. "Three Concepts of Dignity in Constitutional Law." *Notre Dame Law Review* 86: 183–272.

Rawls, John. 1999. *A Theory of Justice*. Cambridge, MA: Harvard University Press.
    2005. *Political Liberalism*. New York, NY: Columbia University Press.
    2003. *The Law of Peoples: With "The Idea of Public Reason Revisited."* Cambridge, MA: Harvard University Press.

Raz, Joseph. 2001. *Value, Respect, and Attachment*. Cambridge: Cambridge University Press.

Ripstein, Arthur. 2009. *Force and Freedom*. Cambridge, MA: Harvard University Press.

Rodriguez, Philippe-André. 2015. "Human Dignity as an Essentially Contested Concept." *Cambridge Review of International Affairs* 28 (4): 743–56.

Rosen, Michael. 2012. *Dignity*. Cambridge, MA: Harvard University Press.

Rousseau, Jean-Jacques, and Donald A. Cress. 2011 *Basic Political Writings*. 2nd ed. Indianapolis, IN: Hackett.Ruskin, John. 1985. *Unto This Last, and Other Writings*. London: Penguin Books.

Shelby, Tommie and Brandon M. Terry, eds. 2018. *To Shape a New World: Essays on the Political Philosophy of Martin Luther King, Jr*. Cambridge, MA: Harvard University Press.

Skinner, B. F. 2007. *Beyond Freedom and Dignity*. Indianapolis, IN: Hackett.

Tomasi, John. 2012. *Free Market Fairness*. Princeton, NJ: Princeton University Press.

Vallier, Kevin. 2014. *Liberal Politics and Public Faith: Beyond Separation*. New York, NY: Routledge.

Veblen, Thorstein and Martha Banta. 2009. *The Theory of the Leisure Class*. Oxford: Oxford University Press.

Velleman, J. David. 1999. "Love as a Moral Emotion." *Ethics* 109 (2): 338–74.

Waldron, Jeremy. 2015. *Dignity, Rank, and Rights*. Edited by Meir Dan-Cohen. Oxford: Oxford University Press

   2002. *God, Locke, and Equality: Christian Foundations in Locke's Political Thought*. Cambridge: Cambridge University Press.

   2012. "How Law Protects Dignity." *The Cambridge Law Journal* 71 (1): 200–22.

   2014. *The Harm in Hate Speech*. Cambridge, MA: Harvard University Press.

Weil, Simone and Siân Miles. 2000. *Simone Weil: An Anthology*. New York, NY: Grove Press.

White, Stephen K. 2009. *The Ethos of a Late-Modern Citizen*. Cambridge, MA: Harvard University Press.

Williams, Kipling D. 2001. *Ostracism: The Power of Silence. Emotions and Social Behavior*. New York, NY: Guilford Press.

Wolterstorff, Nicholas. 2008. *Justice: Rights and Wrongs*. Princeton, NJ: Princeton University Press.

INDEX

Lightning Source UK Ltd.
Milton Keynes UK
UKHW032313300921
391417UK00004B/51